PEOPLE IN POWER

FORGING A GRASSROOTS DEMOCRACY IN NICARAGUA

HONDURAS

• Jalapa
• Ocotal

• Jinotega
Estelí •   • Matagalpa

• Chinandega

Corinto   NICARAGUA

León
Managua ★ L. *Managua*
    • Santo Tomas
Masaya
• Granada
Rivas   L. *Nicaragua*

PACIFIC
OCEAN

Puerto Cabezas

CARIBBEAN
SEA

MOSQUITO COAST

Bluefields

COSTA RICA

PEOPLE IN POWER
FORGING A GRASSROOTS DEMOCRACY IN NICARAGUA

GARY RUCHWARGER

BERGIN & GARVEY PUBLISHERS, INC.
MASSACHUSETTS

First published in 1987 by
Bergin & Garvey Publishers, Inc.
670 Amherst Road
South Hadley, Massachusetts 01075

789   987654321

Printed in the United States of America
Library of Congress Cataloging-in-Publication Data

Ruchwarger, Gary.
  People in power.

  Bibliography: p. 328
  Includes index.
  1. Political participation—Nicaragua.   2. Nicaragua—
Politics and government—1979–   I. Title.
JL1616.R82   1987   324'.097285   87-12623
ISBN 0-89789-129-5 (alk. paper)
ISBN 0-89789-130-9 (pbk. : alk. paper)

Contents

PREFACE

Although the literature on the Nicaraguan revolution is expanding rapidly, few works examine the revolution's efforts to build a participatory democracy. And no book offers a comprehensive account of the institutional vehicles forging this democracy—the Sandinista mass organizations. I therefore approached this study with the aim of providing a detailed analysis of the history, structure, and tasks of Nicaragua's neighborhood committees, women's association, and unions.

To gain first-hand knowledge of these organizations, I conducted sixteen months of primary research from 1983 to 1986, attending dozens of base-level meetings and interviewing scores of grassroots activists. This book is the fruit of that research. After discussing their pre-triumph origins, it examines the mass organizations' relationship to the Sandinista party and the revolutionary state. The book also explores the development of democratic practices within the popular associations and the power they wield in the revolution.

I am greatly indebted to the national and local leaderships of the Sandinista mass organizations for the complete cooperation they granted me during the past three years. They were always quick to give me access to documents and never turned down a request for an interview. At the same time they have never tried to control or even monitor what I was writing.

Special thanks must go to Hugo Saenz, CDS coordinator in barrio Georgino Andrade in Managua; Rafael Flores, president of the Gamez-Garmendia cooperative in Estelí; and numerous officials in the ATC, AMNLAE, and UNAG zonal and regional offices in Estelí, especially Vivian Perez, Luz Florian, and Roberto Laguna.

I am also indebted to Sylvia Maxfield and Jonathan Fox for their helpful suggestions concerning the structure of this book.

Among the various people who assisted me with specific research I would like to acknowledge Emily Schnee, Barbara Stahler-Scholk, and Paula Worby.

While writing this book I was frequently invited to lecture on its contents by the staff at the NICA Spanish school in Estelí. Many of the comments and questions that the NICA students raised during these talks stimulated my research.

A number of people made direct contributions as a result of reading a part or all of the manuscript at some stage of its development: Leslie Baum, Chris Boyer, David DeLeeu, Sonia Diaz, David Forbes, Richard Harris, Phil Martinez, David Smith, Ken Strauss, and Steve Watrous.

I am particularly grateful for the extensive editorial assistance of Dan Pharaoh who read most of the manuscript and improved my style.

Jim Bergin and Sophy Craze at Bergin & Garvey provided me with useful advice regarding the logistics of handling a manuscript produced in Nicaragua. Sarah May Clarkson did a superb job copyediting the final draft.

Finally, I wish to thank the many residents of Georgino Andrade in Managua whose dedication to building a new Nicaragua kept me inspired during the course of my work. To them it is warmly dedicated.

ACRONYMS

AMNLAE	Asociacion de Mujeres Nicaraguenses 'Luisa Amanda Espinoza'	Association of Nicaraguan Women 'Luisa Amanda Espinoza'
AMPRONAC	Asociación de Mujeres Ante la Problematica Nacional	Association of Women Confronting the National Problem
ANDEN	Asociación Nacional de Educadores Nicaraguenses	National Association of Nicaraguan Teachers
APP	Area de Propiedad del Pueblo	Area of Public Ownership
ARE	Asamblea de Reactivación Economica	Economic Reactivation Assembly
ATC	Asociación de Trabajadores del Campo	Rural Workers' Association
CAS	Cooperativa Agricola Sandinista	Sandinista Agricultural Cooperative
CAUS	Central de Accion y Unidad Sindical	Federation of Trade Union Action and Unity
CBS	Comite de Barrio Sandinista	Sandinista Barrio Committee
CCS	Cooperativa de Credito y Servicios	Credit and Service Cooperative
CDC	Comite de Defensa Civil	Civil Defense Committee

CDS	Comite de Defensa Sandinista	Sandinista Defense Committee
CGT-I	Confederación General de Trabajo-Independiente	General Confederation of Labor-Independent
COIP	Corporación Industrial del Pueblo	People's Industrial Corporation
COSEP	Consejo Superior de la Empresa Privada	Higher Council of Private Enterprise
CST	Central Sandinista de Trabajadores	Sandinista Workers' Federation
CTN	Central de Trabajadores de Nicaragua	Workers' Federation of Nicaragua
CUS	Consejo de Unificación Sindical	Council of Trade Union Unification
ENABAS	Empresa Nicaraguense de Alimentos Basicos	Nicaraguan Basic Foods Marketing Company
EPS	Ejercito Popular Sandinista	Sandinista People's Army
FER	Frente Estudiantil Revolucionario	Revolutionary Student Front
FETSALUD	Federacion de Trabajadores de la Salud	Health Workers' Federation
FSLN	Frente Sandinista de Liberación Nacional	Sandinista National Liberation Front
GPP	Guerra Popular Prolongada	Prolonged Popular War (FSLN Tendency)
MAP	Movimiento de Acción Popular	People's Action Movement —Marxist-Leninist
MDN	Movimiento Democratico Nicaraguense	Nicaraguan Democratic Movement
MICOIN	Ministerio de Comercio Interior	Ministry of Internal Commerce
MIDINRA	Ministerio de Desarollo Agropecuario y Instituto Nicaraguense de Agraria	Ministry of Development and Agrarian Reform Institute
MPS	Milicias Populares Sandinista	Sandinista People's Militia
MPU	Movimiento Pueblo Unido	United People's Movement

PCD	Partido Conservador Democratico	Democratic Conservative Party
PCN	Partido Comunista de Nicaragua	Communist Party of Nicaragua
PLI	Partido Liberal Independiente	Independent Liberal Party
PPSC	Partido Popular Socialcristiano	People's Social Christian Party
PSC	Partido Socialcristiano	Social Christian Party
PSD	Partido Socialdemocrata	Social Democratic Party
PSN	Partido Socialista Nicaraguense	Nicaraguan Socialist Party
UNAG	Union Nacional de Agricultores y Ganaderos	National Union of Farmers and Ranchers
UPE	Unidad de Producción Estatal	State Production Unit

INTRODUCTION

July 19, 1979, dawned on a liberated Nicaragua. In the early morning hours, Radio Sandino woke the nation with Sandinista hymns and songs of triumph. The broadcast called upon everyone to "be calm, act with maturity. The moment is coming when all Nicaraguans . . . can go into the streets together and rejoice." Radio Sandino instructed the National Guard: "You have no reason to fight. Somoza . . . and the entire command have gone. There is nothing to defend. Don't lose your life unnecessarily. Go to the nearest church or Red Cross and surrender."[1]

While the joyous music and instructions continued into the day, Nicaraguans from as far away as Chinandega and Estelí poured into Managua. As Managuans romped in celebration, trucks packed with *muchachos* (Sandinista fighters) jammed the streets. Church bells rang in the border towns and refugees began crossing into the newly proclaimed *territorio libre* (free territory). The new governing council left León and headed for Managua. Hundreds of thousands of ecstatic, tearful Nicaraguans welcomed them with ovations, gathering at the soon-to-be-named Plaza of the Revolution outside the National Palace. Here the Nicaraguan people confirmed the power of the Government of National Reconstruction.

But how did such a poor, oppressed people defeat the Somoza dictatorship, a regime backed by the Nicaraguan National Guard, Central America's best-equipped and best-trained military force? The answer is *participación popular* (popular participation): the organized, militant participation of Nicaraguan citizens in a "people's war" against a brutal and ruthless tyranny. Assisted by the Sandinista National Liberation Front (FSLN), Nicaraguan social groups organized themselves into separate,

1

but mutually supportive, *organizaciones de masas* (mass organizations). From September 1978 to July 1979, these organizations launched a series of insurrections against the National Guard that ultimately forced the collapse of the Somoza dynasty.

Mass organization members performed a wide range of activities to sustain the anti-Somoza uprisings. Neighborhood residents in Civil Defense Committees built barricades, administered first aid, and supplied combatants. Peasants and farm workers in the Rural Workers Association demonstrated against hunger, blocked roads, and seized *Somocista* property. Urban and rural women in the Association of Nicaraguan Women Confronting the National Problem protested in the streets, hid provisions, and transported weapons. Students in high school and university associations occupied schools, led demonstrations, and built barricades. Urban workers in clandestine unions organized strikes, sabotaged production, and forged weapons. In addition, members of all these organizations engaged in armed combat against the National Guard.

In short, the Nicaraguan people as a whole, not a small guerrilla elite, cooperated to overthrow the Somoza dictatorship. The FSLN, the revolution's military wing, recognized the critical role of the masses.[2] Immediately following the victory over Somoza, Humberto Ortega, a Sandinista leader and Nicaragua's Defense Minister, acknowledged the FSLN's dependence on popular participation:

> The truth is that we always took the masses into account, but more in terms of their supporting the guerrillas, so that the guerrillas as such could defeat the National Guard. This isn't what actually happened. What happened was that it was the guerrillas who provided support for the masses so that they could defeat the enemy by means of insurrection.[3]

Popular participation in the Nicaraguan revolution did not end with Somoza's downfall. On the contrary, since July 19, 1979, *el pueblo* (the people) have expanded their participation, contributing to Nicaraguan political, social, and economic life. Through various grassroots organizations, Nicaragua's citizens—peasants, workers, artisans, small merchants, civil servants, and professionals—make decisions at their workplaces, fashion laws that strengthen social bonds, enhance the well-being of their communities, and contribute to the nation's educational and health programs.[4] In this way, the people of Nicaragua have a strong voice in determining the course and shape of local and national policies.

Yet Reagan administration officials and many American journalists project a different image of Nicaragua. They argue that the Sandinistas are totalitarian rulers who have betrayed the original democratic goals of the revolution. In an April 1985 speech advocating military aid to the Contras, President Reagan asserted:

> The truth is, there are atrocities going on in Nicaragua. But they are largely the work of the institutionalized cruelty of the Sandinista Government—cruelty that is the natural expression of a Communist government, a cruelty that flows naturally from the heart of totalitarianism. The truth is Somoza was bad, but so many of the people of Nicaragua know the Sandinistas are infinitely worse.[5]

In contrast, the Sandinistas insist that they are developing a democratic, not a totalitarian, society. But how do they define democracy, and how are they actually building a democratic society? In his classic work *Democracy, Capitalism, and Socialism*, Joseph Schumpeter defines democracy as "that institutional arrangement for arriving at political decisions in which individuals acquire the power to decide by means of a competitive struggle for the people's vote."[6] This electoral definition of democracy is the dominant conception in capitalist countries.

The main problem with the electoral view of democracy is that it places scant emphasis on the role of participation. Many political theorists, such as Jean-Jacques Rousseau and John Stuart Mill, argued that ongoing participation in all aspects of public affairs is crucial to the creation and maintenance of a democratic society. It was Rousseau and Mill's contention that constant participation in decision-making engenders "public spiritedness," which is the necessary condition for genuine democracy. Individuals who participate in public affairs learn to gain other people's cooperation by considering matters beyond their own private interests. Moreover, both Rousseau and Mill held that a participatory form of democracy is self-sustaining because the more individual citizens participate the better they are able to do so.[7]

The Sandinistas subscribe to these main tenets of participatory democracy. Indeed, they make the principle of "popular participation" central to their conception of governance. Speaking at the close of the national literacy campaign in August 1980, FSLN leader Humberto Ortega defined the Sandinista viewpoint this way:

> For the Sandinista Front democracy is not defined in purely political terms, and is not reducible to popular participation in elections. It is something more, much more . . . . It must be said once and for all: democracy neither begins nor ends with elec-

tions. It is a myth to try to reduce democracy to that kind of condition.

Democracy first appears in the economic order, when social inequalities begin to diminish, and when the workers and peasants improve their conditions of life. That is when true democracy begins, not before. Once these goals are attained, democracy immediately spreads to other areas: the field of government is broadened; the people exert influence over its government, determines its government, whether that is agreeable or not.

At a more advanced state, democracy means workers' participation in the management of factories, cooperatives, cultural centers, and so on. In short, democracy is mass intervention in every aspect of social life.[8]

In a July 1983 speech, Sergio Ramirez, the current vice-president of Nicaragua, offered another formulation of the FSLN's notion of democracy.

> For us, the efficiency of a political model depends on its capacity to resolve the problems of democracy and justice. Effective democracy, like we intend to practice in Nicaragua, consists of ample popular participation; a permanent dynamic of the people's participation in a variety of political and social tasks; the people who give their opinions and are listened to; the people who suggest, construct and direct, organize themselves, who attend to community, neighborhood and national problems; a people who are active in the sovereignty and the defense of that sovereignty and also teach and give vaccinations; a daily democracy and not one that takes place every four years, when at that, or every four, five or six years when formal elections take place; the people don't go as a minority but in their totality, and they consciously elect the best candidate and not one chosen like a soap or deodorant, a vote freely made and not manipulated by an advertising agency, a vote for change to improve the nation and not in favor of a transnational finance company or an industrial military trust. . . . For us democracy is not merely a formal model, but a continual process capable of giving the people that elect and participate in it the real possibility of transforming their living conditions, a democracy which establishes justice and ends exploitation.[9]

On November 4, 1984, the Sandinistas and the Nicaragua people showed their respect for the electoral aspect of democracy by going to the polls to elect a president, vice president, and National Assembly. Seventy-five percent of the eligible voters participated, and the FSLN received 67 percent of the votes cast in a field of seven parties. Because of the United States government's anti-Sandinista campaign, few Americans realize that the Sandinistas' electoral victory was the result of their popularity, and not political manipulation. By parroting Reagan administration cries that the Sandinistas are "Marxist-Leninists,"[10] American journalists ignored the fact that the FSLN is the first Nicaraguan revolutionary party to gain power in this century and promote genuinely free elections.[11]

Some European correspondents, on the other hand, acknowledged the Sandinistas' precedent. "By putting everything inside a U.S. or East-West context," said Luccia Annunciata, Central American correspondent for the prestigious Italian daily La Republica,

> the American press missed a very important story. Nicaragua is not a traditional left-wing country. It isn't Maoist, Stalinist, or Leninist. They are trying to pick the best elements of the democratic system in Western countries—elections, free speech, unions—and combine them with collectivism and some form of socialism. By choosing a National Assembly, the election in Nicaragua has already made the first break from the conception accepted in every single left-wing country, that the party is the state. This first great break was not understood by the American press. They simply didn't care about it.[12]

The Sandinista conception of democracy, with its emphasis on massive and ongoing citizen participation, falls squarely within the Western democratic tradition. In both theory and practice, the Sandinistas, and the people of Nicaragua, are proving to be the political heirs of Rousseau and Mill. Moreover, the Nicaraguan revolution has created specific institutions through which poder popular (people's power) is exercised: the Sandinista mass organizations in which approximately one-half of Nicaragua's adult population participate. Many individuals are simultaneously active in at least two organizations. But what exactly are mass organizations and what role do they play in a revolutionary society? A mass organization is a collective association that represents the fundamental interests of a particular social or demographic sector of society. There are five principal Sandinista mass organizations: the Sandinista Defense Committees, the National Union of Farmers and Ranchers, the Sandinista Workers Federation, the Rural Workers Association, and the Luisa Amanda Espinosa Association of Nicaraguan Women.[13] These organizations are identified with the Sandinistas because they recognize Nicaragua's ruling party—the Sandinista National Liberation Front (FSLN)—as the guiding political force in the country. Whether they are members of the party or not, people use the term "Sandinista" to identify themselves and their associations as nationalist and anti-imperialist, two central political ideas of Augusto Cesar Sandino. Sandino was the "General of Free Men" who fought against U.S. military intervention in Nicaragua from 1927 to 1933.[14]

Grassroots organizations serve as the principal vehicles through which Nicaraguan citizens are attempting to build what political scientist Carole Pateman calls a " 'participatory society': a society so organised that every individual has the opportunity directly to participate in all political spheres."[15] In a century when most, if not all, revolutionary experiments have led to a centralized, hierarchically organized state machine, a participatory society seems beyond reach. Indeed, many political theorists believe that social revolutions in less developed countries inevitably lead to the creation of elitist, bureaucratic states.[16] Nicaragua's attempt to forge a grassroots democracy therefore represents a radical departure from the path taken by other contemporary revolutions. Should the Sandinista experiment in participatory democracy enjoy even partial success, it will be an accomplishment of world-historical significance.

1

THE FSLN AND THE MASS MOVEMENT

The revolutionary process in Nicaragua was set in motion by diverse forms of struggle over a long period of time. Moreover, the revolutionary movement passed through several phases, correcting itself, altering its course, dividing and converging for the final assault on the Somoza dictatorship. The organization that guided the war against the autocratic regime was the Sandinista National Liberation Front (FSLN), whose origins and development are rooted in the Nicaraguan revolutionary experience of the 1920s and 1930s and in more recent Latin American history.

The origin of the Sandinistas' strategy lay in the relationship between their organization and that of the mass movement against Somoza. This dynamic unity provided the necessary counterweight to the highly-trained and better-equipped National Guard, which outnumbered the Sandinistas ten to one at the time of the revolution. The FSLN realized that victory depended not on its own members, but on the tens of thousands of Nicaraguans who also fought the dictatorship. Humberto Ortega, Nicaragua's current defense minister, emphasizes the centrality of the mass movement in this way:

> It is very difficult to take power without a creative combination of all forms of struggle, wherever they can take place: countryside, city, town, neighborhood, mountain, etc., but always based on the idea the mass movement is the focal point of the struggle and not the vanguard with the masses limited to merely supporting it.[1]

7

THE HISTORICAL BACKGROUND

Nicaragua in the nineteenth century was undermined by violent feuds among the country's backward elite, who were weakened socially by frequent foreign interventions and economically by the pressures of the world market.[2] The upper classes—cattle ranchers, merchants, and the coffee-based "plantation bourgeoisie"—acquired fortunes at the expense of the peasantry, and dominated the country's political life. Yet they were politically divided into the fiercely antagonistic Liberal and Conservative parties, neither one of which was capable of providing effective resistance to United States' intervention in the late nineteenth and early twentieth centuries. A knowledgeable observer summed up the situation in 1926: "Concessions of utterly ruinous character have been given to powerful American concerns, which have merely exploited the natural resources of the country for their own benefit without any benefit whatsoever to Nicaraguans."[3] Systematic injustices engendered considerable unrest in the country, especially among the rural poor who suffered the greatest oppression. Consequently, the United States sent in troops to ensure "stability" and protect their "interests."

Only the peasant army led by Augusto Cesar Sandino between 1926 and 1934 defended Nicaragua's sovereignty against the United States Marines and Anastasio Somoza's American-trained National Guard. A populist and militant nationalist, Sandino pledged to wage guerrilla war until the Marines departed. When United States troops left Nicaragua, Sandino and his followers agreed to lay down their arms, as promised. Somoza then lured Sandino to a banquet at the presidential palace in Managua, where he was murdered on February 21, 1934, by National Guard soldiers. Somoza went on to establish his personal dictatorship in 1936.

Following Sandino's death and the intense repression that accompanied the formation of the *Somocista* regime, Nicaraguan revolutionaries had difficulty mobilizing the masses against the dictatorship. The anti-Somoza movement, reeling from government attacks and lacking effective organization, soon became subordinated to the Conservative Party. Indeed, during the period between 1934 and 1956 even the Nicaraguan Socialist Party collaborated with traditional opposition politicicans. Ortega confirms that this era represented a "difficult stage (1934–1956) of decline of the popular movement."[4]

Rigoberto Lopez Perez's 1956 assassination of Somoza Garcia halted this decline, and as the FSLN would later assert, marked the beginning of the end of the Somoza dynasty. Perez's bold action dramatized the weakness of the conservative opposition. In the words of Jose Benito

Escobar, an early Sandinista leader, this killing brought "an end to the traditional methods of opposition which the bourgeoisie had imposed on our people," and demonstrated "that the forms of struggle to be employed to attain liberation should be those which correspond to the needs of the people."[5]

Somoza Garcia's assassination unleashed a wave of repression that culminated in the imprisonment, torture, and exile of many opposition leaders. Nevertheless, a new period of revolutionary struggle ensued, characterized by numerous acts of popular resistance which expressed the growing political and social rejection of the dictatorship.

During the late 1950s, a sharp drop in cotton prices contributed to a stagnant Nicaraguan economy, and as unemployment rose dramatically, strikes increased, followed by additional suppression. Although students and workers conducted significant protests at the end of the decade, the demands of the popular sectors did not become part of a larger struggle. The bourgeois opposition carried out unsuccessful armed adventures and continued to pursue inconseqential political strategies, but Nicaragua lacked a cohesive, revolutionary force capable of directing the disparate and spontaneous struggles of the masses.[6]

The Founding of the FSLN

The death of Somoza Garcia and the failure of the conservative opposition to provide an alternative to the dictatorship sparked the student population that had been active in the earlier part of the decade. The students' rekindled activism coincided with the revival of Sandino's writings. One student, Carlos Fonseca Amador, recognized the importance of Sandino's message and set out to demonstrate the relevance of Sandino's teachings to the Nicaraguan reality.

The success of the Cuban revolution in 1959 inspired this generation of Nicaraguan revolutionaries. Reinforcing the beliefs of Fonseca and other young leftists, the Cuban victory underscored the importance of building a base of support among the local peasant population. In addition, the legacy of Sandino provided the necessary elements for a national identity epitomized by Nicaragua's history of intervention and resistance.

When Carlos Fonseca Amador and two fellow students, Tomás Borge and Silvio Mayorga—met in Tegucigalpa, Honduras in July 1961 to discuss the creation of a national liberation movement, they had already absorbed the lessons of the Cuban struggle as well as Sandino's writings. The outcome of the meeting was the establishment of the Sandinista National Liberation Front (FSLN). The founders insisted that this new revolutionary organization be called "Sandinista" to honor Sandino's struggle. Sandino's ideas were to serve as the foundation for the FSLN's activities. Bayardo Arce, a member of the FSLN's National Directorate, explains what Sandino meant to the young revolutionaries:

> Our movement gathered the essence, the best of the patriotic movement which developed between 1927–1934, and articulated this to modern-day political theories . . . which analysed the social reality to the people. This is what Sandinismo means in the present time, a combination of our forms of traditional struggles—which had their maximum expression in Sandino's movement and the scientific theories of revolution.[7]

The FSLN adopted not only the ideological but also the military content of Sandino's struggle, that is, the guerrilla strategies that had been so effectively employed by Sandino in the 1920s.[8] Symbolic acts such as recruiting Colonel Santos Lopez, a veteran guerrilla of Sandino's army, established a direct link to Nicaragua's revolutionary past. Consequently, the FSLN maintained continuity between the basis of their political program and that of Sandino. This program centered on the fundamental contradiction of people versus dictatorship/imperialism. The FSLN clarified the necessity of developing a broadly-based national liberation movement to resolve this contradiction. Jaime Wheelock, a member of the FSLN's National Directorate, explains: "The enemy of the Nicaraguan people was the Somocista dictatorship . . . an intermediate power of imperialism . . . It was necessary to amass all the people's forces against the dictatorship, to unite all the people."[9]

The tasks of the FSLN, however, transcended those which Sandino had set for himself. Victory would not be focused primarily on the removal of foreign domination, but also on the creation of a new society. Such a society, as envisioned by the Sandinistas, would have a *socialist* content that would be adapted to the specific reality of Nicaragua. Carlos Fonseca set forth the FSLN's position on socialism: "We are conscious that socialism constitutes the only perspective that the people have in order to achieve a profound change in their conditions of life. . . . We identify ourselves with socialism, without giving up a critical approach towards the socialist experience."[10]

Fonseca developed a socialist ideology based on Sandino's writings and Nicaragua's historical experience, emphasizing the *class* nature of the popular struggle against the dictatorship. The Sandinista leader identified two oppressed classes—peasants and workers—as Nicaragua's revolutionary classes. Fonseca asserted that a strategic alliance between these two classes served as the social basis of the revolution, and that the FSLN functioned as the revolutionary movement's vanguard—its political leadership.

During the 1960s, the FSLN consolidated its ideology on the basis of Fonseca's central ideas.

> The ideological achievements in this period of expansion consist in having shattered the ideological and cultural hold existing from 1934 over our working classes by imperialism and its local expression—the Somocista dictatorship; increasingly, we have been able to diffuse among the masses the political and military thought of Sandino in close and dialectical combination with the scientific doctrine of the proletariat, the confirmation of the *Frente Sandinista* as a political organization with a clear revolutionary ideology capable of absorbing the inheritance of Sandino and giving a true class content to the popular struggle.[11]

The FSLN fused socialist ideological elements with the essence of *Sandinismo*—its broad popular basis, its anti-imperialism, and its reliance on armed struggle—to create the driving revolutionary ideology of the next twenty years.[12] This ideology, notes Henri Weber, the French political observer, touched the national aspirations of the Nicaraguan people:

> By draping its undistorted programme and methods of struggle in the cloth of Sandinism, the FSLN leadership was able to turn the formidable weapon of patriotism against the whole bourgeoisie. In fact, the upheavals of the previous thirty years, involving the disruptive penetration of the American way of life in Central America, had provoked a grave crisis of identity in Nicaraguan society and rendered the appeal of patriotism even more potent than in Sandino's time.[13]

The Sandinistas derived their initial strategy from the experiences of the Cuban revolution and the writings of Che Guevara. They considered guerrilla warfare the appropriate means of achieving political change and they were convinced that a revolutionary struggle based in the countryside, relying mainly on the support of the peasantry, would eventually lead to the overthrow of the dictatorship. Consequently, when workers, students, and members of the middle class joined the FSLN, they were transferred to the politico-military structure in the mountains.

In the 1960s, FSLN leaders believed that only the hardships of guerrilla life could forge true revolutionaries. Tomás Borge expresses this Sandinista article of faith:

> Colonel Lopez would tell us that the troops of Sandino had never suffered the incredible hardship that our guerrilla group had . . . for example, it was impossible to protect ourselves from the cold, from disease, to obtain the necessary food . . . there were many comrades who never gave up. . . . Only with men like these was it possible that an organization such as the FSLN could exist.[14]

And Henry Ruiz of the FSLN's National Directorate says that "the mountains represented at that time a laboratory for the revolutionaries, a kind of crucible in which were forged the best qualities of the revolutionaries."[15]

Legalistic Interval (1963–1967)

Reliance on a strategy centered solely in the mountains, however, tended to isolate the revolutionary movement from most sectors of Nicaraguan society. The FSLN's military defeats in Rio Coco and Rio Bocay were made worse by the absence of strong links with the masses.[16] The *Frente* later acknowledged that during this period their military operations had an "invasionist character," that is, Sandinistas would enter a rural area without having conducted prior political work there, which failed to win the support of the local population.

The FSLN abandoned its "foco" strategy and decided to initiate forms of struggle that organically linked the strategy of armed struggle to the participation of the oppressed majority of the population.[17] The Sandinistas began to build ties with urban workers and students by creating a clandestine and semilegal urban network designed to furnish logistical and political support for the armed struggle.

But the FSLN faced serious difficulties in establishing an urban base during this period. With few material resources, the *Frente* faced an uphill struggle. "After the Bocay," remembers Sandinista veteran Jacinto Suarez, "we carried out work among the masses. These were years when we had nothing. It must be said, we didn't have a thing: a wooden mimeograph, a safehouse, a pencil factory, a few yards of cloth, at most two pistols, and a great desire to work."[18] Because of their limited resources, the FSLN joined forces with the Nicaraguan Socialist Party, the only other organization in the country that was working for fundamental social change. But the Sandinistas soon found themselves in a subordinate position to the socialists, thereby facing serious limitations on their urban activity. According to Borge, "the direction of that activity,"

> was not in the hands of the *Frente Sandinista*. It is important to remember how these parties were formed—their economistic

character, their form of struggle for social gains, and, moreover, their electoral style. We went to the barrios and did not succeed in giving the struggle a revolutionary character. We did not succeed in giving it a political character; instead, the desire for immediate gains prevailed: street lights or drains had to be installed; the water company needed to come and wet down the streets because of the dust; there was no water, or it was too expensive; a bus needed to be routed here or there . . . things of this type. It wasn't bad to fight for all this, but these were the only things that we fought for.[19]

Although their presence in the urban poor neighborhoods remained weak between 1963 and 1967, the Sandinistas made substantial gains among the student population through the *Frente Estudiantil Revolucionario* (Revolutionary Student Front or FER). A high school student at the time, relates his experience:

I remember that in 1963 we revived the FER and gave it a Sandinista character. I had the opportunity to participate in this. The *Frente* decided to expand the involvement of the university, the work of the students, and that of the FER to encompass the high schools. The FER had been founded the year before and the high schools were incorporated into what was called the Second National Congress of Revolutionary Students.[20]

With many of its key militants in the cities, however, the FSLN was unable to sustain continuous political organizing among the peasants of the north. Some peasants received political instruction in the *Frente's* urban cells, and others were sent in groups to departmental capitals to protest against working conditions and land evictions.[21] But the Sandinistas lacked both adequately trained cadres and the necessary determination to organize both the urban and rural struggles. Consequently, the FSLN was unable to project itself to the masses as a viable political force.

The Sandinistas drew two principal conclusions from their experience between 1963 and 1967. First, they felt that their work in the countryside had suffered as a result of too much legal political work. Second, they criticized their devotion to short-term goals and their failure to advance a long-term revolutionary struggle. Fonseca summarized the organization's shortcomings during the mid-sixties:

In the years 1964 and 1965, practically all the emphasis was put on open work, which included legal work among the masses. Clandestine tasks were carried out, above all in the countryside, but the main emphasis of the work during that time was legal. Reality showed that legal work carried out in that manner did not serve to accumulate forces and that the progress achieved was minimal. Neither can it be overlooked that the legal work through the now disappeared Republican Mobilization group, the student movement, and peasant movement suffered from lack of discipline, audacity, and organization.

One must also conclude that revolutionary work (whether it be public, legal, or clandestine), cannot be advanced in an accelerated way if the armed revolutionary force is lacking. It was the lack of such a force that determined the extreme limitations of the legal work carried out in the years 1961–65.[22]

A new strategy emerged from this evaluation: *guerra popular prolongada*—prolonged popular war, or GPP. The GPP strategy centered on the rural proletariat, the largest sector of the working class. With recruits from this social base, the FSLN sought to develop a popular army in the countryside. Given the political backwardness of the agricultural working class and the strength of the ruling regime (which had been aided by the United States, reactionary Central American governments, and the national bourgeoisie) the Sandinistas stressed that the struggle would necessarily be a war of attrition.

From Pancasan to the Urban Experience (1967–1974)

In 1966, the FSLN leadership decided to resume the armed offensive.[23] The Sandinistas strengthened their guerrilla units in the area around the mountain of Pancasan, about thirty miles east of Matagalpa. A series of FSLN bank raids assisted the buildup in that area and local peasants provided considerable support. Problems remained, however, in the integration of peasant recruits into the regular guerrilla formations.

> The militants who came from urban areas generally possessed a higher revolutionary consciousness than the peasants as a whole, who became demoralized when faced with the first difficulties that we ran up against: scarcity of supplies, certain slow marches, and the first rumors of the presence of enemy soldiers on nearby roads. This obligated the leadership to send back the majority of the peasants, although there were honorable exceptions of peasants who firmly refused to be let go and who are an example of the combative possibility of this sector.[24]

The formation of the Pancasan guerrilla columns marked a significant advance for the Sandinistas. Fonseca saw this development as "a notable step forward organizationally because it did not follow the usual practice of preparing the armed movement in a neighboring country, which had provided distance from the enemy's observation; rather it was preparation of an armed movement in mountains situated in the very center of the country."[25]

The FSLN leadership arrived to direct the training and education of new peasant recruits who were now fighting with the *Frente*. But at the end of August 1967, the National Guard detected the guerrilla columns and launched an attack against them. For the FSLN, the attack on Pancasan was a severe military defeat—thirteen experienced members of the organization had been killed. Even though Pancasan was a military defeat for the Sandinistas, it was a political victory. Because the *Frente* had received considerable notoriety as a result of the battle, students and workers engaged in solidarity actions with the organization. Although the FSLN did not yet appear as an alternative to the dictatorship or to the nonrevolutionary opposition, Pancasan demonstrated that, unlike other guerilla organizations destroyed throughout Latin America in the disastrous years of *foquismo*, the FSLN was alive and gaining strength.

The surviving leadership of the FSLN quickly sought to achieve political gains from the military action. Their objective was to prove that Pancasan was merely the armed manifestation of a united mass struggle. No longer would they enter political alliances with the Socialist Party or other groups on the left. Instead, the FSLN moved to bolster its direct ties with the people. The strategy was to establish "intermediate organizations" which would be affiliated with the *Frente*, but would not bear its name.

"After Pancasan," recalls Borge, "we began the silent accumulation of forces which gradually formed an organic structure in the barrios."[26] In fact, the first violent demonstrations in support of FSLN actions occurred in the barrios. On July 15, 1969, the National Guard discovered and then attacked an FSLN safehouse in Managua, killing five Sandinista militants, including Julio Buitrago of the national leadership. When the National Guard refused to turn over the bodies, FSLN cadres and collaborators organized a protest.

> We held a public vigil for unreturned bodies of the fallen *compañeros*. During this vigil the people demonstrated something we had always believed: their sympathy for the *Frente Sandinista*, their faith in the *Frente Sandinista*. In this symbolic vigil the street vendors covered us with flowers. Afterwards we arranged gigantic demonstrations, five and ten blocks long, something never before seen in Managua. We first organized protests against the unreturned bodies and later supported the denunciation which

Doris Tijerino made concerning the torture she suffered in the office of security. It was also the first time that we attempted to set vehicles on fire during this type of demonstration. The people were scared a little and ran—rather we all ran. But we observed then the first use of violence, albeit timid, but accepted by the demonstrators.[27]

The attack on the Managua safehouse, however, revealed the Sandinistas' weakness in urban areas. Recognizing their vulnerability, which was exacerbated by the absence of fixed guerrilla camps, the FSLN national leadership ordered in 1970 that the organization go completely underground and only enter into combat as a last resort.

With the FSLN underground, the role of intermediate organizations became more crucial than ever. The Sandinistas carried out intense organizing efforts in the factories and working-class barrios, winning over many ex-members of the Nicaraguan Socialist Party. Because many of these new FSLN recruits were factory workers, a foundation was established for subsequent gains in Sandinista trade union organization.[28]

The Sandinistas also extended their influence in the universities. As more and more middle-class high school and university students slipped away from home on weekends and evenings in order to attend clandestine meetings, the student organization FER renewed its activity: "The student movement with FER at its head—the one with the most prestige among the intermediate organizations of our Sandinista youth—was consolidated as a student union . . . and in this period came to control the major organization of the student movement, the CUUN (the student council of the National University)."[29] The FER and other intermediate organizations put forth FSLN demands in communities and work sites, presenting—to the extent conditions permitted—the political line of the underground leadership. Furthermore, each time the National Guard lashed out at the FSLN these organizations led demonstrations to protest the Guard's repression.

During this period, Nicaraguans began to lose their fear of the Guard and became more willing to confront the regime directly. In May and June 1970, mothers and students launched a hunger strike in support of political prisoners, and in September a massive national protest movement erupted in all the major cities. In January 1971, students and workers in León demonstrated against increases in public transportion costs. Carlos Nuñez recalls the sudden increase in mass activity:

Everything began to happen at this moment: the first street demonstrations, the closing of schools. A climate of agitation began to be felt throughout the country. Public and private high schools got involved. In León almost all the schools were occupied—private church schools and public schools. Large numbers of students just stayed inside the schools. In León, these actions were directed by Carlos Roberto Huembes, Efrain Fajardo, Omar Cabezas, Agustín Lara, Edgar Munguia, and a number of other compañeros.[30]

The occupation of the high schools led to church occupations. Relatives of political prisoners held protest demonstrations to pressure the government. Repressive acts soon followed: students were dragged out violently, beginning with those who were occupying the public high schools. But as the repression increased the protests became more frequent.

Growth of the Mass Movement and Repression (1974–1977)

Somocista repression in this period was extremely severe. In 1972, Somoza proclaimed that the National Guard had eliminated the Sandinistas. Many believed him until the FSLN struck suddenly and boldly. On December 27, 1974, a Sandinista commando unit took twelve of Somoza's inner circle hostage at a Christmas party, and ultimately exchanged them for the freedom of fourteen political prisoners. In addition, the government was forced to broadcast and publish a lengthy FSLN position paper. The Sandinistas' December action had an effect on the residents of Managua's poor neighborhoods.

The residents of OPEN 3 were "filled with jubilation" when the report came in over the radio. Said one Maryknoll sister, "it was like hearing our own salvation history" as they listened to the FSLN leaders review the preceding twenty years of Nicaraguan history, detailing injustices of the regime and the struggle of the opposition. With this success the Frente gained stature in barrios such as OPEN 3, Riguero, 14 de Septiembre, and San Judas, while Somoza "lost face" and ordinary people had a glimpse of the possibility that popular opposition could be effective against his regime.[31]

New attacks from the mountains demonstrated the growing strength of the *Frente*. The regime responded to the offensive with a ferocious reign of terror. Somoza ordered the creation of a counterinsurgency unit and hired mercenaries trained in guerrilla warfare. Guard detachments were sent to the rural north with road-building equipment, helicopter

gunships, and American military "advisers." With the country under
martial law, all constitutional guarantees suspended, and strict press
censorship, the government conducted a ruthless campaign against the
guerrillas' base of support in the countryside. During 1975 and 1976
approximately 3,000 peasants were murdered, and thousands more were
imprisoned or forced into exile.[32]

Although the FSLN's December action served as an important stim-
ulus to the mass struggle, government repression and the Sandinistas'
internal weaknesses prevented the Frente from taking full advantage of
it. Sandinista leader José Valdivia recalled that the December action

> was of the greatest importance for us. A wave of enthusiasm in
> favor of the Frente Sandinista arose in Nicaragua and elsewhere.
> But the organization did not have the ability to channel this
> enthusiasm because the necessary structures did not exist. That
> is, we lost the initiative—we struck once and we couldn't strike
> again later. The Guard maintained the offensive, continually
> pounding us and our structures, especially the structures which
> we had in the mountains. The mountains endured nearly all the
> repression.[33]

The FSLN Splits

The enforced clandestinity and unrelenting repression between 1974 and
1977 destroyed the cohesiveness of the Frente.[34] As a result, its rural
guerrilla units were isolated from its urban cadres, and much of the
leadership was in exile or in hiding. The vital link between the mountain
and the city had been severed. Moreover, just when the objective conditions of the war called for a variety of strategic choices, factions of the
FSLN were working in different locations, with different class forces,
different forms of military tactics, and different agendas. They were unable to maintain communication with one another and coherent unified
discussions on future strategy were impossible to arrange. Valdivia describes the situation in 1975:

> Communicating with the city from the mountains took time. We
> were able to communicate once a month, every two months, or
> even less often. Thus, it was difficult to elaborate a general
> political line or to reach an agreement with the city in order to
> implement the offensive in a coherent way.[35]

At the same time that the Frente confronted these communication
difficulties, the FSLN was faced with basic questions of strategy and

tactics: Should the *Frente* concentrate its work in the cities or the countryside? Was the struggle against Somoza to be a protracted one, to be won by sticking to the established mode of rural guerrilla warfare? Should the political or the military aspect of its efforts be dominant? What relationship should exist between the bourgeois opposition and the FSLN? What demands should be put forth by the mass movement? Did the situation already exist for an insurrection?

Disagreement over answers to these questions led to the creation of three separate factions within the FSLN. They were the *Tendencia Proletaria* (Proletarian Tendency—TP); the rural *Guerra Popular Prolongada* (Prolonged Popular War—GPP); and a third group, the partisans of broad class alliances who supported a rapid overthrow of Somoza, the *Tendencia Insurreccional* (commonly known as *Terceristas*).

The Proletarian Tendency argued that the guerrilla army was operating in isolation from the urban working class. Pointing to the relative decline of the agricultural sector in the 1960s and the rapid growth and new militancy of the urban proletariat, the *Proletarios* held that only a Marxist-Leninist party of the proletariat could guide the revolutionary struggle. Without such a party, the workers' movement would be confined to economic demands and *anti-Somocismo*. Consequently, the Proletarian Tendency focused its efforts on political, educational, and agitational work with urban working class cadres and the marginal barrio dwellers of Managua's outlying slums. They also carried out organizing activities among the agricultural workers of the Pacific Coast and in the sugar refineries and cotton-processing plants of the departments of León and Chinandega.

The Proletarians began two publications, the ideological *Causa Sandinista* and the military *El Combatiente Popular*. In the second issue of *Causa Sandinista*, they put forth this position:

> We must promote the formation of unions, peasant leagues, professional associations, democratic organisations of workers, women and youth—every kind of legal, illegal, open or clandestine organisation. Without mass organisation, the revolutionary struggle against the dictatorship has no effective underpinning.[36]

Each of these organizations, the Proletarians emphasized, must maintain its class independence from the bourgeoisie.

Proponents of the original Prolonged Popular War strategy remained faithful to their position. Although recognizing the importance of the urban struggle, they viewed the guerrilla units as the vanguard of the revolutionary process; mountain strongholds and the rural proletariat would prevent the bourgeoisie from coopting the revolution. They held that the rural guerrillas had weakened the regime and its repressive apparatus, thereby promoting the work in the cities. In defense of their concentration on military action, the GPP argued that the National Guard had to be contained militarily before effective political work could be carried out among the masses.

In the period before the split, the Sandinistas used the phrase "prolonged popular war" to characterize mainstream FSLN strategy. A Sandinista communiqué once defined the phrase as "the political and military confrontation of the organised people against their foreign and class enemies during the time required for careful preparation and development before the final battle."[37] During the period that the FSLN was fragmented, the GPP still thought that a final insurrection against Somoza was a distant goal, and that the dictatorship would wither away slowly in the face of organized mass action. Furthermore, they were convinced that only a long struggle would foster socialist consciousness among a working class kept politically backward by forty years of Somocismo.

During Somoza's intense counter-offensive, communication broke down within the National Directorate, the leadership body of the FSLN. The positions of all three tendencies became fixed and arguments among them were bitter and polemical. In October 1975, elements of the leadership expelled the Proletarians who subsequently operated independently but retained the name of the FSLN.

At this juncture, members of the leadership in exile, acting as a "third force," tried to reconcile the two positions. In 1976, two members of the FSLN's ten-person National Directorate, Carlos Fonseca (General Secretary) and Eduardo Contreras, attempted to end the split. But the third force, the *Terceristas*, was unable to resolve the dispute and soon emerged with its own "insurrectionist" strategy.

The *Terceristas* did not agree with the Proletarians and the GPP that the struggle must be a protracted one requiring the gradual accumulation of forces. On the contrary, they claimed that a revolutionary situation already existed: anti-Somoza sentiment had spread throughout the society and the popular sectors were ready to revolt. The *Terceristas* proposed a series of military strikes that would spark a popular insurrection. The insurrection's success, according to the *Terceristas*, rested on gaining support from all anti-Somoza sectors, including factions of the bourgeoisie whose economic pressure (through strikes) would coincide with armed activities. Only a broad-based coalition under FSLN hegemony, founded on a program of progressive reforms, could isolate the regime and engineer its collapse. Somocismo would be replaced by a provisional pop-ular-democratic government with FSLN participation.

By 1977, a distinct majority of the FSLN leadership favored the insurrectional strategy. Although the Terceristas' name never appeared in *Frente* documents, the National Directorate became clearly identified with the insurrectional tendency. In mid-1978, the national leadership summarized its goals this way:

> The armed insurrection of the masses is a means to achieve the revolutionary overthrow of the Somoza dynasty and open up a process of popular democracy, which will allow our people to enjoy democratic liberties, a more favourable framework in which to accumulate the revolutionary energies required for the march towards full national liberation and socialism.[38]

To ignite an "armed insurrection of the masses," the Terceristas had to initiate a dramatic armed offensive that would encourage the people to take to the streets.

Toward the Offensive (1977)

In 1977, much to the surprise of the FSLN leadership, Somoza again proclaimed that the FSLN had been liquidated. The United States Embassy agreed, and in March 1977 issued the following confident statement: "Nicaragua should continue to enjoy political stability for some time to come. . . . During 1976 the government inflicted heavy blows on the local guerrilla organization and now faces no serious threat from that quarter."[39] Somoza, in response to United States pressure, ended martial law and censorship for the first time in three years.[40] But that concession led directly to a massive outburst of anti-Somoza activities. A new wave of strikes, increased student protest, and press exposure of government corruption and torture combined to inspire the *Terceristas* into action. In mid-October, well-armed *Terceristas* attacked several towns, including Masaya, just thirty miles from the capital.

Immediately after the attack, a highly respected group of Nicaraguan intellectuals calling themselves the "Group of Twelve" released a state-ment from Costa Rica urging the population to support the Sandinistas, praising their "political maturity," and declaring that the FSLN would have to participate in any solution to Nicaragua's problems.[41] The Costa Rican government also lent its tacit support to the *Terceristas* by per-mitting them to set up their bases inside Costa Rican territory.[42]

The GPP did not fight in the *Tercerista* actions, but it did continue to carry out a small-scale offensive in the northern mountains, seizing small towns, destroying Somoza properties, and ambushing military convoys. In the cities, the Proletarians organized the class-based Revolutionary Workers Committees. Pro-FSLN students led demonstrations to demand freedom for imprisoned Sandinistas and the prosecution of Guardsmen responsible for the "disappearance" of 350 campesinos. Somoza responded to the opposition with an unprecedented reign of terror in the countryside, designed to end peasant support of the FSLN.

The Chamorro Assassination

On January 10, 1978, Pedro Joaquín Chamorro, a leading Somoza opposition figure and editor of the daily La Prensa, was assassinated. His death served only to intensify and extend the popular struggle against the dictatorship. Massive nationwide demonstrations, backed by the church and the traditional opposition parties, erupted during the next few weeks. In addition to the mass protests, the business community called a general strike, sending workers home on full or partial salaries.

Chamorro's assassination was a critical turning point for the FSLN and the mass movement. After his murder, large numbers of Nicaraguans began to join the insurrectional process. By January 28, protests flared in Matagalpa and Diriamba, followed by large demonstrations in Managua, Masaya, and San Carlos on the Costa Rican border. Within two days the National Guard responded, attacking women with tear gas at a large peaceful demonstration at the United Nations building, and assaulting 3,000 students protesting at the National University. The next day large crowds erected street barricades in León, Jinotega, and Chinandega. Escalating the level of violence, the Guard beat, arrested, and shot dozens of demonstrators. The students tried to win over some members of the Guard with slogans such as "Guards, control yourselves, don't kill your own people," but the soldiers ignored their pleas. At night women marched through the streets pounding pots and pans, and during the day young people built barricades and set fire to tires on street corners. In response, the Guard increased its armed patrols, often shooting people on sight, or, as in the Managua barrio of Open-3, beating protestors in full view of the public.[43]

In February, when popular resistance was at its peak, Tercerista units from Costa Rica attacked Peñas Blancas and Rivas. In Granada, the Sandinistas trapped the Guard in its barracks and conducted a popular assembly in which they explained the goals of the revolution. At the same time, GPP squads struck Guard strongholds in the north.

The most dramatic expression of mass outrage in this period took place in the Indian community of Monimbó. At the end of January for four days, the population battled the well-equipped National Guard with homemade bombs, clubs, machetes, 32-caliber rifles, handguns, and boiling water. The Guard responded by using tanks, helicopter gunships, and armored cars against the protestors. Although the Indians suffered hundreds of casualties, only weeks later Monimbó revolted again with even greater intensity.

> On February 22, Monimbó's men, women, and children de-
> fiantly challenged Guard control of their barrio. Using the tools
> of their trade, the weapons available to the poor, and their artisan
> creativity, they confronted the Guardsmen. With sticks, clubs,
> machetes, and brick barricades, the very young and very old
> guarded strategic street entrances. With eight 22-caliber rifles,
> four 38-caliber pistols, two grenades, and an arsenal of fused
> fireworks and home-made "contact bombs," the residents seized
> control of the barrio. Forcing the National Guard out of their
> streets and past the barrio entrance at the San Sebastian Church,
> the residents took possession of the plaza. Gathering with their
> home-made weapons raised victoriously, they shouted in unison,
> "Not even death will deter us!" The Guard continued its brutal
> repression, combining aerial bombardment and ground attack,
> and refused Red Cross entry into the barrio, while it sought to
> re-take the area. La Prensa headlines of February 23 read: "Mon-
> imbó: the neighborhood struggles house by house."[44]

By February 1978, a prerevolutionary situation had emerged in the country. Isolated revolts had begun to merge and identify themselves as Sandinista. The requirement of the moment was a strong organization to conduct a coherent military and political war against the regime. The FSLN faced the task of converting prerevolutionary conditions into a revolutionary crisis. But the Sandinistas were not yet prepared to effectively guide the upsurge in the mass movement.

> The vanguard . . . hadn't been able to make contact in a more
> organic form with those sectors of the masses with the greatest
> political awareness. The actions of that sector, encouraged by
> the telling blows dealt the National Guard by the FSLN, in the
> midst of the Somoza regime's political crisis and the country's
> social and economic problems, surpassed the vanguard's ca-
> pability to channel all that popular agitation.[45]

On the Road to Insurrection (1978)

As popular demands for arms, leadership, and organization grew, the need for unity among the revolutionary forces became paramount.[46] As the mass movement developed numerically and politically, internecine conflict declined considerably among the FSLN tendencies. Differences narrowed as each tendency displayed a new strategic and tactical flexibility.

The Proletarians, although focusing on the urban proletariat, extended their organizing efforts to radicalized farm workers and landless peasants. In March 1978, the Proletarians consolidated the Rural Workers Association (known by the acronym ATC) as a public organization.[47] Devoting increased energies to military matters, they formed a grassroots militia—Revolutionary People's Commandos. The Proletarians never renounced their goal of building a vanguard party, but the crisis situation demanded more immediate action in other areas.

At the same time, the Prolonged Popular War tendency strengthened its urban organization, particularly in the north. The mass actions of January and February 1978 had convinced GPP partisans that mass sentiment existed for insurrection, but they felt that popular organization was still inadequate. Nevertheless, with tens of thousands now looking to the FSLN for leadership, the continuation of the insurrection was imperative. In the past, both the Prolonged Popular War tendency and the Proletarian tendencies had insisted that an insurrection, without the presence of strong mass organization, would only benefit Somoza's conservative opponents and the United States, by then eager to replace Somoza.[48] But the conservative opposition remained too deeply divided to take advantage of the situation.

The weakness of the bourgeoisie lent credibility to the *Tercerista* argument that the revolutionary forces would gain hegemony within a broad, anti-Somoza coalition.

The Tercerista attacks in October and February, notes Nicaraguan historian Alejandro Bendaña,

> had escalated the struggle. Their strikes had forced the regime
> to strain its repressive might, fueling greater resistance and win-
> ning support for the Sandinistas as the only truly popular force.
> Tercerista tactics were not above criticism: they had underesti-
> mated the fighting capacity of the Guard, and its loyalty to So-
> moza; they had overestimated the strength of spontaneous
> insurrectionist forms. Nonetheless, their actions had propelled
> the mass movement forward, kept the initiative in revolutionary
> hands and expanded the mass base of all three tendencies.[49]

In June 1978, the three tendencies signed agreements on immediate military action. They established a national Sandinista coordinating committee, with the understanding that tactical agreements were the first step toward ultimate formal unification. Each tendency recognized that important ideological disagreements remained, that reunification would be long and arduous, but that the revolutionary process depended on the unity of Sandinismo.

Immediately after the FSLN achieved tactical unity, the Sandinistas created the United People's Movement (MPU). The three FSLN tendencies joined with the Communist Party of Nicaragua, the traditional left, and more than twenty student, labor, women's, and civic organizations to develop a concrete plan for mass opposition to Somoza.[50] Unified in the MPU, the popular sectors pressured Somoza to allow the Group of Twelve to return from exile. Despite government intimidation, thousands of Managuans welcomed them at the airport—clear proof of popular support for both the Twelve and the FSLN. Sergio Ramírez, one of the Twelve, notes that "it was the first time the people had the opportunity to express themselves en masse in favor of the Sandinista Front, and there were more than 150,000 people amid the tremendous agitation that was produced in Managua that fifth of July."[51]

On August 22, the Terceristas attacked the National Palace in Managua. Disguised as Somoza's personal military guard, they managed to seize the entire building and more than 1,000 hostages, including key government officials and several Somoza relatives. The dictatorship had no alternative but to meet the Sandinistas' demands. An attempted coup by hard-liners inside the Guard during the palace takeover laid bare divisions within Somoza's forces and revealed the erosion of his political authority.

The palace seizure was crucial and accomplished all three of its principal aims: to give immediate publicity throughout Nicaragua and abroad to the FSLN's political demands; to inspire a national insurrection; and to gain the release of key FSLN leaders. Thousands turned out to give the commandos moral support as they headed to temporary refuge in Panama. The Sandinistas were now hailed as national heroes.

As demands to oust Somoza reached an unprecedented level, a new general strike was launched—this time with labor as the principal participant.[52] The Sandinistas now had to decide when and how to begin the general offensive. The GPP and the Proletarians maintained their doubts about an insurrectional strategy, pointing to insufficient organization as an obstacle to success. But the Tercerista attack on the National Palace had inspired the population, and all three tendencies mobilized their combat units.

On September 9, the FSLN leadership issued a communiqué that began with these words:

> The hour of the Sandinista popular insurrection has come. Every-
> one on to the streets. The Sandinista army, the Sandinista militias,
> and the Sandinista people must take up arms against the National
> Guard of Somoza. Everyone to organise around the provisional
> government headed by Las Doce.[53]

To trigger the insurrection, the FSLN coordinated attacks that were
launched on army posts in Managua, Masaya, León, Chinandega, and
Estelí. They distributed arms to a population that had previously fought
only with stones, hunting weapons, or no weapons at all. Before the day
ended, the Sandinista and popular forces had either captured or surrounded the garrisons of four provincial cities and established popular
emergency administrations.

In Masaya, the people again took over the central section of their
city as well as the entire barrio of Monimbó.[54] In Managua, crowds seized
four sections of the city and burned National Guard barracks. In the
north, the FSLN first occupied the town of Chichigalpa, and then with
the help of urban militia and townspeople, seized the city of Chinandega.
In León, a joint attack by the townspeople and Sandinista forces held
Nicaragua's second largest city for days.

These initial gains, although dramatic, were quickly lost as the
people's struggle turned into a defensive "war of positions." As the
National Guard regrouped and began to recapture one city at a time,
the FSLN, not yet prepared to confront a standing army, had to retreat.
The urban "muchachos" were left alone to face the National Guard. The
Guard was able to reenter the cities, but only after Somoza's air force
had subjected them to intensive and systematic bombing against the
Sandinistas. The Guard entered what remained of these cities with orders
to "take no prisoners." Mass execution was the order of the day. One
refugee later commented that it was "a crime to be a male between the
ages of 12 and 30 in Nicaragua."[55] The Guard burned down entire
neighborhoods in retaliation for support given the Sandinistas.

Although thousands of Nicaraguans lost their lives in the September
1978 insurrection, the FSLN regarded the uprising as a political victory.
And once again the Sandinistas had to acknowledge that the people were
the driving force in the fighting.

> In the final stages, the peasants came down to join the struggle
> in the cities. In Chinandega, the safe houses were filled with
> people taking three-hour classes. The people were going to take
> to the street: The people were the ones in the vanguard of that
> struggle. There was no alternative but to put oneself at the head
> of that upsurge and try to obtain the most positive outcome.
> We placed ourselves at the head of that movement and led it

in five cities. It was the first national uprising led by the FSLN but that was chiefly due to pressure by the masses.[56]

January 1979 represented a political watershed in the popular struggle against Somoza. To strengthen its confrontation with the regime, the FSLN created an alternative political structure: the *Frente Patriotico Nacional* (National Patriotic Front—FPN). The FPN shared the Sandinista perspective and accepted the three fundamental points of the Sandinista program: disbandment of the National Guard, nationalization of all Somocista business and property, and establishment of a democratic popular government. With the exception of the financial capitalists, most of the bourgeoisie, the working class, the peasants, the marginalized population, and the intellectuals coalesced in the FPN.[57]

While the FSLN launched its political offensive, Somoza tightened the grip of military control. In the north, the dictator's forces conducted a fierce campaign of terror, murdering entire families in the countryside near Estelí, and randomly firing on civilians in urban areas. International press cables reported that 200 Nicaraguans died during the first twenty-four days of 1979.[58] The Guard's repression, however, failed to deter the mass movement, which was quick to capitalize on Somoza's weakening political position. On the anniversary of Chamorro's death, The Popular Unity Movement and other civic organizations announced their intent to hold a memorial march. On January 6, Somoza banned the proposed march, but reversed his decision three days later when the people threatened to ignore the dictator's command. The MPU viewed Somoza's reversal as a major victory for the people, and on January 10 the country conducted a general work stoppage and 30,000 people marched through Managua.

Immediately after its conception, the National Patriotic Front began an intense organizing drive through its different commissions. The Urban Workers Commission, for example, successfully formed a Workers Defense Committee that united unions such as the National Association of Teachers, the People's Union Movement, and the National Employees Union. When Somoza devalued the cordoba by 43 percent in May 1979, the Workers Defense Committee staged a major protest. This committee also campaigned against poor working conditions and low wages. Other FPN commissions campaigned against unemployment, lack of urban housing, and poor public transportation.[59] Now unified, the popular opposition was prepared for the next stage of the revolutionary war.

The Reunification of the FSLN

The FSLN did not regard its retreat from the National Guard in September 1978 as a defeat, but rather as a calculated tactical withdrawal. It was able to regroup its forces in the mountains where the Guard could not reach them, and reflect on the lessons from September. The Sandinistas did not consider the results of the uprising as evidence against the efficacy of insurrection as a military tactic. But they they did acknowledge that the popular forces were insufficiently organized and that the vanguard was fragmented; the FSLN could not challenge the Guard until these shortcomings were corrected. In late 1978, Sandinista militant Giaconda Belli evaluated the situation:

> The present situation calls for a tactical retreat in the military sense, to reorganize our forces, move to new forms of struggle, and unleash guerilla actions throughout the country. On the political plane, this is a time for an offensive in order to qualitatively transform the enthusiasm and heroism [of the people] into popular organizing. By developing them militarily and politically, this process of organizing the masses is precisely the guarantee of triumph for the guerilla movement.[60]

To the *Frente*, "organizing the masses" meant three things: military leadership, grassroots organization, and political education. After September, the FSLN trained combatants and new recruits in both political theory and military tactics. Thousands learned to handle both the sophisticated and makeshift weapons that the FSLN now had at its disposal. Clandestine editions of Sandino's works were studied, together with the *Frente*'s internal communiqués and the theoretical journal *Pensamiento Critico*.[61]

It was not enough, however, to train the people; the FSLN itself had to be reunited. During October and November 1978, the three tendencies held meetings to resolve their differences. They based their unity on the following seven-point program originally drawn up by Sandino:

1. Establishment of a popular and independent government
2. Cooperative management of the land to benefit those who work it
3. Suppression of all reactionary treaties that have been forced upon the nation
4. Integration of continental organizations that work for Central American interests, without Yankee or other foreign power involvement
5. Recovery of our national riches and resources to benefit the great majority of our people
6. Respect for our national values
7. Maintenance of a popular army[62]

On December 7, 1978, "somewhere in Nicaragua" the GPP, Proletarian, and *Tercerista* tendencies announced their agreement:

> [We] have decided to unite our political and military forces to assure that the heroic struggle of our people shall not be mocked by the machinations of Yankee imperialism and those sectors of the local bourgeoisie who have sold out on our country. We will unite our forces in order to advance the revolutionary armed struggle until the Somocista military dictatorship is definitively defeated and we have installed in our country an authentically democratic regime, one which guarantees national sovereignty and the socio-economic progress of our workers. This Sandinista unity which we hereby commit ourselves to reinforce more and more each day, will be the unquestionable guarantee of popular victory.[63]

This first move toward unity required a gestation period during which the leadership could communicate the agreement to each tendency's wider membership. In the meantime, the GPP worked to fortify its urban base, and the Proletarians launched a new campaign to win over peasants and rural workers in the major production centers of the Pacific Coast. With their formation of the Revolutionary People's Commandos, the Proletarians thrust headlong into the military struggle in the fight against Somoza.

On March 8, 1979, the three FSLN tendencies completed their "program of national unity" signed by the "Joint National Leadership of the Sandinista National Liberation Front (FSLN)."[64] The Sandinistas asserted their unity and further clarified certain fundamental points in their plans for a future government. Specifically, they set out to establish: 1. a provisional government of national unity; 2. a program of national reconstruction; 3. a foreign policy of nonalignment; and 4. the expropriation of all of Somoza's properties.[65]

While the FSLN was resolving its internal difficulties, the crisis of the dictatorship deepened. In May 1979, the Sandinistas outlined their view of the regime's plight:

> The fact that the Somoza military dictatorship and the opposition bourgeoisie have been unable to resolve their crisis because they could not eliminate the FSLN and the popular forces, and the fact that the FSLN and the popular forces have been able to maintain their legitimacy and popular support, and build sufficient forces to defeat the dictatorship, and establish a Government of National Unity under the popular hegemony, gives this crisis the nature of a "revolutionary crisis."[66]

But before the Sandinistas could launch a final offensive against the Somoza regime, they had to 1. consolidate the FPN, granting the MPU the key role within the new front; 2. complete the international isolation of Somoza and gain international recognition for their provisional government; 3. intensify the combativeness of the people until they were prepared for war; and 4. attack and unremittingly weaken the National Guard.[67]

In order to disperse the regime's forces, the Sandinistas had to combine different forms of guerrilla warfare and popular insurrection. Regular forces on the regional fronts had to be strengthened and the militias, people's brigades, and urban commandos had to be improved. And this military restructuring could not be allowed to distract from the Sandinistas' sustained harassment of Somoza's troops. At the same time, the FSLN began to form the nucleus of a regular army. They sought to multiply the military resources and tactics available for the coming offensive, and provide a ready-trained people's army that could replace the defeated National Guard.

In late March, the Sandinistas conducted their first joint guerrilla operation, seizing the small town of El Jicaro in the northern province of Nueva Segovia. This attack was strictly diversionary, drawing more Guard troops into the mountain stronghold of the guerrillas. The united FSLN launched their second attack less than a month later in Estelí. According to the original plan, the Carlos Fonseca Amador columns were to have diverted the Guard with a series of hit-and-run assaults throughout the Estelí zone; but when guerrilla patrols entered the city to collect weapons and supplies, thousands of residents spontaneously revolted, just as they had the previous September. After gaining control of the city, the people of Estelí asked the Sandinistas to stay and support them. The Sandinistas consented, but were soon surrounded by the National Guard. To distract the Guard, one FSLN commander carried out a swift diversionary operation, allowing the escape of both the attack unit and hundreds of new recruits.[68]

> After that came another of the Guard's famous "Cleaning-Up Operations," and that was important for the consciousness of the people here. We were the only city that went through three separate uprisings and three waves of National Guard barbarity. April meant that there was no-one at all left in Estelí who didn't support the Frente. When the call came for the final insurrection in June, everyone was ready.[69]

As the time for the final offensive approached, the FSLN prepared the integration of its three weapons—a national strike, popular insurrection, and military attacks—into a unified strategy. The Sandinistas had used each of these weapons before, but never all three simultaneously. To coordinate them, the FSLN established a communications network via radio (Radio Sandino) that linked the rural guerrillas to the urban militias, the United People's Movement to the Civil Defense Committees, and the FSLN high command to the people. By May, Radio Sandino was functioning effectively: "The means of communication were . . . of vital importance: wireless for coordination among the various fronts, and the radio. Without them it would have been impossible to coordinate it [the final offensive] either from a political or military standpoint. We succeeded in organizing Radio Sandino, which was the main means of propaganda for the uprising and for the strike."[70]

With their communications link in place, Sandinista strategists put the finishing touches on their plans for the final offensive. They agreed that the offensive should begin in the north; there was also consensus about the need for a general insurrection. As before, the FSLN aimed to divert the National Guard forces to prevent them from concentrating their forces as they had in September.

The National Directorate chose Jinotega for the final attack of the preoffensive period. In the attack, the FSLN suffered a serious loss with the death of German Pomares, one of the Sandinistas' most effective commanders. But because the National Guard had to transfer elite units to the north, the FSLN succeeded in depleting the dictator's forces on the southern frontier.[71]

The FSLN learned from the Jinotega experience that its forces alone could not defeat the National Guard. Victory could be won only with the efforts of the so-called Internal Front: the popular forces that would lead the urban insurrection. Between the end of May and early June, everything would depend on the people. Ortega explained the FSLN's strategy:

> The way we saw it, the insurrection had to last, at a nationwide level, for at least two weeks in order to give the guerrilla columns a chance to regroup and go into action at the right moment, making the enemy's situation completely untenable and subjecting the enemy to a constant strategic siege, with victory only a question of time, of wearing down the enemy before launching the final attack.[72]

Final Sandinista Offensive against the Somoza Dynasty

In the unanimous view of the FSLN National Directorate all the necessary conditions had been met for the start of the final offensive by the third week of May. On May 14, the International Monetary Fund approved a 66 million dollar loan to Nicaragua, but the national economic austerity measures that were enacted following the loan award angered nearly all Nicaraguans. Within days of the IMF announcement, Mexico broke off diplomatic relations with Somoza because of the "horrendous acts of genocide" committed by the National Guard. All the FSLN's guerrilla units were battle-ready, and the Internal Front provided a political and military leadership flexible enough to combine the three elements of the struggle in the major cities: a general strike, mass insurrection, and military action. The Civil Defense Committees and the United People's Movement were ready, and the political consciousness of the people matched that of their organizational preparedness.[73]

The final Sandinista offensive to overthrow the Somoza dynasty occurred in three distinct phases: 1. May 29 to June 8: attack on all fronts, popular insurrection, and general strike; 2. June 9 to June 25: battle of Managua and the Southern Front feint; and 3. June 26 to July 12: taking of Carazo and consolidation of the northern cities. Unlike the spontaneous and disorganized insurrection of September 1978, the strategy of the final offensive was to attack on all fronts at once.[74]

The FSLN began the final offensive with a successful attack on the National Guard barracks in El Naranjo, located in southern Nicaragua. Sandinista combatants in the northern front first seized Ocotal and the town of El Viejo, north of Estelí. The main offensive in the north, however, was aimed at capturing Matagalpa, where some of the most bitter street-by-street fighting went on for weeks. When the National Guard sent 250 reinforcements to Matagalpa, they were ambushed by the Sandinistas. Such ambushes became a key part of the offensive because they enabled the FSLN to disrupt or seize control of many Nicaraguan roads and highways, slowing down National Guard movements. By the end of the first week of fighting, the FSLN controlled most of the residential neighborhoods of Matagalpa.[75]

On June 2, Radio Sandino called upon the Internal Front to launch a "mass insurrection throughout the country."[76] The response was swift and effective. The high degree of organization within the Civil Defense Committees allowed FSLN military units to quickly gain strategic positions in León, Chichigalpa, Matagalpa, and Masaya. On June 2, the main Sandinista forces entered León and in two days had gained almost complete control of Nicaragua's second largest city. In Masaya, Civil Defense Committee leaders organized the collection and egalitarian distribution of food, strengthened the barricades, and created a popular tribunal of justice to judge Somocista criminals and delinquents.[77]

On June 4, the FSLN called a general strike. Within two days the shutdown was almost complete. Somoza ordered an immediate state-of-siege that included arrest without warrant, detention without charge, press censorship, and restrictions on civilian movement. But the state-of-siege backfired: it crippled the economy and converted the entire nation into a war zone. By the end of the first week of June, the Sandinistas claimed control of León, Matagalpa, and Chichigalpa.[78]

In Managua the FSLN's strategy was to win time not territory. By tying down Guard troops in the city and exhausting Somoza's resistance and credibility, the FSLN converted the capital into a frontline battle zone, and thereby exposed the war to the foreign press and international community. At the time of the national strike, the Sandinistas controlled one-quarter of Managua's streets, houses, stores, and supply centers. On Sunday, June 10, Radio Sandino called for immediate action: "Open ditches! Build barricades! Immobilize the enemy in the streets."[79] Thousands worked feverishly to build barricades, filling the streets with tree trunks, rocks, overturned cars, and broken bottles. Within two days, insurrectionists gained control of the entire eastern sector of Managua, a total of twenty-five barrios.[80]

The Sandinistas' military success in Managua increased its international political legitimacy. On June 18, the FSLN announced the formation of the new provisional government council, and the Andean nations (Venezuela, Columbia, Ecuador, Peru, and Bolivia) formally recognized the FSLN as a "legitimate army."[81] Having achieved their goal of pinning down the National Guard in Managua, the Sandinistas departed during the night of June 21. Black described their tactical retreat to Masaya:

> The plan was to take all the regular and militia forces, with any civilians who wanted to leave, to evacuate all the wounded, and to reach Masaya in twelve hours on foot. All this to be done without revealing the plan in advance to those who would participate—the risk of discovery was too terrible to contemplate. When the Guardia launched its habitual morning attack on the 28th, they were met with sporadic gunfire from isolated snipers left to cover the retreat. As it died down, Somoza's men took stock of the situation. The eastern barrios were deserted. Under cover of night three columns—containing 6,000 people instead of the 1,500 originally planned—had left Managua in single file. In the darkness they had become hopelessly lost, but despite taking 30 hours to cover the distance and being sighted on the volcanic flatlands of Piedras Negras by six aircraft, the columns reached Masaya with only six dead and sixteen wounded. "If we can do that," said one man, "we can do anything."[82]

The Managua strategy was successful: the Sandinistas departed with overwhelming popular and international support; Somoza and the National Guard were left defeated and internationally condemned. The FSLN had converted their withdrawal from Managua into another victory. Between June 25 and 27, they strengthened their grip on Masaya and Diriamba, where they outnumbered the National Guard. Shortly thereafter, the Sandinistas moved west to seize the town of Jinotepe and within a week consolidated control over the entire Corazo region. Retaking Managua had severely damaged Somoza's northern forces. The Guard could no longer send reinforcements to the field: "The National Guard has been weakened [in the countryside] by wide-ranging guerrilla attacks. With heavy government troop concentrations in Managua commanders were aware that outnumbered posts outside the capital often are left to fend for themselves."[83]

The FSLN's dispersed attacks destroyed Somoza's strategy of dominating rural zones. Many Guard units had to concentrate on the Sandinista-held cities or were trapped in their own barracks within liberated territory. Even in areas where the Guard could move freely due to their superior firepower, the FSLN received virtually total support from the peasants.

By early July, the FSLN moved to solidify its control in Chinandega and Somotillo in the west, in Ocotal and Estelí in the north, and in Granada and Rivas in the south. The Sandinistas and the local population had already liberated Matagalpa, and revolutionary forces dominated the Carazo region. A desperate Somoza vented his resentment on everyone: fleeing civilians, Sandinista muchachos, liberal sympathizers, and conservative industrialists. Nicaragua became an inferno during the last days of the insurrection as the dictator ordered his troops to murder civilians and his air force to bomb rebel cities indiscriminately.

The popular forces demonstrated their ingenuity in the southern town of Rivas, where pro-Sandinista elements had captured the town center. Even though they were encircled by some 1,000 Guard troops, the armed population and Civil Defense Committee activists were more concerned about aerial bombings. The combatants were especially worried about the 450 patients in the Rivas hospital, and decided to evacuate them. They directed the patients out, single file, through openings that CDC members had carved through the hospital's walls, and then through house after house, past the National Guard, to safety.[84]

By July 12, the war was almost over. Sandinista forces had liberated León, Chinandega, Estelí, Matagalpa, and Masaya. The FSLN immediately prepared its forces for the final assault on Managua. Somoza, reeling from the Sandinista victories, threatened to shoot down any plane attempting to bring a "rebel government" into Nicaragua; but his days were numbered and he knew it. Shortly after 5:OO A.M. on July 17, Somoza, a few family members, and a hundred Guard officers, flew to Miami in a private jet.

On July 18, National Guard forces sought their vengeance on liberated cities, looting and bombing them all night. But the next day Sandinista forces entered Managua. Before the guerrilla forces arrived, the people of Managua had captured the city. They first took the Basic Infantry Training School and First Armored Battalion installations, then the smaller barracks, until it seemed that the entire population of the capital was armed and firing rounds in the air from their liberated weapons. On July 20, the streets were filled with family reunions after years of clandestinity and combat. Chaos reigned for a few days—the chaos that only the removal of an entire state structure can bring. As one member of the National Directorate concluded, "the dictator's departure confirmed our theory that Somocismo was a coherent structure. We took the heart and the body fell. Now we must fill the empty space."[85]

2

THE MASS
ORGANIZATIONS EMERGE

The Sandinistas and other early activists had to overcome tremendous obstacles to create the mass organizations that supported them. Both FSLN cadres and non-FSLN organizers were operating in a society with no history of mass organization, amid a climate of intense National Guard repression. They were also working with a population that possessed little education, and, initially, minimal political consciousness. Nevertheless, the Sandinistas and their collaborators succeeded in organizing the Nicaraguan masses—landless peasants, farmworkers, urban workers, women, students, and neighborhood residents—into dynamic and militant popular associations which played a decisive role in the victory over Somoza.

ORGANIZING THE PEASANTS AND FARM WORKERS

Of the 500,000 Nicaraguans engaged in agriculture during the late 1970s, approximately twenty percent were landless wage workers who could find employment only four months of the year during the coffee, sugar cane, and cotton harvests. These agricultural workers were primarily victims of a period of expanded cotton production in the 1950s and 1960s, when landowners expelled tenants and sharecroppers from the haciendas: similar "land clearance" occurred in the sixties and seventies with the expansion of cattle ranches. In addition, the vast majority of peasants who possessed land did not have sufficient land to meet their subsistence needs. Consequently, they were compelled to work for the big landowners during the harvest season. In total, almost eighty percent of the rural labor force was engaged in wage labor.[1]

Orlando Nuñez, a Sandinista economist, points out that this agricultural work force was characterized by a forced mobility.

> Although the seasonally-employed agricultural proletariat might be the most numerous group during four months of the year . . . , they survive unemployed or as semiproletarians, going from the cotton, coffee, and sugar harvests on the plantations back to their peasant plots, from the countryside to the city where they struggle for survival, unemployed or underemployed.[2]

This very mobility tended to draw together some of the most oppressed sectors of the population. Deere and Marchetti note that most peasants shared the same fate as the rural workers.

> Middle peasant farmers who have sufficient access to land are organizationally isolated from one another. While they are also exploited by merchants and usurers, their exploitation is not so easily identified. In contrast, the vast sector of smallholders without sufficient access to land migrated for four months out of the year to the harvests to engage in wage work. There they lived in the most wretched conditions and worked 12 to 15 hours a day picking coffee or cotton only to be cheated out of a day's work by crooked measuring scales. For these months of the year, their conditions were one and the same with the landless rural workers and those workers either permanently employed on the haciendas or who were given access to land on the haciendas as sharecroppers or renters.[3]

In short, "the material conditions for the rural worker-peasant alliance were provided by the pattern of Nicaraguan agrarian capitalist development."[4]

Although the FSLN sought to develop a rural worker-peasant alliance based on the two classes' common interests, its efforts to organize peasants and rural workers had only mixed results in the 1960s. Between 1964 and 1967 urban cadres made important contacts with the peasant sector in the northern region of the country. The Sandinistas studied the peasants' problems and attempted to organize a revolutionary movement in the countryside. During this period, however, the FSLN was unable to adequately mobilize the peasantry, and the low level of political activity that did occur failed to gather strength.

Winning the support of the rural population in those years was no easy matter. Deprivation and isolation had made the Nicaraguan peasant withdrawn and taciturn, wary of strangers. Despite a lingering sympathy for Sandino, many peasants were loyal Somocistas, while others were at

least to some degree influenced by the dictatorship's ideological hegemony. For the Sandinistas, the problem was to distinguish between these
two types of peasants in order to avoid the constant danger of being
uncovered and reported. Because family relationships are the essence of
Nicaraguan peasant communities, FSLN cadres were fully accepted only
after they had completely integrated themselves into the family and community life of the peasants. Black describes this painstaking process:

> After the mid-1960s, no recruit entered the FSLN without a com-
> mitment to live as the campesinos did, sharing all their privations
> and so gaining their confidence. For most of the guerrilleros,
> urban middle-class youth, it meant abandoning the class of their
> birth, with no turning back. Support from the campesinos came
> in a slow chain-reaction. In each new village or hamlet, a single
> slowly built friendship brought the sympathy of an entire family;
> every political contact brought three or four more. Gradually,
> the network of support swelled, an infinitely patient and arduous
> process guided by every combatant's belief in ultimate victory.
> The guerillas came and went, getting to know the lie of the land,
> establishing arms caches, teaching the peasants a political un-
> derstanding of their situation. Recruitment of peasants became
> easier. Many of the peasants captured by the National Guard
> admitted to cooperating with the Frente because the guerrillas
> had taught them to sow their crops better, taught them to read
> and write, given them medicine or clothing. And National Guard
> repression in turn only increased peasant sympathy for the mu-
> chachos.[5]

For many years, however, National Guard repression stymied FSLN
efforts to organize in the countryside. For example, when peasants and
farm workers attempted to form a union in the cotton-growing region of
Chinandega in 1963, the National Guard intervened and slaughtered 300
people.[6] "In contrast to most of Central and South American countries
with long histories of rural movements, the National Guard's political
repression and Somoza's private agro-business expansion effectively
thwarted any efforts to organize campesinos until the 1970s."[7]

The FSLN's first real successes in the countryside occurred in the
north-central region of the country, once Sandino's base of operations.
In 1974 German Pomares, a Sandinista leader of peasant origin, established guerrillitas de campo, units of part-time peasant guerrillas who
later served as a rear guard for major guerrilla actions.[8] By the end of
1976 the drive to incorporate peasants into the armed struggle had gained
considerable momentum; Hugo Torres of the FSLN would later comment

that the six urban cadres in Victor Tirado's rural guerrilla column were considered an excessive number.[9]

During these same years two religious groups, the Agrarian Promotion and Educational Center (CEPA) and the "Delegates of the Word," made the first concrete attempts to ameliorate the living and working conditions of Nicaraguan peasants and agricultural workers.[10] CEPA, founded by the Jesuit order of Catholic priests in 1969, was a rural pastoral program that trained leaders in the theory and practice of organizing "grassroots communities." From 1970 to 1976, CEPA conducted workshops mainly for priests and coffee plantation workers. These workshops attempted to integrate biblical reflection and technical agricultural training. Those who attended these training sessions later shared their skills and helped expand social awareness within their own communities.

Many of the participants in CEPA's seminars were part of another Catholic movement, "Delegates of the Word," that also sought to improve peasant conditions throughout the country.[11] In response to the comprehensive reforms proposed for the Catholic Church at the 1968 Medellin Conference of Latin American bishops, Nicaragua's Catholic hierarchy sought ways to identify the Church with the poor. Faced with a shortage of priests to carry out this task, the Church offered basic training to lay people who became known as Delegates of the Word, and returned to their own communities with this socially-oriented gospel.

Although not originally intended to have radical political influence, the religious training of lay people fostered a heightened social consciousness. By the mid-1970s, the FSLN had come to recognize that religious training could lead to political awareness and action. Dodson and Montgomery explain why the CEPA self-help programs radicalized certain Church activists:

> In time, these efforts came to center on organization as it became clear that peasants could not improve their conditions without organized, collective political action. When this awareness took hold, it raised the level of theological reflection among people in the Church. They perceived the need to assist peasants in organizing to defend their interests within the context of a society which was controlled by Somocismo and fundamentally hostile to peasant interests. In this manner, a number of Christians working in CEPA became sharply politicized and militantly anti-Somocista.[12]

Influenced by CEPA's reflection/training seminars and the Delegates' social work, plantation workers in Carazo and Masaya formed Committees of Agricultural Workers that demanded higher wages, decent food and housing, and sanitary facilities. The National Guard moved swiftly to crush the Committees' organizational work. But Somocista repression only reinforced peasant resistance:

> This intense peasant repression actually backfired on Somoza. Thousands of peasants had already labelled Somoza the "enemy" because of his take-overs of their land. These landless peasants wanted their land, and they wanted to get even with Somoza. When they found their comrades and families bearing the brunt of the National Guard's systematic "clean-up," they escalated their organizing. Committees of Agricultural Workers spread from the Pacific region's coffee plantations to cotton and sugar plantations. By late 1977, the northern Pacific zone was the most militant sector of the population.[13]

The FSLN joined the Committees' organizing efforts in 1975 when the Proletarian Tendency decided to begin working with peasants. One important case of peasant unionization occurred on the massive San Antonio sugar plantation and mills. During the long struggle to organize its workers, the enterprise dismissed strikers and organizers, and the Guard used force against strikers. Despite such repression the struggle culminated in a 1977 walkout by approximately 5,000 workers, mostly cane cutters, who won wage gains and improved working conditions.

La Asociación de Trabajadores del Campo (Rural Workers Association—ATC) emerged from the San Antonio strike. Promoted by the FSLN and staffed in part by former CEPA organizers, the ATC began to organize peasants in other areas of the Pacific Region, concentrating on day laborers in sugar, cotton, and coffee. By the end of 1977 the ATC had united all the Committees of Agricultural Workers in the departments of Carazo, Masaya, León, Chinandega, and Managua. The ATC's ultimate goal was to unite all semiproletarianized peasants and agricultural workers around demands for improved living conditions, year-round employment, and an end to political repression in the countryside.

Taking advantage of the shared economic conditions of small peasants and landless rural workers, the ATC created a political alliance that would go beyond immediate demands to confront the dictatorial state. As one Association document asserted,

> neither the struggle to organize as groups on plantations nor the struggle in the fields offered us great possibilities for throwing off the exploiters who had robbed us for so long. It became clear to us that we needed to organize as a social class, organize on every plantation where the salaries were so poor, where the

struggle was direct and focused. Where the political development was broadest among the plantation and farm workers, this
was where we united.[14]

Peasants and agricultural workers formed additional committees during 1977, extending south to the department of Rivas and north to Chinandega, now including sugar cane and cotton plantations as well as the
coffee plantations. By the end of the year, the struggle in the countryside
had established links to the growing urban revolutionary movement.
Members of the ATC went to Managua in December, joining the anti-
Somoza rallies that Sandinista militants organized in a number of barrios.
These protests faced National Guard tear-gas attacks, beatings, and even
open machine gun fire. After the murder of Pedro Joaquín Chamorro in
January 1978, ATC members seized major roads and highways, virtually
paralyzing the mobility of the Guard.

By March 1978, ATC representatives had established an organizational network to coordinate the efforts of the Association's different zonal
branches. The ATC established subcommittees to coordinate security and
defense, finances, political education, and public information. Many
regional committees began to demand workers' control over the farms
in their areas. Furthermore, urban workers—originally from the countryside but now working in small factories, public transportation, and small
shops—had joined the ranks of the Association. In April, the ATC published its first national newsletter, El Machete, which enhanced members'
political awareness and extended the Association's prestige.

In its first public act as an organization, the Association carried out
a march and hunger strike in Diriamba on April 9, 1978, to protest the
debilitating conditions of the peasant population. The National Guard
harassed and terrorized ATC members the week preceeding the demonstration, and on April 8 captured several important leaders. Nevertheless, the ATC proved its capacity to organize peasants and rural
workers by mobilizing 1,200 members and supporters for the march.

Although the Guard dispersed the demonstration, a strong feeling
of solidarity developed among other anti-Somoza forces. Women from
AMPRONAC, high school students, and university opposition groups
launched hunger strikes throughout the country to show their support for
the militants in the ATC. The hunger march and the subsequent hunger
strike propelled the Association into political alignment with the FSLN.

The grassroots committees of the ATC thus became committees
in support of all out war (against the dictatorship) and carried
out their political line in conjunction with the FSLN. During

May, June, July, and August, hundreds from the ATC armed and organized themselves in popular militias, while others continued their work on plantations and farms. Their homes became virtual Sandinista strongholds and their goal was one and the same with the FSLN: "Death to the dictatorship; Death to Somocismo."[15]

The insurrections of September 1978 and May-July 1979 demonstrated that "the ATC was able to convert itself into a powerful force of the FSLN, not only in building the armed struggle but in organizing political action by workers and peasants in the rural areas."[16] The Sandinistas began to organize military training schools for ATC committees in response to National Guard repression of land take-overs and peasant demonstrations, and by September 1978 ATC military contingents had assumed an active combat role. Armed only with outdated weapons, Association combatants provided cover for the *Frente*'s withdrawal from the cities of Chinandega and Carazo, and throughout 1979 carried out a series of harassment operations against Somoza's troops.[17]

The early history of the ATC exemplifies the dynamic relationship that developed between the FSLN and the masses. Spontaneous peasant struggles were given form and direction under FSLN leadership, and a coherent class-based organization emerged: formally independent of, but intimately linked to the FSLN.

ORGANIZING THE LABOR MOVEMENT

One of the most significant features of the Nicaraguan revolution is that it succeeded despite having one of the smallest and traditionally worst-organized urban proletariats of Latin America. The division within the working-class movement and the economistic nature of its demands (a result of oppression, disorganization, and leadership failures) were a source of strength to the Somoza dictatorship for decades. The Nicaraguan working class was the product of a century of violent dispossession of peasant farmers and was linked to the incorporation of Nicaragua as an agro-export producer within the world economy.[18]

Nicaragua's working class is concentrated in the western departments of Managua, León, Chinandega, and Carazo. The capital alone houses a quarter of the population, containing 65 percent of Nicaragua's industry and 60 percent of the country's commercial activity. From 1960 on the urban population has steadily increased, from only 41 percent in 1960 to 52 percent of the total population in 1980. In 1979, 343,000 people were employed in agriculture, 90,000 in industry and construction, and 228,000 in commerce and services.[19]

The urban working class, employed in industry, construction, and mining, constituted only 16 to 18 percent of the economically active population in 1975. Few factories employed more than 100 to 500 workers. Under Somoza, urban workers were largely unorganized: only ten percent of the work force belonged to trade unions, and these were scattered among five federations, one of which was controlled by Somoza.[20] The dictatorship often adopted a paternalistic style in an effort to win over workers. But even though Somoza granted a social security system, an annual bonus of one month's pay, and other fringe benefits, the growth of inflation and unemployment in the 1970s led to a considerable movement for workers' demands.[21] This movement, however, was not a revolutionary one; as Orlando Nuñez said, it

> was characterized by a consciousness, organization, and form of mobilization that was essentially economistic and was controlled by reformist or doctrinaire parties that never thought that the revolution would come so soon. This was the case until the working class and the union movement linked up with the FSLN.[22]

The Nicaraguan Socialist Party (PSN), founded in the early 1940s, had failed to provide a revolutionary leadership for Nicaraguan workers. The PSN collaborated with Somoza Garcia briefly during his populist period then went underground following the 1948 persecution and constitutional ban on a communist party.[23] Even though its was struggling, the PSN maintained its base in the urban working class, especially the construction trades. In 1967, the PSN participated in the Conservative-led National Opposition coaltion that fielded the presidential candidate Fernando Aguero against National Guard leader Anastasio Somoza Debayle. Fonseca explains the reason for the PSN's collaboration with the Conservatives:

> It's necessary to explain that this very grave error was not the result of simple bad faith by the leaders. . . . The Marxist leadership did not possess the necessary clarity in the face of the Conservative sector's control over the anti-Somozaist opposition. It could not distinguish between the justice of the anti-Somozaist opposition and the maneuvers of the Conservative sector.[24]

As the FSLN increased its influence in the 1960s, the PSN suffered deep divisions concerning its relationship to the armed struggle. In 1967, most of the original leadership was expelled because of opposition to any cooperation with the growing guerrilla movement. Three years later the expelled group established the *Partido Comunista de Nicaragua* (Nicaraguan Communist Party—PCN). This party was outspokenly anti-Sandinista and claimed allegiance to Moscow, although the Soviet Union related only to the PSN.

After the split, the PSN continued to criticize the FSLN: "They—the Sandinistas—tried traditional *foquismo,* at other times putschism, suffering Maoist, almost Trotskyist influences."[25] Few were surprised, therefore, when the Socialist Party joined the bourgeois-led UDEL coalition in 1974.[26] At the same time, the PSN and its labor federation, the CGT-I, proposed many of UDEL's most progressive demands for labor reform. As the dictatorship reached a crisis stage, the Socialist Party sought a working agreement with the Sandinistas, and in 1977, when the *Terceristas* argued that the time was ripe for an insurrectional strategy, both the FSLN and the PSN took concrete steps to reach a rapprochement.[27]

In the 1970s, two strikes revealed both the weakness of the working-class leadership and the militancy of the rank and file. After the earthquake of 1972, the expanding construction industry offered favorable employment conditions, good wages, and the opportunity for workers to effectively organize. Building workers in the General Confederation of Workers-Independent (CGT-I), linked to the Socialist Party, went on strike in 1973. But after four weeks their negotiators agreed to a mere 10 percent wage increase and dampened the workers' growing militancy. The strike was an important experience in mobilization, but did not go beyond economic demands, and when the construction boom died out the following year, building workers lost much of their political dynamism.[28]

During the same period, 5,000 workers at the country's largest sugar refinery, the Ingenio San Antonio, walked off their jobs. The workers, mainly cane cutters, were subjected to a whole range of management strike-breaking tactics. By expelling union activists, the factory owners dismantled the workers' unions. The National Guard then attacked the strikers and management tried to halt the work stoppage by conceding minor wage hikes. The cane cutters, however, retained their resolve, drawing encouragement from the peasant land invasions in nearby Subtiava and Chinandega.[29]

Although the Sandinistas recognized the importance of mobilizing the Nicaraguan working class, they had difficulty uniting a fragmented trade union movement. The pressures of National Guard repression and high unemployment reinforced labor's historical weakness. The Socialist CGT-I, with which the FSLN maintained an uneasy collaboration, was only one of five labor federations in Nicaragua. The other four were the Council of Trade Union Unification (CUS), tied to the American Institute for Free Labor Development (AIFLD); the Workers' Federation of Nicaragua (CTN), linked to the Social Christian Party; the Federation of Trade Union Action and Unity (CAUS), loyal to the Nicaraguan Communist Party; and the General Confederation of Workers-Official (CFT-O), loyal to the Somoza regime.

As the dictatorship entered its crisis stage, radical workplace organizations began to appear. Among these, the FSLN devoted particular attention to what they regarded as incipient factory councils, Workers' Fighting Committees, that included workers from various political tendencies. As worker involvement in the revolutionary struggle began to intensify, the FSLN launched a vigorous discussion and reassessment of its rural-based strategy, seeking ways of directing the militancy of the urban proletariat. As Chapter 1 noted, the Proletarian Tendency of the FSLN even argued for a new party of the urban proletariat. Autonomously, the Proletarians created the Revolutionary Workers' Committees in factories and barrios, and in 1977 helped establish the Workers Commission that was linked to the National Patriotic Front.[30]

The Sandinistas' internal debate over the importance of organizing urban workers was acrimonious but necessary. In the three years from 1975 to 1978, a historically weak and fragmented working class movement, recently energized by economic collapse, repression, and the visible decay of the dictatorship, had to be transformed into one of the principal forces of the anti-Somoza movement.

The Sandinistas, however, never consolidated their position among urban workers during the war of liberation. This was largely because the FSLN's political work among the working class started much later than its efforts among students, peasants, and urban poor. Furthermore, urban workers remained seriously divided throughout the period before the triumph. "We should recognize," declared a 1982 Sandinista Workers Federation document, "that during the entire period preceding the overthrow of the dictatorship, one could observe the divisions within the workers' movement."[31]

WOMEN'S ROLE IN THE STRUGGLE: AMPRONAC

Throughout the 1960s, the FSLN sought to increase the participation of women not only within the vanguard but within all sectors of Nicaraguan society. The successful organization of women on a large scale, however, came relatively late in the struggle against Somoza. Until the earthquake of 1972, class differences between women, and the low level of consciousness among women of all classes, kept women divided and unorganized.

Bourgeois women were notorious for their condescending attitude towards the poor. They did charity work that reinforced their feelings of superiority toward poor women. Wealthy women had developed the notion of women's rights, but identified with their oppressed sisters only after the 1972 earthquake, when Somoza's greed began to threaten the economic power of the Nicaraguan bourgeoisie.

Middle-class housewives in particular had little political consciousness, due partly to their isolation and individualistic lifestyles. These women viewed society as a cluster of "familial nuclei"; their world was reduced to their homes, families, and individual problems.[32] Only when the repression became unbearable did these women change their view of society and join the revolutionary struggle.

Peasant women, often heads of households, suffered unemployment, illiteracy, and sexism. As part of the itinerant agricultural work force, women and children worked full-time only four months of the year and eked out an existence during the other eight months.[33] Unable to survive in the countryside, many peasant women and children moved to the towns. Thousands of women found work as domestics or street vendors and many others were forced into prostitution.[34] The daily struggle to care for and feed their families, coupled with a high illiteracy rate, made organizing peasant women difficult.

Many working-class women were also heads of households, engaged in unskilled work such as street vending or market vending. Elizabeth Maier, who has spent years studying the Nicaraguan women's movement, argues that such occupations fostered an individualistic outlook:

> In a country such as Nicaragua, where the majority of women are in unskilled labor or are "walking vendors," their experience only reinforces their individualist view of the world, even when they leave their houses to work. Factory conditions, where the labor process is a collective force that enables the workers to share their experiences, present collectively their complaints, worries and demands, are absent from the work life of a great percentage of women workers.[35]

The situation of most Nicaraguan women grew even worse during the period after the earthquake because it had occurred in the middle of a two-year drought, which had ruined staple food production. Peasants, hungry and unemployed, made their way to the capital where they endured terrible living conditions.[36] Increasing numbers of peasant and working-class women became the sole supporters of their families. Consequently, they were often the first to be affected by unemployment and inflation.[37] Without sufficient income or access to social services, many of their children died from lack of food and health care. Peasant and working women were also frequently tortured, raped, and murdered by the National Guard.

Although bourgeois women were not targeted by the Guard, they were horrified and outraged by its atrocities. They also recognized that Somoza was busily engaged in accumulating more wealth after the earthquake, which threatened their own economic position.[38] These two factors combined to change their attitude toward the poor. By 1977, significant numbers of women from all classes were demanding solutions to the country's problems.

In some barrios, women formed discussion groups to analyze what they could do about the national situation. Maier emphasizes the political significance of these discussions:

> Housewives met in Mothers' Clubs in search of a collective solution to their needs. They discussed and described their situation, analyzed its origins, and were gaining consciousness. For the majority of these women, this experience was their first attempt at socio-political practice. It was the first time they collectively handled their overwhelming problems, which they were able to then remove from a family context and place within a global context of historical development.[39]

The FSLN began to consider the formation of a woman's organization in 1977, an attempt which led to large-scale, cross-class organizing. In 1977, Jaime Wheelock, leader of the Proletarian Tendency of the then-divided FSLN, sent a note to Lea Guido (who would become minister of health) suggesting the establishment of a women's organization. Guido gives these comments on the *Frente's* efforts:

> It was in April 1977 when I received a note from Comrade Jaime Wheelock. He suggested we organize a work commission to look at women's problems and work toward the creation of a broad-based women's association. The Sandinista National Liberation Front had already failed in two previous attempts to organize women. This attempt was to be successful . . . To begin with we set up a collective inside the FSLN to write something on the importance of organizing women. . . . We knew it was important to bring women from different sectors together to deal with this problem—the total lack of human rights in the country, which was epitomized so clearly by the horrible conditions and the torture our comrades were being subjected to in the prisons.[40]

Soon after Somoza lifted the state of siege in September 1977, a small group of women created the *Asociación de Mujeres Ante la Prob-*

lematica Nacional (Association of Nicaraguan Women Confronting the National Problem—AMPRONAC). The majority of the founders were bourgeois and middle-class women, but a few FSLN members and sympathizers also joined the ranks.[41] The association's program included the following objectives: 1. to encourage the participation of women in the resolution of the problems of the country; 2. to defend the rights of Nicaraguan women in all sectors and in all aspects—economic, social, and political; and 3. to defend human rights in general.[42] The program's goals combined women's concerns with those of the Nicaraguan people as a whole. Bourgeois women played a crucial role in AMPRONAC's work, especially in its first few months. Their class position and the dictatorship's image of women as harmless made it possible for them to meet with government officials. Without threat of arrest or torture, these women could work effectively on both the national and international level.[43]

AMPRONAC's policies and strategies were aggressive. Its members demonstrated constantly, always carrying militant banners and posters.[44] The Association organized dozens of meetings in which it condemned National Guard atrocities committed against women and children. Members also conducted investigations into the cases of prisoners and disappeared persons.[45] An initial membership of only twenty-five women carried out all these activities. Although small, AMPRONAC was a very visible organization.[46]

The murder of Pedro Joaquín Chamorro in January 1978 triggered demonstrations across the country. Shouting slogans and raising their banners, AMPRONAC members protested the slaying at the hospital where Chamorro lay.[47] Later that month, AMPRONAC led the occupation of the United Nation's offices in Managua. Designed to protest disappearances and urge the release of political prisoners, the occupation succeeded in mobilizing large numbers of peasant women. During the twelve-day sit-in Association members distributed leaflets and organized daily pickets.

On the final day of the protest, AMPRONAC called a meeting to support the occupation; more than 600 attended, including many upper-class women upset by Chamorro's death.[48] The bourgeoisie demanded justice only in the case of Chamorro, but AMPRONAC members put forth a more radical demand with their new slogan: "Where are our *campesino* brothers and sisters? Let the assassins respond!" The National Guard dispersed the peaceful protest with tear gas and beatings. But the women did not leave without a fight: "Our sisters fought back. When the troops bombed us with tear gas, we threw the cannisters right back at them. It was a really militant demonstration."[49]

After the failure of the first FSLN-supported national strike in January, AMPRONAC members met to evaluate their association's role in the struggle. They concluded that the situation called for a new type of organization: a mass organization consisting of both urban and rural women.[50] Women in the Managua chapter established a number of base committees, including a very effective propaganda committee.[51] The propaganda committee initiated a massive educational effort and launched a national campaign to defend citizen's rights. In response to appeals from rural women, AMPRONAC leaders created local Association chapters in the countryside.[52]

By midyear, AMPRONAC posters were appearing throughout the country, calling for a women's movement to fight for both women's liberation and the liberation of the Nicaraguan people. The following is an excerpt from the program:

Only the full participation of women within the political, economic, and social life of the country can guarantee us the total destruction of the system of discrimination and oppression of women. This is why we women are organizing ourselves separately, because we are the ones who can best defend the rights of Nicaraguan women. This is why we are struggling for the growing participation of women in the political, economic, and social life of our country.[53]

In accordance with its program, AMPRONAC set forth the following demands: 1. an end to repression; 2. freedom of association; 3. freedom for political prisoners; 4. prosecution of those guilty of crimes and barbarities; 5. no rises in the cost of living; 6. the repeal of all laws that discriminate against women; 7. equal pay for equal work; and 8. an end to the commercialization of women.[54]

During March and April 1978 AMPRONAC carried out a number of activities, employing more agressive methods to express the outrage and concern of Nicaraguan women. Visits to ministers gave way to public meetings and members occupied Red Cross offices in different areas of the country.[55] On Mother's Day, AMPRONAC activists circulated leaflets against the objectification and commercialization of women, and their slogan for the day was, "The Best Gift Would Be A Free Country."[56]

On April 9, AMPRONAC joined the ATC hunger march in Diriamba. The National Guard killed one woman and injured many others in their attack on the demonstrators. Undeterred, the Association then joined ATC-initiated hunger strikes throughout the country and held press conferences in rural areas to publicize repression against the *campesinos*.[57]

Through such activities, AMPRONAC played a key role in consolidating the urban and rural struggle against the dictatorship.

During this period, AMPRONAC experienced a rapid growth in membership, absorbing many women sympathetic to the FSLN. By July of 1978 the Association claimed more than 1,000 members.[58] The influx of hundreds of radical women precipitated an intense political debate between Sandinista sympathizers and supporters of the bourgeois opposition.[59] The FSLN adherents envisioned AMPRONAC as a militant mass organization committed to the transformation of Nicaraguan society, but the followers of the bourgeois opposition did not fundamentally question *Somocismo*. This political split led to a special conference in which 150 delegates representing the 1,022 members voted on AMPRONAC's future political direction. The pro-Sandinista women prevailed: AMPRONAC consolidated its identity as an anti-imperialist, anti-Somoza, anticapitalist, and antisexist women's organization. Soon afterward, AMPRONAC joined the United People's Movement.[60]

In August 1978, the regime raised the price of several basic consumer goods. The Association responded with demonstrations at which women wore aprons and carried saucepans or empty shopping baskets. In the barrios, AMPRONAC presented skits with titles such as "Our Children are Hungry." By focusing on the role of mothers, such activities were extremely effective in mobilizing women. AMPRONAC members were able to link their activities as women to the popular struggle against economic and political repression.[61]

At the end of August, the United People's Movement organized a national strike. AMPRONAC was instrumental in parlaying the strike into another victory for the mass movement. Moreover, as Lea Guido affirms, the strike taught AMPRONAC members how to maintain their organization amid chaos:

> During the strike our association learned to function in an emergency situation. We learned how to keep going, keep operating, no matter what kind of a situation we found ourselves in. We suspended the base committees with their headquarters in the neighborhoods and organized a more centralized structure. We developed a chain whereby only one comrade from each neighborhood would have contact with other areas. Only the leadership met together. We also modified our leadership structure; there was no longer a president, only a co-ordinator in charge of finances and another in charge of security and health. This clandestine operation was crucial to our survival through this period of increased struggle and repression and into the future.[62]

The movement against Somoza culminated in the September 1978 insurrection. The FSLN coordinated its military actions with popular uprisings in several towns. Although AMPRONAC members did not have time to sufficiently prepare themselves for the September revolt, they provided some support, conducting first-aid courses and furnishing several barrios with medicine and supplies. Some members participated directly in the street fighting. Despite a lack of preparation, the Association's members demonstrated their ability to effectively mobilize large numbers of people. Lea Guido offers her assessment of AMPRONAC's role in the September insurrection: "I believe our greatest contribution was helping organizing the masses. By this time all our neighborhood women knew how to organize people, which was something that many of the students, for example, didn't. AMPRONAC stood out for its mobilizing and organizing capacities."[63]

Having played an important role in the insurrection, AMPRONAC suffered the brutal repression that followed. Many women were arrested and tortured, and some of their husbands were murdered by the National Guard. Almost destroyed, the organization was forced underground. In Managua a core group of women regained contact with a small number of remaining members, and began working more closely with the United People's Movement.[64]

Although in early 1979 government authorities believed they had destroyed the Association, AMPRONAC was secretly preparing itself for the final insurrection: members taught first aid classes, prepared storehouses with food and medicine, and collected and hid material for contact bombs and molotov cocktails.[65] When the final insurrection began, AMPRONAC's infrastructure in the poor barrios proved indispensable, and its members participated in every necessary activity: constructing barricades; hiding combatants, weapons, and medicine; giving first aid; sending messages; transporting weapons and bombs; preparing food; and engaging in combat.[66]

AMPRONAC's strategy of raising women's concerns to create a mass political movement was successful. It helped overthrow the dictatorship, developed feminist demands later met by the new government, and gave women a sense of confidence in their ability to influence national events. It also changed the nature of the national liberation struggle from one in which women were merely helpmates to one in which they were fighting on their own behalf.[67] As Lea Guido put it: "we were successful because we learned how to involve women in the national struggle while at the same time organising around problems specific to women. We always looked at the situation from a women's point of view. If we hadn't what meaning would it have had us to organise women?"[68]

STUDENT MOBILIZATION AGAINST THE DICTATORSHIP

The student struggle against Somoza took place primarily in the cities where the majority of the high schools and universities are located.[69] Between 1963 and 1978, the high school age population exploded, growing at an annual rate of almost 17 percent. Yet many youths were unable to continue their education, having dropped out during primary school to help support their families. For many who managed to remain in school it was difficult to study. In 1976, Doris Tijerino, a Sandinista leader, enumerated some of the students' problems:

> In Nicaragua it's very common these days for the students in the public schools or institutes to faint because of not having eaten breakfast, or fail to be able to carry out their assignments for lack of a notebook, and most of the time they can't study because they don't have the necessary books . . .
> Then there are the conditions under which a middle-class or proletarian student has to study; he or she generally has a very large family, irritable parents and a very small house. Almost everything keeps him from studying, from being able to concentrate.[70]

Among upper-class students, the situation was quite different. These young people attended private schools, and most went on to attend foreign universities. When they returned to Nicaragua they were culturally alienated and distanced from the realities of their own society.[71] Yet a significant number of young revolutionaries emerged from these social sectors. Once they came to realize that their privileges were linked to the oppression of their compatriots, many Nicaraguan youths began to work for the complete transformation of their society. These young people established the student organizations that played such a vital role in the overthrow of Somoza.

The year 1959 is often regarded as the beginning of the revolutionary student movement in Nicaragua. In mid-July, the National Guard destroyed a guerrilla unit in El Chaparral, and university students in León organized a protest demonstration on July 23. The Guard savagely attacked the demonstrators, killing four university students and injuring hundreds of townspeople. A witness emphasizes the importance of the July 23 demonstration:

> The Chaparral affair was a popular movement that had no connection with the conservative oligarchy or with the opposition

bourgeoisie and so they tried to ignore the real reason for the demonstration of July 23, 1959. It is very important to remember that date; those were the first street demonstrations in support of the popular liberation movement of the Nicaraguan people.[72]

Classes were cancelled at the León university after the July 23 shootings, and when they began again in September the students launched a campaign to expel military personnel studying at the school. Sergio Ramirez, now vice president of Nicaragua, describes the students' efforts:

First, we staged a sit-in, the first to be held at a public institution, and then we took over the university. After a hunger strike . . . we held an assembly and decided to simply stay there. We locked ourselves in, until we could get the military expelled from campus. The Guard surrounded us and there was a lot of tension. But we finally won; Somoza decided to remove the military and send them to foreign universities to study, especially to Spain. So that was a battle won.[73]

On July 23, 1960, the student movement organized demonstrations to commemorate the four fallen students. In Managua, thousands of people gathered at the chapel of the General Hospital. As the Church mass began, both the Guard and the police arrived and dispersed the congregants. Street battles ensued and during the melee a police patrol fired at a handicapped student who was merely watching the activity. The boy, Julio Oscar Romero, died instantly.[74]

The people's fury increased when they saw the crime committed against that boy. Demonstrations were organized all that day and night, and people came to stand guard at the place where comrade Julio Oscar Romero had fallen. He was buried the next day.
     That was one of the greatest demonstrations against the regime of the Somozas. I remember the funeral demonstration—from beginning to end it was some five or six blocks long . . . The streets completely filled with people, the people composing slogans, singing the hymn, singing revolutionary songs, and on every block, on every corner, there was a student or a worker or a woman . . . I don't think there was any exploited or oppressed sector of the Nicaraguan people who were not pronouncing judgement on, or denouncing that assassination.[75]

In 1966, the Revolutionary Student Front participated in the student elections at the National Autonomous University in Managua. Although its candidate lost by seven votes, the FER used the elections to measure the FSLN's support among the student body. The FER then led students in a hunger strike to protest the Liberal Party's convention held to nominate Somoza for the presidency. During the entire four-day convention students, joined by union leaders and leftist political activists, carried out the first student-led strike to protest the corruption of Nicaraguan party politics.[76]

No account of the revolutionary student movement in Nicaragua can ignore the important contribution that the *Movimiento Juvenil Cristiano*, Christian Youth Movement, made to the liberation struggle. Rooted in the Christian student protests that began in 1970, this movement provided the Sandinistas with indispensable support after the 1972 earthquake. In 1970, students at the Jesuit-run Central American University challenged the conservative orientation of the university, and when the authorities refused to discuss the situation they occupied it. A group of students and priests occupied the cathedral of Managua in August, protesting human rights violations. By the end of 1970, the dictatorship had imprisoned almost 100 students associated with the Christian student movement.[77]

In November 1971, a group of six university students who had participated in the Managua cathedral occupation decided to form a "Christian community" in the El Riguero barrio under the direction and support of Father Uriel Molina.[78] Father Molina was a radical priest who taught at the Central American University and preached in El Riguero. Why did they select El Riguero? Roberto Gutierrez, one of the original members of the community, explains:

> We chose that neighborhood because it had all the conditions which would allow us to live the way we wanted. First, it was a working-class neighborhood and we very much wanted to be near the working people. Secondly, we found Uriel, who came to play a very important role in our lives. He was a serious theologian and was up-to-date on all the new ideas of liberation theology. We found the right atmosphere and a sounding board in Uriel.[79]

Raised in bourgeois families, these students wanted to change their lives and work for justice among the oppressed sectors of the Nicaraguan population. They were also Christians who were in the process of changing their understanding of religion: "We saw the need to regard faith not as an individual question but a collective one. We came to see that one's faith could not be authentic except around those who are poor and exploited. At that point we did not think of Nicaraguan society in terms of classes; we thought we were concerned for the poor."[80]

Once the community was established in El Riguero, the students worked in different areas. Some worked with a youth group, others worked with the Christian base communities. They saw their task as that of trying to present a new, revolutionary vision of Christianity. They also realized that they, too, would be educated from their work and contact with the people of the barrio. Because each of the groups in the neighborhood was isolated from one another, the students decided to organize a leadership structure that could coordinate the work of the different groups. This structure laid the groundwork for people with organizing abilities to develop as leaders of the community.

The students then formed a neighborhood association to which everyone eventually belonged. They organized a delegation that visited Somoza's light and power company and asked that electricity be provided to the neighborhood. They also sent a group to request the repair of potholes and the fumigation of buildings in the barrio. All these social demands strengthened the organizing efforts in the neighborhood. By the end of 1972, the community was thriving and the FSLN was emerging as the leading force in the struggle against the dictatorship. The members of the community were aware that they would have to offer a political alternative to people who could no longer tolerate the unjust structure in their country.

> We knew we weren't any kind of political alternative for our country. The only way to effect real change was to be a militant in a political party aimed at taking over power. So we set out to examine the political organizations that did exist in the country. The Liberal Party? The Communist Party? The traditional left? And the Sandinista Front? It is interesting that our link to the Sandinista Front came through a cold, calculated analysis, beginning with strictly defined political and ideological questions. We didn't join because of personal connections, but rather by putting all the cards on the table and trying to examine what we saw.
>
> So we set out to find out about the Front: what they thought and what their strategy was. It is interesting that our decision to find out more about the FSLN coincided with the Sandinistas' interest in us. They had heard that some Christians living in the barrio were doing mass organizing. This was tempting to the FSLN. Our class background meant that we'd have access to material resources: houses, cars, farms to use as training centres, etc. And we had dozens of people organized into circles from

which cadres might be recruited. We had developed a kind of political structure throughout the neighborhood.[81]

Some of the members formed a *Frente* cell and began to meet and study FSLN documents. But it was only in the weeks following the December 23, 1972 earthquake that the link between the Christian Youth Movement and the Sandinista Front was solidly established. The Riguero community played a central role in this relationship. Alvaro Baltodano, now head of the Sandinista army's office of combat preparedness, explains:

> After the earthquake we had stronger links with the Front. We made arrangements to read the first documents and a little manual about security. We did that as revolutionary Christians, convinced that Christians in Nicaragua had to participate with the Front because no other party presented a real alternative. There were no possibilities of bringing the people to freedom except through armed struggle. The FSLN was the only organization that presented a just alternative and had demonstrated revolutionary honesty. It had been consistent and always shown honest and revolutionary attitudes. Why should you start something new if there was already an organization with experience? Besides, even at that time, we admired the fighters in the Front. For us it was inspiring to speak of Carlos Fonseca, to speak about the Ortega brothers, Jose Benito Escobar, Commandante Borge. We admired the struggle in the mountains. And as Christians we decided to join the Front and keep working and organizing.[82]

After the earthquake, the Christian groups and many unorganized youths began intensive humanitarian work in all the barrios of Managua. They established strong links with large numbers of people and the Riguero community became a center for both the political activity of the barrio and all the youths who were there. At the same time, the Christian students in the FSLN continued their political development.

> Our FSLN cell meetings were held in a nuns' retreat house in Las Palmeras. We discussed several documents analyzing the national reality and concluded, first, that it was necessary to get better organized ourselves; and secondly, that we had to help organize the whole people. We decided our work should not be confined to the university or the student milieu and instead had to be mainly in working class barrios. We came up with the idea of organizing a Christian Movement for Revolution and so began to re-establish links with all those we'd contacted through the December protests.[83]

Led by Luis Carrión and Roberto Gutierrez, the Christian Youth Movement coordinated organizing work that quickly expanded to other Managua barrios. Movement members carried out investigations into the water, electricity, transportation, and health problems in each barrio, and mobilized people to work for solutions. They also sought to radicalize the religious conceptions of each community, advancing a more political reading of the Bible, and connecting that interpretation to discussions about the problems in the community. The Christian students wished to transform the Christian base communities into neighborhood organizations that would begin to deal with the barrio's problems. Gutierrez describes the importance of these organizing efforts:

> That work in the barrio had a tremendous impact on the people and the political struggle in Nicaragua. It was not well known because most of the work had to be clandestine, even when the comrades didn't belong to the Front. The repressive conditions in Nicaragua forced us to work secretly, underground. We recruited many of those involved in the base communities to the Front and others became collaborators by lending their houses, etc. This experience was particularly important because at the beginning the Christian movement had been a petit bourgeois movement. This was changing as a result of the work in the barrios, which was more and more under the leadership of the FSLN.[84]

The collaboration between the Christian student movement and other student organizations backed by the FSLN eventually bore fruit: the national student movement against the dictatorship was consolidated by April 1978.[85] This was the result of sporadic but increasing student rebelliousness during the state of siege between 1975 and 1977. During these years, protests were led by high school students in the Association of Secondary Students and the Secondary Student Movement, reflecting the GPP and TP tendencies, respectively. These organizations mobilized student groups under the slogan, "Don't allow a single act of repression or a single crime by the dictatorship to go by without denouncing it everywhere."[86]

This growing student movement was centered in the departments of Managua and Carazo, and to a lesser degree in León, Chinandega, and Estelí. In its earlier period, the movement was weakly organized and suffered, in part, from the FSLN divisions that became increasingly public during 1976 and 1977. From 1977 on, the secondary students from the Cristobal Colon and Andres Bello schools in Managua gradually established links with the students at the Central American University. They worked together until, by the end of 1977, rallies numbered as many as 2,000 students. During that year, growing National Guard repression forced the students into using specialized resistance techniques: pickets in front of schools, street bonfires, "lightning meetings," and spray painting of political slogans at night.

The first successful political action led by students came in the summer of 1977, when the government raised bus fares by 40 centavos (5 cents) per ride. This decision fell heavily on the poor and produced widespread outrage. Students decided to lead the protests against the fare hike, channeling public anger by letting air out of tires, breaking bus windows, and strewing wooden boards filled with nails on streets and highways. Bus transportation came to a halt and commercial business suffered. This campaign brought students off campus and into the streets, forcing them to interact with working people and deepening their understanding of the economic struggle of the masses.

In December 1977, students launched protest actions around urgent political issues: the increased numbers of political prisoners and the repression of campesinos. After the FSLN's October attacks, the National Guard expanded its operations throughout the country. Students responded to the Guard with protest demonstrations at which they carried placards reading: "Where are our campesino brothers and sisters?" and "Christmas '77 without political prisoners!" In this atmosphere, acts of protests against human rights violations quickly turned political. Students not only demonstrated in the streets; they began to occupy churches and schools which they sometimes held for days. National Guard efforts to end these occupations compelled students to learn how to defend themselves against tear gas attacks, prepare supply caches before taking over buildings, establish communications systems, and set up street barricades.

The assassination of Pedro Joaquín Chamorro in January 1978 led to even more student resistance. The December actions had prepared the students for leadership roles after the assassination. During January and February, three other pro-Sandinista student organizations became politically active: the Revolutionary Student Front, the Nicaraguan Revolutionary Youth, and the University Center for Popular Solidarity. During the Chamorro funeral period, students established contact with trade unions and individual factory committees; for the first time students and workers marched together in political protests. The National Guard responded with new tactics including the increased use of the Special Brigades Against Terrorist Acts. Guardsmen, usually traveling four in a jeep, arrested and shot students and young people on sight. In turn, the students adopted more aggressive countertactics.

The students' militancy reached a peak during the period from April 6 to May 9. During these thirty-three days of continuous struggle, students and young people became the vanguard of the civilian revolts in many cities. The event that led to this period of organized rebellion started at the end of March 1978 when Albertina Serrano, a widow, began a hunger strike to protest the solitary confinement of her son Marcio Jaen, and that of FSLN founder Tomás Borge. Both AMPRONAC and the students at the National Institute of Masaya backed this hunger strike. In addition to demanding the release of Jaen and Borge, the institute's students demanded that the faculty remove all teachers who were working as Somocista spies, and denounced the National Guard's widespread distribution of marijuana and other drugs as a tactic intended to weaken the students' organizing capabilities.

The largest and longest student strike in the history of Nicaragua began on April 6. Within two days, students had seized some twenty schools and institutes throughout the country. This led to battles between students and the Guard, with the soldiers recapturing several educational centers and turning them into military headquarters. It was during this time that students convinced their parents to become active and mobilized the parent-student organization "Family Parents."[87] By the end of the strike many previously traditional and conservative Catholic schools had become militant anti-Somoza centers.

The national strike, which included 60,000 students, crippled the entire educational system. Somoza could not employ extreme tactics against the students because they had a favorable image with the general population and because nearly all of them came from middle class and upper class families. Nevertheless, in several cities, including Diriamba, Jinotega, and Estelí, the National Guard used tear gas, mustard gas, and random shooting to smash pickets and force students out of buildings. In these attacks, hundreds of students were arrested, wounded, or killed.[88]

Despite the growing ruthlessness of the Guard, the students maintained their militancy. On July 9, four students were killed during a march against Elena de Porra, Somoza's representative in the Ministry of Public Education. During a massive funeral procession held for the murdered students, more than 10,000 cordobas were collected and used to buy arms for the next battle. Typical of these student struggles is a May 1978 account of a student uprising in Estelí.

A student center in Estelí had been taken over by young people (including children 6–10 years of age). These youngsters were violently forced out of the buildings and an unimaginable number were beaten, or shot. This act moved the citizens of Estelí to realize they must respond in like manner. They destroyed the property and houses of Somoza officials in retaliation. Recovery of arms became commonplace. One military armory was totally emptied of arms as the people prepared to follow the insurrectional leadership of the FSLN vanguard. All these events helped create the material conditions for the moment when the entire nation would initiate its final struggle for liberation.[89]

Thus the students became the leading force in the urban struggle against the dictatorship. More than any other sector, it was the students who laid the foundation for the September insurrection in the poor neighborhoods. It was these students, and youth in general, that made up the squads, brigades, and guerrilla units. As Orlando Nuñez has emphasized, these students were "the enthusiasm of the revolution."

Not only did the students demonstrate, participate in ambushes against the National Guard, provide urban and rural support for the guerrillas, and serve as a reservoir for cadres for the organization of the FSLN, but through their actions they also enriched the mobilizing power of the revolution among the population. Their forms of struggle and, accordingly, the ideological content of their demands progressed daily. From assemblies, they progressed to demonstrations; from rocks thrown against the police, they graduated to contact bombs; from pamphlets to guns; from student organizations to mass organizations and those of the revolutionary vanguard; from questioning the principal of the school to confronting the Minister of Public Education; from questioning the regime to questioning the system; from the fight against Somoza to the struggle against imperialism and the questioning of capitalism; from the defense of their interests to the defense of those of the peasants and workers and the exploited population in general; from the questioning of capitalism to the struggle for the construction of socialism.[90]

ORGANIZING THE NEIGHBORHOODS

Although the Sandinistas began their struggle against the dictatorship in the countryside, they knew that the target for the conquest of power was fundamentally urban. The FSLN's early attempts to organize the urban neighborhoods, however, met with little success. In 1964 and 1965, the *Frente* created the Popular Civilian Committees. These committees were primarily concerned with making basic social gains. But the lack of strong ties with the people in the barrios posed a serious problem for the Sandinistas.

The fact is that you arrived in the *barrio* and didn't live with the people—you always arrived with a paternalistic attitude. This was a fairly common phenomenon. You almost always came with that attitude, but after coming in contact with the misery, with the problems of the barrio, you became sensitive. You tried to better understand the people. For us, communication was made more difficult, at times, because of the differences in vocabulary and also, at times, because we did not truly understand the way of life of these people.[91]

The efforts of the FSLN to organize the urban barrios were without success until 1972, when the student movement actively campaigned against milk and gasoline price increases. The price of milk rose exorbitantly during 1971 and 1972. The Somozas had part of their capital invested in the milk monopoly and made considerable profits from these price increases. Rising gas prices also had an impact on the majority of the people, especially the working class. All those who relied on public transportation vehicles as well as taxi drivers who owned their own vehicles were affected by the high gasoline prices.[92] The two struggles were waged simultaneously, and all the social sectors harmed by the price increases carried out massive demonstrations. The student movement assigned its activists to work in the marginal neighborhoods, organizing them to struggle against the dairies and gasoline processors, and against the government.[93]

The greatest opportunities for organizing in the barrios came after the December 1972 earthquake. This earthquake caused enormous destruction in Managua. Approximately 8,000 people were killed. Of the total affected area, estimated at thirty-three square kilometers, over 80 percent was damaged. The central core of the city, representing 40 percent of the area, was decimated. Up to 75 percent of the residential housing was destroyed or seriously damaged, leaving about 250,000 people homeless.[94]

Harvey Williams outlines the ways in which the 1972 earthquake affected the urban development of Managua:

First, the nearly complete destruction of the central core, its subsequent demolition, and the government's interdiction against new construction there until an urban reconstruction plan could be developed accelerated the trend toward decentralization and deconcentration. The narrow streets, congestion, high-density housing, and small commerce found in other cities was no longer to be found in Managua. Second, the earthquake destroyed much of the older housing. In most cities, such housing has been converted into high-density tenements, or *vecindades*. In Managua, this possibility was eliminated. Finally, the disaster increased the housing deficit by some 40,000 units.[95]

The authorities decided that Managua would be reconstructed on the same site rather than relocated. But the government agencies that planned and directed the reconstruction failed to control corruption and private interests.[96] The United States government donated wooden houses that were put up in the outlying districts of Managua.[97] To assemble these houses the Housing Institute required land. Cornelio Hueck, president of the House of Deputies, bought a parcel of undeveloped land after the earthquake for $17,000 and immediately sold it to the Housing Institute for $1.2 million.[98]

Priests and religious persons working in the poorer communities of Managua experienced firsthand the connection between the Somocista political structure and the suffering of the poor after the earthquake.[99] The case of the Maryknoll Missionaries in the OPEN 3 neighborhood is illustrative in this regard. Displaced persons flooded into OPEN 3 during 1973 and a Maryknoll-operated Youth Club distributed relief supplies. The government then took over the relief effort, hoarding and selling the supplies which virtually ceased the flow of aid to OPEN 3. Both the Maryknoll sisters and the barrio's Christian youth responded by intensifying their organizing efforts, preparing the neighborhood for a series of battles with the government.

During the summer of 1976, OPEN 3 residents waged a campaign to reduce water prices that the government had raised only in the poor neighborhoods. The Youth Clubs, the Christian community, the local worker association, and a women's organization worked together to carry out the "water fight." The Church used the local parish center's mimeo machine for announcements and its building for meetings. After three months, the neighborhood won a reduction in the price of water. This experience taught the residents how to organize politically and it prepared them for future battles. For the Church, it was a lesson in supporting the people in their fight for self-determination. One Maryknoll sister assserted that participation in these struggles "carried the Church into the stream of history."[100]

The most intensive neighborhood organizing took place after the September insurrection when the United People's Movement and the FSLN created the Civil Defense Committees (CDCs) to coordinate and concretize civilian resistance. The MPU organized the CDCs by block, with neighborhood and zonal steering committees. Neighborhood residents elected the directors and representatives to the steering committees.

The CDCs adopted the following goals: 1. to effectively coordinate the urban population for defense against the National Guard; 2. to place all resources and people at the service of the popular brigades and armed forces combating the dictatorship; and 3. to establish a base that would ensure that the people retained power in a new social and political structure.[101]

Between October and December, the urban population carried out intensive clandestine organizing. MPU representatives visited neighborhoods to pass on their organizing techniques and to give instructions in tackling the National Guard. The CDCs stored medicine and medical supplies, and trained older men and women in basic first aid skills. CDC activists collected food and prepared reserve water supplies. The CDCs also set up "Sandinista dining rooms" where the combatants could eat during the fighting, and "security houses" where FSLN leaders could meet. A CDC organizer in a Masaya neighborhood explains the procedure for identifying security houses:

> The first thing we did when we arrived in a barrio was to make a map. We detailed all the houses that existed in each block. We noted which houses belonged to Somocistas and which were houses of trustworthy people, and we drew up dossiers on these people . . . and on this basis we organized the CDCs. So we already knew from which house we could operate and which house to avoid.[102]

The majority of adults in each neighborhood participated in one or another CDC task. Some observed and reported National Guard troop movements. Others followed the activities of Somoza's spies. Older persons and young children carried messages between the Committees in different blocks and neighborhoods. The Popular Brigades (combatants who had not formally joined the FSLN) readied themselves for the task of digging street trenches and stored bricks to build barricades.[103] Many residents fabricated weapons such as Molotov cocktails and contact bombs. Students established arms caches at key points throughout the barrios. Because the National Guard frequently raided private homes, and often bombed or burned whole neighborhoods to force people into the streets, CDC members created evacuation passageways by connecting each house with hidden wall openings and tunnels.

Though the FAO and the business opposition feverishly attempted to strengthen its forces after the September insurrection, the MPU and CDCs unified poor neighborhoods into a clandestine civilian and political force. From January 1979 to the final insurrection of June and July, the Civil Defense Committees proliferated throughout the country, distributing food, organizing health care, and forming popular militias to oppose the National Guard. As Ortega observed afterward, "what happened was that it was the guerrillas who provided support for the masses so that they could defeat the enemy by means of insurrection."[104]

A coalition of social groups ousted the Somoza dictatorship. The Sandinistas united around its political leadership all the major sectors of society: the radical church, the peasantry, the working classes, women, the student movement, the urban poor, and the "patriotic" sectors of the bourgeoisie. It was this pluralism, notes Panamanian economist Xavier Gorostiaga, that distinguished the Nicaraguan revolution from others:

> The Sandinista Revolution is not the product of a proletarian revolution directed by a party, nor is it a peasant revolution, nor does it correspond to the typical model of the seizure of power in a socialist country, like Cuba or China. Rather the revolution is the product of a prolonged war with massive popular participation, a revolution characterized by a strong pluralist content in the manner in which power was taken.[105]

Indeed, the massive popular participation in the overthrow of the dictatorship provided the Sandinistas with the basis for their postvictory legitimacy. The FSLN and different sectors of the mass movement had developed a close working relationship during the war against Somoza, and it was this relationship that laid the foundation for the subsequent ties between the FSLN and the grassroots organizations. Because the organized masses toppled the autocratic regime, the embryonic popular associations were prepared to assume a central role in the revolutionary process after July 19, 1979.

3
THE SETTING

The Sandinista victory over the Somoza dictatorship on July 19, 1979, inspired millions of people in the Third World, especially Latin Americans. The Nicaraguan revolution demonstrated that with sufficient organization and determination a united people can defeat even a well-armed and well-trained military force. In addition, the FSLN proved that a revolutionary organization, able to build patiently on the existing levels of a mass movement's mobilization and consciousness, can achieve victory in the face of tremendous obstacles. Finally, the Sandinistas' merciful treatment of captured National Guardsmen in the aftermath of the war showed that a long-oppressed people need not seek vengeance after overthrowing a hated dictatorship.[1]

This chapter outlines the context in which the mass organizations operate, surveying the central developments of the Nicaraguan economic, political, kinship, and cultural spheres.[2] Such an overview will help clarify the unique aspects of the Nicaraguan revolution, and the tremendous constraints that inhibit its development today. We will then be ready to examine the popular associations' vital role in the revolutionary process.

THE ECONOMIC SPHERE

After Somoza's overthrow the Nicaraguan people inherited a devastated economy. Somoza's looting had left only $3.5 million in the treasury, not enough to pay for two days' worth of imports. Somoza's bombers had destroyed schools, hospitals, and workplaces in Nicaragua's major towns, including several dozen factories owned by opposition industrialists. Capital flight during the civil war had also damaged the economy: $220 million in 1978 and $315 million in the first half of 1979. In Managua, more than one-third of the labor force was unemployed. Production levels had regressed to those of 1962. Because of the fighting, 70 percent of the cultivable land had not been sown, affecting both cash crops and food staples. A foreign debt of $1.64 billion was the highest per capita in Latin America. Even before Somoza's fall, the situation was becoming desperate for most Nicaraguans.[3]

> In mid-June, famine had appeared in the cities and towns as the last bits of hoarded food ran out. The starving populace had then sacked every food store and warehouse in Managua for supplies that ran out within days. Fuel supplies too were virtually exhausted. The Nicaraguan Red Cross and international agencies had begun to distribute food in early July. In Managua alone, a hundred thousand a day had lined up for rations; a family of eight received daily one kilogram (2.2 pounds) of rice and a half kilogram each of sugar and milk. Nevertheless, relief workers estimated that six hundred thousand hungry people received no relief at all. Various epidemics had spread as the public water supply became contaminated, health services broke down, and medical supplies ran out. By 19 July, bodies of the thousands of recent dead were decomposing in Managua's streets and in the rubble of houses, spreading contamination and disease to the living.[4]

The new revolutionary government that took power on July 19, 1979, faced a formidable economic crisis. It set three major goals for the economic system: 1. to rebuild the devastated economy; 2. to redistribute income and economic influence toward the workers and peasants; and 3. to dismantle the economic base of the old regime.[5] One of the new government's first acts was the confiscation of properties and enterprises that had formerly been owned by Somoza and his collaborators.[6] The new government also nationalized the bankrupt financial system, the insurance companies, foreign trade, and the country's run-down mining sector. These confiscated properties and holdings formed the foundation for the new state sector of the economy, called the *Area de Propriedad del Pueblo* (Area of People's Property—APP). The government turned over management of the confiscated agricultural holdings to the new *Instituto Nicaragüense de Reforma Agraria* (Nicaraguan Institute of Agrarian Reform—INRA), and placed most of the manufacturing plants in the hands of the new *Corporación de Industrias del Pueblo* (Corporation of

People's Industries or COIP). The revolutionary state thus assumed control over a major proportion of the means of production and took responsibility for reorganizing and reactivating the economy.

The new government, however, made no attempt to socialize the entire productive process or eliminate private capital. Rather, the government offered guarantees to the private sector that private property would be respected and that private enterprise would be encouraged to take part in the reactivation and development of the economy. Since the early days of the revolution, the political leadership has stressed that the elimination of private enterprise and an extensive socialization of the means of production have not been among their goals. According to Jaime Wheelock, Minister of Agricultural Development and Agrarian Reform,

> It is important to understand that the socialist model is a solution for contradictions that only exist in developed captialist countries. Now, for a series of reasons, many of them political, and others having to do with hunger and desperation, certain peoples have made a revolution in the worst conditions of social development . . . This is our case. Even though we have socialist principles, we cannot effect the transformation of our society by socializing the means of production. This would not lead to socialism, rather, on the contrary, it could lead to the destruction and disarticulation of our society.[7]

The Sandinistas, therefore, do not think it is possible to socialize all the means of production in an underdeveloped country such as Nicaragua. Consequently, they seek the cooperation of private enterprise in the development of a "mixed economy," which includes five forms of property: state, cooperative, small private, medium private, and large private.

The Mixed Economy

The state sector now comprises approximately 40 percent of the gross domestic product (GDP) and the three froms of private production account for the remaining 60 percent. In agriculture and manufacturing—the two main productive sectors of the economy—private producers generate an even larger proportion of total production. The place of private property in Nicaragua's mixed economy is therefore more significant than most outsiders realize. In fact, revolutionary Nicaragua has a smaller state sector than Peru under General Velasco's reformist military regime, or Argentina under Peron's populist regime, or even Chile under Allende's Popular Unity government.

On the other hand, capitalists are not free to set the pace for the Nicaraguan economy. The government possesses an array of powers that act to restrain and reduce subversion of the Sandinista economic program. The Central Bank regulates the allocation of credit and foreign exchange to both the private and the APP sectors. And though the various banks operate semi-independently from each other, they do so because they are specialized in different areas.[8] In addition, all Nicaraguan exports and imports are under the control of various bodies within the Ministry of Foreign Trade. The government, with its national import and export companies and its control over foreign exchange, regulates the volume and nature of investment in the entire productive sector. This, together with state administration of the credit structure, allows the government to influence the form and structure of private sector development, and to plan economic growth in terms of social need. Consequently, the revolutionary government "goes against the logic of capital accumulation without breaking it."[9]

The Sandinistas stress that their support of a mixed economy does not contradict the revolution's primary commitment to defend the interests of the country's poor majority, especially the peasants and workers. In February 1983, Sandinista leader Tomás Borge revealed the meaning of the mixed economy in the Nicaraguan context:

> Mixed economies in other countries that have not had revolutions are not the same as the one in Nicaragua. There are more private enterprises here, relatively speaking, than in Venezuela, for example, but here political power is not in the hands of the businessmen. The revolution wants to cooperate with them in production and economic planning. In Nicaragua there does exist a truly mixed economy, within the revolution. We provide the businessmen with many concessions, credits, facilities, but many of them remain discontented. They will not resign themselves to losing political power![10]

Class Structure

Insufficient data exist to elaborate a detailed analysis of Nicaragua's class structure. Nevertheless it is possible to draw an outline of the country's social classes. In 1985 government calculations showed that the economically active population (EAP) stood at 1,045,000, out of a total population of 3,100,000.[11] The class structure of the EAP looks something like this:

Agricultural EAP
large agrarian bourgeoisie—1,500[12]
middle agrarian bourgoisie—40,000[13]
rich peasants—30,000[14]
medium peasants—55,000[15]
poor peasants—135,000[16]
agricultural workers:
   permanent workers—70,000
   temporary workers—70,000

Nonagricultural EAP
large urban bourgeoisie—620[17]
middle urban bourgeoisie—3,500[18]
highly-paid managers, professionals, and technicians—15.000[19]
lower-paid managers, professionals, and technicians—60,000[20]
industrial workers—100,000
white-collar workers—80,000
petit bourgeoisie—35,000[21]
shopkeepers, vendors, and artisans—95,000
subproletariat (unemployed, domestic employees)—140,000

Due to historic underdevelopment, Nicaragua's unproductive or "informal sector" is quite inflated. Nearly half of the urban EAP survive as commercial intermediaries and vendors. Since 1984 the unproductive sector has drawn thousands of rural dwellers to the city who are attracted by the possibility of selling scarce products outside of the regulated markets. Because of high defense expenditures the government is unable to expand the productive sector and can offer few alternatives to this large group of small speculators. The development of agrarian reform will lower the migration rate from the countryside to the city, but it will not address the needs of the multitude of people already located on the outskirts of the main cities who act as commercial middlemen.

Since the revolution stripped Nicaragua's capitalists of political power, the question of which class shall rule has come to the fore. One thing is clear: the Sandinistas rely increasingly on a group of managers, professionals, technicians, and party and trade union functionaries to run the mixed economy and administer revolutionary projects. Considerable evidence exists to show that this social group represents an embryonic ruling class made up of people who earn at least four times more than the average wage for a manual worker, enjoy job tenure, and wield considerable decision-making power. So although Nicaragua's workers and peasants exercise considerable economic and political power in the new society, they must share this power with an emerging group of administrators and professionals.[22]

Changes and Crisis

The revolution has brought about major changes in the consumption factor of the economy. Public consumption increased from 8 percent of the GDP in 1977 to 25 percent in 1982, and private consumption of basic goods and services also increased, from 35 percent of the GDP in 1977 to 43 percent in 1982. At the same time, private consumption of nonessential goods such as appliances and automobiles, declined from 38 percent to 22 percent of the GDP. This transformation stemmed from the government's efforts to restrict the consumption of nonessential goods and increase the poor majority's consumption of basic goods.

The revolutionary state strictly limits luxury imports and all other nonessential goods. Until February 1985, it rationed and subsidized the prices of basic goods and services to ensure that workers and peasants gained access to them. To guarantee equitable consumption patterns, the government also attempts to restrict wage and salary increases. E.V.K. Fitzgerald, a top government economic adviser, explains: "The lesson of the Chilean experience, and to a certain extent in Cuba as well, was that nominal salary increases only served to increase the prices of food to the disadvantage of the popular classes. Therefore, in Nicaragua it was decided that the only way to produce changes in the economy which would improve the distribution of incomes was through increasing the supply of wage goods."[23]

The changes in consumption patterns have aided the poor majority, but the Reagan Administration's economic war against Nicaragua has greatly hindered Sandinista policies. Historically, all revolutionary societies have confronted major economic problems as they attempt to restructure their socioeconomic systems. The United States has often aggravated these difficulties by withdrawing aid and financial credit and by enforcing trade embargoes and economic boycotts. To destabilize and ruin the Nicaraguan economy, the Reagan administration has backed the contra (counterrevolutionary) campaign of economic sabotage, and has also orchestrated a systematic campaign to cut off Nicaragua's sources of international financial aid.

By December 1985, Nicaragua had lost $1.3 billion in the Contra war, three times more than double the value of the country's annual exports.[24] The destruction of the oil refinery in Corinto and the CIA mining of the harbors were the most dramatic forms of economic sabotage, but the Contras' more traditional techniques, such as destroying power lines, storage facilities, and vehicles, have also taken a considerable toll. Since 1983 the Contras have attempted to disrupt the coffee harvest, Nicaragua's largest source of foreign exchange.

In 1984 and 1985, the government imposed drastic austerity measures to deal with Nicaragua's deepening economic problems. To reduce
expenditures on food subsidies, the government doubled the prices of
basic goods in early August 1984. The government also sharply raised
consumption taxes on soft drinks and beer to help reduce the national
deficit. After five years of maintaining the official exchange rate at 10
córdobas to the dollar, Nicaragua devalued the official value of the
córdoba to 28 córdobas to the dollar in February 1985. The government
also designed a new currency exchange system to maintain different rates
for exports and imports in order to stimulate production and curb the
black market for dollars.[25]

In 1984 and 1985 shortages became more acute, principally because
of the war effort and the lack of foreign exchange. As much as half the
nation's corn and bean crops were lost because they had been grown in
war zones, and peasants often could not plant or harvest them. "This is
a war economy," declared Fitzgerald in November 1984, "and all war
economies involve shortages and hardships."[26]

In early February 1986 President Daniel Ortega announced further
economic adjustments as part of the government's continuing efforts to
regulate controlled economic variables. The government devalued the
córdoba by 150 percent and increased bank interest rates by 100 percent.
The new exchange rate was not a real attempt to achieve economic
equilibrium because the trade balance had surpassed $530 million, ex-
ports had fallen below $350 million, and the foreign debt had climbed
to more than $5 billion.[27] Rather, the measures were an attempt to
politically balance the role played by different social sectors in an economy destabilized by the war, the world economic crisis, and the economic structures inherited from Somoza. "We are waging the battle for
military defense with great effectiveness, but the economy is more complex and difficult," declared President Ortega when he announced the
new exchange rate.[28]

Although the revolution made substantial military advances in 1985,
they can be attributed to the mobilization of a significant part of the
workforce and resources to the war fronts. This mobilization inflated the
fiscal deficit which in turn fueled a huge increase in the amount of money
in circulation that was not backed by a corresponding increase in production. Prices rose dramatically leaving salary adjustments, exchange
rates, and bank interest rates far behind.

In 1985 inflation became a virtual war tax that weighed most heavily
on those whose income—derived from selling either their labor power
or their products—could not keep up with rising costs. Inflation hit wage
workers with the most force. Wages increased in 1985 by an average of

140 percent, but prices for basic consumer goods shot up by more than 300 percent.[29] In the first three months of 1986 the government announced two wage increases totalling 135 percent. The salary hikes, however, were absorbed quickly by an inevitable rise in prices stemming from the devaluation of the córdoba and the higher interest rates.

The escalation of U.S. aggression has forced the government to maintain a budget deficit which is not economically productive. The government is unable to expand social services and can invest only modest sums in the productive sector; defense costs eat up more than 50 percent of the budget. This means that the "war tax" will continue. In February 1986 Barricada Internacional summed up the economic situation:

> At present the economically productive sectors carry the weight of the war, of an administrative apparatus that is frozen but still oversized, and of an enormous intermediary commercial layer with few prospects in production. The policy of adjustments is in reality a political measure aimed at making this burden more tolerable and achieving a more equitable balance within the limitations imposed by the nation's difficult economic situation.[30]

THE POLITICAL SPHERE

By 1979 the FSLN was the predominant political organization in Nicaragua. After the victory over Somoza, the FSLN worked to expand and to integrate its own mass base of supporters in order to compete successfully with other political groups. During the revolution's first five years, the Sandinistas established an elaborate party organization stretching from its Managua headquarters to every corner of the nation. The national headquarters generates copious literature, propaganda, plans, and programs.[31] Although the pro-Sandinista popular associations are organizationally independent of the FSLN, but most association members provide the party with its mass support. In the November 1984 general elections the Frente received 67 percent of the popular vote, falling just short of a two-thirds majority in the new National Assembly.[32]

The FSLN defines itself as "the vanguard organization of the Nicaraguan people." "The FSLN," says Comandante Carlos Nuñez,

> came to be and is the vanguard of the Nicaraguan people not only for having defined the correct way of struggle, but also for having clearly defined that the masses were the force capable

of moving the wheel of history. If yesterday, oriented and directed by their vanguard, they were the motor of the overthrow of the dictatorship, then today, directed by that vanguard, they are the motor of the revolution.[33]

As Richard Fagen notes, the Sandinistas' definition of vanguard entails a "double imperative":

> First, it implies a continuing dominant place for the FSLN in Nicaraguan politics. It is a claim that FSLN hegemony . . . ought to be a structural, not just a temporary, feature of the political economy of the nation. Second, it implies that membership in the FSLN must be strictly controlled. Not everyone can belong, no matter how heroic he or she might have been during the final insurrection.[34]

Indeed, it is extremely difficult to become a Sandinista party member. The *Frente* has two types of members: aspiring militants and militants. Aspiring militants must be active at their workplace, involved in their community, familiar with Nicaragua's political problems, and trusted by other party members. Furthermore, a person attains the status of aspiring militant only upon recommendation by an FSLN base committee and approval by both the zonal and regional party offices. Aspirants must then wait from six to eighteen months to gain the status of party militant. To become a militant, a member must be outstanding in carrying out party duties, disciplined in personal behavior, and manifest a "great love for the people."[35]

The party has a five-tiered organizational structure. Base committees are the elemental party organs, charged with maintaining the *Frente's* links with the country's working people. Zonal offices coordinate the work of these committees, and regional offices monitor the activities of the various zones. At its September, 1980, National Assembly, the FSLN formed the Sandinista Assembly, a 105-member advisory council to the National Directorate. The Assembly, made up of the party's best militants, approves FSLN programs and statutes, periodically reviews party strategy, and helps determine the party's mass line and political education policies. The FSLN National Directorate is the organization's highest leadership body. Based on the principle of collective leadership, the National Directorate makes all major party decisions, and acts as the guiding force for the Sandinista Popular Revolution, the FSLN's official name for the revolution.[36]

Although their critics charge that the Sandinistas are orthodox Marxist-Leninists, the FSLN differs markedly—in both theory and practice—

from contemporary communist parties. Unlike Marxist-Leninist parties in socialist countries, the FSLN has not fused its party apparatus with that of the state. Daniel Ortega and other Sandinistas now control the government's executive branch as a result of the 1984 election, but the state bureaucracy consists mainly of non-Sandinistas. As stated earlier, the FSLN has no intention of nationalizing the entire economy, and continues to foster private enterprise. Ideologically, the FSLN adheres to *Sandinismo*, a complex mixture of nationalism, anti-imperialism, Marxism, liberation theology, and classical liberalism. Untouched by the militant atheism that characterizes communist parties, the *Frente* sees no contradiction between Christianity and revolution, and a majority of its members are Catholics.

The Executive Branch before 1985

The Governing Junta of National Reconstruction was the principal executive council of Nicaragua until January 9, 1985.[37] It was a collegial presidency that included major leaders of the FSLN. Served by a large staff of technical experts, trained public administrators, and social scientists, the junta developed public policy along the lines determined by or with the FSLN National Directorate, and executed that policy through the various government ministries. During its first year, the junta legislated by unappealable decree under emergency powers. The junta usually made decisions by consensus and without formal votes. Although an exchange of ideas took place between the FSLN Directorate and the junta, the Directorate set the general guidelines for the revolution and the junta worked to execute details of those guidelines. Between February 1981 and January 1985, Daniel Ortega, as junta chairman, was the link between the Directorate and the junta.[38]

The Cabinet and the Council of State

During the years between 1979 and 1985, the Nicaraguan government executed policy through various ministries such as foreign relations, internal commerce, and defense, as well as autonomous agencies such as the Central Bank and the International Reconstruction Fund.[39] Cabinet members included a number of Somoza opponents and many officials who did not have previous ties to the Sandinistas. Cabinet reorganization through 1981 maintained this pluralism while increasing FSLN influence. Non-Sandinistas occupied the more technical, less political portfolios, and FSLN leaders headed such critical ministries as defense, interior, agrarian reform/agricultural development, and planning.

On May 4, 1980, the revolutionary government of Nicaragua inaugurated its consultative representative assembly, the Council of State. The broad revolutionary alliance originally negotiated the Council's membership before Somoza's fall, but the Sandinistas modified it in April 1980. The Council was originally designed to have thirty-three representatives: twelve for the FSLN and its closest political allies. The FSLN Directorate and the junta later added fourteen new delegates, twelve from pro-Sandinista organizations.[40]

The Council of State played a "co-legislative" role, sharing a consultative and legislative function with the junta. Corporatist in representation—delegates represented organizations rather than geographical electoral districts—the council at first reviewed proposed legislation and recommended modifications; but in 1985 and 1986 it initiated a considerable amount of legislation. The council had no representative from the formal opposition because it included no sector opposed to the ouster of Somoza or to major reforms, and because the government's revolutionary aims required national unity and consensus building. An opposition to the FSLN did begin to form in late 1980 and 1981, led by the Nicaraguan Democratic Movement and included business associations and other small parties. In late October 1981, the MDN, the Social Christian Party, and the Social Democratic Party began to form the Nicaraguan Democratic Coordinating Committee (CDN). Some of the opposition representatives boycotted their council seats for extended periods to protest FSLN policies. Generally though, the council provided a forum for public discussion of issues, and effective consultation took place among the interests represented, often producing substantive changes in proposed legislation.

The 1984 Elections and the New Government

The general elections held in Nicaragua on November 4, 1984, were the first since Somoza's overthrow.[41] The FSLN had included elections as part of its platform even before Somoza's fall. On July 20, 1979, the day after the Sandinistas took power, the government junta proclaimed a "Fundamental Statute" that specified that "to the extent that the conditions of national reconstruction permit it, general elections will be held for the constitution of a National Assembly . . . in accordance with the Electoral Law which shall be promulgated at an opportune time."[42] In a speech on August 23, 1980, celebrating the end of the national literacy campaign, Comandante Humberto Ortega pledged that elections would occur within five years, and that the Council of State would begin formulating the country's electoral laws in early 1983.

In March 1981, the Council of State began to discuss various drafts of a law on political parties. The debate on this law continued into 1982, but was suspended in March of that year when the junta declared a state of emergency in response to an increase in counterrevolutionary activity. (In December 1981, President Reagan approved an initial expenditure of $19 million for the "secret war" against the FSLN government.) The Council of State finally approved the Political Parties Law on August 17, 1983. On February 21, 1984, the junta issued Decree Number 1400 which set November 4, 1984, as the date for elections. Thus, it was affirmed by the Latin American Studies Association delegation to the Nicaraguan elections that "the 1984 elections had been in the making for more than five years, and the Sandinistas had essentially adhered to their own publicly announced schedule for holding them."[43]

The Electoral Law

Nicaragua's 1984 electoral law established an electoral system derived from the classical liberal-democratic concept of territorial representation and "one citizen, one vote."[44] The law calls for presidential government, and the separation of powers between executive and legislative authorities and functions. The electorate is defined as all citizens sixteen years of age or older. In the November 1984 elections, voters cast one ballot for the offices of president and vice president and one ballot for a predetermined, party-specific list of candidates for the National Assembly.

In the short term, the major governmental institution is the National Assembly, since it functions as a constituent assembly charged with defining and promulgating the basic constitution of a new political system. The National Assembly is a unicameral body with ninety-six members (ninety regular members plus the defeated presidential candidates of the six opposition parties, who are entitled by law to hold a seat in the Assembly) all of whom serve six-year terms.

The Assembly will function as a constituent assembly until January 1987, and then become a legislature unless the Assembly itself, acting in its constituent role, changes its own term, powers, and functions. Under the law, the Assembly could dissolve itself and call new elections as soon as another constitution has been drafted and declared. The FSLN, however, has discounted the possibility of new elections in the near future.

The election of the Assembly was based on the principle of proportional representation. The electoral law divided the country into nine territorial districts with a varying number of members per district, apportioned according to population. Each legally registered party chose an ordered list of candidates to present to the electorate, and each party won seats in the Assembly according to the fraction of the vote won in each district. "The choice of this kind of proportional representation system is significant," writes the Latin American Association Studies delegation, "because it tilts the National Assembly toward political pluralism, by assuring the representation of a wider range of interersts and opinions within the electorate than would be achieved under a U.S.-style single-member district system. Proportional representation should also encourage the institutionalization of a multi-party opposition in the legislature."[45]

In its first two years, the Assembly's duties will include determining the functions and powers of the executive branch. The constitution-making process also established the powers of the National Assembly itself. The Assembly has the right to full disclosure of the national budget and the power to enact laws regulating foreign investment. Furthermore, the constituent assembly is responsible for redefining the basic rules for the future relationship between the state and the private sector.[46]

The Political Opposition

The Nicaraguan Democratic Coordinating Committee (CDN) is the principal opposition group in Nicaragua. The CDN is composed of members from the Superior Council of Higher Enterprise, the largest private employer group in Nicaragua, three right-wing political parties, the Social Democratic Party (PSD), the Social Christian Party (PSC), the Constitutionalist Liberal Party (PLC), and two small unions [the AFL-CIO affiliated Confederation of Trade Unions (CUS) and the Nicaraguan Workers Federation, (CTN)]. Since its formation in October 1981, the CDN has become increasingly critical of the Sandinista government. Many former CDN leaders have left the country to join the Contra cause abroad. Since November 1983 the CDN has called for a "dialogue" with the Contras. Indeed, the CDN conditioned its participation in the 1984 elections on the government's willingness to negotiate with the Contra.

The CDN strengthened their alliance with the Contras when the electoral campaign began during the summer of 1984. Both major Contra organizations, the Nicaraguan Democratic Front (FDN) and the Revolutionary Democratic Alliance (ARDE), appointed the CDN to negotiate on their behalf and agreed to lay down their arms if Arturo Cruz, the CDN's presidential candidate, would be permitted to run for office. For his part, Cruz demanded that FDN leader Adolfo Calero and ARDE leader

Eden Pastora be permitted to return to Nicaragua and participate in the elections. The government refused to accept these conditions and the CDN abstained from the elections.[47]

In January 1985, CDN leader Cruz called for a resumption of United States aid to the Contras. On March 2, Cruz and Calero signed a joint document demanding that the government engage in immediate negotiations with the Contras and schedule new elections. And one month later, on April 4, President Reagan met with Cruz and Contra leaders Calero and Robelo and proposed that $14 million in U.S. aid to the contras would be used for nonmilitary purposes if the Nicaraguan government negotiated with the Contras for at least sixty days. In 1986 the Democratic Coordinating Committee continued to echo the main political line of the Contras.

The FSLN also confronts a parliamentary opposition made up of the six political parties that competed in Nicaragua's November 4, 1984 elections: the Democratic Conservative Party (PCD), the Independent Liberal Party (PLI), the Popular Social Christian Party (PPSC), the Communist Party of Nicaragua (PCN), the Nicaraguan Socialist Party (PSN), and the Marxist-Leninist Popular Action Movement (MAP-ML). These six parties all saw the elections as their best opportunity to have some political influence on the course of the revolution. Although these parties were sharply critical of the FSLN during the election campaign, none of them opposed the fundamental framework of the new historical period that began in 1979. Together the six opposition parties received a total of 33 percent of the vote. Twenty-seven percent corresponded to the three parties to the right of the FSLN: the PCD with 14 percent, the PLI with 9.6 percent, and the PPSC with 5.6 percent. The remaining 4 percent went to the three parties representing positions to the left of the FSLN: the PCN, the PSN, and the MAP-ML.[48]

Since the 1984 elections the six opposition parties have conducted a fierce battle with the FSLN in the National Assembly to challenge the Sandinistas in their efforts to draft the new constitution. The first draft was presented on February 21, 1986 during the opening of the Assembly's second legislative session. The Assembly's Special Constitutional Commission was made up of twenty-two representatives from six of the seven parties represented in the Assembly. Much to the discouragement of the Constitutional Commission, two of its members—from the Democratic Conservative Party and the Marxist-Leninist Popular Action Movement— refrained from signing the draft document.[49] During the plenary debate on the draft in August 1986 each party fought for its version of the constitution. The Constitution was formally ratified and signed in December 1986.

THE KINSHIP SPHERE

A key element in the unprecedented participation of women in the Nicaraguan revolution is their role as "pillars of their families."[50] This is the
basic reality of life for Nicaraguan women. They don't view themselves
merely as housewives caring for their children, attending to domestic
concerns, and subordinating themselves to their husbands. Women are
the center of their family—emotionally, ideologically, and economically.
This is especially true of working-class and peasant women.

Single mothers abandoned by their husbands constitute 34 percent
of urban households in Nicaragua.[51] Even when husbands remain with
their families, the high rate of both seasonal and permanent unemployment among men places the burden of family survival on women. This
daily struggle to survive is responsible for strong, well-developed, and
determined personalities among Nicaraguan women.

The participation of women in the war against Somoza strengthened
their character even further, and precipitated many changes in their views
on traditional gender roles. AMPRONAC, the organization that mobilized
women against the dictatorship, offered its members a crucial vehicle
for participation by encouraging women to break from their prescribed
roles to become politically active anti-Somocistas. For many women,
political activism led to conflicts within the home, even separation from
husbands and children. Indeed, many women engaged in a double clandestinity: hiding their political involvement from their husbands and the
National Guard. But as men began to recognize the important role that
women were playing, they came to treat women with new respect.

Gloria Carrión, one of the founders of AMPRONAC, describes the
effect that women's political involvement had on relationships between
men and women:

> Women began to develop their own points of view on issues
> and began to express their ideas. In homes where both the hus-
> band and wife lived together new relationships developed.
> Women started to make their feelings and opinions known. They
> would disagree with their husbands on issues where they never
> had before. And as women got involved in activities outside the
> home their time was less fully devoted to the home and the
> division of labour within the family began to change. All this
> demanded a re-evaluation of the family situation.[52]

Participation in the struggle against Somoza also brought a sense of self-
respect to many women. One domestic worker who had raised nine
children alone declared: "Women weren't aware of anything; they only

washed, ironed, cooked, had children and that was it. But now, I tell you, we're awakened."[53]

Even in revolutionary movements, however, there is no guarantee that participation will lead to a permanent political role in the new society, or that it signifies a genuine step toward emancipation. History has many examples of societies in which women participated in social and political conflicts only to be forced back into traditional roles when the crises subsided.[54]

Although thousands of women developed a feminist consciousness during the revolutionary war, sexism still thrives in Nicaragua. The battle to end the oppression of women is an arduous and protracted one that is only just beginning. Women still maintain primary reponsibility for child-rearing and housework; initial attempts to liberate women from such traditional tasks face immense obstacles. In addition, transforming patriarchal ideology and behavior—challenging men to change relationships from which they have gained definite privileges—is a difficult task in any society. In a 1984 speech delivered in the United States, AMNLAE's Magda Enriquez spoke of the ideological constraints faced by Nicaraguan women:

> Many people think that because there is a revolution there is an ideological change just like that. Political and economic structures that are corrupt can be destroyed rather quickly. But mental structures—culture, ideology, education—that is not so easy. That's a longer process. So that's why many times friends that worked with us side by side in the mountains and never thought of us as being a woman or a man because his life depended on me and my life depended on him—that's why men will fully agree that all the women in the world should have an equal participation, but when it comes down sometimes to his little wife, things kind of change . . . And they get nervous and the ideological floor shakes a lot.[55]

Legislation

The legal reforms passed in revolutionary societies have brought a significant improvement in the status of women, particularly in the area of family law and the laws of personal status. As Maxine Molyneaux observes:

> In many Third World countries where customary, tribal, and religious laws defined women's position as inferior and clearly subordinate to men, depriving them of many of the rights enjoyed

by men, the very granting of formal legal equality between the sexes (as between castes) has represented a significant break with the past. Indeed, by establishing formal juridical equality for all citizens the new states have undoubtedly weakened, if not abolished, traditional structures of hierarchy and privilege.[56]

At the time of Somoza's overthrow, Nicaraguan women were subject to gross legal discrimination. In March 1980, Maria Lourdes Vargas, then an official of the Socio-Legal Department of the Ministry of Social Welfare, described women's legal situation.

If we are to speak of women's legal status, we must note that the laws of Nicaragua reflect the interests of a capitalist system. Therefore, they should be thoroughly examined—little by little, since this is an immense task. It is within the general context of Nicaraguan legislation that the legal situation of women must be examined.

According to our laws women are at a clear disadvantage at all levels, including those levels where they are most directly affected, such as marriage, divorce, patria potestad [laws giving husbands and fathers extensive authority over wives and children], abortion, and rape.[57]

The revolutionary government took the first step toward eliminating discriminatory laws against women just two days after the fall of Somoza. On July 21, 1979, it issued the Fundamental Statute, stressing the equality between men and women before the law. And on August 16, 1979, the government decreed a media law prohibiting the depiction of women as sex objects: "The use of women as a sexual or commercial object is prohibited, eliminating once and for all those infamous commercial advertisements which always associated women with the consumption of alcoholic beverages."[58] This law has been quite effective. People who object to particular advertisements can complain to the government director of communications, who has the power to prohibit their dissemination.[59]

In Nicaragua, the *Patria Potestad* that was recognized in the civil code was based on the absolute dominion of the father over the family and its possessions. The law also stipulated that only children born within a legal marriage had legal rights. Even though a legally married mother may have been the only one to concern herself with the education and development of a child, she had no legal decision-making power in the life of her children. For example, if a son wanted to leave the country to go abroad, he had to obtain the father's permission, even if the father was not living with the son.[60]

The new Law on Relations between Mother, Father, and Children calls on fathers to share child-rearing responsibilities with mothers. It requires parents to ensure the material well-being of their children, and discusses the love that parents should demonstrate in order to guide and instruct their children. The law also restores mothers' rights concerning their children in cases of male abandonment, and it eliminates discrimination against the child born outside legal marriage.[61]

In addition to proclaiming women's equality with men in all areas, the Nicaraguan Fundamental Statute grants women the right to work, the right to enjoy equal conditions of work, and the right to an equal salary for equal work. Women receive special mention in the new codes on land use and allocation, and these measures grant women the right to membership in agricultural cooperatives and state farms. Furthermore, new employment laws ban discrimination against pregnant women, and guarantee ninety days of fully-paid pregnancy leave.

The Family

The family is the core of Nicaraguan society.[62] It serves as social network, support system, and unit for child-rearing. Women play the central role in the Nicaraguan family—a role that can inhibit their ability to be workers, activists, and soldiers, but which makes them essential in other ways. Women maintain the labor force, raise children, clean up neighborhoods, care for the sick and provide reproductive resources. Women serve as unpaid social workers, thereby aiding a country too poor to pay for many such public social services.

Most Nicaraguan women experience the family as something changeable and unstable, quite different from the durable nuclear model. Few women get married, but nearly all begin bearing children between the ages of fifteen and nineteen. Women head 40 percent of the families in the country, rearing their children without a male partner. Because a large percentage of women have to work outside the home, relatives often take charge of the children. In many cases, though, children are left to take care of themselves.

Although women play the dominant role in the upbringing of their children, men wield tremendous power within the family, controlling the household finances. Even families with an absent father can feel his presence. For instance, the mother tends to speak favorably of the father to her children and often portrays herself as "helpless" without him, thereby reinforcing sexist family stereotypes. Deighton et al., a team of English feminists who interviewed scores of Nicaraguan women in 1982, describe the ways in which sexism permeates the Nicaraguan family.

Machismo, which is deeply ingrained in Nicaraguan men, underlies relations between them and their families. A display of male superiority, one of its characteristics is the assumption of male privilege and power in the family: the man is 'master' of his 'own' woman—to the point even of physical violence. Women are defined essentially in terms of their reproductive functions and as mothers are expected to bear the practical responsibility for bringing up a family. The cult of virility dictates that a rigid division of sexual roles must be maintained and housework is left entirely to women. Though men often expect their women to bear many children, quite often they simply abandon their families, often described as 'irresponsible paternity.'[63]

The extended family provides Nicaraguan women with a crucial support system. Most homes comprise parents and children as well as grandparents, aunts, uncles, and other relatives. As an interdependent unit, the extended family furnishes women with both economic and emotional sustenance. A woman's relations with her sisters, brothers, and mother are often more important than those with her male partner.

Yet the Nicaraguan family is subject to substantial pressures. In the countryside, most men who journey to other jobs during the year maintain relations with a second or third woman in the area of their seasonal work, and frequently they have children with these women. Many men in urban areas also have relationships and children with more than one woman. The lack of privacy in town and city dwellings can strain family relations. In the poor neighborhoods of Managua, 65 percent of the houses have only one bedroom, in which as many as six or seven family members sleep.[64] This often contributes to spousal conflicts, jealousy, alcoholism, fatigue, and promiscuity.

Researchers with the Instituto Historico Centroamericano observe that

despite all these difficulties that affect family stability, the Nicaraguan family sees itself as a monogamous unit. This is the ideal to be striven for, a sign that things are getting better, a life style in which people will be happier. There is a certainty that it will mean greater emotional stability for both couples and their children, as well as a way to achieve greater economic stability. In spite of all the present ruptures in family life produced by the revolution—that has also entailed a revolution in morals, in cultural patterns, and in collective ideals—the goal continues to be a united family.[65]

Nicaraguans view the family as the focal point of social and personal interests. As the elementary cell of society, they contend, the family contributes to social development and plays an important role in the upbringing of coming generations. The Fundamental Statute embodies this concept of the family: "The family is the natural element of society and has the right to protection from society and the state."[66]

Aside from pragmatic reasons, ideological motives also underlie the revolution's commitment to both the nuclear unit and the stem family (children, parents, and grandparents). Catholicism's traditional attitudes toward the family have profoundly influenced the family policies of both the FSLN and the government. In addition, the stable family represents normality and calm after the upheaval and chaos of the civil war.

CULTURE, COMMUNITY, AND RELIGION

Somoza ruled Nicaragua by combining coercion with consent. For decades the dictator's media disseminated capitalist values and a fierce hostility toward socialism. During the prerevolutionary period, the FSLN developed a parallel ideological and cultural hegemony that definitively broke the legitimacy of the Somoza state. Combining the legacy of Sandino with elements of liberation theology and Marxism, the Sandinistas hope to create a new national culture that will facilitate the psychological, economic, social, and political well-being of all Nicaraguans. As John A. Booth, a political scientist at North Texas State University, elaborates:

> Selfless and socially responsible collaboration should replace individualistic striving. Nicaragua should become an integrated whole, incorporating fully and equally such marginal zones as the Atlantic region and such long-victimized social groups and strata as women, Indians, peasants, and the urban poor. The revolution should be both truly revolutionary (not reformist) and Sandinist, with the FSLN as the vanguard, arbiter, and main agent of social change within an environment of political liberty and ideological pluralism.[67]

To disseminate these cultural goals for the country, the FSLN has carried out an intensive propaganda campaign. The *Frente* conducts its ideological activities through its newspaper, *Barricada*, its broadcast media, the publications of the Secretariat of Propaganda and Political Education, and the mass organizations. The Ministry of Culture runs the nationalized television channels and radio stations, subsidizes the arts, organizes historical and cultural programs, and operates museums.

The Sandinistas' most ambitious socialization effort was the 1980 National Literacy Crusade that taught basic reading and writing skills to 52 percent of Nicaraguans aged ten or older who were found to be illiterate in a late 1979 census. Student volunteers, trained by the Ministry of Education, were the main teaching force in the crusade. The educational materials used pro-Sandinista messages to teach illiterate Nicaraguans the principal tenets of the FSLN vision of the "New Nicaragua." The literacy primer *El Amanecer del Pueblo* (Dawn of the People) included the following chapter titles: "Sandino, Guide of the Revolution"; "The Popular Masses Made the Insurrection"; "The Sandinista Defense Committees Defend the Revolution"; "Agrarian Reform Will Restore to the People the Production of the Land of the People"; and "Our Democracy is the Power of the Organized People."[68]

One cultural goal difficult to achieve was the integration of the Atlantic zone into Nicaragua.[69] The Atlantic region had long been isolated from the populous Pacific region. The various Indian groups (Miskitu, Sumu, Rama, and others) and English-speaking black Protestants of the zone had historically regarded the Spanish-speaking population as alien exploiters. Under the Somoza regime, foreign mining, fishing, and lumber companies provided many jobs, and Anastosio Somoza Debayle had cultivated the zone's Moravian missionaries, who promoted anti-FSLN sentiments among the population.

After the fall of the dictatorship many "Spaniards" from the Pacific region entered the Atlantic region and disrupted established patterns. In particular, the nationalization of the mines, labor operations, and fisheries made the government solicitous of newly-organized unions demanding numerous improvements in wages and working conditions. Other conflicts arose over the MISURASATA (Unity of the Miskitu, Sumu, Rama, and Sandinistas) Indian organization's demands for recognition of land titles dating back to the British protectorate era, and over the local black commercial elite's resentment of "Spanish" control over many new government agencies. Resistance broke out in 1980 and 1981, including riots in Bluefields and Puerto Cabezas and an abortive consipiracy to kill FSLN leaders. This outburst against the revolution stunned government and Sandinista officials, very few of whom had come from, or even visited, the Atlantic coast before the victory.

Tensions in the Atlantic region grew again in 1981 and 1982 as counterrevolutionaries based in Honduras took advantage of anti-Sandinista feelings in order to expand their sabotage and raids within Nicaraguan territory. The government then increased the number of Sandinista Army troops in the area. When counter revolutionary activity escalated, the government began to transfer some of the indigenous population to camps away from the fighting along the Honduran border. In early 1982, Reagan administration officials displayed photographs that allegedly proved that the Sandinista Army was systematically killing and torturing the Miskitu Indians. The Sandinistas were able to prove that the photos actually dated from the Somoza era, and Nicaraguan and international observors who visited the Atlantic region also denied United States accusations of torture and murder. Nevertheless, the relocation program alienated numerous Indians and added to an escalated state of tension in the Atlantic zone.

The Sandinistas now concede that they had originally tried to impose their revolutionary ideas on Atlantic Coast residents, thereby angering many members of the region's indigenous communities.[70] But the FSLN learned from its mistakes, and in 1983 began to take a different approach to the Indian and black populations of the area. In late 1984, the Sandinistas established a joint commission comprised of FSLN representatives as well as Indian and black leaders, to draft proposals for an autonomous government on the Atlantic Coast. Initial plans call for two regional governments: one in the north where most of the Miskitu Indian population lives, and another in the south which is predominantly black. The local population will elect these governments which shall have the authority to set economic priorities as well as the administrative and security policies for the region. The proposed constitution will institutionalize these autonomy measures as well as guarantee the rights of the indigenous communities to cultural expression and the protection of their historical and religious heritage.[71]

Autonomy for the Atlantic Coast would represent a key advance in the revolution's attempt to accommodate the country's ethnic diversity. No other government in Latin America or the Caribbean has ever allowed its ethnic minorities the degree of autonomy that is being proposed for the Atlantic Coast population in Nicaragua.

Religion and the Revolution

Nicaragua's Christians, both Catholics and Protestants, were heavily involved in the revolutionary struggle.[72] Church men and women condemned the abuse of human rights, and secured international publicity for these atrocities. Priests fought, and lost their lives. At the grassroots level, the church had been the only organization that could exercise the tradition of Sandino by creating cooperatives and encouraging popular education. Many FSLN militants had been participants in church youth organizations in the 1960s, and some of the mass organizations of today have their origins in Christian groups. When the bishops confirmed the right of the people to join the insurrection, and when priests said mass in the guerrilla camps, these were revolutionary acts which absolved the people from the sin of "communism" and sanctioned the use of arms.

After the revolution, the anti-Somoza alliance began to fragment in the church as it did elsewhere, to the point where it is now possible to talk of two churches: one, the hierarchy, led by Cardenal Obando y Bravo, and most of the bishops who are supported by Rome; and second, the people's church, many of them priests, men and women in orders, and lay people of all classes who identify with the revolution. Organizing through base communities in rural and urban communities, the people's church promotes involvement in the popular associations and campaigns, and carries out its own work of politicization. The ministers of culture, education, and foreign relations are priests, as is the ambassador to the Organization of American States. Other priests pursue theological studies on the compatibility of Christianity and Marxism, and their findings often reinforce aspects of popular education.

The FSLN recognizes that through its traditional authority and cultural influence, the church can often legitimize the revolution at a popular level more effectively than Sandinista cadres. This interest in the church is not cynical: the members of the National Directorate maintain a profound respect for the people's faith. Tomás Borge, an FSLN founder and minister of interior, asserts that there is "no alliance, but integration between Christianity and the revolution."[73] In October 1980, the FSLN published its "Official Statement on Religion," a document that breaks with the traditional Marxist stance on religion. In nine points the Sandinistas detailed their position on religion which can be summarized as follows:

1. The FSLN guarantees the "inalienable right" to freedom of religious faith.
2. Although "some authors" see religion as a "mechanism of alienation"—understandably given the conditions of their age—the FSLN's experience is that people can be Christians and revolutionaries. (This statement was a clear rejection of militant atheism, breaking a tradition going back to Marx himself.)
3. All who agree with FSLN objectives and principles may participate in it, whatever their religious beliefs.
4. Within the party limits of the FSLN there is no room for proselytizing, but elsewhere Christian militants may express publicly their convictions. (Points 3 and 4 were a clear divergence from Marxist practice—in Cuba, for example.)

5. The FSLN "has a deep respect for all the religious celebrations of our people and is making efforts to save their true meaning, attacking the vice and corruption imposed on them in the past." They should not be used for commercial or politicking purposes.
6. Religious discussions are proper to the church; no Sandinista speaking for the FSLN should participate in them.
7. Contrary to reactionary ideologues, the FSLN is not trying to divide the church. "If there is division it is independent of the will and action of the FSLN."
8. The priests and religious in the government are exercising their rights as citizens and have carried out an "extraordinary labor." Should they withdraw for personal reasons, that would be their right.
9. The origins, purposes, and spheres of the action of the revolution and the state are different from those of religion, which is a personal matter, proper to individuals, churches, and religious associations. Like every modern state, the revolutionary state is a lay state and cannot adopt any religion, since it is the representative of the whole people, believers and nonbelievers.[74]

Ten days after the FSLN document on religion was published, the Nicaraguan Bishops Conference issued a reply, which, despite admitting that the FSLN had provided a "basis for dialogue," strongly attacked the revolution.[75] Indeed, since late 1980, the church hierarchy has waged a steady campaign against the Sandinistas, accusing the FSLN of totalitarian tendencies and a manipulative attitude toward religion. The hierarchy has supported the removal of priests from ministerial positions, secured large sums of money from American business interests to finance an "evangelical crusade" of traditional religiosity, and joined the Democratic Coordinating Committee and the Superior Council of Higher Enterprise in attacks on the government in La Prensa. In early 1986 both Cardenal Obando y Bravo and Bishop Pablo Antonio Vega traveled to the United States to meet with contra leaders and support their request for additional military aid from the Reagan administration. And in July 1986 the Sandinistas expelled Bishop Vega for his defiance of the national emergency law. Thus the political conflicts that grip Nicaragua are reflected in the church.

The Nicaraguan people have refused to follow any models in forging their revolution. Indeed, the Sandinistas often say, "We don't want to create a second Cuba; we want to create the first Nicaragua." They insist that people judge the revolution by its real social achievements and not by the ideological labels that some obervers try to pin on it. Drawing from the positive experiences of twentieth century revolutions, the FSLN has also learned from its predecessors myriad mistakes. The Sandinistas' commitment to a mixed economy, political pluralism, religious tolerance, and indigenous rights represents a radical departure from the practice of other contemporary revolutionaries. Furthermore, the Sandinistas' support for independent and dynamic mass organizations could be the most important modern attempt to build a revolution on a democratic foundation. This attempt will be the subject of the remaining chapters.

4

DEVELOPING A NATIONAL PRESENCE

The FSLN rose to power through the mass participation of hundreds of thousands of Nicaraguans. But until the last stages of the anti-Somoza war, Nicaragua had one of Central America's least advanced popular movements. The movement possessed neither a strong organizational base nor a developed political consciousness. These weaknesses were due to the tremendous repression of the National Guard, the penetration of Somoza's virulent anticommunist propaganda, and the historically low level of industrialization and urbanization. "In the past," observes Silvia Reyes, a Sandinista militant, "many people remained unorganized for fear of repression or for lack of political clarity."[1]

At the time of Somoza's overthrow, the Nicaraguan masses lacked the political experience and the organizational capacity to consolidate their position in the revolution. The arduous struggle against the dictatorship had engendered broad anticapitalist sentiment among the popular sectors, but they were not prepared to launch a full-scale socialist project. Consequently, the Sandinistas devised a transitional strategy, one which allowed for the continuing participation of privileged social classes, but which promoted the well-being of the country's poor majority.

The FSLN adopted a transitional strategy to reconstruct the country's war-devastated economy.[2] To reactivate the economy, the FSLN and the Governing Junta of National Reconstruction called for the participation of all social sectors. The revolution needed administrators for their managerial expertise, professionals for their technical abilities, and capitalists for their financial resources. The Sandinistas developed a policy of national unity to ensure that each social group would play a role in reconstructing the war-torn land. But the Sandinistas also reiterated what they had emphasized before the victory: that they sought to build a social system that would end illiteracy, disease, malnutrition, and slum housing—a system that would bring genuine economic and political power to Nicaragua's workers and peasants.

Indeed, the popular classes—brought together in the mass organizations—were determined to assume a key role in the revolutionary process. During the first year of the revolution, the strength of the popular associations grew dramatically. By mid-1980 the Sandinista Workers Federation numbered 80,000 workers, the Rural Workers Association 106,000 rural laborers, the Nicaraguan Women's Association 25,000 women, and the Sandinista Defense Committees 220,000 neighborhood and village residents.[3] More important than their numerical growth, however, the mass organizations established a strong national presence within the new Nicaraguan political system. To consolidate their national presence, the popular associations strengthened their organizational structures, gained entry into the Council of State, and participated in the national literacy and malaria campaigns.

ORGANIZATIONAL CONSOLIDATION

The Sandinista Defense Committees

Immediately after Somoza's fall, the CDCs—renamed *Comites de Defensa Sandinista* (Sandinista Defense Committees or CDSs) in 1986—advanced throughout the country and tackled the emergency situation left by the war. Continuing and expanding the tasks they had carried out during the insurrection, the CDSs filled the vacuum left by the disintegration of the Somocista state and economy. The neighborhood committees distributed food to the needy, treated the ill and injured, found housing for the homeless, and began the process of reconstruction. In addition, the CDSs helped the militias organize neighborhood security to defend against the continuing threat from ex-National Guardsmen and common criminals. Finally, the CDSs served as channels for the new government's announcements and decrees to people throughout the country.[4]

Self-defined as "the primary and elemental connection between our people and the Revolution," the CDSs (then and now) remain open to all Nicaraguans older than fourteen.[5] They include men and women, workers, and peasants, urban dwellers and rural inhabitants. The CDSs are organized by block, rural district, or village. During the revolution's first year, fifteen to twenty urban CDSs formed a neighborhood committee, over which stood zonal and municipal committees. In the countryside, the organizational structure varied according to the size of the rural communities. The CDSs held weekly meetings in which they discussed economic and social problems, evaluated their activities, and planned future projects.[6]

In cities with a history of intense struggle during the insurrection, the CDSs developed easily and effectively. In Monimbó, for example, the experience of the insurrection had a lasting effect on community participation. As a Monimbó shoemaker and CDS activist testified:

> It's a funny thing: people tend to think that the Monimbosenos were always revolutionary. Well, it was just the opposite. We weren't born Sandinistas, we became Sandinistas. Political ignorance was tremendous. . . . It's hard to overcome that, to learn that we're capable of thinking for ourselves. But in the war we had two advantages: we had a sense of community, and we were good with our hands. So we turned our skills to making arms, improvising weapons like the contact bombs.
>
> All that has stood us in good stead. As we began to organize the CDCs, the process taught us our own power, what we could achieve by being united. We used my own house as a medical centre in the war, and my *compañera* still works on medical care with the CDS. She's giving courses on vitamin injections now. I ended up as *coordinador de manzana* [block coordinator]. The committees are even more vital to us now. Attendance hasn't fallen off.[7]

In their first year, many neighborhood committees confronted problems and limitations. Some of these problems stemmed from the original tasks assumed by the CDSs—tasks which became sources of conflict. CDS control of security and individual movement, for example, was controversial. At first the CDSs had wide security powers to detect escaped National Guardsmen and infiltrated Somocistas; they frequently processed the exit visas that citizens required to travel from one area to another. But some committees abused their powers in carrying out this duty, and detained residents without just cause. In addition, some CDS officials used their positions to settle personal and domestic disputes by denouncing their neighbors as Somocistas.[8] At the end of 1979, the neighborhood committees' national office conducted an inquiry into the abuses of local CDS officials and issued the following evaluation: "A whole series of abuses were evident which were harmful to the people, for example the refusal to give letters of reference because of petty personal enmities. At the same time, many CDS officials and activists fell into arrogant ways, believing that their responsibilities turned them into the lord and master of the barrio and not the servants of the community."[9]

In addition to abuses of power and personal conflicts, many CDSs lacked effective communication between the rank and file and the top leadership. Other neighborhood committees suffered from insufficient grassroots participation in the assignment of tasks or from the continuing presence of "last-minute Sandinistas"—opportunists.[10]

In many neighborhoods, problems emerged only after an initial period of enthusiastic participation. In the Masaya barrio of San Juan, for example, people from all social sectors—artisans, professionals, and civil servants—at first participated actively in CDS activities. Juan Jose, the barrio's CDS coordinator, describes the initial outburst of activity in his neighborhood:

> People here are very spontaneous and show a lot of curiosity. The CDS was a novelty. I'm not sure exactly what people were looking for. Some were simply opportunists who may have felt a certain guilt about their dealings with the dictatorship. Others perhaps believed that through the CDS certain problems could be solved. It's a question of awareness. Others wanted to find out what people were saying about them, for now and then they would be accused of being Somocistas.[11]

Eight months later, however, many personality conflicts broke out, disrupting the work of the CDS. In addition, the neighborhood's CDS coordinators had to battle against political apathy and individualistic attitudes. Juan José faced such a situation:

> Although there are a large number of tasks, there isn't always enough participation to guarantee that they get done. There are even people who used to come to meetings but now refuse to participate. Here too, we suffer from problems that could be solved with greater collective participation. For example, the septic tanks. The ones we have are too small for large families. People have talked about the problem a lot, but when we asked for help in solving it nobody responded. Only one person was willing to work.[12]

Nevertheless, most neighborhood committees achieved the bulk of their original goals, especially those concerning health care, food supplies, and education. By mid-February, the CDSs had organized polio vaccination campaigns that reached 80 percent of the country's children under five. Fourteen neighborhood committees clustered around Managua's northern highway jointly constructed a maternity hospital in the La Primavera barrio. To improve food distribution, the national CDS office promoted the establishment of 200 basic food supply centers in Managua and 450 others throughout the rest of the country.[13] The CDSs also adopted educational tasks. Miguel de Castilla, the vice minister of education, noted in an interview: "This is the hour of non-formal education in Nicaragua. The educational system is like a tidal wave, which shows itself in the mass media, in CDS meetings, in every facet of the class struggle. The school as an institution has lost forever all the mythical prestige it enjoyed in the past."[14] And Glenda Monterrey, a member of the FSLN's National Commission on Organization, asserted: "The committees will be the basic vehicle for the people's political education."[15]

Other early achievements of the neighborhood committees included the creation of approximately 15,000 CDSs throughout the country; the reconstruction of many homes, streets, and sewage systems; the enforcement of price control; the formation of production collectives; and neighborhood cleanup and sanitation campaigns.[16] The CDS' apt slogan during this first year was "Organización, Organización, y Más Organización" ("Organization, Organization, and More Organization").

The Evolution of AMNLAE

Within two weeks of the Sandinista victory on July 19, 1979, the Nicaraguan Women's Association began contacting the members who had dispersed to participate in the final insurrection. Having achieved its original goal of helping to topple the dictatorship, AMPRONAC began to reconstitute itself as a mass organization which would work to strengthen the revolution and to confront the problems of Nicaraguan women. To reflect the organization's new objectives, its leaders changed the name to Asociacion de Mujeres Nicaragüenses "Luisa Amanda Espinosa" (Luisa Amanda Espinosa Association of Nicaraguan Women— AMNLAE). Luisa, a seamstress, was the first woman killed fighting with the FSLN in 1970 and had become a symbol for the struggle facing contemporary Nicaraguan women.[17]

During its first year, an original group of twenty women in Managua and Matagalpa organized chapters of AMNLAE consisting of thirty to one hundred members in ten departments, and established embryonic organizing committees in five others. In Matagalpa, for example, AMNLAE established six local chapters in the city and one in the countryside. In April 1980, AMNLAE had 17,000 members. By October of its second year, 25,000 women were active in 420 rural and 382 urban chapters.[18]

In 1979 and 1980, the Association participated in all the major national campaigns, recruiting its members for the coffee and cotton harvests, the literacy campaign, and the vaccination programs.[19] To combat the sexist image of women, AMNLAE prepared weekly radio and television programs, published a newspaper, La Voz de la Mujer (The Women's Voice), and screened textbooks and other teaching aids. As part of its organizing tasks, the Association gathered detailed information on the working conditions of urban and rural women. With one seat on the Council of State, and with the aid of a team of experienced lawyers, AMNLAE planned to employ this information in its efforts to replace Somoza's sexist laws.[20]

AMNLAE organized a music festival in November 1979 to raise money for the literacy campaign. Women in Matagalpa obtained a grant from the Dutch government and established the city's first child care center. Working with the Ministry of Health, a number of AMNLAE members received training in public health care. These women eventually served in poor neighborhoods and rural areas where health facilities had always been primitive. Mobile units of women trained in preventive medicine traveled with Ministry of Health personnel in remote rural districts to prepare a census, conduct seminars on hygiene, and vaccinate the population.[21]

The Association accomplished much, but also had its share of problems. According to Gloria Carrión, general coordinator during AMNLAE's first year, the women's organization lacked a detailed plan of action and failed to properly coordinate its relations with state ministries. This led to duplication of services and a waste of scarce resources. AMNLAE also found itself competing for members with other mass organizations. With the farm workers' and industrial workers' unions available to peasant women and working women, the Association had difficulty recruiting these women. Furthermore, those women who did join were heavily committed to other organizations—the FSLN, the government, and the CDSs—and had few opportunities to contribute to AMNLAE projects.[22] Latin American history professor Susan E. Ramirez-Horton cites further difficulties that AMNLAE faced:

A lack of funds and communication problems with some of their less-educated, rural sisters . . . limited activities. Imagine how difficult it was to organize peasant women when some asked what the word "organization" meant! Other affiliated women in departmental capitals and cities wanted to do more, but hesitated to act because they felt disoriented. They clamored for more training, which, for lack of funds, was still unavailable. Further complicating AMNLAE's task were lingering male suspicions of a "women's" organization and a still too vague notion of "liberation" and its consequences.[23]

According to Margaret Randall, "none of the things they were able to achieve seemed to be very remarkable or seemed to many of us and to the leadership of AMNLAE to seek the answers that we really needed to women's problems here."[24] Activists felt AMNLAE had duplicated much of the work of other mass organizations, and that the mass organizational structure was inappropriate to the particular nature of women's oppression, which cuts across all social sectors and class lines:[25]

> Most women identified more closely with, say, their CDS than their local AMNLAE group. Moreover, AMNLAE had managed to mobilise thousands of women around specific tasks but, unlike the CDSs and the unions, it did not arrange for its constituents to tackle their own problems on an ongoing basis. Nor had it used its mobilisation of women to encourage them to group together to confront their everyday problems, in particular the topics of male violence, sexuality and birth control which most women are shy about talking about publicly.[26]

Therefore, AMNLAE began a pervasive internal debate. This discussion led to the decision to redefine the Association's structure. During a series of meetings that culminated in a December 1981 Constitutional Assembly, AMNLAE women presented and defended a new approach for the organization. Most AMNLAE members wanted their association to become a political movement with characteristics that differed from the other mass organizations.[27] "Work committees" of politically committed AMNLAE members would agitate within other popular organizations for women's rights. Thus AMNLAE would make its presence felt wherever women toiled: factories, neighborhoods, and state farms.[28] An AMNLAE spokeswoman explained the organization's new course:

> The new AMNLAE line is that we should concentrate on promoting the involvement of women and their demands within the mass organisations. We are not interested particularly that there should be a separate group [of women], but that women should be involved at all levels, politically and socially, that women take on more responsibilites within their trade unions and that all women take prominent positions within our revolution.[29]

In addition, AMNLAE leaders began to define their organization as a "movement" that would no longer compete for members with the other mass organizations.

To some observers, AMNLAE's new line represented a positive development, a change that strengthened the Association:

> In this new capacity the women can organize and function within all areas of national life: among workers, peasants, students, professional women, housewives, Christian communities and others. They can become an agent for women's rights as well as for their coordinated support of the revolutionary process as a whole. It is this dual consciousness—revolutionary and feminist—that characterizes the women's movement here, and assures it a strong future.[30]

Other observers, however, viewed AMNLAE's shift in emphasis as a retreat for the organization. Deighton et al., issued this critical assessment of AMNLAE's new stance:

> The new structure will very likely undermine the possibilities for women to take action for themselves. It follows the policy of "integrationism" to its logical conclusion: integrate the association as well as individual women into the main labour and governmental institutions. AMNLAE has effectively dissolved its independent national structure. While its new strategy may enable the association to reach out to women in factories and farms, it may also turn AMNLAE into little more than a pressure group. Given the historical indifference of the unions to women's issues, it is likely that the work committees will see their demands submerged in general union or neighborhood issues.[31]

At the core of these different interpretations of AMNLAE's new structure is the question whether or not AMNLAE is an independent women's organization. All too often in revolutionary societies male-dominated political parties have subordinated women's concerns to "more important national priorities"—priorities set by these same parties.[32] As the threat of destabilization increases in Nicaragua, the pressure grows for the government to put defense and production ahead of all other concerns, including those particular to women. Already feeling the weight of this pressure in 1981, FSLN political secretary Marta Cranshaw avowed:

> Women in Nicaragua are not totally emancipated; they have only achieved what people generally have gained . . . they must still break a social, psychological and economic dependence. But we have serious problems—like the threat of an invasion. So if we had to choose between discussing women or external aggression, we would discuss the problem of aggression.[33]

The Rural Workers Association—ATC

As of July 1980, the ATC had organized almost one-third of Nicaragua's economically active rural population: 110,383 workers out of 350,000. At the time of the 1979 victory over Somoza, the ATC had affiliated regional committees in only four of the country's fourteen departments: Carazo, Masaya, Chinandega, and Managua. In mid-1980, it could claim members in all fourteen, having made its presence felt even in the economically backward areas of Río San Juan and Zelaya.[34]

Because four basic forms of production existed in the countryside, the ATC created different types of union locals to represent the state-farm workers, the private-farm workers, the small independent peasants, and the peasant cooperative members. The Association then organized these local unions and base committees into municipal committees with their own elected executive councils. Delegates from these councils participated in departmental assemblies, which in turn elected the departmental executive councils. The national council, which set the general policies for the Association and selected its national executive committee, was the highest body in the ATC.[35]

The composition of the ATC demonstrated an imbalance in its strength on state and private farms: 48,712 of its members were organized in 397 credit and service cooperatives, 30,844 in 472 state farms, and 21,552 in 621 private farms.[36] In 1980, exploitation of workers often continued as before on privately-owned farms, and the ATC at the time lacked sufficient union strength to fight for basic worker rights, including the implementation of minimum wage levels.[37]

Nevertheless, the Association's phenomenal early growth earned it the respect of the Nicaraguan Institute of Agrarian Reform (INRA), the state body charged with running the 2,000 farms (all ex-Somocista) expropriated immediately following the fall of Somoza. The ATC's heavy presence in the countryside allowed INRA to determine the needs of peasants and farm workers and aided the implementation of the agrarian reform. Jaime Wheelock, head of the Nicaraguan Insitute of Agrarian Reform, stressed the ATC's importance in a speech delivered to the ATC Constituent Assembly in December 1979:

> It is vital to realize that agrarian reforms can never be made from above, that agrarian reform is a combination of great effort from the grassroots and the organizational efforts of their representatives at the superstructural level. I stress the importance of organization. The ATC has a permanent place in INRA. You are the real power there, and what you say in INRA is as good as law.[38]

INRA organized the state farms in a three-tiered management system.[39] Geographically contingent farms were grouped into 1,200 production units or *Unidades de Producción* (UPESs). The Agrarian Reform Institute grouped these units into 170 complexes, called *Complejos Agrícolas*, organized by product. The Institute then gathered the regional complexes into twenty-seven state agricultural enterprises, known as *Empresas Agrícolas*. INRA established this three-tiered structure to take advantage of both centralized and decentralized forms of management.

The large state farms that included an industrial processing plant were under the responsibility of Agro-Inra, a special subdivision of INRA. Agro-Inra organized these farms by product. In 1980 Agro-Inra managed ten enterprises that included sugar, rice, tobacco, cotton, coffee, meat slaughtering and packing, hog production, food processing, and animal feed enterprises.

The ATC rapidly organized the vast majority of workers on the state farms. From the outset, the union helped INRA administer this sector. Workers elected representatives to production consultation councils that were responsible for planning and evaluating the production process. INRA consulted with the union federation before appointing directors of complexes and production units.

In a major step toward worker participation in management, the ATC had decision-making powers concerning the surplus produced on state farms. Writing in 1980, Deere and Marchetti explain the new system of distributing this portion of Nicaragua's agricultural surplus.

Previously, profits were appropriated by a small minority and often just one man. Now, that surplus is to be utilized to benefit both the workers and the surrounding rural population. In this initial period, part of the surplus is, in effect, being returned directly to the workers through higher wages due to compliance with minimum wage regulations that went unheeded under the dictatorship. It is planned that a larger share of the surplus will go into social services such as health, sanitation, housing, and education, which were ignored under the Somoza regime. The increased provision of social services is to form a significant aspect of the higher standard of living of rural workers. It is also hoped that, by planning the delivery of services at the regional level, inequalities in access to resources in the countryside can be ameliorated, and the provision of social services will serve to raise the standard of living of the rural population as a whole. Finally, a portion of the surplus will form the investment fund, in the short run, directed toward the reconstruction of the agrarian infrastructure and in the medium run, channneled to intensify production and generate more employment with the people's sector.[40]

On most state farms, the Rural Workers Association held two or three political meetings a week, teaching members how to formulate their demands in light of the new political and economic realities in the country. On the one hand, the ATC had the difficult task of showing that the new state was not a traditional instrument of exploitation; but on the other hand, the Association had to maintain its independence from the state and forcibly assert the demands of its constituency. The ATC leadership therefore emphasized labor discipline and worker productivity to comply with the state's economic reactivation plans, but at the same time worked hard to remove uncooperative bureaucrats in various state agencies, such as the Nicaraguan Basic Foods Company, the National Development Bank, and the National Coffee Enterprise.[41]

Within the state sector, the ATC unions pushed for a variety of social services including health care, country stores, schools, and better housing. In the large, agro-exporting complexes, such demands led to rapid social gains.[42] At the German Pomares sugar refinery, for example, the Association gained a health clinic staffed by fourteen social workers, a commissary selling seventy-five basic products at ENABAS-controlled prices, and a production collective making clothes at no cost to the sugar workers and at little cost to their families. The ATC also created union-managed stores on the state complexes to supply workers with basic goods at low prices; sixty were in operation by mid-1980. At this early date, then, the ATC had already demonstrated what strong organization could achieve.[43]

On national issues, the ATC leadership tended to advance demands only when the rank and file applied pressure. When the Workers' Front, an ultraleftist labor federation, attempted to achieve political gains by organizing sugar workers around demands for 100 percent wage hikes, the ATC did not try to compete with them. Although farm workers averaged only 636 cordobas a month, the ATC decided to wait until higher wage demands emerged from the local affiliates. Only when this occurred in May 1980—three months after the Workers' Front conflict—did ATC executives press the Junta for wage increases.[44]

Of all the mass organizations, the ATC had the most effective internal relations during the first year of the revolutionary process. This was largely due to the mutual trust between the organization's leadership and its rank and file. The ATC has a firmly-rooted historical relationship with the labor force in the major agro-exporting plants, and faces little competition from other unions in the rural sector.[45] Consequently, the Association was free to devote its efforts to achieving important worker gains during the revolution's early period.

The Sandinistas Workers Federation—CST

Immediately following Somoza's overthrow, the insurrectional Workers' Fighting Committees (CLTs) formed the nucleus of the new Sandinista labor federation. They adapted their role to the requirements of the new revolutionary state, but remained independent of it. On July 27, 1979, newly formed committees and the old CLTs in factories throughout the country adopted the name *Comites de Defensa de Trabajadores Sandinistas* (Sandinista Workers' Defense Committees). At the national level, these committees became the *Central Sandinista de Trabajadores* (Sandinista Workers Federation—CST).[46]

During its first year, the CST set for itself four strategic objectives: the fulfillment of working class demands that transcend the economistic basis of traditional Nicaraguan trade unions; support for the revolutionary transformation of the state; increased levels of worker participation and control of production, especially in publicly owned enterprises; and, above all, the fight for the class independence and unity of the urban proletariat.[47]

Under Somoza, a main obstacle to working-class coordination was the prohibition of national craft or industry-wide unions. The organization of plant-based unions had continued during the revolution's first year; nearly all of the new CST-affiliated unions were plant-based. Clearly, few workers realized the advantages of industry-wide unity. The situation in the mines of the northern Atlantic Coast was typical:

> In the last months of 1979, separate unions sprang up spontaneously in the major mining settlements of Bonanza, Siuna and Rosita. When CST officials and local miners' committees made an exhaustive study of working conditions and wage rates in the three mines, the effects of these divisions became clear. Not only did salary levels vary from one mine to another, but there were also discrepancies within the same mine, unequal pay for equal work, often on a racial basis. Wage parity in the mining sector is now a reality for the first time, and the first result of coordinated action came when the unions at the three mines joined forces to negotiate large cuts in ENABAS [National Basic Foods Company] prices for beans, rice and sugar.[48]

In addition to pressing for unity within individual industries, CST unions began to unite on a regional basis. On March 7, 1980, immediately following serious disputes with the Communist-led CAUS, the Social Christian CTN, and the Workers' Front, twelve factories in Managua's industrial center formed a "regional trade union bloc."[49] The unions involved—all CST affiliates—asserted that the bloc arose "as a necessity in the face of the destabilizing campaign being waged by the CIA and certain pseudo-leaders of the workers' movement."[50] The CST unions aimed this barb at the CAUS leadership. The twelve factories included El Caracol, the important food-processing plant, and the Standard Steel factory.[51]

The CST led other unions in signing collective bargaining agreements, which workers were ratifying at the rate of more than one a day during January and February 1980.[52] In negotiations with management, the CST-affiliated unions demanded increased worker participation in factory management and its control over production, the need for job security, and better health and safety provisions.[53] The CST also demanded that the government penalize those owners who decapitalized their factories or who failed to participate in the reactivation of the distribution system.[54]

In July, 1980 the CST outlined its *Plan de Lucha*—the federation's platform for future action. The plan included the enforcement of minimum wage levels and recently decreed wage increases; compliance with the terms of the collective agreements signed by management, workers, and government; full respect by management for newly won trade-union rights; a revision of the existing Labor Code (enacted under Somoza); the organization of voluntary trade union work brigades; and the establishment of factory outlets to distribute food at regulated prices.[55]

In addition, the CST took the first step toward urban working-class unity. But from the outset, the CST came into conflict with the other urban labor federations. Henri Weber, a French political observer, relates the details of the CST's confrontation with SCAAS, the construction workers' union linked to the Socialist Party.

> Under the very popular leadership of Alejandro Solorzano, a communist PSN leader and general secretary of the CGTI, this organization had waged a number of major struggles under the dictatorship. It therefore had a legitimate claim to constitute the framework for unity in the building and public-works sector. But there was no avoiding the fact that it was led by PSN and CGTI members. Unlike the PCN (the other, equally pro-Soviet Communist Party), the PSN applied a tactic of keeping as close as possible to FSLN policy, instead of seeking to outflank it. And yet, however accommodating they might be, these SCAAS leaders still belonged to a political party with which the FSLN was

in conflict. The Sandinist Front thus tried to build a rival union based on workers employed by the Managua Municipal Junta. The Ministry of Labour naturally hastened to recognize the new CST union as the only authorized partner in talks. When Solorzano refused to bow to its ruling, he was jailed for a few days in October 1979.

In January 1980, several thousand building workers took up the struggle to increase their wages and force recognition of the SCAAS. On 9 January they demonstrated in front of the Ministry of Labour, whereupon Minister of the Interior Tomás Borge and war heroine Comandante Dora Tellez began to suggest that talks be held. The workers' pay was increased towards the end of the month, and by giving up its legal entitlement, the CST union opened the way for recognition of the SCAAS as the single building-workers' union. This trial of strength actually deepened the workers' suspicions, and could have been avoided easily enough.[56]

Weber's criticism is justified insofar as both the CST and the FSLN miscalculated the mood of the SCAAS workers and mistakenly employed heavy-handed tactics at the beginning of the conflict. But he fails to give an accurate picture of what occurred at the end of this episode: part of the strike settlement included a call for new union elections February 3. On that date 90 percent of the 3,000 building workers who voted approved a joint list of CGT-I and CST candidates. This successful resolution of the dispute led to closer relations between the CST and PSN-backed unions, and both the FSLN and PSN hailed the election as a major triumph.[57]

At the same time, the CST continued to promote the unification of the workers' movement. After a number of abortive attempts, the CST brought together 200 delegates representing virtually all of Nicaragua's trade unions and union federations in a November 1980 conference. The conference, which established the ongoing *Coordinadora Sindical de Nicaragua* (Nicaraguan Trade Union Coordinating Committee, CSN), represented the first organized discussion among the various labor federations since the fall of the dictatorship.[58] The delegates represented the CST, the ATC, the CGT-I, the CAUS, the Workers' Front, the health workers union, the CUS, the teachers' union, and the Union of Nicaraguan Journalists. Union delegates discussed the social problems facing the revolution and workers' attitudes toward those problems. The conference concluded by adopting a joint program of action concerning four points of discussion proposed by the CST. The four points were: 1. increasing production and productivity; 2. improving working conditions and social services, and increasing wage levels; 3. maintaining strict discipline in the workplace; and 4. resolving labor conflicts without halting production.[59]

The formation of the Nicaraguan Trade Union Coordinating Committee was an essential step toward the unification of the workers movement, and proved the influence that the CST had gained among the country's urban workers. In 1979 and 1980—the peak period of the unionization of urban and industrial workers—seventy-five percent of the new unions were affiliated with the CST.[60] Thus, by the end of 1980, pro-Sandinista workers dominated the Nicaraguan labor movement.

MASS ORGANIZATIONS GAIN ENTRY TO THE COUNCIL OF STATE

The rapid growth and expansion of the mass organizations in the weeks and months after the dictatorship's collapse greatly influenced the FSLN's decision to postpone and restructure the Council of State. The Sandinistas announced the original composition of the Council, which was to share legislative powers with the Junta of National Reconstruction, in their June 1979 government program.[61] The Council that was originally proposed included representatives from twenty-three organizations. Yet no plan existed to allocate the thirty-three seats designated for the Council, and none of the newly formed mass organizations were represented. In its original form, the Council would have given Nicaragua's business sector seventeen seats, a number out of proportion to their political weight in the post-Somoza period. When the Sandinistas were negotiating the future structure of the Council in June 1979, they had anticipated the survival of some elements of the Somoza apparatus, and felt compelled to approve such a power-sharing solution. But by July 19, the seizure of Managua by FSLN guerrillas and militia radically altered the balance of forces in favor of those social sectors represented by the grassroots organizations. Committed to a legislative body that would fairly represent the new alignment of political forces in the country, the Sandinistas were determined to include the mass organizations in the Council of State.

On October 22, 1979, the FSLN officially announced its decision to postpone and restructure the Council of State. The FSLN declared that the popular associations would receive sixteen seats in a forty-seven-member legislative body, and that the Council of State would be installed on May 4, 1980, the "Day of National Dignity,"—so named to commemorate Sandino's refusal to sign the Pact of Espino Negro.[62] The opposition was enraged:

COSEP [the Higher Council of Private Enterprise] immediately launched a furious attack on the government, which the Right accused of violating the alleged Pact of Puntarenas which they suggested the government Junta had signed in the presence of Costa Rican and Venezuelan officials, giving guarantees of rapidly institutionalized structures of bourgeois democracy. The government and Frente denied that any such pact existed, but the COSEP tactic was clear and consistent—to accuse the FSLN and Junta of "illegalities" which might discredit it in the eyes of uncommitted middle sectors and the deeply ambivalent U.S. Government.[63]

In contrast, the mass organizations, offered a significant position within the new Council, applauded the Sandinistas' decision. After vigorously campaigning for full representation, the popular associations viewed the FSLN decision as a vindication of their recent struggles in support of the revolution. Edgardo García, secretary general of the ATC, expressed the attitude of his membership at a November 3 news conference: "The ATC, vanguard of the farm workers, has to make it known that . . . the Council of State must be comprised of those organizations that represent the interests of the people and that are dedicated to carrying forth the tasks of the Revolution at any cost."[64] Another typical reaction was that of the CST executive committee in Chinandega on November 4:

> The reactionary sectors, without possessing any legitimate popular support, want the immediate installation of the Council of State without any alterations in its composition, that is to say as it was originally conceived before the revolutionary overthrow of the dictatorship. They want to hide the irrefutable and undeniable fact that political and social conditions have changed profoundly since the revolutionary triumph, that the majority of those organizations that existed before the overthrow of the tyranny have disappeared today. The immense majority of Nicaraguans have formed new mass organizations such as the ATC, CDS, and AMNLAE, that currently gather the popular masses of the country in their ranks.
> A Council of State cannot be conceived today without the direct and representative participation—according to its membership—of the working people and the people in general who have organized since the revolutionary triumph.
> We declare our decisive and militant support to the just and correct decision of our Government of National Reconstruction to install the Council of State on May 4, the day of National Dignity.[65]

Having won the right to participate in the nation's co-legislative body, the mass organizations began the process of selecting their representatives to the Council. The CST and the ATC were allotted three delegates each, AMNLAE one, and the CDSs—the largest organization in the country—nine.

The Sandinista Workers Federation held its delegate elections to the legislative body only two days before the May 4 installation. Eighty-eight delegates chosen by the rank and file of CST-affiliated unions attended an electoral assembly held in Managua. These eighty-eight workers represented regions of the country with the highest concentration of urban workers. Before the final election, twelve candidates ran for the Council seats: six from Managua and a total of six from the departments of Estelí, Granada, and Chinandega. Each of the eighty-eight delegates then voted for the six candidates of their choice—three representatives and three alternates.[66]

When the votes were tallied, Denis Melendez of the CST national executive committee declared that the elected delegates would represent the interests of all Nicaraguan workers, not just the interests of workers in the delegates' unions or regions. Melendez asserted that the workers' representatives would have to take the lead in promoting the tasks of the revolution. "If not," he cautioned, "it will be the workers themselves who will replace them with new comrades in the Council of State." Melendez went on to say that "these comrades will work to distribute the social wealth in a reasonable and just manner, seeking solutions to the problems of the our people."[67]

The Rural Workers Association selected its Council representatives on April 28. At a press conference the day before, Francisco Lopez, the ATC's national secretary of organization, declared that for the first time in history Nicaragua's working people had the opportunity to elect representatives who would raise their principal demands in a national legislative body. Lopez also noted that the Council reflected the revolution's commitment to political pluralism because it included sectors sharply criticial of the FSLN. The secretary emphasized that the ATC had gained the right to participate in the Council of State through bloody sacrifice.[68]

The ATC chose its three representatives at an assembly of 370 delegates representing the country's fourteen departments. Local unions elected these individuals because, in Barricada's words, they were "among the most indefatigable defenders of the interests of farmworkers and peasants."[69] The ATC selected the following slogan for its electoral assembly: "FOR THE CONSOLIDATION OF DEMOCRACY AND THE PEOPLE'S FREEDOM, THE RURAL WORKERS WILL MARCH TO THE COUNCIL OF STATE."[70]

AMNLAE selected its two delegates—one representative and one alternate—at a national assembly held on May 2. Monica Baltodano, head of the FSLN's Secretariat for Mass Organizations, delivered the keynote address at the assembly. Baltodano asserted that AMNLAE's delegates would faithfully represent the Association in the Council of State because AMNLAE leaders knew how to make demands that correspond to rank-and-file aspirations. Baltodano also emphasized that the women's association represented all those interests that favor workers and peasants, "the protagonists and guardians of the Revolution."[71] From their new position in the Council of State, "women would continue struggling for the freedom of all, because only with the freedom of all would women achieve their own liberation."[72] Gladys Gomez, a member of AMNLAE's national executive, closed the Assembly with these words: "Women, whose lives have always been framed by domestic work, who have had an extremely disheartening history, now, through the struggle, are in the vanguard. What we are doing here today is a an historical event."[73]

The election of nine CDS representatives to the Council of State was the culmination of a democratic restructuring of the Sandinista Defense committees at a national level. First, CDS members in small barrios, those with less than fifteen CDSs, elected one representative from each CDS to form a Comite de Barrio Sandinista (Sandinista Barrio Committee—CBS). In larger neighborhoods, members elected secretaries to CDS executive councils made up of one elected secretary for each of the CDSs' areas of responsibility.[74] Each barrio elected two delegates to the next level, the Zonal Council. For the Council of State elections, zonal delegates selected their representatives to regional assemblies, which in turn received nominations for the nine seats on the Council. On May 2, the national Executive Committee of the CDSs announced the names of the nine elected delegates. Of the nine, two were accountants, two students, two peasants, one was an office worker, one a tailor, and one a factory worker.[75] The FSLN lauded the mass organizations' democratic selection of delegates. In an April 11 editorial, Barricada summarized the Sandinistas' position.

Until now, the mass organizations have been been a factual expression of the new foundations of Nicaraguan democracy and popular participation. However, both with respect to their internal organization and the expression of their interests, there is a long way to go. But it is most important to note the experiences they have accumulated up to now: the full exercise of democratic freedoms with which the workers are daily strengthening themselves, and the class character of the organizations that guarantee the masses a steadfast representation of their interests in each of the struggles and affairs carried forth by their representatives.

In a few weeks, that which has been a de facto democratic participation will acquire an institutional channel through the installation of the Council of State. Here, the representatives of the workers, the peasants, women, youth, teachers, and other authentically popular groups, will be able to express their interests through proposed legislation. Therefore, it is of utmost importance to accelerate . . . a preparatory campaign to prepare all the mass organization activists for their participation in the Council of State.[76]

Pro-Sandinista representatives viewed the Council of State as a body in which the majority of the population could express its interests.[77] The Sandinista Workers Federation viewed the Council of State as the embodiment of the class struggle in Nicaragua. "For the CST, the aim was to elect as delegates the most responsible comrades, those who had a critical vision and firmly rooted class consciousness. Because the Council of State would give us the chance to confront the exploiting classes face to face: the bourgeoisie, the gentlemen of COSEP [the Higher Council of Private Enterprise]."[78] Comandante Hugo Torres, the Sandinista Popular Army's representative, insisted that Council of State delegates were responsible to the people: "If we make a mistake and pass a law which is against the interests of the people, then the people must protest. And if we fail them . . . they must go as far as exercising their right to dismiss us as their representatives."[79]

PARTICIPATION IN THE NATIONAL LITERACY AND MALARIA CAMPAIGNS

In August 1979, less than a month after Somoza's fall, the new government of Nicaragua embarked on an ambitious national project to plan, organize, and complete a literacy campaign involving more than one-half million people—all within twelve months.[80] In the face of the country's devastated post-war situation, such a campaign seemed foolish to many observers. Yet the government had a number of pragmatic reasons for immediately implementing a national literacy campaign. The Sandinista regime sought to dramatically improve the situation of Nicaragua's poor majority and bring it into the reconstruction process. With the national treasury empty, a nationwide literacy program would have to depend on volunteer labor from the citizenry as well as financial support from the international community. In addition to practical considerations, a literacy campaign met other more essential requirements. Valerie Miller, an American who assisted the Ministry of Education in the literacy campaign, outlines what was uppermost in the minds of Sandinista leaders.

> If the human energies of the country could be mobilized for national reconstruction and a means found to promote popular participation, the foundations for a system of equitable development could be established. Motivated by this challenge, the new leadership oriented its policies and programs toward the poorest sectors of the population. They understood that such a developmental strategy, in large part, depended upon the participation of an educated populace—people able to analyze, plan, think and create; people motivated by a sense of social responsibility rather than personal gain. A literacy campaign, implemented through a volunteer teacher corps, was seen as a fundamental first step in achieving these aims. Such a program would provide an opportunity for people to develop the skills and attitudes necessary to meet the development challenge.[81]

The 1980 literacy crusade was inspired by the liberation struggle begun by Sandino in the 1920s. Despite the obstacles involved in creating an educational program under the conditions of war, General Sandino was committed to teaching his men the basics of literacy. He always attempted to provide them with learning opportunities, as he explained in the following account: "When General Pedro Altamirano first joined us he did not know how to read or write but . . . during the fighting and only because I insisted on it, Altamirano learned. He stumbled and mumbled as he went along and yet despite his age, he has made great strides since then. Now, amazing as it may seem, he actually knows how to type—even if it is only with one finger."[82] The rigors of war and the shortage of people available to teach, however, prevented Sandino from launching a widespread literacy effort.

The founders of the FSLN adopted Sandino's aspirations. In the 1960s, Carlos Fonseca told Sandinista militants not only to teach people military skills, but also how to read and write. The Frente conducted clandestine literacy classes throughout those years. In early July 1979, the FSLN selected a team of Nicaraguan educators to plan the national literacy program. On the day of victory, July 19, the educators completed a draft proposal calling for the immediate establishment of a nationwide literacy campaign. Fifteen days after the victory, the Junta of National Reconstruction chose Father Fernando Cardenal to direct the program, and in April 1980 Nicaragua's Literacy Crusade began.

The planners of the literacy campaign designed a national training program to prepare the literacy volunteers in the use of the campaign's methodology and for the new type of educational role they would be expected to play. The literacy campaign "orientation notebook" told volunteers, "You will be a catalyst of the teaching-learning process. Your literacy students will be people who think, create and express their ideas. Together, you will form a team of mutual learning and human development. . . . The literacy process is an act of creation in which people offer each other thoughts, words, and deeds. It is a cultural action of transformation and growth."[83] To prepare the literacy teachers, the training program emphasized small-group study, collective problem-solving, peer teaching, and educational methodologies that fostered participation and creativity. The training workshops used a variety of teaching techniques: role playing, debate, simulation, group discussion, and different forms of artistic expression.

To train the tens of thousands of *brigadistas* (literacy volunteers) the campaign planners developed a decentralized four-tiered program. The program relied on a multiplier effect. Beginning with a core group of eight, four months later it had more than 80,000 teachers. In December and January, Ministry of Education personnel trained the core group of eighty teachers and university students. In February, that group taught 600. In early March, the 600 prepared approximately 12,000, of which most were teachers, and in mid-March, the 12,000 trained tens of thousands more who were mostly university and high school students. In addition, teaching supervisors conducted Saturday workshops for the volunteers. A daily radio program on all national radio stations also provided instruction to literacy volunteers.

A massive organizational system was required to support and administer the work of thousands of teachers. Following the insurrectional strategic model, campaign planners established a structure based on widespread popular participation, coordinated and directed by a central collective leadership. The campaign consisted of a national system of state agencies, mass organizations, professional associations, and religious organizations. One central executive body, the National Coordinating Board, managed the entire effort. To evaluate the campaign, the Board organized literacy congresses that originated first at the community level and extended upward to the zone, department, and region, culminating in two nationwide conferences. An estimated 100,000 people participated in the literacy process.

In rural areas, the logistics of transporting 60,000 teachers around a mountainous country with poor transportation and communicatio were complex. The task fell largely to the mass organizations. Because 60 percent of the *brigadistas* were female, AMNLAE played a crucial role, providing support to the teachers in the field through the *Comités de Madres* (Mothers' Committees). The Sandinista Youth organized the rural teacher corps: the Popular Literacy Army. ANDEN, the teachers' association, organized and coordinated the 10,000 teachers who participated as educational supervisors. Both the CST and the ATC joined the educational army with their "literacy militias." The ATC also furnished transport in isolated communities that were linked to neighboring communities only by river or horse trail. In the northern departments of Madriz, Nueva Segovia, and Jinotega, where there were problems with food distribution, Rural Workers Association members established small stores.[84]

In the cities, there were two groups of teachers: the CST's workers' literacy militias and the "urban literacy warriors" of AMNLAE and the CDSs. These 25,000 teachers were housewives, factory workers, government employees, professionals, and students. The urban campaign also included educational programs for children: the Quincho Barrillete project held literacy, cultural, and sports programs for child street vendors, and the "Rear Guard" project conducted a summer daycamp for school children. The ubiquitous CDSs dealt with parents' concerns by holding public assemblies to discuss all aspects of the campaign.

Among its many other accomplishments, the Crusade demonstrated the enormous capacities of the mass organizations. Their size, organizational cohesiveness, and resourcefulness all contributed to the literacy campaign's central achievement: some 400,000 Nicaraguans learned elementary reading and writing skills, and studied their history and revolution in the process. Basic illiteracy was lowered from 50 to 13 percent, and more than 50,000 urban youths and their families who served as literary volunteers learned about rural poverty and peasant culture. Finally, in the course of the campaign, volunteers also participated in a nationwide malaria control program, myriad local community development projects, and surveys that gathered valuable information for future national developmental planning.

The literacy campaign was a difficult challenge for the mass organizations, testing their capacity to mobilize their constituencies. Popular association participants in the campaign developed both leadership and organizational skills. "The remarkable accomplishments of the Crusade," writes Miller, "were testimony to the creative power and potential of the popular organizations and the hundreds of thousands of individual Nicaraguans who participated in the program. The success of the campaign also clearly demonstrated the capacity of the government to inspire and mobilize large sectors of the population and to organize and administer national development programs."[85]

The Antimalaria Campaign

During the literacy campaign, the Ministry of Health (MINSA) administered and supplied the *brigadistas* with enough prophylactic antimalarial medicines to last five months.[86] This was the first attempt in Nicaragua to conduct a mass drug administration campaign among a special sector of the population. Health authorities considered it a success because few cases of malaria were registered among the literacy volunteers. During this same period, however, the incidence of malaria among the general population was rising. The Ministry of Health commented, "The transmission of the disease is most intense in rural areas and peripheral sections of the cities . . . because primitive housing is found close to water sites where the mosquitoes breed. The disease favors the dispossessed classes . . . and it is this vicious cycle of poverty and illness that must be broken."[87]

The war had disrupted traditional malaria control measures. Vehicles and spraying equipment had been lost or destroyed, and malaria workers had to be organized and trained. MINSA viewed the literacy campaign as an opportunity to promote malaria control: "In our effort to fight this disease, we have tried to use all available resources. We have sought ties with the mass organizations and have made use of the national literacy crusade to make volunteers work to control this disease."[88]

The United Nations Development Program aided Nicaragua in its first attempt to involve the general population in malaria control after the Sandinista victory. In late 1980, MINSA set up case reporting posts along the 35 kilometer northern edge of Managua. By January 1981, residents in this zone were removing mosquito breeding sites and killing larvae with insecticides. The popular associations were directly involved in these early efforts. MINSA's director of preventive medicine affirmed that "the mass organizations have given their full support via their participation in the malaria control program."[89]

In 1980, the Ministry of Health established a division for health education: *Oficina de las Jornadas Populares de Salud* (Popular Health Campaigns Office—JPS). Initially a small unit, this division became the largest office in the Ministry by the end of 1981. The Popular Health Campaigns' Office promoted community participation in health care, which was a basic goal of the Ministry of Health. Through a series of workshops, the JPSs trained 11,000 volunteers to serve as health auxiliaries during the literacy campaign. After the campaign the JPS planned a series of single-theme health programs to be implemented in 1981.

In order to formally coordinate activities between the government and communities, MINSA created the Popular Health Councils in 1981.

The councils took charge of organizing and implementing health campaigns in their local communities. Members included representatives from MINSA, the health workers federation, the FSLN, and all the mass organizations. To facilitate coordination with the Ministry of Health, the councils established a three-tiered structure: local, regional, and national levels that paralleled MINSA's structure. Although the Ministry of Health offered the councils technical advice, they were responsible for developing all aspects of the upcoming campaigns. Representatives of the councils' regional and national entities coordinated the distribution of MINSA's materials and resources, and activists on the local councils decided how best to implement the campaign at the grassroots level.

MINSA set ambitious goals for the 1981 antimalaria campaign. The campaign sought to administer antimalarial drugs to the entire Nicaraguan population over one year of age. Rather than provide temporary protection to the persons taking the drugs, the campaign sought to reduce the transmission of the disease rapidly so that conventional methods would then be more effective in achieving long-term control. MINSA aimed to reduce malaria cases from 50,000 in 1981 to 4,000 in 1982, and to eliminate entirely the incidence of malaria mortality. Other campaign goals included: 1. teaching communities about malaria and improving their preventive activities; 2. expanding community participation in health tasks; 3. improving interministerial and inter-organizational coordination in health care; and 4. bolstering the organization of the Popular Health Councils.

Employing again the multiplier technique that was so successful in the literacy campaign, the Ministry of Health conducted training workshops to prepare the 85,000 *brigadistas* who were to work in the antimalaria campaign. The first meetings held for new recruits began with a discussion of the severity of the malaria problem in Nicaragua, its effects on economic and social development, and the campaign's goals. Subsequent workshops centered on the contents of training pamphlets that had been distributed throughout the country. Published in comic book form, the pamphlets discussed the value of prophylactic medicines and dosage schedules, and responded to common misgivings concerning the administration of medicine. The workshops also employed role playing, sociodramas, and question-and-answer sessions.

Once national leaders of the mass organizations announced their support for the campaign, many local activists volunteered to serve as *brigadistas*. Many representatives from grassroots organization representatives attended the first training workshops and became leaders of the malaria campaign in their communities. Because many of these same leaders had participated in other revolutionary projects such as the literacy campaign and the agrarian reform, the campaign quickly gained acceptance by residents in most communities.

The mass organizations' degree of participation in the campaign varied with their presence in the different areas of the country. The ATC provided 25,000 *brigadistas* for rural areas—one *brigadista* for each small farm that the union organized. The popular associations were less active on the Atlantic Coast where churches traditionally did most of the social outreach work. *Brigadistas* on the Atlantic Coast were mainly recruited from religious groups and from the Ministry of Education. In Managua, many thousands of *brigadistas* volunteered for the campaign: 15,000 were members of the Sandinista Youth; 3,400 were CST members, 1,300 represented ANDEN, and 10,000 were CDS activists. Nationally, women played a predominant role in the campaign. Approximately 80 percent of the *brigadistas* and 75 percent of the training staff were women, thousands of which were AMNLAE members.

MINSA planners decided to administer a three-day antimalaria dosage. This required more than eight million medicine packets, which included a total of twenty-five million chloroquine and ten million primaquine tablets. The drugs were divided into doses according to the day of administration and the age of the recipient. MINSA volunteers, militia members, and mass organization activists placed the nine dosage schedules into color-coded envelopes and then distributed them throughout the country.

To handle the counting, packing, distributing, and training, the Popular Health Councils added Coordinating Commissions to their structure. The Commissions functioned at the departmental and municipal levels and were responsible for the daily operation of the campaign. At the departmental level, mass organization leaders, mainly AMNLAE and CDS activists, comprised the majority of Commission members.

Richard Garfield, an American public health worker who studied the campaign, summarizes the results of the campaign:

> The mass drug administration of November 1981 appears to have been largely successful in overcoming the disappointments and disorganization which were problematic for prerevolutionary health programs. . . . the high level of participation evoked in this campaign, which required a more active response from the population than did pre-revolutionary health activities, suggests that the apathy of the past had been overcome. More than 85 percent of the estimated population was counted in the malaria census. A little over 80 percent of these participated in drug administration, comprising 70 percent of the country's total population. . . . the decentralized campaign structure, dependent

primarily on local mass organizations, was key to the malaria campaign's success.[90]

Once again, the popular associations had proven capable of mobilizing their members for a complex, national campaign. Government officials learned they could rely on the assistance of mass organizations in additional health campaigns and, in subsequent years, Nicaragua has conducted a series of highly successful campaigns against polio, tetanus, and dengue fever.[91]

In less than two years the popular associations had succeeded in developing a national presence. Through diligent organizing efforts, the grassroots organizations expanded their memberships and penetrated most of the population centers of the country, with the notable exception of the Atlantic Coast (for example, as late as 1981 AMNLAE had no chapters on the Atlantic Coast).[92] In addition, all the mass organizations consolidated their organizational structures, usually establishing a four-tiered structure of base, municipal, departmental, and national levels. Their tremendous growth and successful adaptation to the radically new tasks they had assumed in the first two years of the revolution earned the mass organizations sixteen seats in the forty-seven member Council of State. For the first time in Nicaraguan history, democratically-elected delegates represented the popular sectors in a national legislative body.

Finally, because of their participation in the literacy and anti-malaria campaigns, the mass organizations demonstrated their capacity to assist in the planning and execution of national projects. Indeed, neither campaign could have been carried out without the involvement of the popular associations' immense constituencies. By the end of 1981, members of mass organizations were learning how to participate in a revolutionary process that was more and more a process of their own making.

5

BUILDING INTERNAL DEMOCRACY

The Sandinista mass organizations serve as "schools of democracy" for their members. Since the collapse of the dictatorship, the popular associations have experimented with internal democratic processes, the first such participation the masses have ever experienced in Nicaraguan history. Such experiments have centered on their ability to 1. democratically select their leaders; 2. participate in decision making; 3. to ensure the accountability of their leaders; and 4. guarantee the political equality of all members. This chapter details the achievements and failures of these experiments in democracy.

ORGANIZATIONAL PRINCIPLES AND STRUCTURE

The mass organizations are open to all Nicaraguans who have a social affiliation with them. A single person may belong to more than one association. Despite such open acceptance, disruptive or ambitious individuals sometimes forfeit their membership.

> Many such individuals did join the mass organizations in the early days—in many cases causing these organizations to commit excesses and abuses of power. Thanks in part to the criticism leveled at these abuses by all three major newspapers, and the internal practice of self-criticism, trouble-making individuals were gradually weeded out and there was a progressive improvement in mass organization] behavior.[1]

The popular associations strive to maintain three principal channels of communication:

116

1. *From bottom to top:* the grassroots members convey their desires, criticisms, and suggestions to leaders in the mass organizations, the FSLN, and the government.
2. *From top to bottom:* the leadership submits its proposals and directives to the grassroots for their discussion.
3. *Lateral:* the mass organizations attempt to maintain coordination among themselves to avoid unnecessary duplication of effort and to maximize joint action.[2]

In performing their tasks the grassroots organizations follow six fundamental principles:

1. Democratic centralism. Though members freely discuss issues and make decisions based on majority opinion, the mass organizations centralize the administration and execution of policy decisions. Once made, all decisions are expected to be carried out with discipline.

2. Collective leadership. The popular associations follow the collegial leadership model of the FSLN's National Directorate. They believe that collective decision making prevents the concentration of personal power and enriches decisions with broad support. Although the collective actually makes decisions, the responsibility for executing mass organization policies rests with each individual.

3. Representativeness. Mass organization representatives, elected by the grassroots, must periodically undergo rank and file scrutiny and are subject to immediate recall by the membership.

4. Criticism and self-criticism. To resolve problems rapidly and publicly, the popular associations encourage continuous self-evaluation. All criticism is meant to be constructive—honest and open with concrete suggestions for improvements.

5. Division of labor. The grassroots organizations divide their tasks into different categories, delegating them to individuals with the appropriate skills.

6. Planning of labor. Popular association activists carefully plan their organizations' activities: they prioritize tasks, allocate human and material resources, and assign time schedules to attain goals.[3]

The many different popular associations share certain structural similarities. They all maintain a four-tiered organizational network. Base units are formed by block (CDS), place of work (CST), neighborhood and work site (AMNLAE), hacienda and rural district (ATC), or individual farm and cooperative (UNAG). Above the base level are the zonal, regional, and national levels of the mass organizations, reflecting the 1982 administrative division of the country.[4] Each level has an executive committee, headed by a secretary general or coordinator, and made up of a number of commissions and secretariats concerned with tasks such as organization, propaganda and political education, economic affairs, social defense, and sports and culture. Another institution common to the mass organizations are the councils. These bodies exist parallel to each level of the association, acting as consultants to each of their corresponding leadership organs. The executive committees direct the councils, which are made up of the top coordinators at each level of the organization. For example, the CDS National Executive Committee presides over the CDS National Council, which is comprised of the regional coordinators who are the highest-ranking CDS officers in each region of the country.[5]

AUTHORITARIAN LEADERSHIP SELECTION

Today all the mass organizations employ democratic procedures to select their leadership. But during the inital post-Somoza period there was a tendency to appoint executives rather than elect them. This led to authoritarian practices in some mass organizations, alienating sectors of the rank and file. The Sandinista Workers Federation, for example, exhibited authoritarian conduct during its bitter struggle against ultraleft union federations in 1980.

In the period immediately following the overthrow of the dictatorship, the FSLN insisted that the union movement make an active contribution to the country's economic recovery. For the FSLN, such a contribution entailed not only careful monitoring of the economic performance of the bourgeoisie, but also strengthening labor discipline and subordinating wage demands to national reconstruction. Given the country's dire condition, a rapid increase in wages would have fueled inflation, which was already high as a consequence of the civil war.[6]

Both the CST and ATC leaderships supported the Sandinista position on wage demands. But for many workers who had expected significant wage increases after the victory, this approach was disappointing. Nor were they swayed by the state's policy of responding to popular demands by subsidizing basic goods and extending social services—known as the "social wage" at that time. The union federations to the left of the pro-

Sandinista federations took advantage of this worker discontent, moving rapidly to win over rank-and-file industrial workers by emphasizing bread-and-butter issues.[7] Carlos Vilas, an Argentinian political scientist, outlines the motivations that drove these federations to pursue an anti-FSLN policy.

> They viewed Sandinista requests that the workers moderate their demands as having the effect of protecting capital's rate of profit and consolidating bourgeois political influence. What was for the FSLN "national reconstruction" was interpreted by CAUS, the Frente Obrero . . . the Nicaraguan Communist Party, and the . . . Popular Action Movement as the promotion of the interests of the bourgeoisie. And labor discipline was perceived as exploitation of the proletariat. In response to the political line of the FSLN, these organizations made radical labor demands and strongly attacked the CST and ATC for their lack of combativeness.[8]

Both the CAUS and the Workers' Front demanded 100 percent wage increases for industrial workers. In February 1980, after management at the Fabritex textile factory in Managua offered only a six percent wage increase, the CAUS convinced the workers to walk off their jobs. Within hours, workers at Plasticos Modernos and sixteen other smaller factories with CAUS-affiliated unions had walked out in sympathy. After arguing with local CST union members and CDS activists, all the workers went back to work, with the understanding that their demands were economically impossible and that their methods were incorrect.[9]

By June 1980, however, strike activity had spread to state enterprises with CST-affiliated unions. At the Plywood S.A. factory in Tipitapa, which was under 61 percent public ownership, the 600 workers struck over a 43 percent wage demand that would have brought them up to the then standard 40 córdoba ($4.00) daily rate. Other factories with CST locals also experienced walkouts over wage claims. In all cases, plant unions decided to strike against the advice of the CST leadership. Because of the economic crisis, the CST national executive committee was unable to resist pressure from its own rank and file. Furthermore, the CST recognized the legitimacy of the lowest-paid workers' wage claims. In some cases, state factory directors met the workers demands, but in others, the government responded by boosting the "social wage." The Labor Ministry paid such "wages" by providing free transportation to work, reducing factory lunch prices, increasing labor inspections, enforcing health codes; and job training and skill upgrading.[10]

In one factory, however, the effects of inflation on wage levels triggered an open rupture between CST-affiliated workers and the CST leadership: "Among some workers where the CST (in line with government policy) made a concerted effort to deny the workers their right to petition for salary increases, it led to a major rebellion within the factory, leading to the eventual displacement of the Sandinista leadership, their replacement by a new independent slate, and disaffiliation from the CST."[11] This incident occurred at the country's only cement-producing factory.[12] Originally owned by Somoza, the state expropriated the factory after the revolution and within three months it was producing cement at the prewar level. The enterprise employed 443 workers, only eleven of whom left after the fall of Somoza. Management encouraged the workers to participate in plant administration, though not in areas affecting hiring and firing. The workers' position was essentially consultative; management had the final say on investment decisions. In the immediate postwar period, these workers formed a trade union with a pro-Sandinista leadership and the local affiliated with the CST.

After suffering an inflation rate of 65 percent in 1979 and 35 percent in 1980, the cement workers demanded a 40 percent wage increase in June 1980. This and other demands led to an open break between the rank and file and the union leadership. The following account, based on an interview by James Petras, with seven members of the new union leadership, reveals the full details of this conflict:

> The trade union before the revolution was a bosses' union. It had no respect for the workers. The only part we had was to pay two córdobas dues monthly. We didn't have any autonomy before. The power of the bosses was based on money. Everything was in the hands of the boss. If you protested, you ran the risk of being fired. In August of 1979, after the triumph of the revolution, we began to form a trade union—in a moment of euphoria. The new leadership was advised by the CST. The workers met in assembly to discuss with the new union leadership a set of social benefits. We put forth a demand for salary increases, but the leadership did not respond to these demands. Political courses were set up for the workers but only the leaders were invited. The workers were marginalized from education.
>
> The local advisor (*orientador*) of the CST was badly trained. He got an office job at the plant. He preached labor discipline but he showed up at work at 10 and left at 3. The relations between this advisor and the workers was unfavorable because every worker grievance was considered negatively. It got to the extreme where he threatened to arrest workers with grievances. He acted very arrogantly at a meeting between leaders and work-

ers, and the adviser became hostile to all those workers who differed with CST policy. He acted in an undisciplined way.

The workers had no way to press demands because the leadership would not listen. They took a position and called the workers to inform them. As a result, workers in each of the 23 sectors of the plant elected representatives and started to press issues. The demand was for a salary readjustment of 40 percent to keep up with inflation. In the end, we secured a weekly "bonus" worth 62.4 córdobas to purchase food at the state store. [This was equivalent to a 21 percent raise for the poorest paid workers and nine percent for the better paid workers.]

After securing the bonus, the workers called a new assembly to elect a new leadership. On July 4, 1980, 406 workers voted in a new 11 man leadership—there were three slates and the winners got 200 votes. The old leadership abstained and got 30 or 40 votes. We were elected because we represent workers' interests, resolving immediate problems—dealing with working conditions in each section and increasing social benefits. The old leadership was unable to solve immediate problems. All our demands were relegated to the dustbin. The government launched a campaign attacking the workers' demands. The workers were accused of being agents of the CIA, Somocistas by the same representatives of the Ministry of Labor.

In contrast, negotiations arranged between the administration of the company (representatives from the Corporacion de Industrias del Pueblo) were cordial. Relations between the administration and the workers are good. Worker participation in the firm is good when there are good relations with the administration and when there are no anti-working class attacks. Wherever there are good relations, there is good production.

Today workers are better informed about the operations of the firm. Workers are consulted on new hiring and wage rates. This is a positive change [in relation] with the past. A new cafeteria and library is being constructed, and a typewriting class is being formed. We are asking for scholarships for workers to attend the university to develop technical education. Sanctions against workers are decided by the trade union.

The revolutionary government is very good in all its goals. There are errors within this process, these errors are being corrected. The objectives of the revolution are the liberation of the workers and peasants and employment for all. The revolutionary government has good intentions but there are persons who direct organizations who have weaknesses that create a bad image for the government. The CST created a bad image through the adviser who was sent here. He should have come to unify and present the just social demands of the workers. For the time being we have decided to remain independent.[13]

The CST's strict interpretation of national policy and its rigid opposition to worker initiatives led to considerable conflict between the rank and file and the Workers' Federation during the first year of the revolutionary process. The CST later conceded that its loss of prestige in that period could have been avoided if it had adopted a more flexible and less bureaucratic approach.

In October 1980, the CST Secretariat published a self-critical document in which it acknowledged the inexperience and inadequacy of its union leaders, the tendency of union cadres to act without consulting the rank and file, and the existence of "bureaucratic centralism" and "paternalist" traditions in the worker's movement. The document declared that

> in essence organizational work was entrusted to a small number of fringe cadres lacking in both quantity and quality. The leaders of union branches were not invested with the highest responsibilities. In many cases the Regional Executive Committees were not representative of the rank-and-file. . . . So, we can see why many disputes expressing genuine grievances did not receive the support of a number of leaders. This led to a situation in which other federations were able to capitalize on the workers' just demands.[14]

As a corrective measure, the CST Secretariat recommended the development of union democracy, a struggle against "bureaucratic centralism" and "paternalism," and a policy of voluntary, democratic unification for the workers' movement. "Leaders should not make decisions on behalf of the working class. Working people should make their own decisions and choose their real leaders. . . . Concrete proof that we have left behind the old style of work will be the formation of cadres from rank-and-file members steeled in day-to-day union activity. Such leaders should be placed in the highest positions of regional responsibility."[15]

DEMOCRATIC LEADERSHIP SELECTION

The Rural Workers' Association avoided the early errors committed by the CST. Indeed, the ATC was the first mass organization to replace appointed officials with elected ones. In December 1979, 250 ATC members from fourteen departments of the country gathered in a constituent assembly to draft the association's statutes and replace the appointed executive with an elected leadership. Prior to the assembly, the Association held 660 local meetings, allowing the entire membership to discuss all the issues before they were raised at the National Assembly. Association members elected both the delegates to the National Assembly as well as the local officers of their base committees.[16]

The ATC's Declaration of Principles, adopted at the constituent assembly, later served as a model for the other mass organizations. Article 4 declared:

> The ATC adopts as its own the principles of our vanguard, the FSLN, with regard to working methods and decision-making mechanisms which will guarantee internal democracy and the effective participation of the bases in the life of the Association. For that reason, we highlight the importance of criticism and self-criticism in the relationship between the grassroots and the leadership, and of the principle of democratic centralism, which means that rank and file opinion will be consulted and taken into account in all the Association's major decisions at every level.[17]

ATC executive member Francisco Lopez emphasized that the Assembly itself was the culmination of series of local elections.

> All rural workers affiliated to the ATC took part in assemblies where the objectives of this event were explained and 664 candidates were nominated to attend. Of these, 250 were elected as delegates to this Assembly. . . . There are 100 delegates representing the municipal, departmental and national offices of the ATC, which means that 60 percent of the delegates are direct representatives of grassroots bodies.[18]

In 1983, the CDSs restructured their organizational apparatus at the zonal and regional levels to match the state's decentralization process. A regional CDS secretary in Las Segovias explains how the rank and file in his region chose the executive committee according to the new organization.

> We have a system of popular democracy. At the zonal and regional level, we are approved or rejected in public assemblies. Our record of struggle against Somoza is taken into account, as well as our level of acceptance by the people. All block, neighborhood, rural district, and community leaders participate. So in this zone four hundred CDSs and two thousand people can

participate. In October 1983 the regional assembly met and chose the regional secretaries. Each zone put forth two or three candidates that were chosen at the base level. Seven people were elected and we then decided among ourselves who should be responsible for each position.[19]

Members of the National Association of Farmers and Ranchers (UNAG) established their organization's structure and leadership through a democratic process. Until the founding of UNAG, the Rural Workers Association had organized those peasants with small- and medium-sized landholdings. But by 1980 many farmers had come to feel that the ATC could no longer respond to both their needs and those of landless agricultural workers.[20] Consequently, in late 1980, many landholding peasants began to meet on their own to discuss the establishment of a new organization. In late 1981, some 10,000 *campesinos* attended five regional assemblies and on April 25 and 26, 1981, 360 delegates met in Managua to form the UNAG. In addition to adopting member-supported resolutions, the delegates elected a national council and a governing board.[21]

PARTICIPATION IN DECISION MAKING

How the mass organizations handle decision-making power is another test of how democratic they are. Are leaders the only ones who set priorities, assign tasks, and design the mechanisms used to carry out these tasks? Or is a genuine effort made to distribute responsibility to the base in order to allow the organization to work in a truly democratic manner?

There is no simple answer to these questions. The popular associations seek to incorporate Nicaragua's workers, peasants, artisans, and poor merchants into the decision-making process at all levels. Power-sharing within the grassroots organizations depends on both the leadership and the rank and file. On the one hand, leaders must do everything possible to encourage the development of those members who are not as self-confident, articulate, or politically sophisticated as others within the organizations; on the other, base-level members must constantly monitor the leadership to guarantee that tasks are rotated, debates open, and technical training available to all interested members.

Decision Making in the CST

In January 1983, six weeks before its first Constituent Assembly, the CST launched a discussion of a draft proposal called the "Declaration of

Principles of the CST."[22] The proposal included a description of the union federation, its goals, and the statutes that govern the life of its affiliated unions. The disucssion over the proposal was designed to increase workers' knowledge of the CST's role and to augment their participation in developing a new structure for the Federation. Remberto Mena Brenes, CST secretary general in Masaya, summarized the goals of the discussion: "We believe that this discussion constitutes an extensive democratic participation in the life or our union federation. It is also the first such discussion in the country because no other union federation has discussed its statutes with its locals before being approved in a national constituent assembly."[23]

Local unions met in departmental assemblies throughout the country to elect 285 delegates to the Constituent Assembly. In addition, workers at these assemblies chose their departmental councils and departmental executive committees. After wide-ranging discussions, the workers approved the declaration of principles, permanent tasks, and CST statutes. And many workers took the opportunity to express criticism of the CST National Executive Secretariat, and insisted that union delegates air their criticisms at the Constituent Assembly.[24] Finally, workers demanded that the CST Executive pressure SINAFORP, the government's technical training agency, to reveal its plans for upgrading the training of innovadores— workers who adapt, refurbish, repair, or maintain productive equipment.

Federation leaders considered the constituent assembly a major step forward in democratizing workers' participation in the life of the CST. In February 1983, Trabajadores, the CST's national newspaper, issued the following editorial lauding the federation's achievement.

> The democratic opening, backed by the Sandinista Workers Federation, is the product of a historical necessity that arose from the workers themselves who demanded a greater responsibility for the Nicaraguan working class.
>
> On February 26 and 27, the CST will culminate its first project in democratic practice when representatives from all its affiliates approve the statutes, general tasks, and principles of the organization that leads the workers' movement in our country.
>
> The leadership structures that the CST are organizing constitute a new practice within . . . the workers' movement that opens possibilities for greater achievements by union cadres, from the rank and file to the members of the National Assembly.[25]

Training for Participation in Decision Making

The mass organizations confronted three key problems during the revolution's first year. First, their rapid growth led to poor internal coordination and control. In a December 1979 *Barricada* interview, Patricia Orozco, then general secretary of the CDSs, acknowledged: "There is no relationship between number and quality of members." Orozco also identified the second series of problems: the lack of a politically trained leadership due to the death of many activists during the insurrection, the enormous demand for trained personnel in government, and the tremendous expansion of the popular associations. Luis Serra, an Argentinian political scientist, outlines the third major problem: "There was a lack of understanding at the grass-roots level about the nature and importance of participation in the mass organizations due to general educational and political backwardness, the lack of information, rumor-mongering by counterrevolutionaries, and errors committed by some novice or opportunistic leaders."[26]

Obviously, these three problems inhibited members' participation in the mass organizations. To overcome the obstacles, the popular associations launched intensive programs to enhance the political capacities of their memberships. Each organization created a secretary in charge of propaganda and political education at each level of its structure. These secretaries are responsible for providing members with information concerning the history and structure of the grassroots organizations, technical training in skills relevant to the members' needs, and basic reading and math skills.[27]

The mass organizations use a variety of means to develop their members' political abilities, including publications, rallies, assemblies, special leadership courses, radio and TV advertisements, articles and ads in the two main newspapers supporting the revolution, cultural events, and constant discussion. AMNLAE, for example, uses all these methods to "warn about aggression and integrate women into vigilance."[28] In June 1983, AMNLAE's monthly magazine, *Somos*, conveyed the Association's determination to fight CIA-sponsored aggression.

> We must conduct an intense and daily effort of ideological work among men and women to neutralize and defeat the enemy, to demonstrate consciously that the women of Nicaragua are ready to sacrifice ourselves, with the firmness, ideological clarity, morale and combat disposition necessary to block whatever act or method the CIA may employ, following the example of our heroes and martyrs.[29]

AMNLAE sponsors a notable example of organization-supported participation: the Committees of Mothers of Heroes and Martyrs are made up of women whose children have died in the war against Somoza and in the contra war. On July 9, 1983, these Committees held a National

Assembly dedicated to defending the gains for which their children died: "We will work so that the blood of our children will germinate into schools, roads, and highways."[30] The spirited chanting of political slogans marked the assembly: *No pasaran*—They shall not pass; *Patria libre o morir*—Free homeland or death; *Todas las armas al pueblo*—All arms to the people; *Por esos muertos, juramos defender la victoria*—For the dead, we swear to defend the victory; *Sandino se siente en la lucha por la paz*—Sandino is present in the struggle for peace; *Los hijos de Sandino no se venden ni se rinden*—The children of Sandino neither sell out nor surrender; *Sandino vive, vive, la lucha sigue, sigue*—Sandino lives, the struggle continues; and *Si la revolución necesita combatientes, aquí estamos las madres siempre*—If the revolution needs fighters, we mothers are here."[31]

The peasants' union also works to promote the political development of its constituency. In a January 1984 interview, Octavio Obregon Blandon, UNAG regional secretary of propaganda and political education, reported that regional training teams hold workshops for union members on Nicaraguan history, the goals of the revolution, the agricultural cooperative movement, and the aims of the agrarian reform. He went on to list the team's specific tasks:

1. to inform members about what UNAG is and why it exists
2. to teach them about the FSLN as vanguard, why it fought against the dictatorship and what it is today
3. to explain to peasants how a cooperative should function: that the farmers themselves must manage; that everyone has the right to their opinion; that tasks must be shared; that the members must dominate their own destiny; and that the cooperative should be run democratically
4. to educate members about the historical period through which we are living[32]

The training team holds weekly orientation workshops for new members, periodic seminars for cooperative presidents, three-month animal husbandry classes for ranchers, and taxation workshops for small farmers. Blandon stressed that the members often select their own themes for educational sessions. "We're a popular school," he declared, "where the students learn from us, and we learn from them."[33]

UNAG's national Publicity and Training Commission conducts a nationwide program to strengthen the union's municipal councils. The program consists of a series of training workshops designed to deepen activists' familiarity with the aims and structure of their organization. In the third workshop, for example, participants study a booklet called "Our

UNAG Municipal Branches," which refers to the union's intermediate organizational level. The booklet contains five themes: 1. "The Situation of our Base and Municipal Branches"; 2. "The Importance of Organizing Ourselves in the UNAG"; 3. "Our Role as UNAG Leaders" 4. "The Functioning of the Municipal Branches of UNAG"; and 5. "Improving our Organization."[34]

In studying the third theme, "Our Role as UNAG Leaders," members must devote one hour to reading and discussing the answers that three UNAG activists gave to the question, "What makes a good UNAG leader?" These answers reveal the values that the union attempts to encourage among its membership:

> A good leader is someone who is dynamic enough to enlighten those of us who live in the countryside. For example, over in my region where there are a lot of reactionary families, an UNAG leader came and in four days he had them all going to a patriotic demonstration that the people held in town. Just think—this man would come out every day, banging a can to call people to a meeting. We took some tires to sit on while he talked to the people. So in four days he was able to move all those confused people, something that no one had ever done before. There are a lot of good speakers, but to raise people's spirits you have to be a good leader.
>
> For me, a good leader is that individual who is popular with his people, someone able to lead them in crucial moments. It is important that the people believe in their leaders, that they have confidence that this man is going to lead them in a correct manner, and that they can see that what we are doing is for the good of all the people. The leader has to make the people see that this Revolution was made so that all of us could have rights. And if the leader fulfils his duties to the people, then they will follow him in doing whatever task is necessary.
>
> A revolutionary leader, whether from the base, municipal, or national level, must be fraternal with the rank and file, talk to the heart of the peasant, take him by the hand if necessary. There is a saying that says "Food must be given to the hungry and that one must overcome the bad with the good." So if there is a compañero that turns against us, we should not contradict him, but rather treat him in a fraternal way so that he understands us and we understand him.[35]

The CST also has a very active political education program aimed at preparing its own cadres. Trade unionists attend day schools that offer some forty courses on the history of the Nicaraguan and world labor movements, labor legislation, the national economy, Sandinista history, and world labor currents. In cooperation with the Ministry of Education, the CST also promotes adult education via the Centers of Popular Education. On the day-to-day level, the CST conducts discussions on current events, and monthly union meetings include workshops on the economy and international politics.[36]

THE ACCOUNTABILITY OF LEADERS

Mass organization members can ratify or reject their leadership in assemblies held at the base, zonal, regional, and national levels. To assess the behavior of their base-level executive officers, members periodically hold evaluation sessions in which they discuss their leaders' job performances and suggest how the leaders can improve their responsiveness to constituents.

In principle, all mass organization leaders are subject to immediate recall for abuses of power or negligence, and members do not hesitate to employ this measure when necessary. In October 1982, for example, CDS members removed many of their leaders after an intensive nationwide investigation of abuses committed by CDS coordinators. This investigation was launched on the basis of a letter that Commander Bayardo Arce of the FSLN's National Directorate sent to all CDS coordinators in the country. Because of the letter's importance, it is quoted here in its entirety.

The FSLN National Directorate sends greetings to the 459,750 CDS members throughout the country, who on a daily basis are strengthening the defense and preserving the gains of our people by carrying out their tasks. That is precisely why we want to repeat to you the concepts outlined by your national coordinator, Commander Leticia Herrera, and by Sergio Ramirez, at the commemoration of the CDS's fourth anniversary.

We affirm that the entire CDS membership, fully involved in their tasks and continually working to become more responsible, contribute decisively to the way in which the Sandinista people's revolution confronts the difficulties inherited from the past. The same holds true in regard to the problems brought in by the war policies that have sought to strangle our aspirations to be respected, sovereign, and independent.

We firmly believe that the CDS leadership and membership must express qualities that can be measured by:
— participation in defense activities;
— respect for the revolution's laws;

— discipline and respect in carrying out the directions of their immediate superiors; and

— willingness to be the best servants of the people, avoiding and combating opportunism, favoritism and bossism.

In this framework, a concern has arisen that troubles the National Directorate. We consider it an unavoidable duty to present it to you. There are signs that many coordinators have not accurately understood the line of the revolutionary directives. Based on its persuasive character, this policy has the aim of attracting the sympathy of sectors that, because of their situation, ought to be in favor of defending the revolution.

We refer to arbitrary attitudes and actions that have effects that are contrary to Sandinista principle. For example:

— Authorization of arbitrary land or building seizures despite the fact that all legal efforts are being made to give a plot of land to everyone who need and deserve it.

— Witholding the sugar distribution card from someone who has still not come to understand the Revolution, instead of using the revolution's achievements to raise his or her consciousness. We know that this method is used at times to pressure people into doing CDS tasks, which are supposed to be voluntary.

— Harassment by words and deeds of citizens who profess another ideology, religious or political, or who work with persons or institutions not identified with the revolution.

— Arrogant and haughty attitudes, taking on a kind of authority that only discredits the organization; creating small elite groups; and fostering divisiveness and intrigues between neighbors in a community.

— Misusing of one's position in order to transform personal problems into problems of the organization, or promoting destructive campaigns to discredit persons with whom one has conflicts.

— Falling into an abuse of authority and using a responsible post in the organization as a way to enjoy personal and family privileges. A concrete case, for example, would be to award lots to close relatives, bypassing the directives of the revolutionary state. This only encourages and puts into practice notions left over from *somocismo*.

— To tolerate and lead in abusing revolutionary vigilance [voluntary night-watch duty] especially through taking repressive measures against those who still have not joined in this task. (In some cases this has gone so far as the breaking of someone's door, or the casting of doubt on them, forgetting the fact that all CDS tasks are voluntary.)

It is absolutely necessary that we review our positions and make corrections. We have been thinking that we ought to meet in the near future to discuss these matters internally. Today, more than ever, national unity is the determining factor in defense. That is why we have put forward these ideas, upon which you surely will reflect.[37]

Between mid-October and early November 1982, an organizational restructuring of the CDSs occurred throughout Nicaragua. During that time, CDS members gathered in elective assemblies to reaffirm or to replace the old leadership at all levels of the organization: block, zone, barrio, and municipality. The rank and file often cited Arce's letter during evaluations of their leaders' behavior in office. On November 1, an election assembly for CDS leaders took place in Ciudad Sandino, a poor barrio on the outskirts of Managua. After reading the letter, one woman asserted, "We should make copies of that letter and give it to everyone. Here our rights are underlined. And we ought to show it to our leaders often so that they fulfill them faithfully."[38]

One of the most significant points of the letter is the affirmation that leadership is "service" to the people. All the abuses of leadership described in the letter stem from the mistaken belief that the individual who leads has certain special rights or powers in their social and even personal relations. But this document is based on a quite different concept of leadership, which has been expressed in the phrase, "their disposition to be the best servants of the people." The premise here is that leadership is a function and a service—not a privilege. The mass organizations have tried to inculcate this concept of leadership within their ranks. Given the need for national unity and the fact that many Nicaraguans tend to judge the success of the revolution based on the actions of their CDS leaders, Arce's letter served as an important educative tool during a key period of the revolution. It also encouraged the CDSs' rank and file to rid themselves of unscrupulous officials.

But by August 1985 the abuse of power among CDS leaders had again became a major issue. The National Executive Committee of the CDS underwent an intense self-criticism during a three-day conference in Managua. In a September 9 speech commemorating the seventh anniversary of the foundation of the CDSs, General Secretary Leticia Herrerra made public the principal results of this self-evaluation. She admitted that the CDS leadership had become isolated from the masses, and attributed this failure to the leadership's concentration on structural problems during the first stage of the revolution. "We were more interested in the organizational problems of the base structures than in providing solutions to community problems. We have fallen into a growing bureaucratism and consequently into a nearly total isolation from the masses," Herrerra confessed. She called on CDS members to elect leaders who were representative of the masses, who wished to learn from the masses, who understood their problems, and who would struggle to resolve their problems. Herrera insisted that there was no room in the CDSs for leaders who enjoyed giving orders and who ran their neighborhoods like kings.[39]

Shortly after Herrerra's speech, CDSs throughout Nicaragua held workshops in which activists evaluated the successes and failures of their organization and studied the national leadership's recommendations for restoring the CDSs. The need for effective leadership was a principal theme of the workshops. A discussion document studied at the workshops included the following section on leaders:

What qualities are important in a CDS leader?

The CDS leader should be a person who inspires participation in the community, and who is eager and willing to work for the community's goals. He or she must be able to relate well with all the neighbors, without making any distinctions among them. Most importantly, a CDS leader must lead by persuasion rather than imposition.

It depends on all of us to choose a block leader with the necessary qualities to inspire our participation. It will also be up to us to point out his or her errors, if and when they occur. . . . It is especially important that all of us assume the responsibility for asking: who can best fulfill the honorable role of leadership in such a way that the united community exercises popular power, the power that we won with the revolution.[40]

In a September 11 article *Barricada* reported that many Managua residents were dissatisfied with their current CDS leaders, and had accused them of authoritarian behavior. Two activists in Barrio México complained that the members of their barrio committee often declared "we are the authority," and refused to give authorization letters to residents who declined to participate in revolutionary vigilance and other CDS activities. A CDS member in Barrio Ariel Darce asserted that bad leaders needed to be replaced by people who would be dedicated to resolving their community's problems. Another CDS activist in the same neighborhood called for the election of CDS leaders who were "humble, honest, good workers, and committed to resolving the community's problems in cooperation with its members and not separate from them."

By mid-November 1985 thousands of neighborhoods throughout Nicaragua had formed election commissions designed to supervise CDS elections and guarantee their fairness. And on November 24, many of these same neighborhoods held their CDS elections. In Region I, 20,000

CDS members went to the polls to elect a total of seventy-three leaders from a field of 292 candidates. In the city of León scores of barrios carried out CDS elections that were accompanied by treasure-hunts, piñatas, music, and popular dances.[41] In their acceptance speeches most of the winners spoke of the importance of nonhierarchical leadership and reaffirmed their commitment to lobby for neighborhood improvements such as street repairs, child care centers, water and electricity, sewage systems, and new housing.

POLITICAL EQUALITY

The issue of political equality raises two questions: 1. Do the mass organizations provide their members with equal treatment according to the standards of their own internal regulations? 2. Do the popular organizations grant their members equal opportunity to participate politically in these organizations?

These questions are particularly relevant to those mass organizations with members whose political ideologies vary widely. To be a member of the UNAG, for example, one need only be an agricultural producer, or someone who doesn't yet own land but would be ready to produce if given land. Although UNAG members are expected to support the revolution's general goals, they do not have to be revolutionaries. Roberto Laguna, UNAG secretary general in Region I, elaborates:

> We have members of different political parties in UNAG. You have to produce efficiently but in UNAG you don't have to participate in revolutionary tasks. We defend members as long as they produce and therefore our members feel represented. So we do have some contradictions with other mass organization members who accuse our members of being *contras* because they don't participate in revolutionary activities. But we say that they are not, as long as they don't collaborate with the contras.[42]

Daniel Nuñez, UNAG's national coordinator, also stresses the broad nature of the union's membership.

> The UNAG . . . is a broad organization. It is what its name implies, the National Union of Farmers and Ranchers. And who should be in the UNAG? Those who were ashamed of *somocismo*. Those who were not involved with theft, or contraband, gambling, or prostitution. The noncorrupt elements, because we need to build a prestigious organization. Here we want neither opportunists nor lazy people. Nor do we want people who want

us to go to them to solve their problems, but rather those who want to confront the problems together with us.

Therefore, we say: Good, the UNAG has room for those sectors. It even has room for those who are capable of saying, I was wrong and now I see that the revolution is good for everyone. But we cannot bring in those who are for the aggression, those who are for the intervention, those who support the policies of destabilization, because we cannot join God with the devil.[43]

Within the UNAG, then, there is an effort to afford full political rights to those who meet the union's fundamental criteria for membership.

In all the mass organizations—with the obvious exception of AMN-LAE—the women's association,—women face obstacles participating equally with men. Women must confront entrenched sexism within the mass organizations as well as in the society at large. For example, although women make up almost half of the rural labor force, only six percent of the agricultural cooperatives' members are women.[44] Furthermore, a large majority of CDS activists are women, yet women hold less than half the leadership positions at the zonal and regional levels of the organization.

However, all the popular associations are taking measures to augment the participation of women. At a conference in the city of Granada on April 10, 1983, AMNLAE representatives and women from the ATC met to discuss the situation of women farm workers.[45] The meeting focused on the their political, organizational, labor, and social problems.

Women's familial responsibilities, delegates complained, prevented them from participating fully in the life of their union. They also criticized husbands for failing to understand their desire to be involved in union activities. Many of the women explained that union leadership positions were beyond their grasp so long as they remained barely literate. Women who care for children could not attend adult education classes because they are held at night. Furthermore, some delegates accused two state farms of failing to grant women equal pay for equal work, a practice contrary to Nicaraguan statutes. Other delegates reported cases of discrimination in hiring and training, and instances where women were prevented from joining the union. Finally, conference participants reported that some pregnant women miscarried during the coffee harvest because they had been assigned to work on difficult terrain.

Many of the delegates offered suggestions to overcome these problems, including an educational campaign to inform women of their rights under the law, and a proposal that guaranteed women access to technical training courses. The ATC studied and debated the concerns raised at the conference, and adopted measures to address some of the problems faced by women in the union. One regional office decided to guarantee 20 percent of its leadership positions to women, and to hold training courses for women only or with women comprising the majority of students.[46] In the meantime, women at all levels of the ATC are applying pressure to gain equal rights in the union.

Popular association members' attempts to build democracy within their organizations have met with mixed results. After an initial period of authoritarian tendencies and abuses of power, all the mass organizations developed democratic procedures to select their leaders. Grassroots organizations have also made some progress in granting decision-making powers to the rank and file through discussions and elections held at the base levels. Moreover, all the popular associations conduct ongoing educational campaigns designed to increase members' abilities to contribute to the political life of their organizations. And the associations are now addressing the problems faced by women in gaining full political equality.

But fostering democratic participation in the mass organizations is an arduous undertaking, especially in a society emerging from four decades of dictatorial rule. Luis Serra's words, written in 1980, summarize the difficulties:

> It would be wrong to project an idyllic image of the mass organizations since ". . . true revolutions . . . and Nicaragua's is one of them, are full of contradictions. They draw their sustenance from them, they live on them."[47] It would be strange if a people, accustomed to exploitation and marginalization dating to the Spanish Conquest, could develop a political system of full democratic participation in one short year. As the leaders of the FSLN noted on many occassions, the 19th of July 1979, was only **one** victorious battle in the ongoing war for the liberation of the Nicaraguan people. How could the enormous weight of behavior, attitudes, and values nourished by the old social system be thrown off overnight? How could corruption, alcoholism, apathy, egoism, individual lust for power and riches, *machismo*, violence, and authoritarianism be erradicated? If the experience of other countries in transition to socialism teaches anything, it is that old ideological legacies have much more weight than revolutionary theory supposes.[48]

Nevertheless, the revolution has made significant progress inculcating democratic values and practices to the population. Through their involvement in the day-to-day life of the popular associations, hundreds of thousands of Nicaraguan citizens are receiving training in democratic participation. Theorists such as Rousseau and Mill argue that such participation in all aspects of public affairs is the only way to create and maintain a democratic society. Individuals who participate in public affairs learn to gain other people's cooperation through the careful consideration of matters beyond their own private interests. Moreover, this participatory form of democracy is self-sustaining because the more individuals participate, the better they are able to do so. It is precisely through participation that cultural change and individual development—necessary ingredients for democracy—can happen. Thus, if democracy is to flourish in Nicaragua, the mass organizations must continue to serve as training grounds for democratic participation.

6

RELATIONS WITH THE PARTY AND STATE

The relationship between the mass organizations and the two other power centers of the revolution—the party and the state—raises a number of fundamental questions. Does the FSLN encourage the mass organizations to function as a parallel source of power in the revolution? Or do the Sandinistas manipulate the mass organizations from above and deny these organizations an independent role in the new regime? Do the constituencies of the popular associations regard the FSLN as their vanguard, and, if so, what action do they take when they oppose party positions? Does the state permit popular participation in the formation of government policy, or does it employ the mass organizations merely as instruments to implement executive decisions? Do the mass organizations carry out their tasks in close collaboration with the government, and, if so, how does such collaboration affect their ability to act as an objective watchdog of the state? An attempt will be made to answer these basic questions in the pages that follow.

MASS ORGANIZATIONS AND THE FSLN

The relationship between the mass organizations and the FSLN is complex. Although the popular associations receive political and ideological guidance from the party,[1] they maintain organizational and financial independence from the FSLN.[2] The grassroots organizations often serve as a rearguard and support system for Sandinista projects, but they sometimes oppose party positions and challenge the FSLN in various forums. The following discussion outlines both the cooperative and conflictual aspects of the mass organization/party relationship, focusing on the extent to which the popular associations exercise autonomy vis-à-vis the *Frente*.

FSLN's Conception of the Mass Organizations

The FSLN had no coherent plan for the role of the mass organizations in the early period of the revolutionary process. In fact, a number of Sandinista leaders asserted that the mass organizations ought to evolve independently, without the FSLN imposing a blueprint on their development. In early 1980, Comandante Monica Baltodano, then head of the FSLN's Secretariat for Mass Organizations, asserted, "We were working to give answers to problems as they presented themselves. But we didn't have lines laid out."[3] Even if they had sought to exert their influence while the revolution was young, the Sandinistas lacked the politically experienced cadres to guide the transformation of semi-autonomous, embryonic committees into independent and mature national organizations.

Indeed, in the first year of the revolutionary process, FSLN militants often used the word "embryo" to characterize the mass organizations, especially the Sandinista Defense Committees.

> We in the FSLN do not see ourselves as the final repository of revolutionary ideas. That would be dogmatic, and we do everything possible to avoid dogmatism or the rigid application of any political theory in our vision of future political power. That principle has guided the FSLN throughout its history as an organisation. We look to the masses constantly to enrich our vision, and when we talk of the CDSs as the "embryos" of popular power, it is because we have no preconceived idea of what that power will look like. The CDSs are the best current example we have, because they involve the whole people and function in a highly democratic way which guarantees a continuous dynamic interplay between the vanguard and the masses and avoids the risk of bureaucratisation. The actual structures of popular power in the long term will be forged through necessities and experience.[4]

In a November 1979 interview with the FSLN weekly *Poder Sandinista*, Jaime Wheelock, speaking for the National Directorate, capsulized the importance of the popular associations: "The organizations of the working class in trade unions will be the basic support of the Revolution, and likewise the rest of the mass organizations. The organized people must prepare themselves to run the state, through all the channels which the Revolution is creating."[5]

The phrase "prepare themselves" is instructive. The FSLN had no intention of employing the grassroots organizations as extensions of the party that would execute party directives. On the contrary, the Sandinistas encouraged the mass organizations to assert the demands of their own constituencies. In a speech to the Sandinista Workers Federation in October 1979, Carlos Nuñez expanded on this theme:

> The CDS . . . what are they but the result of all the efforts of the FSLN and other revolutionary organizations to give the popular classes a form of organization through which then can express their concerns, their worries, their criticisms, and say how far they want to take this revolutionary process? . . . This happens in the context of creating organizations with a true class character which embrace the productive sectors of the nation.[6]

The Sandinistas did not view the popular associations as agitational agents, nor as vehicles to communicate party policy to various other sectors of the population. Although the mass organizations partially served these functions, FSLN leaders insisted that the grassroots organizations act independently on behalf of their members. In another speech delivered on April 20, 1980, Nuñez defined the party's position on mass organization autonomy:

> We would like to generate the consciousness within the mass organizations that they should work to preserve the revolutionary political project and that they also should be instruments capable of autonomously expressing the demands of the sectors that they represent. And they have to express these demands employing methods ranging from the most usual to the most unusual.[7]

In addition to supporting the independence of the popular associations, the FSLN views the organized masses as the "architects of history" in the new Nicaragua. Agustín Lara, a Sandinista regional political secretary, underscores this idea:

> The FSLN has the conception that the role of the masses in the revolutionary process is something fundamental; it is not an accessory nor something secondary. The masses themselves have demonstrated that they themselves are the principal agent in revolutionary transformations; they are the active and conscious agents of the revolution. As a political organization we relate ourselves to them.[8]

Maintaining the Party-Masses Relationship

The FSLN relates to the different mass organizations according to whether or not the party feels that revolutionary action is necessary. But the party's involvement with an organization can depend on its relationship to the members. Between the October 1977 FSLN attacks on National Guard barracks and the final insurrection, the Sandinistas' relationship with the populace alternated between that of initiator and coordinator of mass action. Over time, the FSLN learned when the people needed inspiration through example, and when their revolutionary potential surpassed the leadership's expectations. During their first year in power, the Sandinistas used this knowledge to strengthen their relationship with, and understanding of, the Nicaraguan people.

> The spontaneous energy which abounds in Nicaragua today is the FSLN's most powerful asset, but there has been a strict avoidance of spontaneism determining the overall policy and direction of the Revolution. In the insurrection of September 1978, there were critical moments in which leadership and spontaneity were out of phase, but the still fresh memories of the results of spontaneous action at that time have helped to discipline acts whose tactical importance has changed radically with the taking of power.[9]

The rural poor, for example, employed land takeovers as a demonstration of their struggle during the final months of the war against Somoza, but land seizures were discouraged during the first year of the government's agrarian reform plan. ATC political education work largely eliminated the peasantry's initial confusion at the apparent contradiction in FSLN policy—approval for land seizures before the triumph, but prohibition after the victory—and land invasions were infrequent in the first year. Both the ATC and the CST had to explain to their constituencies that even though land seizures and factory strikes might ease immediate exploitation and improve living standards, the use of such tactics in the postwar reconstruction period could critically wound the revolution.[10]

During the early days of the revolutionary government, the FSLN engaged in constant, patient, and detailed explanation of all new policy measures. The Frente seldom acted without consultation and explanation, and it recognized the dangers of moving ahead of the development in working-class political consciousness. Above all, the FSLN sought to avoid lapsing into elitism, and dedicated itself to constantly renewing its popular support and moral authority. Borge put it succinctly: "We cannot simply capitalize on the prestige which we won in the war and think that this is enough. We have to win the support and respect of the masses every day, each minute, by knowing how to interpret the interests of the working people."[11] And "knowing how to interpret the interests of the working people" meant that the Sandinistas had to maintain continuous contact with the mass organizations and monitor their reactions to FSLN and government decisions.

Because the party often calls on the population to publicly demonstrate their support of revolutionary programs, the FSLN is able to gauge mass sentiment by the turnout at demonstrations.

> In mass demonstrations, whether to mark anniversaries, repudiate the activities of the CIA in Nicaragua, condemn the manoeuvres of ultra-left trade union groups, or support a new government decree, their presence and numbers are vital in gauging approval and understanding of measures taken. If a demonstration is small, it is direct evidence that policy should be rethought.[12]

Both party leaders and mass organization officials attempt to coordinate the developed centralism of the FSLN with the more decentralized structure of the popular associations. "Following the leadership of the FSLN," observes former CST Secretary General Ivan García,

> doesn't mean, for example, that the FSLN imposes its criteria over the workers in authoritarian fashion. To the contrary, the FSLN enriches its political conceptions and strengthens its position as vanguard by understanding the concerns of the workers and applying them to the real conditions in a way that aligns those concerns to the development of the revolutionary process.[13]

Mass Organization-FSLN Communication

The Sandinistas and the mass organizations have formalized their means of communication. Zonal and regional officials of the grassroots organizations regularly send written reports to the party's zonal and regional offices. These reports detail both the achievements and problems of the popular associations. In turn, the FSLN sends *orientaciones* (orientations) to the mass organizations' various leadership bodies. Orientations are transmittals that either notify pro-Sandinista organizations of the party's policy lines, or request the popular associations to perform a specific revolutionary task. The *Frente* delivers orientations only after holding prior face-to-face consultations with mass organization officials.[14]

The FSLN frequently proposes that the mass organizations meet certain goals in conducting their activities. For example, in February 1984 an FSLN zonal office in Managua asked the Sandinista Defense Committees to recruit one hundred additional volunteers from each barrio to carry out "revolutionary vigilance," a nightly five-hour neighborhood watch program. But before the FSLN established this goal, it conferred with CDS zonal leaders to see if the request was realistic. Only after the neighborhood officials told the party that its proposal was feasible did the FSLN officially submit the orientation.[15]

Vivian Perez, an ATC zonal secretary, describes how the farm workers association coordinates its work with the FSLN:

> We make a weekly work plan, then try to add to this the tasks that the *Frente* sends us. For example, we set production as a priority and then the *Frente* sends us an *orientacion* asking for 32 volunteers for the reserves and the militia. But we may see that this is not possible because the men are needed for production. So we send a written report to the FSLN explaining why the 32 men cannot be mobilized. This happened only this week.
>
> Each Monday there are zonal meetings with the FSLN secretary of propaganda and political education in the zonal offices of the the *Frente*. Representatives from the ATC, CST, AMNLAE, UNAG, CDS, JS 19, FETSALUD, UNE, and ANDEN attend the meetings. Here we discuss the new lines. We may discuss the lack of manpower for the harvest of a product. We discuss what mechanisms can be used to get more workers to participate in the harvest. For example, right now we need more people to harvest beans. The Juventud Sandinista will guarantee a brigade of students for a *roja y negra* ["black and red"—a volunteer work day]. After the meeting the *Frente* sends us the orientations based on these discussions.[16]

Because the mass organizations set their own priorities, their representatives sometimes reject FSLN proposals. One regional CDS secretary stresses that his organization does not regard FSLN orientations as imperatives: "If the *Frente* has a task for us we talk with them and decide whether we can do it on not. We negotiate with them to see whether its possible. We are an autonomous organization. We don't have a vertical relation with them."[17]

Conflicts

Three episodes of conflict that have occurred between the party and the grassroots organizations verify the assertion that the popular associations' relationship to the FSLN is not "vertical." These disputes have involved key revolutionary policies.

One such conflict occurred in 1980. In the months following the defeat of Somoza, the Rural Workers Association engaged in a series of spontaneous land takeovers of non-Somoza farms.[18] The Association argued that land seizures were the just, heroic response of the rural majority. The Sandinista leadership, concerned with maintaining the support of large landowners, tended to oppose ATC land takeovers.

By early 1980, tensions over land occupations were building toward a dramatic climax. In late 1979, the courts moved to return to owners those farms and ranches that ATC members had seized, if it could not be shown that the owners had been linked to Somoza. For the Association, however, any return of land to private owners symbolized an end to the process of agrarian reform at a time when thousands of workers and peasants expected its continued advance.

Carrying banners and machetes, more than 30,000 peasants and landless rural workers from all over Nicaragua converged on Managua's Plaza of the Revolution on February 17, 1980, to submit their demands to the Government of National Reconstruction. Speaking to the gathering, Edgardo García, secretary general of the ATC, demanded that all land then under the control of the agrarian reform agency be legally transferred to the *Area de Propriedad del Pueblo* (Area of Public Ownership—APP). García insisted that "not one inch of land be returned" to the original large landowners.[19] The ATC also demanded the reduction of land rental prices and a more liberal credit policy for peasant producers.

Shortly before the ATC rally, the FSLN relinquished its previous position and decided to support the Association's demands. Jaime Wheelock, the minister of agriculture, made an appearance at the demonstration and declared: "We know that your demands are just, and this march gives us the confidence to advance and make further transformations." Although Wheelock stressed the need for the agrarian reform to follow an orderly path, avoiding "anarchic and spontaneous actions," he affirmed that "there are elements among the landowners who must be hit hard if their lands are left idle."[20] He promised that the state would move quickly to meet the ATC's demands. At the same time, Sergio Ramirez of the governing junta announced that a new decree was imminent. Issued on March 3, the decree ordered the immediate confiscation of all the intervened lands, excluding those owned by small producers.[21]

Another conflict between a mass organization and the FSLN centered on the law establishing a compulsory draft. Until January 1984, Nicaragua's primary defense had been provided by two volunteer forces: the Popular Sandinista Army and the Sandinista Popular Militias. Although the Sandinistas had been discussing a compulsory draft since the victory over Somoza, they waited until August 1983 to introduce legislation calling for obligatory military service.

All the Sandinista popular associations strongly backed the draft proposal. But AMNLAE objected to that part of the law that made a distinction between men and women, excluding the latter from the draft. The women's association launched an attack against the draft legislation and a rigorous debate ensued. Glenda Monterrey, then general secretary of AMNLAE, expressed the Association's position: "We all have limitations, and we run into obstacles. This does not mean that our society can adopt a law that includes discrimination on the basis of sex. . . . Women are demanding the right to take an active part in the service that is being organized."[22]

During the month of debate over the law, AMNLAE members campaigned vigorously for their position. They argued that many women had combat roles during the struggle against Somoza, and that thousands of women were defending Nicaragua's sovereignty in the war against the contras. Military participation by women was, and is, high: between one-third and one-half of the militia members are women, and women comprise about 30 percent of the reserve battalions engaged in combat with the counterrevolution.[23] AMNLAE's arguments were persuasive: women won the right to be included in active military service as volunteers, but such service would be compulsory only for men. In November 1983, several thousand women throughout Nicaragua registered for active service.[24]

During the 1984 election campaign, another conflict arose between the FSLN and the mass organizations. All the opposition political parties accused Sandinista supporters, primarily CDS activists, of harassing their party militants as they conducted their campaigns. Even the Socialist Party, a staunch ally of the FSLN, criticized the behavior of neighborhood association members. Domingo Sanchez, the PSN's presidential candidate, registered this complaint: "The CDSs leave much to be desired. Their lack of orientation and political capacity leads to abuses. We have told the FSLN that they have given the CDSs too much power for their capacity at this time. They commit abuses. However, this is a natural part of a revolutionary process."[25]

Throughout the campaign, the FSLN sought to end the abuses of the popular associations. In August, Commandante Carlos Nuñez wrote three articles in *Barricada*, imploring the mass organizations to respect the rights of the opposition parties. Though Nuñez acknowledged the difficulty of establishing the proper atmosphere for a political campaign after decades of dictatorship, he emphasized that the FSLN as a party did not support the harassment.[26]

In a speech to the Sandinista Police on August 27, 1984, Tomás Borge, the minister of interior, described the electoral process as part of the overall revolutionary process.

> It is easy to deduce the importance for Nicaragua of an impeccable electoral process, where all the registered political parties have the broadest liberties to compete, to criticize, to demonstrate, to make their programs known, to publicize their programs. To restrict the liberty of the registered parties is obviously to play into the hands of the enemies of Nicaragua who are trying to portray an image of an electoral process in which repression and fraud predominate.
>
> In the development of the electoral process, problems have arisen . . . some of the accusations are true. In a few cases there have been excesses on the part of the authorities who have the institutional authority to guarantee the electoral process . . . We must direct them so that they contribute energetically to building respect for liberties, within the limits of the electoral law, of all the registered parties.[27]

Although the FSLN leadership decried the abuses, they continued, albeit at a reduced level. Virgilio Godoy, the leader of the Independent Liberal Party, admitted afterward that matters had improved in the period just before the election.[28] One election observer noted that the Contra war had fostered an atmosphere that led to mass organization abuses.

> The *contras* launched explicit campaigns to disrupt the elections. In July they attacked and killed three CSE [Supreme Electoral Council] officials as they atttempted to carry out voter registration. On August 25 they castrated and murdered a local election official in front of his wife and six children. On September 8 ARDE troops kinapped FSLN National Assembly candidate for the Atlantic Coast Ray Hooker.
>
> In this context, the harassment of the opposition by supporters of the FSLN is less surprising. . . . the FSLN retains a large base of dedicated supporters. Many have lost family members in the fights against first Somoza and now the *contras*. They view opposition to the FSLN as a threat to what they have sacrificed for and resent it. Because of this, the position of the FSLN leadership on harassment did not end all abuses.[29]

In advancing the interests of their constituencies, the mass organizations sometimes enter into conflict with the FSLN, which is charged with mediating the interests of the revolutionary process as a whole. The degree of openness about these conflicts and the fact that the FSLN encourages the popular associations to express their divergent views and demands—in spite of the pressures of the war and the economic crisis—demonstrate the degree of autonomy that the grassroots organizations possess. But, as the case of AMNLAE and national military service shows, the mass organizations are not always successful in winning their demands.

Overlapping Memberships

The FSLN draws most of its new members from the ranks of the mass organizations. For example, in the northern city of Estelí, a Sandinista stronghold, four of the five AMNLAE zonal officers are FSLN militants[30] and six of the eight regional CDS leaders are members of the party.[31] Agustín Lara describes the attributes that the party looks for in its recruits:

> The FSLN is a political organization that nourishes its ranks with people from different social sectors, but largely from among the peasants and workers. From the mass organizations [we recruit] . . . the excellent leaders who wish to join. To be an aspiring member you must be 18, and be recognized in your sector as being capable, honest, and so on. Without having authority, prestige, and love from the masses you can't enter. You must be an example: last in gaining privileges and first in making sacrifices. These requirements demonstrate to the people that the *Frente* chooses the best people from the masses.[32]

Lara emphasizes that in most cases the new recruits maintain their active participation in the mass organizations.[33]

But because both the party and the popular associations lack a sufficient number of politically trained cadres, conflict sometimes arises over the recruitment of new members. If the FSLN recruits an ATC activist, for example, and then assigns that person to a task unrelated to the union's activities, the ATC not only loses a valuable member, but must then spend considerable time and effort training a replacement.[34]

The FSLN's continuous recruitment of new members from the mass organizations reinforces the close link between the party and the grassroots organizations. But there is also the danger that the Sandinistas could one day unwittingly control rather than guide the mass organizations. If the Sandinistas ever lost the support of Nicaragua's popular sectors, they could take advantage of their presence among the mass organization leadership by falsely influencing the popular associations.

Edgardo García, is both general secretary of the ATC and a member of the Sandinista Assembly.[35] When asked whether he thought there was any danger in Sandinistas holding dual memberships, he responded, "I don't have any fear in the overlap of members of the *Frente* and the mass organizations. I don't have any fear of this. Remember, Nicaraguans of the popular classes don't mind taking on anyone, including militants who have the most experience in the guerrilla and in the FSLN."[36]

Mass organization autonomy will face its greatest challenge as the institutionalization of the revolutionary process unfolds. Until January 1985, the mass organizations maintained their own elected representatives on the Council of State, the nation's co-legislative body. But because only political parties were allowed to field candidates in the November 1984 elections, the popular associations lost the power to choose their own legislative representatives. Although many FSLN delegates to the National Assembly are mass organization leaders, they could face a serious dilemma: a conflict of interests.[37] As Sandinista militants *and* popular association members, these delegates may have to vote on legislation backed by their party, but opposed by the constituencies in their popular associations. It remains to be seen whether FSLN delegates who are also mass organization leaders will be able to effectively represent their memberships.

The mass organizations have displayed a considerable degree of autonomy from the FSLN, sometimes even opposing the *Frente* in order to meet the demands of the sectors they represent. For the most part, the Sandinistas have encouraged the autonomous development of the mass organizations, preferring to let these organizations develop theie own role in the revolution. But when the grassroots organizations press demands that conflict with the party's policy of national unity in the face of military aggression and economic crisis, the FSLN may withdraw its support. For example, some observers speculate that the FSLN opposed AMNLAE's proposal to extend the draft to women in 1983 because it would have alienated certain Catholic sectors who have so far supported the revolution.

The party's stand on independent action by the mass organizations sometimes appears contradictory. For example, Jaime Wheelock warned the ATC in February 1980 against "anarchic and spontaneous actions" in pressuring for agrarian reform. Two months later, Carlos Nuñez stressed that the popular associations must assert their demands in the face of state inflexibility. On the one hand, the FSLN urges the mass organizations to employ all means at their disposal to meet their needs, but on the other, cautions them against unsanctioned actions. This may seem contradictory, but it also reveals the Sandinistas' simultaneous commitment to Nicaragua's workers and peasants, and to the preservation of national unity.

Enough evidence exists to demonstrate that both the FSLN and the grassroots organizations are conscious of the need for popular association autonomy. The key question for the revolution is how to translate this consciousness into concrete practices or guarantees that such autonomy will be respected. With the current political institutionalization process now underway, the Sandinistas have a unique opportunity to ensure that the differentiation between the mass organizations and the party becomes a structural feature of Nicaraguan society. For example, the autonomy of the mass organizations could be bolstered if the National Assembly formally recognized their independent status in the new constitution. Such recognition would give the popular associations greater legitimacy and strengthen their hand in the political process. It would also help protect them from any political forces that might challenge their independent status. Moreover, constitutional acknowledgment of grassroots organization autonomy must be accompanied by concrete forms of political power independent of the FSLN.

MASS ORGANIZATIONS AND THE STATE

The relationship between the mass organizations and the state is marked by cooperation as well as conflict. The popular associations officially recognize the revolutionary government as the instrument that directs the administrative policy of the country, and assists the state in planning and executing national policies.[38] Few government programs could be implemented without the cooperation of the mass organizations. At the same time, the grassroots organizations act as a watchdog over state power. Any state requires a bureaucracy and Sandinista bureaucracy can be just as rigid and inflexibile in reacting to popular demands as any government. Therefore, the mass organizations constantly monitor state activites to ensure that it responds to the needs of the population.

Local Government

In addition to meeting emergency needs in housing, food, and medical care during the immediate postinsurrection period, the new government faced a crucial administrative problem as well. Although the Sandinistas had formed a national government representing the unity of anti-Somoza forces, there were no government representatives at the local level. Consequently, amid the destruction and chaos of the first days after the war, the Sandinista Defense Committees took upon themselves state functions. The CDSs had five new and essential tasks to coordinate: distributing food, providing health and hygiene services, identifying medical needs, defending communities, and disseminating information.[39]

Food coordinators worked with the Red Cross, churches, and other emergency aid groups, locating grain and other staples, and determining where they were needed most. The CDS food coordinators also administererd much of the food donated by international agencies, providing meals for voluntary work crews until mid-September, when the first paychecks were were issued.

CDS health and hygiene coordinators worked closely with the Ministries of Health and Social Welfare. They found housing for those people whose homes were destroyed, brought severe cases of malnutrition to the attention of health personnel, and coordinated efforts to make fresh drinking water available.

The medical coordinators identified the sick and wounded in their area who required medical attention. Whenever serums were available, they administered vaccinations to children. In one remarkable accomplishment, the coordinators, working with the Ministry of Social Welfare, located all amputees so that they could be sent to West Germany to receive artificial limbs and rehabilitation.

CDS defense coordinators joined the Sandinista militia in defending the civilian population from uncaptured National Guardsmen. The vigilance coordinators in charge of block security kept watch over suspicious persons and guarded neighborhood meetings. Because all applications for exit visas were processed through local CDS vigilance coordinators, no one left the country without a thorough review by their local CDS. This procedure reduced the number of National Guard escapes, and led to the capture of other Somocistas trying to remove assets from the country.

CDS information coordinators kept residents posted with the latest news. When government officials lifted curfews and announced the removal of other wartime restrictions, the information coordinators reported the details of such changes to their neighbors. With so much political transformation taking place, the FSLN needed a local forum to discuss governmental matters with the people. The information coordinators provided such a forum by organizing meetings and distributing Sandinista statements and declarations.[40]

While the CDSs were conducting their relief measures, the state apparatus emerged at the local level.[41] In the major urban areas that were liberated during the final two weeks of the war, the residents established local councils called *Juntas Municipales de Reconstrucción* (Municipal Reconstruction Councils—JMRs) to direct community affairs. These Councils were comprised of respected and charismatic individuals known for their opposition to Somoza and their commitment to democracy.

During the period of initial recovery from the war the Councils had three functions: to represent broad national unity, to represent the authority of the central government as well as the views of the local population, and to resolve critical postwar problems under emergency guidelines.[42] In October 1979, the Councils shifted their energies to reconstruction. Workers rebuilt factories and refurbished or replaced machinery, and peasants resumed planting on the farms. The government invested foreign aid, principally low-interest loans, in the systematic reconstruction of the six cities that had suffered the most severe war damage: Chinandega, Estelí, Managua, León, Matagalpa, and Rivas. To meet the cost of long-neglected needs, especially in the area of public health, the government channelled additional funds to local municipalities. In only one year, the national government's Secretariat for Municipal Affairs had provided twenty-five times more financial assistance to local governments for improvement projects than Somoza's municipal development agency had financed during its entire two-year existence.[43]

The reconstruction period was characterized by developments that dramatically affected the relationship between local government and the mass organizations. Popular participation began to play a vital role during this phase of the revolution.

> The activities of government were carried out by people representing the popular unity embodied in the revolution, individually without previous experience in government and as a group from classes that had not previously shared in power. It was not to be simply a change in personnel; these people believed in the importance of maintaining and developing the popular participation that had made the revolution possible and should define the priority problems to be solved in the future. Thus, while the concept of reconstruction was fairly straightforward, it was carried out under the control of new political forces, seeking a greater involvement of the mass of the population, resulting in changes in both operations and priorities.[44]

Some municipal juntas had problems handling the demands that stemmed from mass participation. The population considered the Councils responsible for all that occurred in their jurisdiction, and therefore held

Council members accountable for any difficulty that arose, regardless of who was at fault. Consequently, some members resigned, and in other cases the mass organizations exercized their recall powers.

In one large city, the entire Council failed to adjust to the reconstruction period. Nominated during the war, its work centered on the creation of a broad political front, the supply of food, water, and electricity, and the initiation of reconstruction plans. But once the war was over, the Council failed to adapt to the new conditions: the Council coordinator had little contact with the population, and Council members had infrequent meetings with the popular associations; they didn't even attend local political rallies. Moreover, the Council failed to make necessary adjustments in its administrative structure and proved incapable of setting a clear direction for municipal policies.

Whenever Council members resigned, the popular associations met to choose their successors. Municipal government experts Downs and Kusnetzoff describe the selection process in one major city.

The first JMR [Council] resigned at the end of February, 1980. On March 3rd the new JMR was nominated, composed of five members: two for the CDSs, one for the CST, one for the ATC, and one interim member nominated by the FSLN and later elected by the CDSs. The two for the CDSs were elected through a process that began with block level elections, which presented candidates at the barrio level, leaving eight final candidates out of which two were elected by the citywide executive of the CDS. The CST and the ATC each elected their representative internally as well.[45]

Mass participation in local affairs led to significant infrastructural improvements in many communities. Dozens of towns expanded water supplies, paved streets, and built clinics and school buildings. Community involvement in decision making expanded and took various forms: personal contacts, large public meetings, demonstrations, and advisory councils representing local organizations, particularly the mass organizations.

The period of reconstruction drew to a close in the second quarter of 1981. Though not everything that existed previously had been rebuilt, the country now had a material platform upon which future development would be based. Furthermore, the municipal governments and the popular associations learned to combine their forces in order to resolve local problems. Their joint efforts not only achieved concrete gains for the population, but also demonstrated the collective power of the mass organizations and local councils. Working together, they overcame many of the political and material obstacles left by the war as well as various psychological barriers inherited from *Somocismo*.

After sharing experiences in both the emergency and reconstruction periods, popular association activists and local government officials stressed the importance of close relations between the Councils and the organized population. A CDS departmental representative commented that the CDSs, the Councils, and state agencies "should always work closely together . . . In that way both the mass organizations and the Juntas [Councils] will be strengthened, but only to the degree the central government responds."[46] And the coordinator of a small rural municipality asserted that

> the Junta should coordinate closely with the grassroots organizations and not work in isolation. If we work together the responsibility belongs to all of us. The Junta should be closely linked to the mass organizations, but should not be simply an extension of them. It should not simply accept whatever they say, but rather should discuss with everyone how to develop the municipio [muncipality]. The Junta is responsible to make the final decision. The grassroots organizations make mistakes, so one can not simply accept their guidelines. However, the Junta should always function in close coordination with them.[47]

City council and CDS officials point out that such close relations help to 1. strengthen both the mass organizations and the Councils; 2. guarantee the representative nature of local government; 3. furnish support for the Councils in negotations with other governmental and private institutions; and 4. contribute resources and labor to solve local problems.

Government Ministries

Even after the state apparatus began to consolidate itself, the mass organizations found themselves taking responsibility for some state functions. "Largely due to the inadequate nascent state, they [the mass organizations] behaved as parastatal organs," declared Carlos Nuñez. "They failed to find in the state the receptiveness, dynamism, and flexibility required to solve real problems."[48] The FSLN has consistently supported the mass organizations in conflicts with the state, backing the popular associations' attempts to streamline government operations and activities. For example, the grassroots organizations contribute to improving government efficiency in the supply of basic food products. Food shortages have been a long-standing problem in Nicaragua. Under Somoza, the development of an agro-export economy forced peasants to subsist on the most marginalized lands. Inefficient patterns of production and the failure to carry out multicropping further aggravated the problem. Moreover, numerous middlemen plagued the transportation and distribution of food, each trying to maximize their personal profit.

The severe shortage of foreign exchange prevents the government from importing the food, machinery, or spare parts necessary to increase food production. Furthermore, because the purchasing power of most sectors of the population has greatly expanded, there exists considerable consumer and market pressure for food products. Nicaragua's population has also grown by at least 300,000 since 1979, heightening the already scarce food supply.[49] The government's failure to gain control over the allocation of basic goods has exacerbated distribution problems. After Somoza's ouster, the government created the Ministry of Internal Commerce (MICOIN) to guarantee the population's access to basic goods. But direct control over basic supplies is difficult in a mixed economy in which state and private interests must compete for the same products. In late 1983, MICOIN controlled 50 percent of the harvest distribution of beans, 30 percent of the corn, 80 percent of the available rice, 90 percent of the sorghum, and 100 percent of the available oil, laundry soap, salt, and sugar.[50] In the same year, the National Basic Foods Company (ENABAS) controlled 2,647 popular stores, eleven supermarkets, and employee stores in more than 500 workplaces. Although this represented 40 percent of the national distribution network, the other 60 percent was dominated by a traditional network of approximately 37,000 retailers, located mostly in the cities.[51]

The development of two distribution systems (state and private) has created a sort of double market that fosters diverse forms of speculation. In addition, there exists a flourishing black market, centered in Managua, which has fueled tremendous price speculation and inhibited the development of equitable pricing or distribution. The supermarkets located in the middle-class neighborhoods are better stocked than the ENABAS stores in the barrios. Until August 1983, when a consumer protection law went into effect, the supermarkets bought their goods directly from wholesalers or from the factories. The supermarkets were also illegally selling rationed products only on the condition that the consumer buy other goods.[52]

Hoarding by both wholesalers and retailers also plagues the distribution system. Each time there are rumors of shortages, people store large quantities of basic food items, expecting the prices to increase dramatically. In addition, the CDS-controlled rationing system has been subject to manipulation. Many neighborhood leaders have abused the system through nepotism, thereby inhibiting an equitable distribution of limited goods and damaging the integrity of the CDSs.[53]

The government attempts to overcome these problems. State agencies responsible for production, commercialization, and distribution work with the mass organizations to improve the availability of supplies. The Ministries of Internal Commerce, Industry, and Agrarian Reform supervise the provision of basic goods, but alone they are incapable of normalizing the commerce of staple products. While MICOIN, for example, has 512 employees (and only sixty price inspectors), the petty commerce sector constitutes a major source of livelihood. Just one Managua market—the *mercado oriental*—contains products from 8,000 vendor.[54] Not surprisingly, the government relies heavily on the grassroots organizations for assistance with the supply problem.

The CDS, as the largest mass organization rooted in all the communities, plays the major role in distributing consumer products. The CDSs collaborate with MICOIN to secure adequate supplies for the country's thousands of retail outlets. The CDSs also enforce price controls that the government imposes on certain basic goods. In addition, the neighborhood associations maintain a distribution coupon system that allows families to purchase specific quantities of eight basic items each week: rice, beans, sugar, laundry soap, toilet paper, corn, oil, and eggs.

The other mass organizations also assist the state with supply distribution, but in more limited capacities. The women's association coordinates a maternal-child program to aid low-income families suffering from malnutrition.[55] AMNLAE secures medical attention, nutritious foods, and social security benefits for these families. In 1982, AMNLAE initiated a drive to collect containers for preserving fruits and vegetables, and in 1983 launched a campaign to promote the cultivation of family, communal, and collective gardens.[56]

Both the Rural Workers Association and the Sandinista Workers Federation have worked with ENABAS and the Ministry of Commerce to establish commissaries in work centers. As a result, thousands of urban and rural workers now have better access to basic consumer products; they are able to purchase these goods at official prices and can also buy on credit. The CST tracks the volume of products at MICOIN distribution points, allowing the unions to place accurate purchase orders for their members. Direct sales from MICOIN to workers prevent goods from entering distribution channels that are subject to speculation and hoarding.[57] As Nicaragua's economic crisis deepened in early 1985, the CST signed an agreement with MICOIN to help run the commissaries and ensure that goods stayed out of speculators' hands.

The National Union of Farmers and Ranchers (UNAG) maintains

some 300 storage facilities for agricultural products. UNAG farmers attempt to overcome the shortage of basic grains by producing and storing more beans and corn every harvest season. To facilitate the transportation and marketing of its members' goods and products, the peasant union lobbies for the repair and construction of roads. In some zones, where the Ministry of Construction has been unable to send its crews, UNAG relies on its own membership to repair roads and to provide transportion for the most isolated sectors of the peasantry.[58]

The popular associations also aid the government in strengthening the distribution system's retail network. Until recently, many neighborhoods did not have enough stores to serve the needs of the local population, and many store owners lacked sufficient financial resources to purchase enough goods for all their customers. The CDS, MICOIN, and the FSLN studied the problems and in 1983 launched a program to create more retail outlets and to increase financing for retailers. The program's aim was to create stores for every 1,000 to 1,200 people, and to lend retailers money to stock the stores with sufficient supplies of basic products.[59]

These measures have improved matters, but war expenditures, economic difficulties, and bureaucratic deficiencies continue to plague the distribution system. Leonel Quintillana, a CDS regional official in Estelí, explains how the neighborhood association helps retailers tackle bureaucratic problems.

> We still lack enough expendios and a lot of owners still haven't got their loans from the banks. We help owners by giving them information on how to secure loans, and if there are bureaucratic problems we apply pressure on the banks to loan the money. What we do is call on the director of the bank, and if that doesn't work, we petition the Central Bank in Managua. There is a lot of bureaucracy in state offices; there are people who don't have consideration for the problems of the population and people who don't understand the roles they are charged to carry out.[60]

Although CDS activists recognize the adverse impact that the war and the United States economic blockade have on supplies, they blame state agencies for aggravating the shortage problem. Defining the neighborhood organizations' relationship to the Ministry of Internal Commerce, one regional CDS official bluntly proclaimed: "We maintain a belligerent attitude toward MICOIN. We have to pressure them to send products to retail outlets. For example, if cooking oil doesn't arrive we pressure them for more oil."[61]

Mass organizations have continued to combat bureaucratic shortcomings and negligence. In his major speech of April 1980, Carlos Nuñez encouraged the popular associations to be militant when confronted with governmental inaction.

> The mass organizations should gather and make as their own the demands of the masses, of their social sectors, and struggle for their materialization through all the new mechanisms that the Revolution has instituted. But when these channels are closed, when they knock and nobody answers, whether it be because of bureaucracy, whether it be because of liberal methods, whether it be because the problems of the masses are not taken into account, etc., our organizations must move on to other forms of political persuasion.[62]

In many cases, bureaucratic foul-ups and red tape have delayed or prevented the delivery of promised material assistance. The UNAG, for example, must frequently pressure the agrarian reform agency to deliver tractors, seeds, fertilizers, and other materials needed to maintain production on agricultural cooperatives. At the UNAG National Assembly in February 1984, union leaders denounced government mismanagement of programs affecting the small and medium peasantry.[63]

The popular associations and the state have attempted to cut red tape by reordering their respective structures. In July 1982, the state began to decentralize its authority by placing ministerial delegates in the country's various regions and zones.[64] At the same time, the mass organizations began to alter their intermediate bodies—previously established at the municipal and departmental levels—in order to correspond to the new zonal and regional divisions of the country. The restructuring provides a direct link between mass organization leaders and government representatives at each level of the state's administrative hierarchy. For example, if a CDS zonal executive committee needs to discuss its members' housing problems, the committee will arrange a meeting with its counterpart, a zonal delegate from the Ministry of Housing. Both the zonal CDS representatives and the ministry's delegate may have to appeal to higher levels of their respective organizations. But the coordination of structures reduces or eliminates intermediaries between the popular associations and the state bodies, thereby facilitating the implementation of revolutionary projects.

On the local level, close coordination between the state and the mass organizations is crucial to the successful operation of government programs. In the zone of Estelí, for example, the Ministry of Social Security and Social Welfare (INSSBI) administers two programs that depend entirely on popular association support. Relying on CDS, AMNLAE, and

ATC members to identify families with the greatest need, INSSBI delivers basic food packages to unemployed people and the aged. Arquimides Colindus, a regional delegate of INSSBI, stresses the indispensable role that the grassroots organizations play in this program:

> We can only direct our aid through the mass organizations. We make sure to give the food packages to those people who most need them. In urban areas we work with the CDS and AMNLAE. In rural areas we work through the ATC. These people from the mass organizations interview people to determine who needs clothes, food, etc. The mass organizations are our strong aids in this work.[65]

INSSBI also works with the mass organizations in a program designed to protect children who are abandoned, mistreated, or overworked. Again, through information gathered by CDS and AMNLAE activists, the Ministry discovers which children need assistance. If children fail to attend school, INSSBI communicates with their families and attempts to convince them to foster their children's education. They also encourage parents to allow their children to attend comedores infantiles, children's cafeterias, established to help feed children and to provide basic instruction. Volunteers from the Sandinista Youth, AMNLAE, and the CDSs assist paid employees in these cafeterias.[66]

In these two programs, the popular associations and the state enjoy amicable relations. But sometimes a government ministry arouses the ire of mass organization officials by failing to assist their constituents. In August 1984, a zonal ATC secretary reported that the Ministry of Labor (MITRAB) ignored a worker's grievance against a private landowner:

> A man who had worked for eight years for a private farmer registered a complaint with MITRAB. The owner recently sold his farm without paying the worker his last two months' salary and without advance notice of the sale. In this case he was entitled to one month of vacation and one month of bonus pay. MITRAB never helped this worker. He then came to us and explained his situation. We called in the owner and proved to him that he was violating the Labor Code and could be prosecuted by MITRAB. This pressure worked: the worker received all his back pay, another month's pay in lieu of a vacation, and his bonus pay.[67]

The same union official states that MITRAB and the ATC cooperate effectively in most aspects of their relationship. For example, the two organizations cooperate in negotiating and monitoring union contracts. Whenever rural workers formulate a contract proposal, they submit it to the Ministry. MITRAB officials act as facilitators between workers and management during all contract negotiations. After the contract is signed, an ATC leader, two rank-and-file workers, and one administrator form a bipartisan commission to handle any contract disputes that may occur. If the commission fails to resolve a disagreement, MITRAB intervenes to mediate the dispute.[68]

Occasionally, inexperience or lack of assertiveness force the mass organizations into a subordinate role in relation to state ministries where they cannot participate equally in administering revolutionary programs. Through internal evaluation, the popular associations attempt to overcome the obstacles that inhibit the development of their administrative capacities. In March 1984, for example, the grassroots organizations assessed their participation in health administration during the first National Congress of the Popular Health Councils. At the close of the Congress, they published their evaluation in a report entitled, "The Participation of the Popular Organizations in Health Administration." After briefly affirming the extensive participation of mass organization members in the Popular Health Campaigns, the pamphlet targets three aspects of the relationship with the health councils in need of improvement:

1. Our limited experience and ignorance concerning the role of the masses in the state . . . and of the state in coordination with the masses caused us to play a supportive role to MINSA in the first stage of the Councils' work. This is reflected most seriously at the departmental level where the Council has been converted in many cases into a mere instrument of MINSA.

2. We face the necessity of improving coordination with those Ministries that promote health programs in order to avoid the duplication and dispersion of resources.

3. Here it is necessary to point out our lack of belligerency. MINSA was the real force behind the Departmental and Municipal Councils, giving them and the tasks they promote an institutional character; this did nothing to develop the administrative capacity of the masses. This also requires analysis and discussions, and the mass organizations must decide that they will influence their representatives to make adjustments in their work on the Councils.[69]

The mass organizations' representatives also acknowledged their limited ability to influence the planning and evaluation of health programs, noting that the principal emphasis of grassroots participation has been the execution of policies, most of which originated in the Ministry of Health. "We still haven't attained sufficient belligerency that would permit us to switch from being executors of MINSA programs to being genuine managers."[70]

The health activists called on the rank and file in each barrio, hospital, and health center to discuss health problems and then propose solutions that would involve the cooperation of local communities and health workers. Congress participants insisted that Health Ministry personnel listen to the suggestions of the mass organizations, and recognize that such associations are not simply the "propelling force of programs, but rather the transforming force of the society."[71]

That Ministry of Health officials do not yet acknowledge the transformative role of the mass organizations reflects a reality that Argentinian political scientist Luis Serra exposed in 1982: "Some state agencies and administrators tended to view the mass organizations as simple appendages of the government, as instruments for their plans or 'fire extinguishers' for problems they themselves had created."[72] A number of government officials believe that the mass organizations are necessary insofar as they execute state-planned health and education campaigns, but are a nuisance when they take on the genuine functions of government. Popular association activists frequently denounce this elitist attitude, and FSLN leaders echo their position. "In Nicaragua," Agustín Lara stresses, "the problems of defense and production, of education, health, and housing, are gigantic tasks. These problems can only be resolved by a combination of forces, the state and the masses."[73]

The relationship between the mass organizations and the state contains a fundamental tension. On the one hand, the grassroots organizations help the government design and execute revolutionary policy; on the other hand, they monitor the state to ensure that it responds to popular needs and grievances. The latter task is difficult because the revolutionary state is plagued by numerous problems: the scarcity of material resources, inadequate technical and fiscal capacities, poorly trained administrative personnel, and bureaucratic red tape. Confronted with these obstacles, the popular associations must heed the words of Carlos Nuñez: "The mass organizations, acting in the framework of the general line of the revolution, must have sufficient right to resort . . . to private criticism, utilization of all the communications media, and even mobilizations to demand the measures necessary to guarantee that their concerns are heard."[74]

To be sure, the mass organizations alone will not eliminate the deficiencies of the revolutionary state. But their members are determined, and will therefore continue to pursue their role as watchdog of the Nicaraguan state.

7

COMMUNITY DEVELOPMENT: CDSs

On an unseasonably cool and rainy evening in Managua, a group of people gather under a makeshift streetlight in a poor barrio. Dragging chairs from their homes, the group of mostly women forms a semicircle and begins to take their seats. Children settle near or on their parents' laps, dogs run about, fighting and barking, and a young man steps into the light. Calling the group to attention, he leads them in the singing of the national anthem. As the last notes die, people shout slogans in call-and-response form. The young man announces that the meeting will be dedicated to the most recent victims of the counterrevolutionary attacks. These preliminaries over, the business of the meeting begins.

This scene, a neighborhood block meeting to discuss the business of daily life, is repeated weekly in barrios and rural districts throughout Nicaragua: the meeting of a Sandinista Defense Committee. With some 600,000 members—40 percent of the adult population—the Sandinista Defense Committees (CDSs) constitute Nicaragua's largest and most powerful mass organization, which is also its most controversial. Critics from the conservative opposition charge that the CDSs act as an arm of the FSLN, imposing ideological conformity on the masses and intimidating Sandinista opponents. Among the general population, people complain about block coordinators who abuse their power by withholding the letters of recommendation and ration cards of those against whom the coordinators hold political or personal grudges. And in the United States, the CDS is commonly represented as the best example of the totalitarian drift of the revolution.[1]

It is not surprising that controversy focuses on the CDS. Since the Somoza dynasty fell in 1979, the CDS has played a powerful and complex role in shaping the revolution. As a mass organization that excercises certain types of authority ordinarily reserved for government agencies, and which also has strong ties to the FSLN, the CDS is a natural target for people upset about everything from the price of cooking oil to the essential premises of the revolution. Moreover, the size and diversity of its membership, as well as the breadth of its responsibilities, sometimes leads to inconsistency between offical policy and local practice. But the main controversy stems from the role that the CDS plays in politicizing and mobilizing a population which had been kept silent for decades but which is now exercizing its collective strength.

MEMBERSHIP AND STRUCTURE

Unlike the other popular associations, the CDSs are not tied to any particular social sector. Everyone—young and old, men and women, party members and nonmembers, capitalists and workers, Catholics, Protestants, and atheists—can participate in a CDS. Consequently, all the societal contradictions and problems crop up in the neighborhood committees: class distinctions, educational differences, unequal partic- ipation in the insurrection, conflicts between generations, and distinct points of view on the concrete problems that Nicaragua faces. Heter- ogenous in composition, the CDSs are in a constant state of transfor- mation.[2]

The CDSs have altered their organizational structure a number of times since 1979. Currently, the organization is divided into five levels: by block, barrio or rural district, zone, region, and nation. On each level, members choose their leaders by vote. Each block committee elects a representative to the barrio commitee, *Comite de Barrio Sandinista* (San- dinista Barrio Committee—CBS), the barrio committee elects one or two representatives to the zonal committee, and so on. CDS leaders are subject to immediate recall, but their terms of office are not fixed. Leaders at each CDS level are responsible for disseminating information, handling complaints, and taking suggestions from the local to the national level, and vice versa.

SOCIAL DEFENSE OF THE REVOLUTION

As Chapter 4 demonstrated, the CDSs perform a wide variety of tasks. But the power of the neighborhood committees lies in their ability to carry out what Nicaraguans call the social defense of the revolution which encompasses a broad range of CDS tasks: carrying out "revolutionary vigilance," aiding the Popular Health Campaigns, participating in the adult education program, and trying to solve housing problems.

Revolutionary Vigilance

The principal objective of revolutionary vigilance (*vigilancia revolucionaria*) is to prevent all activities that harm the revolution. The CDS national office describes harmful activities as follows: "1. Activities carried out by enemies of our people who are directly tied to the counterrevolution. 2. Activities derived from isolated or organized delinquency, drug addiction, prostitution."[3]

CDS Secretaries of Social Defense recruit volunteers to participate in revolutionary vigilance as members of civilian patrols that guard the neighborhoods. These patrols take two forms: *vigilancia rotativa* or *rondin*, the walking patrol, and *viligancia ocular*, in which residents keep lights on in their houses to watch for unusual activity outside. Often those engaged at *vigilancia ocular* furnish coffee and conversation to those whose turn it is to walk the neighborhood's streets.[4] In urban areas that have been unaffected by armed counter-revolutionary activity, volunteers carry out their guard duty between the hours of 11.00 P.M. and 3:00 A.M. In regions where the contras operate, civilans are often armed as they carry out walking patrols, and revolutionary vigilance may take place as much as twenty-four hours a day.

The American media often reports that revolutionary vigilance is an obligatory task. Despite the fact that social pressure to participate in defense is strong, the task remains voluntary. Even people who sign up to volunteer for night watch duty and then fail to perform it are merely asked why they didn't show up, no sanctions are taken against them. Rebecca Gordon, a United States citizen who carried out a peace vigil in northern Nicaragua in 1984, relates a typical story concerning the night watch.

> Panchita is the *responsable*—the person responsible—for organizing *vigilancia* in her barrio in Jalapa. One day I ran into her as she was consulting a piece of paper. "This is a list of the people who signed up for *vigilancia* but didn't show this week. I'm going to visit them," she said. Ah-ha, I thought. Coercion in action. I asked her what would happen to these missing patrollers. She looked at me, confused and little irritated. "Happens to them? I'm going to talk to them, that's all. Tell them that *hay que ponerse las pilas*—they'd better put their batteries in!" That day in June 1984, 15,000 U.S. and Honduran troops were engaged in the Big Pine military exercises less than six miles away

in Honduras. All Jalapa had been awake for 48 hours, expecting attack at any moment. Even in these extreme circumstances, moral suasion was the extent of Panchita's tools in dealing with her remiss *compañeros*.[5]

To ensure the effective functioning of revolutionary vigilance, the CDSs collaborate closely with the Sandinista Police and State Security. Because CDS activists who carry out the night watch sometimes make "citizen's arrests" of people engaged in criminal activities, the police's cooperation depends heavily on the effective and legitimate functioning of revolutionary vigilance. Yet CDS members frequently complain that the Sandinista Police are not always quick to aid citizens carrying out their night watch duties. On April 14, 1982, *Barricada* reported on a meeting in which CDS activists denounced police officers who failed to work properly with revolutionary vigilance authorities. Some members of the police, according to CDS officials, behaved in an authoritarian manner with the revolutionary guards. Speaking at a ceremony celebrating the fifth anniversary of the Ministry of the Interior, Tomás Borge acknowledged the strains between the CDSs and the Sandinista Police and State Security.

> Here I have a communication from Leticia Herrerra, the national coordinator of the CDS. It says there is still a lack of coordination with and support for the CDSs on the part of the Sandinista Police and State Security. The CDSs point out that on occasion, when carrying out their assigned tasks the Sandinista Police do not give proper treatment to those arrested and to the people in general. The CDSs also believe that at times we place little importance— or do not give an adequate response to—the information and reports that come from the people's organizations.[6]

In addition to performing revolutionary vigilance, the CDSs assist the Sandinista Police through a Volunteer Police program. In December 1984, 10,000 voluntary police were patrolling urban and rural neighborhoods, thereby freeing the regular police to carry out other duties.[7] Both the revolutionary vigilance and the Volunteer Police program have had salutary effects on Nicaragua's crime rate as well as the rate of solved crimes. In 1983 Nicaragua's crime rate was cut to half of the 1982 rate,[8] and in the same year 6,000 out of the 8,400 crimes committed were solved.[9] But the decrease in crime is also the result of the reorganization of Nicaraguan society, of the emergence of a new, collective morality, a morality vigorously promoted by the country's neighborhood associations.

Health Care

The CDSs contribute to health care primarily by aiding the Popular Health Campaigns described in Chapter 4. Since 1983, the Ministry of Health and the mass organizations have restructured the health campaigns in order to promote permanent, ongoing health care. *Brigadistas* are still volunteers, but receive more extensive training in maternal-child health, occupational health, first-aid, and general health assistance. There are now 25,000 of these permanent *brigadistas*, comprising about 1 percent of the total population.[10]

CDS secretaries of community development recruit volunteers to work in health campaigns. The Ministry of Health trains these volunteers in basic health care, offering workshops at the regional, zonal, and neighborhood levels. The workshops are also based on the "multiplier" principle: ten to fifteen instructors each train ten to twelve others who in turn train additional *brigadistas* until there are tens of thousands of people prepared to carry out the upcoming campaign.

In the workshops, *brigadistas* learn how to administer vaccinations, build latrines, and prevent diseases. They also learn first aid skills and how to treat common diseases such as malaria, diarrhea, and parasitic infections. Workshop coordinators encourage the *brigadistas* to discuss the problems facing their communities, to analyze the economic and social roots of the health problems, and to look for solutions in which the community can participate.[11] The workshops emphasize the student mode in health campaign participation: "The teaching methods used encourage creativity and initiative as well as develop organizational and teaching skills. In fact, small groups of brigadistas often study different subjects and then teach each other what they have learned, using theater, demonstrations, puppets, stories, and poems."[12]

Once trained, the health *brigadistas* work with the health secretaries on their CDS. The health secretary is responsible for coordinating the health tasks in his/her area. The secretary usually relies on three or four *brigadistas* and other volunteers to help carry out these tasks. A major part of their effort is devoted to environmental health matters such as eliminating standing water, removing trash, and maintaining an adequate sewage system.

But neighborhood health activists confront serious difficulties in their work. Above all, the *brigadistas* lack sufficient medical resources. Each *brigadista*, after completing his or her basic training, should to receive a first aid kit and be supplied periodically with eight basic medicines. But due to the overall shortage of medicines in Nicaragua, this goal has not been realized. Because many communities lack the resources to construct drainage or sewage systems, health activists' efforts to maintain adequate neighborhood sanitation facilities are limited. During the rainy season both pigs and children wade through the same street puddles. Moreover, without sufficient sources of clean water health problems are compounded. Finally, CDS health secretaries have trouble maintaining an adequate number of health *brigadistas* in each community because many *brigadistas* move on to school work or other revolutionary commitments.[13]

The CDS also plays a major role in national health planning through its participation in the Popular Health Councils. These councils serve to guarantee popular participation in both the planning and execution of national health programs. According to the 1984 publication authored by the National Public Health Council, "The Participation of the Popular Organizations in Health Administration," the CDSs have had the highest level of participation in the work of the Popular Health Campaigns: "The two popular organizations that have contributed fundamentally to the organization and planning of all the Popular Health Campaign mobilizations have been the CDS and AMNLAE. In many municipalities . . . the CDS determines the success of the Popular Health Campaigns."[14] This paper also praises CDS health secretaries for their success in bolstering the level of health training and experience among CDS activists.[15]

CDS participation in health prevention and education activities has contributed to the rapid improvement in the population's health status since 1979. By 1983, infant mortality dropped from 120 to 140 per 1,000 live births to 80.2 per 1000 live births, and life expectancy at birth rose from 52 to 59 years. No polio has been reported since 1982, malaria has decreased by 50 percent, and most other immunization-preventable diseases have been reduced considerably. Diarrhea, previously the leading killer of infants, has fallen from the first to fourth cause of hospital infant death.[16]

Popular Basic Education for Adults

The CDSs' fundamental role in education is to assist the Popular Basic Education for Adults (BPEA), the followup program to the National Literacy Crusade. To counter the danger that new learners will lose their skills through lack of practice, literacy *brigadistas* set up *Collectivos de Educación Popular* (Popular Education Collectives—CEPs) at the end of the crusade. A local coordinator heads each CEP and a promoter oversees the activities of 3 or 4 CEPs in an area.[17] The BPEA consists of six levels and an introductory course for people untouched by the literacy campaign. Students must take an examination before they can pass to the next level in the program; they are also tested each semester in order to judge their progress.[18]

The BPEA has adopted many of the techniques that evolved during the literacy crusade, including the central production of basic materials, the "multiplier" training program, and weekly local workshops for co-ordinators. In areas where professionals, students, or full-time teachers are available to coordinate CEPs, they tend to adopt the traditional role of teacher. But in the vast majority of cases, particularly in the country-side, coordinators tend to be either peasants who took part in the literacy crusade or teenagers who are receiving primary education. In these cases, the peasants are educating themselves collectively with one member of the group coordinating and administering the classes. The coordinator receives support from the promoters who in turn can request assistance from BPEA representatives.[19]

Because CEPs are formed in workplaces throughout the country, the CEPs in the barrios are for younger people, the unemployed, and adults who work alone, such as street vendors and maids. The CDS secretaries of propaganda and political education handle the logistics for the CEPs: they recruit the volunteer teachers, locate places to study (usually private homes), and ensure that the Ministry of Education provides sufficient educational material for all the classes. Most important, the CDS sec-retaries must motivate both teachers and students to maintain their com-mitment to adult education.[20]

The task of motivating CEP participants falls largely on CDS leaders.[21] Nicaragua's situation at present, especially in border areas, is not con-ducive to adult education attendance. Campesinos who participate in the CEPs have often been targeted by the counterrevolutionaries. Since 1982, the contras have murdered dozens of adult education teachers and their technical assistants. Others have been kidnapped and forced to promise they will no longer engage in "politics." Such terror has been effective in many areas. Either out of fear or inability to study due to the lack of materials, more than half of the pupils in border zones have stopped attending classes.

In areas farther from the border, some Protestant religious sects try to discouraged people from participating in the adult education program. Using confusing and discouraging arguments, e.g., "the end of the world is near and war will come as God's punishment," such sects impede all efforts at cultural improvement. Why go on studying, producing, and defending the country if everything is soon going to come to an end? Despite the intimidation of the contras and the religious sects, however, thousands of rural dwellers continue to study. They realize that they can transform their lives and they make the effort, day after day, to do just that.

In the urban barrios, too, students must exert a great deal of energy to attend the daily CEP classes. Many of them work all day, others are married women taking care of a home and numerous children, and still others are single mothers overwhelmed with the problems of family survival. Often a person will begin a semester and then quit because of one problem or another: the illness of a child, difficulties at work, or simple fatigue. Constant military mobilizations also discourage many from continuing their studies in the CEPS; after returning to the city after two or three months in the field, many pupils abandon their classes because they find it impossible to make up the lessons they have missed.

Nevertheless, in certain respects, the incentives to go on studying are greater in the city than in the countryside. In the city, the ability to read and write increases the possibility of finding work or a better-paying job. Literacy allows one to read the newspapers, which circulate more in urban areas. This desire for personal advancement doubtlessly motivates many students in the adult education classes. But the CDS adult education coordinators have worked hard to develop among CEP students a collective desire to understand their education as an instrument for changing their environment and contributing to the goals of the revolution.

In addition to teaching the usual primary education skills, the BPEA has the same aims as the literacy crusade: to teach basic Nicaraguan history, fundamental economic matters, the problems of reconstruction, and an understanding of the alternative strategies for creating a new society. Just as the literacy campaign provided regular workshops for the *brigadistas*, so the adult education program guarantees the continuation of coordinator training through weekly or fortnightly workshops. Promoters, who oversee all the coordinators in a given neighborhood or rural district, support and orient the coordinators. Although the teachers receive training in pedagogy, such training does not compensate fully for their low level of basic education, and the inadequacy of the teachers' education has curtailed the program's effectiveness. For example, the program's planners originally believed that by completing four years of adult education, students would have the equivalent of six years of traditional primary schooling. But by the end of 1982 these objectives had not been reached, and planners added a fifth and later a sixth level to the program. Because teachers' limitations can have a negative effect on the students, the program now strives to improve the teachers' training by raising their basic educational level.

CDSs and Housing

Housing conditions in Nicaragua have always been poor. According to a 1963 national housing census, the country had a housing deficit of 181,700 units, and the government estimated that demographic growth alone would increase the deficit by an average of 10,000 units per year for the next ten years. In its report on the 1971 census, the Nicaraguan Demographic Association outlined the following housing conditions: 61 percent of the residences surveyed had dirt floors; 36 percent lacked access to potable water; 59 percent had no electricity; 46 percent had no sanitary facilities; 68 percent had only one or two rooms; and, in 23 percent, five or more persons lived in a single room.[22]

The 1972 Managua earthquake increased the housing deficit by some 40,000 units. Neither the public nor the private sector could meet the rising demand for housing; consequently, low-income residents constructed more than 50,000 makeshift shelters in the years immediately following the earthquake. "This activity," writes housing expert Harvey Williams,

> did little to reduce the calculated housing deficit, while other factors made the situation worse. Following the 1979 triumph, the new Ministry of Housing and Human Settlements (MINVAH) reported that 4,149 houses in urban centers were damaged severely or destroyed in the prolonged Popular War; and heavy flooding in the northeast coastal area left 30,000 persons homeless in late 1979. Thus the Government of National Reconstruction and MINVAH faced an extremely serious housing situation during the first year.[23]

Following Somoza's defeat in mid-1979, the Government of National Reconstruction announced its Program of Economic Reactivation in Benefit of the People. The program defined the following as major goals for the Ministry of Housing (MINVAH):

> a. Initiation of a territorial ordering of human settlements with the goal of reinforcing production, improving the life condition of the population centers of the interior of the country.
> b. Planning and massive construction of popular housing in the city of Managua in order to attend in part to the deficit inherited from the Somoza dictatorship.
> c. To impel an *Urban Reform* that permits the distribution of the benefits of urbanization to all social sectors.[24]

To implement these policies, the Ministry of Housing relied on the participation of CDS activists. The new policies required communities to channel all requests for improvement through the CDSs, and the CDSs were responsible for including all residents in the planning and installation of such improvements. Because improvement funds came from land payments to MINVAH, the CDSs took charge of encouraging prompt and regular payments.[25]

In late September 1983, the CDS signed an agreement with MINVAH to coordinate responses to the population's housing needs. The agreement created the Regional Committees for the Assignment of Lots and Basic Modules. These regional committees seek to "optimize the effective application of the criteria used to set priorities in the assignment of lots and the distribution of the assigned quota of basic modules and building materials in each region."[26] Each committee consists of the regional delegate to MINVAH, a CDS regional representative, a CST regional representative, a FSLN regional representative, and a regional government representative.

The committees have three basic duties: 1. distributing basic modules within municipalities, barrios, and rural districts in every region of the country; 2. distributing housing lots to various groups based on MINVAH-designed plans; and 3. making decisions concerning special cases that the various member organizations raise with the committee. In all cases of land and housing distribution, the committee must take into account the people and groups with the most pressing needs.[27]

In early 1983, CDSs throughout Nicaragua began a mass discussion and debate over a MINVAH-sponsored housing law.[28] By far the revolution's most radical urban reform yet, the legislation will gradually do away with landlords and rents, but its fundamental aim was to find immediate solutions to the country's housing crisis. In 1981, the housing deficit stood at 240,000 units, and the shortage has been growing by 17,000 units annually. Moreover, in response to earlier urban reform measures, some private interests neglected their properties or even destroyed them, thereby aggravating the housing deficit. Less comprehensive reforms preceding the housing law had already reduced rents by 50 percent, imposed strict rent controls, and suspended all tenant evictions. The Sandinista government constructed more than 12,000 houses during the first five years of the revolution; distributed 25,000 urban lots along with incentives for families to build their own houses; and delivered 21,000 titles to families occupying homes confiscated from fleeing Somocistas and exposed counterrevolutionaries.

Defining housing as a human right and not a commodity, the 1983 law ruled that all dwellings not inhabited by their owners and their immediate family would be expropriated. The former tenants became the owners of these homes, and the government converted rents into 20-year mortgages held by the Ministry of Housing. Tenants who had already paid more than 20 years of rent received titles automatically, and tenants who had rented for less than 20 years had their payments converted into equity. With more than 30 percent of Nicaragua's population paying rent, at least 50,000 families benefitted immediately from the law.

The new law did not mean dispossession. A dwelling's previous landlord receives government compensation, although monthly payments may not exceed $100. The new homeowners have the right to live in the houses as long as they choose, but may not sell them, nor can they pass the houses on directly through inheritance. All real estate transactions now require the approval of MINVAH. Consequently, real estate speculation has ended in Nicaragua.

Before the government presented the law to the Council of State, CDSs in all the major cities organized neighborhood assemblies to promote mass discussion and debate on its provisions. The country's newspapers published the complete text of the law. The Council of State received the final proposal only after public input substantially altered the law. Some CDS members argued that although the law would weaken the power of the big landlords, it could also indiscriminately affect poor and working-class families who rent a wing of their homes or own some extra small property to augment their modest incomes. Others felt that inheritance restrictions might hurt poor families. The government took these criticisms into account and added special clauses and exceptions to avoid adverse effects among the popular classes.

During the debate over the housing proposal, Sandinista leaders acknowledged that the law was not a definitive solution to the housing problem, but rather as one short- and medium-term measure among many that the revolutionary government was taking to relieve those social groups with the fewest economic resources. The housing law has radically transformed urban property relations, rationalizing and maximizing the use of existing housing. It is not a substitute, however, for housing construction.

The CDSs participate in the law's administration through regional committees that deal with problems between landlords and renters. Created in February 1984, these Regional Committees on Housing Affairs are comprised of a president, usually the regional delegate to MINVAH, and two CDS members. Granted powers similar to tribunals, their mandate is to equitably resolve rental problems. At the time of their creation, Perfect Arroliga, CDS delegate to the Council of State, said: "The committees will not only view problems from a legal and administrative viewpoint, but will also focus on them from the angle of popular consciousness. Therefore, the moral credibility of the members of the committees is indispensable."[29] To carry out their housing duties effectively, CDS committee members receive training seminars, organized by MIN-VAH, that explain all aspects of the housing law.[30]

CDSs AND THE SUPPLY PROBLEM

The shortage of food and other basic consumer products is one of the gravest problems facing the Nicaraguan revolution. The major causes for food shortages are a legacy from the days of Somoza.[31] During Somoza's four decades of dictatorship, Nicaragua's development strategy represented a "repressive agro-export model." Since 1950, the country had experienced rates of economic growth that were among the most rapid in Latin America, especially during the period between 1950 and 1970. This growth, however, was based on expansion of export crops: coffee, cotton, sugarcane, and beef cattle. Rapid rates in the growth of the growth domestic product and of exports, however, were not accompanied by the development of a food system meeting the basic needs of the entire population.

Between 1960 and 1976, the production of exportable goods made great strides: coffee production increased by 148 percent, sugarcane by 249 percent, cotton by 282 percent, and beef by 268 percent. During the same period, however, the production of common products such as maize, beans, and sorghum increased by only 60 percent and the average yield of these staple foods showed practically no increase during the 1960s and 1970s. Malnutrition and seasonal hunger were widespread. Restrictions on land access, together with a grossly imbalanced distribution of agricultural income and the country's extremely limited industrial capacity, kept most of the population's effective demand for food at minimal levels. The country's infrastructure—physical, institutional, and social—was also geared to the requirements of the dominant agro-export system. At the same time, the collection, transportion, and distribution of basic foods were in the hands of middlemen who, at each level, tried to maximize their personal profits.

After the fall of Somoza, new problems arose that aggravated the shortage of food and other necessities. In 1981 and 1982, the government spent scarce foreign exchange to import more corn, beans, and small amounts of other foods, because price incentives had failed to spur production enough to meet increasing consumption levels. Disease as well as transport, storage, and marketing problems also plagued the production of basic foods. Moreover, the government-organized popular distribution system was still inadequate to assure stable low-cost access to food for all low-income groups.

The war against the counterrevolution has increasingly complicated the supply problems. Because the Ministry of Defense requires the use of other ministries' vehicles for moving troops and war material (due to its own vehicle shortages), the war has had a negative impact on the transportation sector. The concomitant decrease in the existing supply of private vehicles and a drop in the number of imported small trucks and spare parts has taken its toll on commerce. For example, approximately 2000 small merchants from the area of La Concha, in the department of Masaya, travel to Managua every day. At one time, fifteen buses and 100 small trucks served the region; in 1984 there were two to five buses and fifty small trucks. The situation is similar in the entire metropolitan area of Managua and throughout the country. The results have been a sharp increase in transportation prices, a decrease in the amount of provisions available in urban areas, and a rise in consumer prices.

In fact, since 1984, inflation has become the single most significant factor in Nicaragua's uncertain economic situation. In that year, prices of the twenty-three most basic consumer products rose sharply, crippling the buying power of the majority of the population. An increase in the blackmarket sale of products also occurred in 1984. Inflation in the less essential products rose as well, harming the interests of both merchants and producers of basic goods. In addition, intermediaries are able to manipulate the situation of shortages in a wide range of consumer items and thereby realize tremendous profits, and smugglers engage in contraband trade with Honduras and Costa Rica.

Confronted with these realities, in 1984 the Nicaraguan government launched a major campaign against speculation, a phenomenon that had been undermining the productive capability of the country. The Council of State passed an antispeculation law, ruling that eight basic products would be distributed solely through guaranteed channels. The government turned over major responsibility for enforcing this law to the CDS.

It was natural that the CDS play a central role in the establishment of a more efficient and equitable distribution of food and other basic goods. As the largest mass organization with extensive experience in organizing the distribution of basic necessities, the CDS was in a position to help achieve food security and a sufficient supply of basic consumer items at a time of economic crisis. Indeed, the CDSs had participated in the supply problem ever since the victory over Somoza, principally in four areas: investigative activities, policy planning, policy implementation, and political/organizational tasks.

The CDSs perform the important task of informing the population about all aspects of the supply problem. CDS members are educated about the basic causes of the shortages: the operations of hoarders and speculators, the United States trade embargo, the rise in consumer demand, the lack of foreign exchange, and the problems of institutional coordination and planning. Once they are educated, CDS members work with their leadership to address the effects of the supply problem in their own neighborhoods.

The CDSs also address the psychological and organizational aspects of the supply problem. An excerpt from *Barricada* capsulizes the supply "psychosis" that the CDSs must often confront: "The work of the CDS involves confronting the psychosis concerning supply shortages that affects many consumers. Under these conditions rumors abound . . . concerning an alleged shortage. Merchants and consumers then respond, in an incredibly rapid way, by hoarding and speculating, closing the vicious circle by creating genuine shortages."[32] Through their direct relations with retail traders, especially those in the markets, CDS officials carry out intensive political work: they organize these sectors by incorporating them in the barrio committees and regulating their activities. Such organizational efforts have partially controlled the supply psychosis.

At the end of 1981, the CDSs' role in the supply situation took a qualitative leap when they helped establish a national sugar distribution system. The CDS conducted censuses in the barrios and rural districts to determine the needs of 300,833 families—two-thirds of the national population. The neighborhood committees selected more than 11,000 sugar distribution posts throughout the country and organized a system of distribution cards used by the people to obtain sugar.

CDS involvement in sugar distribution led to the formation of Popular Supply Committees. These committees, which also include ENABAS and MICOIN representatives, evaluate local distribution systems and determine consumption requirements at area distribution centers. They then study the distribution system and make recommendations to overcome deficiencies.

The CDSs can intervene directly in the distribution system through their price control activities. Each CDS chooses a secretary of "economic defense" who checks the prices of goods sold in the distribution centers within his/her territory. This secretary also monitors food distribution to avoid hoarding or favoritism. To assist the CDS secretaries of economic defense, the neighborhood committees maintain a network of "popular inspectors," who are CDS volunteers that inspect local commercial activities. By mid-1986, there were more than 15,000 people working at this task.[33] Finally, the CDSs participate directly in the selection of people who administer *expendios populares* (people's stores). And a CDS authorization is necessary to gain a permit from MICOIN to operate a *tienda popular* (a large, retail store).

In May 1984, as the economic situation worsened and complaints concerning speculation and hoarding became more frequent, the government sought to extend, clarify, and institutionalize its distribution policies. After consulting with CDS national representatives, the government introduced a Consumer Protection Law in the Council of State. At the same time, MICOIN and the CDSs embarked on a massive educational campaign that included pamphlets, house-to-house canvassing, cartoons in the newspapers, and a series of CDS meetings. The campaign attempted to explain the causes of shortages and to prepare people for the new measures.

In July 1984, the Council of State passed the Consumer Protection Law. The law allows MICOIN to fix prices on all goods regarded as "necessary or indispensable for the population." Article 2 of the law requires that the official list of prices published by MICOIN must be posted in a visible place at all retail outlets. Article 3 forbids retailers from selling one product to a consumer only on the condition that the consumer buy a second product. Article 4 restricts the sale of certain basic products to retail outlets designated by MICOIN. In addition, the law strictly regulates the transport of all necessary goods. Penalties for violating the laws' stipulations include stiff fines and cancellation of commercial licenses.[34]

The Consumer Protection Law incorporates fifteen additional "sensitive" products into the nationalized distribution system. These items are either imported or depend on import supplies. Consequently, they are subject to sporadic production and supply patterns as well as weekly fluctuations in rate charged against foreign exchange. The fifteen items include eggs, chickens, light bulbs, batteries, kitchen matches, toilet paper, toothpaste, razor blades, deodorant, powdered milk, detergent, and contraceptives.[35]

The government gave the CDSs responsibility for selecting those neighborhood store owners most likely to cooperate with the new system. The neighborhood committees studied the store owners' past histories with the people in the communities: whether they had speculated in times of scarcity, showed favoritism to certain patrons, been fair about short-terms loans and advances, and other considerations. From a pool of 180,000 retail merchants, the CDSs chose some 6,000 store owners and designated their shops "people's stores." These outlets have special agreements with MICOIN to sell designated product amounts at fixed prices, and to respect the consumer card system. At the same time, the government promised to supply the retailers with necessary quantities of basic items. The owners may conduct the rest of their business as usual.[36]

The law was favorably received by a population fed up with opportunistic retailers and shortages caused by hoarding. Interviews with consumers and retailers during the first weeks after the passage of the law reveal that most people were depending on the CDS to enforce the law. According to Roger Sanchez, the regional delegate of MICOIN in Region II, "The efficiency in the application of the law can only be guaranteed if the organized people within the CDS involve themselves more and more in the enforcement of its articles."[37]

By early August 1984, the CDSs had mobilized their members to perform those tasks that would be necessary to guarantee the provisions of the law. For example, in Region V (Boaco, Chontales, and Central Zelaya), all the CDSs held base assemblies to instruct their activists on how best to end the activities of hoarders and speculators. The popular inspectors attended workshops on the law that prepared them for enforcement duties in collaboration with MICOIN and the Sandinista Police. "Our objective," declared Jaime Espinoza, CDS Regional Secretary, "is to convert ourselves into effective collaborators of the institutions in charge of applying the law."[38]

To be sure, problems continued even after the enactment of the law. In one Managua barrio, residents complained about a retailer in a popular store who refused to sell chickens to the inhabitants of one sector of the barrio, and criticized the zonal CDS office for failing to attend to this problem.[39] Shortages and delayed deliveries continued as well. Meanwhile, the CDSs were always available to provide explanations for of these problems, as one Managua retailer commented: "We continue to have problems: last week eggs and chickens failed to arrive. When such products aren't available I don't have to give explanations because the CDS activists explain the case beforehand."[40]

In July 1984, MICOIN published a comprehensive 24-page newspaper-size pamphlet called "The ABCs of Supply." The section on the "consolidation of popular participation in the organization of supply" calls on the CDSs to carry out the following three tasks:

1. Organize the territorial registration of the population so that every family is registered in an *expendio* or other type of secure channel. It is proposed that each *expendio* will have

the responsibility to attend to the needs of 500 to 1000 people.

2. Increase the number of popular inspectors to watch over official prices, hoarding, and other problems that arise in distribution.

3. Participate in the extension of the system of secured channels [of distribution], selecting people to run the *expendios*, evaluating their honesty and political trustworthiness, and organizing them into associations.[41]

In 1985 and 1986 the CDSs expanded their participation in the organization of supply by training thousands of popular inspectors, reactivating revolutionary vigilance to help control the popular stores, supporting store owners with basic product distribution, entreating barrio inhabitants to grow their own vegetable gardens, and helping the Ministry of Internal Commerce conduct a nationwide census to improve the entire distribution process. With their large membership and presence throughout the country, the CDSs are proving capable of implementing the various measures that regulate internal commerce in Nicaragua.

WOMEN AND THE CDSs

Because the CDSs are based in urban neighborhoods, they have been especially important for women. Traditionally in charge of domestic organization, women have responded enthusiastically to the possibility of improving the quality of everyday life. Through their involvement in the CDSs they have seen how direct participation in community affairs can have an immediate impact on their lives. Women often constitute a majority at CDS meetings, and at the base level they play the primary role, with men sometimes criticized for not taking as active a part. More than half the CDS activists in the country are women, and women comprise approximately 80 percent of the people performing revolutionary vigilance. Although still underrepresented in zonal and regional offices, the national secretary general of the CDS is a woman, and women occupy nearly half of the executive positions within the national CDS office.[42]

For many women, early personal involvement in the CDSs led to broader political commitment. For example, in León, the most active community group is the Mothers Commission, which considers itself both a part of AMNLAE and a part of the CDS. Since the revolution, this Commission has participated in health and hygiene campaigns, and some of its members have worked in the cotton harvest and trained in the militias. In early 1981 members of the Mother's Commission prepared an exhibition in the community center to honor the martyrdom of their children. The exhibition displayed photographs of the dead, and in some cases the clothes they were murdered in. Inspired by the memories of their children, many Commission members went on to carry out other types of political activity.

Mary Solis is a member of the CDS and coordinator of the Mothers Commission of AMNLAE for the barrio of El Coyolar in León. Her experience is typical of many Nicaraguan women:

> I am a widow of Lancer Sandoval. I began participating in the struggle during the September uprising. My son had gone off for two months to a training school in the mountains. I helped with the medicines because I worked in a hospital. Then my son was fighting, but he reappeared around September 26th. Then the fighting got more intense and I had to help hide not only him, but other comrades that he brought to the house. I was scared that he would go off again, so I did what I could to help them, and to keep him there. My house was a "safehouse" for him and others. Five months later, my son was killed. From then on I continued in the struggle. It became a fight for revenge. I knew that I had to take up the fight for his sake. Since the triumph I have got involved in the Women's Commission. I've worked in my neighborhood and I've joined the popular militias. All of us mothers have an obligation, a duty to the country and to our children. We have to continue the struggle for them. The ideological struggle which we now face is very important. There are comrades who don't believe that the revolution is moving forward and will never go back. I am going ahead whatever the cost. If I have to give my life to it, well, I will, because my son fell, and that is a painful thing. I feel proud, even though my son gave his life for the country, and even though I suffer daily. But that's life, and life goes on, and so does the revolution—it has to continue.[43]

León, on the Pacific side of Nicaragua, was a center of anti-Somoza activity throughout the war. The CDS and Mothers Commission activities have inherited that struggle. On the Atlantic coast, however, there was virtually no CDC activity and the CDSs have been much slower to develop there. Towns such as Bluefields were not hit by the fighting, and the men and women there did not become politicized during the pre-triumph period. Consequently, the CDSs in eastern Nicaragua, lacking the revolutionary experience of the Pacific Coast region, have had to start from scratch.

The FSLN has devoted considerable energy to launching the mass organizations on the Atlantic Coast. The Sandinistas seek to bridge the gap between the two sides of the country and provide institutionalized mechanisms for ameliorating living conditions. The task has been difficult. For many *Costeños*—the Spanish name for those living on the Atlantic Coast, the CDSs seem to have been influenced by a foreign government.

Nevertheless, some Atlantic Coast CDSs are active, carrying out many of the same tasks as their western counterparts on the Pacific Coast. Fatima, a resident of Bluefields, discusses her CDS:

> I became a member of the CDS because when the Sandinistas took over they called a meeting with the people of the *barrio*. In that meeting they organised a brigade and I joined the health group. As well as the health group, we've organised a finance group reponsible for money, and a census about how many people live in the *barrio*, how big the *barrio* is, how many children there are . . . In the CDS, men and women participate equally, but the majority are women. This is because men have to go to work, while the majority of women are at home so that they've got the time to take part. If the men do take part, they do so on Sundays when they have their day off.[44]

Although women's participation in their neighborhoods has grown dramatically, sexism continues to act as a barrier to full involvement. Many men feel threatened if "their" women are active outside the home.

> The problem for women in the CDS centers mainly on the attitude of their husbands. Many won't let their wives go out to meetings, so they end up fighting and the women prefer to leave the organization. Liberation from their husbands doesn't exist. This is something which we will obtain bit by bit. At the moment women see themselves as housewives, nothing more, serving their man and living totally immersed in him.[45]

A considerable number of women may challenge such manifestions of sexism, but the government has not launched any systematic effort to combat them. Some women *have* sought, and gained, workable arrangements with their partners. Marta, a CDS activist in Bluefields, had her husband assume the domestic tasks when she attended a health care seminar:

> The Department of Health sent us to Managua for a course. I've got six children. My husband looked after the children—oh he

minded doing it, but we didn't have to argue about it, because
he wanted me to learn something. He likes me to go to meetings.
Yes, I'm lucky, he looks after the kids and the home and everything and I go off. Some men tell their women to do the work,
others like them to go to meetings. Some like everybody to be
for the cause, and maybe some don't like it. They are afraid,
they're scared, but we're the majority.[46]

Aside from AMNLAE, the CDS is the organization most open to
women's advancement. Marta is clearly still an exception, but large
numbers of Nicaraguan women are gaining increasing confidence and
technical competence through their participation in CDS activities. Furthermore, the percentage of women in CDS leadership positions at the
zonal, regional, and national levels is steadily increasing—evidence that
women are making advances in Nicaragua's largest popular association.

CASE STUDY: GEORGINO ANDRADE

Georgino Andrade in Managua is a community of factory workers, artisans, market and street vendors, domestics, and the unemployed.[47]
Located in the belt of neighborhoods, industries, and commercial centers
that sprang up after the 1972 earthquake destroyed the city's center, it
is a sprawling settlement of some six thousand people. Until 1981, the
land on which the barrio is located was vacant. In May of that year a
handful of families from a few of Managua's other overcrowded barrios
decided to build homes there. News of the developing squatter's community spread by word of mouth, and within a month scores of other
families joined the pioneers.

    Although the barrio was settled spontaneously, residents of one sec-
tion quickly organized a CDS. Other sections followed suit, and eventually there were thirty-five block committees, along with a *Comite de
Barrio Sandinista* (Sandinista Barrio Committee, CBS). The CBS serves as
an umbrella organization, uniting all the CDSs in Georgino Andrade and
representing it on the next highest organizational level, the *Comite Zonal*
(Zonal Committee).

    The residents of Georgino Andrade immediately faced a number of
major problems. Three property owners who claimed to own portions
of the land were angered by the squatter's community. In addition, the
spontaneous nature of the settlement meant that the barrio was poorly
laid out. Streets were too narrow or nonexistent, there were too many
houses crowded together, and no space remained for community build-

ings or a recreation area. To make matters worse, some sections of the barrio were located directly on top of earthquake faults.

The process of restructuring and renovating the barrio has been a long and complex one. In late 1981, housing ministry representatives visited the barrio and informed the residents that the layout of houses and roads would have to be changed dramatically. But it was not until the summer of 1983 that the seismographic study of the faults running under the barrio was completed, and the renovations and relocations could begin in earnest.

After numerous CBS meetings, the block coordinators and the barrio's executive committee worked out the problems of restructuring their community. A major concern was that more than seventy families would have to leave the barrio because the required transformations would not leave enough space for all the families within the boundaries of the barrio. The barrio leadership finally decided that an alternative site would be found for these families; they met with MINVAH and received a commitment that the families would be relocated in a new barrio two kilometers away from Georgino Andrade.

There was a high level of participation in this entire process. Long discussions took place during block and barriowide meetings concerning new building materials, loans for families that had to rebuild their houses, and plans for building a new community center to complete the restructuring. The barrio leaders who conducted the meetings never cut off the debates, even when most participants were exhausted. A large majority of those who attended the block and barrio meetings made the effort to express their opinions. It was evident that in a situation where everyone would be affected by the decisions, the CDS members were anxious to be part of the process.

Notes from a CBS meeting

On August 17, 1983, during the period in which residents were discussing the restructuring of the barrio, the author attended a CBS meeting. The following notes from the meeting demonstrate the range of issues that are brought up at neighborhood gatherings and the extent of participatory democracy that exists within the neighborhood organization.

The meeting began with a short presentation by the secretary of political education on German Pomares, a Sandinista hero who died fighting the National Guard in 1979. Hugo, the coordinator of the barrio, then began to talk about the families that had to be relocated. The night before, forty-four houses in one sector of the barrio were chosen to be dismantled and then rebuilt in another location. Several houses in each block of the sector are to be affected. Thus far nearly all the houses that are located on the seismic faults have been selected for relocation. They still have to select the houses that must be dismantled due to the widening of roads and the construction of a new community center.

The secretary of political education then reported that a member of the army's general staff visited the barrio the previous night to explain the current military situation. Most of the CDS in the barrio had sent representatives to the meeting. "We have to promote the development of our territorial militia. Our barrio has to guarantee a company within a territorial unit and we have to do this soon. We have a clear plan to integrate people into the militia."The member of the general staff spoke of the need to strengthen the territorial militia and the importance of giving moral assistance to families whose members are mobilized in the reserve brigades. "Here we have to have the consciousness that it is our land, our country, our children, our families that we are defending."

Next, the discussion turned to the adult education program which was to begin in September. Although the neighborhood had seven coordinators in the program, they were concentrated in only one sector of the barrio. The secretary of political education called for at least two houses and two coordinators in each of the five zones of the community. Workshops for teachers would begin September 24 and classes would begin October 3. It was admitted that the task of popular education was one of the most difficult confronting the neighborhood.

During the question-and-answer period one block coordinator asked why some of the block leaders aren't acting in a more organized way. The answer was the CDS members reserve the right to recall any CDS leader that doesn't respond to the needs of the community. "I don't say this to intimidate anyone," declared the CBS coordinator, "but certain elements of our barrio are boycotting things. We won't permit any CDS to boycott current efforts." [Apparently, members in one block had protested aspects of the restructuring of the neighborhood. A subsequent meeting with the executive committee of the CBS and the inhabitants of this block resolved the problems.]

The coordinator then praised the participation of CDS members in a demonstration held the previous Sunday to celebrate the inauguration of new CDS zonal leaders in the eastern sector of Managua. The meeting, which had lasted nearly two hours, ended with the singing of the Sandinista anthem.[48]

In March 1984, the author attended an emergency block meeting. It was called to resolve a dispute that was causing serious divisions among neighboring families. The dispute concerned the water post used by the block's residents. Each block in Georgino Andrade elects one person to collect money from all the families in order to pay the monthly water bill. Some members of the CDS claimed that the woman who was collecting the money had overcharged various families and pocketed the difference. In addition, the water post would soon be used to meet the needs of the barrio's new preschool, and a second one would need to be installed. The secretary of community development had called the meeting to resolve these problems.

After only a few minutes the meeting turned into a shouting match with one group of CDS members hurling accusations at another group. Meanwhile, the woman who had been charged with corruption had voluntarily resigned her position. Finally, the secretary of community development, Nacho, raised his voice and took charge of the meeting. Nacho pointed out that the shouting reflected a lack of mutual respect on the part of the participants at the meeting, and added that such disunity played into the hands of the counterrevolution. "If we were attacked tomorrow," he asserted, "we would all be carried away in body bags." He went on to suggest that an election be held to choose a new person to deal with the water bills, and that a commission made up of the two quarelling factions be formed to request an additional water post from the government water authority. The residents proceeded to elect a water commission and the meeting ended.

Another incident, which also occurred in March 1984, demonstrates the communal manner in which the residents of Georgino Andrade resolve their problems. Early in 1984, the barrio launched a project to build a preschool in an empty lot one block from the community house. Residents acquired low-cost building materials from the Ministry of Education and a Spanish religious foundation provided funds to pay local construction workers. The construction began slowly and many of the building materials ended up in the living room of a woman named María who had been chosen to supervise the project.

In March, María attended a barriowide meeting and asked for a place on the agenda. When it was her turn to speak, she registered the following complaint.

Listen, when I volunteered to supervise the pre-school project, that didn't mean that I wished to turn my house into a storage shed for building materials. This is not my pre-school—the school will serve all the children in the neighborhood. I have a small house and eight children. The concrete blocks that are now in my living room are making things very difficult in my house. So I would like people to build a storage shed for these materials—as was originally planned. I simply can't tolerate these things in my house any longer.[49]

As María spoke, most block representatives hung their heads in shame, acknowledging the truth of her remarks. When she finished, Nacho called for volunteers to build a storage shed immediately after the meeting ended. Eleven men volunteered and they built the shed in two hours. Maria's reproach of others involved in the building project had accomplished its goal.

The residents of Georgino Andrade began to construct a neighborhood preschool in 1984. The Ministry of Education pledged sufficient funds to cover most of the cost, but the intensification of the contra war prevented the ministry from paying for the full costs. Consequently, the Sandinista Barrio Committee launched a drive to secure foreign donations. In March the Committee sent the following letter to sympathetic groups and individuals in the United States:

March 21, 1984 Managua, Nicaragua Libre

Greetings from our neighborhood organization, the Sandinista Defense Committee (CDS), at a time when we are engaged in the most important tasks of our Popular Sandinista Revolution.

We are writing to the people of the United States and to solidarity organizations that understand the situation of our country, which is struggling for self-determination, to tell you about the work of our CDS and the achievements in our community "Georgino Andrade." We organized after the triumph because of the need and the right we earned to build our homes on idle lands.

We took over this land, an act which would have been repressed in the past by Somoza's National Guard. We organized into Sandinista Defense Committees to demand potable water and electricity. Today, we have potable water that costs 1.2 cordobas [12 cents] per barrel and free electricity. The work of our community of 6,000 people has earned first place in zone 10 of Managua, which includes 36 barrios.

We now have 850 residents who participate every week in "revolutionary vigilance." Many of us are also students in the adult education program. We took part in the vaccination campaigns against polio and malaria, reaching 89% of the children in our barrio. The Revolution inherited a high infant mortality rate and a large number of handicapped children. In the past, the government did not worry about vaccinating children on a regular basis.

Through our organization we have been able to organize food distribution networks that have eliminated speculation and hoarding. We have installed a public phone. Most importantly, the Ministry of Education is helping us build a pre-school for our children.

We need to build a pre-school in our community for the children of working mothers. We have the space for its construction in our communal area but, due to the shortage of our government's resources, we do not have the financial resources to build it. We also have to build a new community house because the existing one will be torn down to make way for a new road through the neighborhood. We therefore solicit your cooperation in aiding this humble barrio.

In spite of the economic difficulties and military aggression, we have survived and repudiated the aggression of the U.S. government against our people. We maintain our vocation for peace but are alert and prepared to repel any type of attack.

Waiting for your response,

Comite de Barrio Sandinista—Hugo Saenz, Coordinator;
Evenor Padilla R., Secretary of Organization;
Armando Vargas F., Secretary of Political Education.[50]

The residents of Georgino Andrade continued their efforts to develop the neighborhood throughout the next year. The government installed an electric transformer and lights. The CDSs conducted successful inoculation campaigns against polio, measles, and tetanus, and completed the third year of adult education classes. With material assistance from CEPAD, a Protestant development agency, the neighborhood committee sponsored a sewing class for more than twenty-five neighborhood women. The neighborhood's major achievement of the year took place in November, when the Ministry of Housing delivered land titles to 70 percent of the barrio's residents.

In January 1986, activists in Georgino Andrade's CDSs participated in a reevaluation of their organization. The reevaluation resulted in the following recommendations:

1. CDS executive committees do not always require a set number of leaders per block. They can get by with a coordinator and a secretary of revolutionary vigilance.

2. Neighborhood committees should try to involve everyone in the problems of each block by encouraging residents to participate in the various CDS commissions.
3. CDS leaders should try to limit all meetings to one hour.
4. Good records should be kept of all CDS meetings.
5. The CDSs must continue to act as an educational vehicle for barrio residents. "Our principle task is to educate ourselves to express what we feel, to encourage people to participate in debates in order to further enrich ourselves."[51]

Georgino Andrade inaugurated its preschool in March 1986 and began to build a classroom for the neighborhood's first grade students. CBS leaders also planned the construction of a health center and a new communal house. Because of its intense involvement in securing land titles for residents in late 1985, the neighborhood organization could not hold CDS elections in November. It therefore devoted the remainder of 1986 to reinforcing its executive committee by training a team of aides that would assist the committee's work. As 1986 drew to a close the barrio's leaders were working to strengthen the CDSs by expanding resident participation in all community activities.

The Sandinista Defense Committees are schools of democracy and instruments of popular power. Through trial and error, hundreds of thousands of Nicaraguans are learning how to cooperatively run the affairs of their own communities. Because of the multitude of tasks they perform, the CDSs represent a new form of organization at the most basic level of Nicaraguan society: an organization that is increasingly capable of both defending the revolution's gains and extending its achievements.

8

WOMEN'S LIBERATION: AMNLAE

The Nicaraguan revolution has improved women's political economic condition, and has brought some changes in the relations between men and women as well. And though these changes certainly haven't spelled an end to patriarchy, it is not yet clear how profoundly the revolution will transform Nicaraguan kinship relations.[1] Although most evidence warrants a cautious appraisal, there are still prospects for an assault on patriarchy itself, and not simply its most extreme manifestations. In the post-revolutionary era, it has fallen to the Nicaraguan Women's Association, AMNLAE, to tackle the country's heritage of economic underdevelopment and deep-rooted sexism.

AMNLAE'S IDEOLOGY

In at least one respect AMNLAE agrees with the orthodox Marxist-Leninist position on women, which attributes the origins of women's subordination to their marginalization from productive work. AMNLAE echoed this view in an important 1980 article.

> At a given moment in the history of the social division of labor, women were separated from production and assigned to domestic labor. With this assignment the world of women was reduced to the atrophying dimensions of the home, to a narrow framework that was limited and individualist. In addition, they were subjected to exhausting and routinized work. This gradually generated in women a political, technical, and social back-

wardness which converted them into objects propelled by history, not subjects forging their own history.[2]

AMNLAE contends that full equality for women—their complete integration into society—can only arise through the consolidation of the revolution. The Association therefore urges women to combine their work to overcome inequality in social and political life with work for the general reconstruction of the country. In the words of a poor Managuan woman:

> We have to root out the bourgeoisie but, at the same time, we have to learn what it means to run things. This is the meaning of the slogan, "Workers' Power." We can't leave the Revolution alone just because we've gotten rid of Somoza; if we do others will take over. This is why we women cannot remain in our homes. We have to work in production, we have to study and learn. As women, we must integrate ourselves into the unions, the CDS, and the other organizations; we must be part of building these organizations.[3]

This "integrationist" approach is fundamental to AMNLAE's strategy for working women. The Association views work as a first step toward women's emancipation, and dedicates itself to encouraging women to work outside the home. Consequently, AMNLAE is committed to policies that free women from household tasks. The Association calls for the socialization of housework and helps establish day-care facilities. The scarcity of resources and the escalating contra war, however, have severely limited such projects.

Although AMNLAE champions women's role in production outside the home, few Association leaders or activists hold to the orthodox Marxist-Leninist view that women's path to emancipation is assured *solely* by participation in the work force outside the home. Rather, many AMNLAE members call for a revolution in patriarchal patterns of thought and action. One Association activist summarizes the views of her sisters:

> We have a great responsibility to push for a change in values. We have to overcome the current situation and make the family a joint responsibility. Children have to receive values from fathers as well as mothers; the formation of a new society is a responsibility of both parents. . . . The patriarchal system is much more difficult to overcome [than capitalism] because patriarchy exists also between men and women who love each other and live together.[4]

Although AMNLAE recognizes that women will gain from Nicaragua's economic transformations, the Association also emphasizes the importance of developing new relations between women and men, and the creation of a new ideology that will liberate women from age-old oppression.

AMNLAE'S ROLE IN LEGISLATION

AMNLAE strongly encourages mass participation in the discussion and revision of proposed legislation affecting women, and in educating the public about these laws after their passage. In a 1984 speech delivered in the United States, Magda Enriques detailed the Association's legislative efforts during the Council of State period.

> To make a law we draft it. We have a group of lawyers, men and women, who help us do that. And then we take it to our grassroots, and we discuss the law. Usually the first thing we do is change the writing because somehow lawyers are specialized in writing things that only they can understand. . . . And then of course, people discuss and some people agree with things, other disagree and things go in and out of the law. And finally when we go to the Council of State we are really representing the voice of a lot of women, and in the case of the Family Laws, men and women, that had become legislators. That for us is democracy.
>
> An important thing is . . . that through the making of the laws not only do we change laws, not only do we make just laws, but we educate people on the law, not as an end in itself but as an instrument of justice. And we also . . . discuss the whole ideological content of a law. And . . . in spite of all the discussions—and some are very heated, some people get very mad— the important thing is that they do get approved. The important thing is that we do have the possibility of building something new.[5]

Because so many different social groups participated in the debates over the new laws, the consciousness-raising aspects of the discussion had more impact than the legislation itself.

AMNLAE established the Women's Legal Office in March 1983 to provide legal services and advice to thousands of women each year. In 1985 the office handled more than 4,000 cases, 1,500 of which dealt with divorce, wife abuse, and alimony. The majority of women who receive the office's legal services are between twenty and thirty years of age and 60 percent are housewives, maids, and office workers.[6]

AMNLAE submitted its proposals to the National Assembly's Special Constitutional Commission that was convened in 1985. The women's organization urged that the new constitution's preamble include 1. a statement underlining the importance of women as a social force in the revolution; 2. an admission that obstacles remain to women's participation in the economic, social, political, and defense realms; and 3. a declaration affirming that the state and society must collectively devote their energies to removing all the impediments that limit the exercise of women's rights.[7]

AMNLAE also proposed that the constitution include provisions that would guarantee women access to employment and leadership positions in the workplace; recognize domestic work as a socially useful activity that must be shared by all family members; prohibit the use of women as sexual objects and terminate sexist arguments that maintain or reproduce prejudices against the abilities of women; prohibit all forms of sexual abuse of women at the workplace; outlaw physical, psychological and moral abuse of women and children within the family; affirm women's political rights to vote, belong to political parties, and hold public office; guarantee women the right to education and technical training; and ensure women's right to own land.[8] AMNLAE also insisted that the constitution recognize women's reproductive rights: the right to decide the number of children they will have and when to bear them; freedom from discrimination against pregnant women and mothers at the workplace; the right to receive prenatal and postnatal medical attention; the right to pregnancy leave and an income subsidy while pregnant; and the right to collective forms of childcare.[9]

AMNLAE AND THE FAMILY

The government and AMNLAE are the guiding forces behind the attempt to strengthen the family. This attempt, as Deighton et al. note, "does not reflect popular clamour for legal reform or a wide canvassing of women's demands but it has been very popular with women."[10] AMNLAE has championed a series of new laws, each with the aim of changing relations within and around the family.

The adoption law, one of the first family laws passed in the Council of State, overcame the legal anomalies that were causing problems during the immediate postwar period. Approximately 40,000 children were orphaned or abandoned during the course of the war. People were caring for them on a provisional basis and families who had taken in children could not formally adopt them. AMNLAE proposed a new law that would eliminate the obstacles to adoption and allow unmarried couples as well as single people to adopt children.[11] The adoption law calls for assistance to abandoned children and their new parents, and reflects the belief that neither the natural mother nor the children should be stigmatized. At the same time, authorities anticipate that future social conditions will reduce the number of abandoned children. In August 1981, Milu Vargas, then director of Legal Services for the Council of State, expressed this view: "We think that at the moment adoption can be an alternative but it isn't a solution. We hope that when the revolution can give all the basic essentials adoption will be less common, because many women in the future will be able to decide whether they want a child or not."[12]

AMNLAE has been the main contributor to the Family Code's reform. The Family Code comprises a collection of patriarchal laws enacted during the Somoza era. The reform of the Code began in September 1981 with intense debate in the Council of State. The Council first abolished the law of *patria potestad*, the archaic law that gave the father sole rights over his children, even though the mother has traditionally been the parent who raises the children. A new law, "The Law of Relations Between Mothers, Fathers, and Children," places the responsibility of bringing up children on both parents, or in the case of a separated couple, on the parent who remains with the children. According to the new law, both parents must 1. take care, raise, and educate their children; 2. provide food, clothes, housing, medicine, recreation, and education; 3. ensure their good behavior; 4. stimulate their capacities for making decisions and taking responsibility; 5. teach them to participate in housework; 6. include them in family decisions; 7. prepare them for socially useful work; 8. help them as dignified members of society; 9. represent them in legal matters; and 10. administer their property.[13]

The family relations law also establishes children's responsibility to their parents, especially if they are old or sick. But the most crucial aspect of the law concerns custody. AMNLAE and the FSLN were on opposite sides of what became a heated national debate as to whether or not the courts should rule in favor of the mother when settling custody disputes. The FSLN favored ruling for the mother in all cases, but AMNLAE contended that such a view would make women's responsibility for children an integral part of the law, thereby harming women's long-term interests. The final version of the law reflects AMNLAE's position.[14]

In August 1982, AMNLAE introduced further, complementary, legislation to the Council of State: the "Law of Nurturance." In a legal sense, "nurturing" represents whatever is necessary for the development of the person, including culture and recreation. Parents, brothers and sisters, and grandparents, in that order, are responsible for the well-being of children under twenty-one years of age and sick family members. The law obliges both parents to guarantee their children food, clothing, health care, housing, and education, and demands familial solidarity with all dependent family members: children, the elderly, and the handicapped.[15]

A hotly-debated aspect of the nurturance law addresses household tasks. The law establishes that "all family members with the economic capacity must contribute, within their means, to the support of the family. This can be in the form of money, goods, or household tasks. And concerning the last category, all family members, regardless of sex, who are capable of doing so, must contribute to household tasks (Article 4)."[16] This latter provision—calling for men to share housework with their wives—caused a national polemic. Rosa Maria Zelaya, director of the Office of Family Protection, comments on the concept of sharing domestic work.

> By introducing the issue, by discussing it, we tried to help men see that domestic work has economic repercussions. In addition, we tried to call attention to the problem of women's participation in economic development. The objective is to include both men and women in productive work. The conflict between the home and production is still being resolved by the woman in very primitive ways: the grandmother or the aunt takes care of the house and the children.[17]

Under the Nurturance Law, a person's responsibility toward his or her family continues after the breakup of a relationship. If a marriage dissolves, wives can claim alimony from their husbands. When unmarried couples separate, the law requires both individuals to provide for their families; and if a man leaves his common-law wife he must support her if she cannot work due to health reasons. The law also does away with the old Civil Code's distinctions between "legitimate" and "illegitimate" children. All children now have equal rights to parental support.[18]

AMNLAE plays a major role in the implementation of these family laws and strives to overcome the irresponsibility prevalent in relations between couples and between parents and children. In the words of one Association activist:

> We have to learn to assume the responsibilities that derive from the relations of couples; both men and women should construct the genuine foundation for new family relations. For this to occur we should be purveyors of new ideas that contribute to the

transformation of the dominant ideology that fosters habits, customs, and prejudices that impede the development of equality between men and women. We must learn to share household tasks as well as the love and the care of our children.[19]

Marriage and Divorce

The majority of Nicaraguan couples have not formalized their union, either civilly or through the church.[20] Civil and church marriages occur among the middle and upper classes, but working-class and peasant couples have de facto marriages. Only one-sixth of Nicaraguan couples are civilly married. New legislation recognizes the de facto marriage and considers it a common-law marriage or a state of companionship. When this relationship takes on permanent characteristics and stability, it receives the same legal treatment as a civil marriage in terms of the couple's rights and obligations, the situation of the children, and the use of material possessions.

There are no reliable figures regarding divorce and separation, making it impossible to ascertain what affect the revolution has had on the stability of couples. But women's increased assertiveness has influenced relationships between couples: it has challenged such sexist practices and beliefs as the physical abuse of women, the father's irresponsibility toward his children, and the man's "right" to have extramarital affairs.

AMNLAE has attacked the Divorce Law, inherited from the Somoza era, because it discriminates against women. The law stipulates that both parties must consent to a divorce. If mutual consent is not provided, six grounds for divorce, three of which are discriminatory against women, may be offered. For example, a man's claim that his wife has committed adultery is considered sufficient proof, but a wife must prove that the man was living with another woman in the same dwelling or that his infidelity is public knowledge. Under the current law, decisions regarding divorce or separation depend on the generosity of the court. Because so few women actually marry, AMNLAE has not pressed vigorously to change this law. But the reluctance to loosen the restrictions on divorce also reflects an increased emphasis on strengthening the family.

Child Care

In Nicaragua, as in other revolutionary societies, the state has assumed a share in the responsibility for child care. The Ministries of Social Welfare, Health, and Agricultural Development and Agrarian Reform have developed a program to establish day-care centers in both the city and countryside. Given the war and the economic crisis, it has been difficult to achieve progress in this day-care program. Nevertheless, at the end of 1985 more than 80,000 children were receiving some form of child care in Nicaragua.[21]

Three basic types of child care centers exist in Nicaragua: preschool facilities, urban child development centers, and rural child services. In Managua, AMNLAE and the CDSs are pushing for the development of "popular preschools": community-run childcare facilities where children can receive a daily meal and basic instruction.[22] Except for a small number of male volunteers from the Sandinista Youth, women provide child care services in the centers. Primary school teachers, secondary school students, and housewives serve the children, in many cases for only two hours a day. According to an official in the Ministry of Social Welfare, many of them lack practical expertise: "The women who work in child development centers would like to have a lot of training; they have low levels of training, but high morale. Most of them are parents who are taking classes to develop their knowledge and convert themselves into professional educators."[23]

Family Planning

Although AMNLAE does not have an offical policy on contraception, in 1983 its monthly magazine, Somos, began to print articles on sexual education, including detailed information on contraception. Few women think of birth control in terms of women's right to control their own bodies. Nevertheless, AMNLAE leaders and activists declare themselves to be fully in support of free contraception. The government has opened a number of women's health centers and contraceptives are available to women who ask for them. Health centers in working-class neighborhoods and the Mother-Infant Hospital in Managua report a growing interest in birth control among young women. The most popular methods of birth control in Nicaragua are the pill and the IUD. Condoms are not commonly used. The government regulates the sale of contraceptives in pharmacies and recommends that people not buy these products in the markets because of the risks involved. Despite these recommendations, some markets continue to sell contraceptives such as Depo-Provera that have been known to cause birth defects. Sterilization is practiced if requested and if certain requirements are met: that both the man and the woman agree on the procedure, that the woman be of a certain age, and that she already have a certain number of children.[24]

During the first six years of the revolution the subjects of birth control and abortion posed problems for AMNLAE. Abortion is not legal in Nicaragua (the abortion law was enacted under Somoza) and there was no public discussion of this issue until November 1985. Individual leaders were in favor of free abortion on demand, but they considered it an issue whose time had not yet come. In a 1982 interview with a British feminist, AMNLAE's Gloria Carrión signaled the Association's differences from western feminism: "When Western feminists come here to interview us, very often the first question they ask is 'What are you doing about abortion or sexual politics?' Of course these are important issues for women, but we have to go one step at a time and our priorities are determined by our historical, social and political circumstances."[25]

During the first six years under the Sandinistas, AMNLAE was not anxious to launch a campaign for legislation on abortion, feeling that such an action might be interpreted as an imposition by Nicaraguan women. "We cannot stir up, start creating a series of demands without the grassroots support of our women," Glenda Monterey asserted.[26] AMNLAE leaders had noted that women were not clamoring for abortions. "There are a few advanced women who do support abortion," said FSLN militant Marta Cranshaw in 1982, "but if you were to take it to the vote most women would be against abortions."[27]

For a number of years AMNLAE considered the provision of health services to mothers and children a higher priority than abortion. In a 1981 interview Gloria Carrión remarked, "The first problem is to ensure that children survive. Of course there are clandestine abortions. The right to abortion is a legitimate struggle, but at the moment it doesn't represent the concerns of the majority of women.[28]

Some foreign observers believed that AMNLAE's close identification with the FSLN prevented it from promoting abortion, because the Sandinistas were reluctant to clash with the church over such an explosive issue. What these observers pointed out was that the Association's stance on abortion may actually prove harmful to all its other efforts.

> AMNLAE's reluctance to actively promote family planning could undermine much of its own and the government's work towards providing equal opportunity for women. . . . By keeping abortion illegal, the government is in effect sending many women into the clandestine world of private abortionists. In doing so, it is perpetuating a structure that, because it is criminal, is in opposition to the government.[29]

On November 19, 1985 *Barricada* launched a series of articles on the subject of abortion. The first article discussed the results of a study on abortion published in early November. The study revealed that between March 1983 and June 1985 one Managua hospital was admitting an average of ten women a day for illegal abortions. A review of 109 illegal abortion cases that involved complications showed the 10 percent of the women died after the abortion and 26 percent became sterile. Each of these cases had hospital expenses of 97,000 córdobas. Eighty-two percent of the women studied opted for an abortion without consulting their partners due to the stigma that is traditionally associated with abortion in Nicaragua.[30]

Barricada followed up its initial article by printing excerpts of an extensive round-table discussion on abortion that included nine doctors, a psychologist, and a hospital official. During the course of this discussion a number of important facts and points of view emerged, including the following:

> — abortion is the principal cause of maternal death in Nicaragua
> — hospital officials will not perform abortions because it is illegal, but know that many women will return to hospital for treatment of injuries sustained during illegal abortions
> — even though the law allows medical-therapeutic abortions, few hospitals perform them
> — the law requires that the parents or the husband must ask for abortion to be performed, but most women don't have husbands and few will turn to their parents
> — women most harmed by illegal abortions are poor women who cannot afford to pay the 25–50,000 córdobas that doctors charge for the procedure. Poor women therefore turn to inexperienced practioners who charge only 2,000 córdobas.
> — the mortality rate due to abortions has risen because of the rising cost of abortions in private clinics
> — the majority of women who have abortions have had at least 3–4 children[31]

Nearly all the participants in the controversial discussion agreed that the government should introduce a comprehensive plan for nationwide sexual education and family planning. But some argued that an immediate solution was necessary to halt the devastating effects of illegal abortions. Dr. Marta Norori, director of the Ministry of Health's Mother Program in the Managua region insisted: "The solution is not abortion but sex education, planning. But, at the same time, an immediate solution is needed because sex education is a long-term project. The law should be revised; if not . . . the majority of those who have abortions will continue to turn to inexperienced practitioners and will continue to die."[32]

Vilma Castillo, a clinical psychologist, responded to the argument that Nicaragua needs to increase its population:

People in our country have always used the argument that we need to populate. What have the results been? Unwanted children, abandoned children, mistreated children. No population nor political law can be defended which manipulates the reproductive capacity of women. INSSBI still doesn't have the capacity to care for these abandoned children. This is the reality. In this country paternal irresponsiblity continues to exist. To have children should be a conscious act.[33]

For a number of years, family planning was seldom mentioned officially. This is partly because the Sandinistas reject theories that tend to explain the economic crisis of Third World countries in demographic terms. Many government officials consider fertility one of the country's natural resources and a key element in its potential development. But there is no state policy designed to increase the birthrate. Miguel Ernesto Vigil, the Minister of Housing, has declared:

I believe that each husband and wife have the right to decide on the number of children that they are going to have, and they should be free to choose the scientific methods that will allow them to control the size of their family. Excessive population growth is not good, for the state does not have the capacity to provide all necessary services. The population pyramid in Nicaragua has an excessively wide base. The economically active population cannot assume responsibility for the health, housing, education, etc. of an increasing number of minors.[34]

An effort is now underway to design an effective sex education program. Government officials believe that such a program takes precedence over legalizing abortion or the dissemination of information on birth control. At the beginning of 1986, the Ministry of Education announced that a new sex education program would be established in the country's schools. The program, first introduced in the Carazo-Masaya region, will include basic information on human sexuality and the reproductive process.[35] Meanwhile, AMNLAE is continuing its drive to sensitize the population a woman's reproductive rights, including the right to control her own body.

EDUCATION

AMNLAE views education as a crucial vehicle for the advancement of women. At the end of the Somoza era, only 21.3 percent of the female population between the ages of thirteen and eighteen had attended secondary school and only 11 percent of the women between nineteen and twenty-four had attended institutions of higher education. In the universities, women pursued studies that led to areas of "female" employment such as teaching, library work, and other careers in the humanities.[36]

The Literacy Crusade marked a major educational advance for Nicaraguan women. The vast majority of the country's illiterate population were women, and in some rural areas few women could read or write. AMNLAE mobilized its members to help advance the achievements of the crusade. Women played a massive and varied role in the campaign, participating as students and teachers as well as working as coordinators and providers of logistic support. Some 60 percent of the members of the Popular Literacy Army were young women, many of whom taught in the most remote areas of the country.[37] AMNLAE's Sylvia Reyes describes the difficulties that women teachers faced.

> The compañeras had many problems. Mountains are difficult regions, sometimes there were problems of adaptation—it depended on the region they had been allocated; we have some regions where it rains for 11 months of the year; vast zones where 'mountain leprosy' was rife, or where peasants live totally isolated. However, they persisted and won the hearts of the peasants . . . In places where the Somocista reaction persisted, they were taken advantage of, and we had entire brigades of 15 women who were raped. We had young compañeras who were assassinated. There were some parts in the mountains where it seemed they would never be able to teach the people to read and write, because of the circumstances for the brigadistas. However, they said that if the Frente Sandinista had spent years in the mountains in order to liberate the country, then surely they could spend six months there, teaching the peasants to read and write . . .[38]

Both teachers and students had to overcome numerous obstacles to the educational process. The daily lesson occurred after a day's work, which for women also included domestic work and child care. Domestic workers in urban areas had special problems. Some employers did not permit "their girls" to go out to classes in the evenings and many domestic workers simply lacked the energy to study. As one literacy brigadista reported: "My student did not make any progress. She seemed intelligent, but she didn't pay any attention and couldn't concentrate. One day I spoke to her. She had been a domestic in the same house since she was 17. She worked 12 hours a day. I was faced with someone totally exhausted, who had no motivation, no energy, no enthusiasm to become literate."[39] Many women were simply unable to attend classes and fulfill their domestic responsibilities. Although some dropped out, others had teachers who made special arrangements for them. People with eye problems could not study the lessons; the literacy campaign planners had not anticipated the problem of bad sight. Although in some areas *brigadistas* were able to provide eyeglasses, most literacy teachers could do nothing about this problem. But despite the many obstacles that students and teachers faced, few people failed to complete the literacy course. Out of the hundreds of thousands of Nicaraguans who became literate there were slightly less women than men: 195,687 compared to 210,429.[40]

The number of professional women in Nicaragua is miniscule. One study on the "Insertion of Women in Social Production" states that in Managua only 4 percent of employed women are professionals and in the Atlantic Coast area the figure is only 1 percent.[41] Furthermore, the relatively few professional women face many obstacles in their work. At a conference of professional women held in September 1983, participants registered complaints concerning the difficulty of attaining leadership positions, the paucity of scholarships available to women for study abroad, and the lack of sufficient technical training courses available to women. The women at the conference resolved to press both AMNLAE and the National Federation of Profesionals to promote and strengthen training programs for professional women.[42]

EMPLOYMENT

Nicaraguan women's intense participation in the revolution is largely attributable to their notable participation in the economy. As Margaret Randall writes: "They [Nicaraguan women] have been continually pushed beyond the narrow domestic scene. While the Spanish Catholic tradition preached of women in the home, passive, dependent and 'ornamental,' the world around them demanded something else. History forced them to assume positions and make decisions which, along with their economic activity, increased their social and political involvement."[43]

Unfortunately, few statistics are available on Nicaraguan women's economic participation. In 1950, women comprised 14 percent of the economically active population (EAP). By 1970 this figure had risen to 21.9 percent and in 1977 it was 28.6 percent. More recent figures reveal that women comprise 40 percent of the urban EAP.[44] Because more than half of the population lives in urban areas, and domestic labor—which still employs many women—is not included in the statistics, this figure provides only a partial analysis of the situation. There are no similar data for rural areas. It is estimated that women make up about 35 percent of the total (urban and rural) EAP.[45]

In Latin America as a whole, women comprise only 20 percent of the labor force. Thus the statistics for Nicaraguan women are remarkably high. Yet this does not mean that women play a significant role in the production process. In a speech celebrating AMNLAE's fifth anniversary, Tomás Borge asserted: "If we analyze the type of work women carry out, we see that a high percentage of these women are really underemployed, and that another large layer is employed in domestic service—work that is not productive and that will have to be regulated and limited in the future."[46]

Of all women who work outside the home approximately 20 percent work in agriculture, 20 percent in personal services, and about 20 percent as market or street vendors.[47] The overwhelming majority of women living in towns—78 percent—work in commerce or services. In Managua, women represent 70 percent of the domestic service workers and 55 percent of the merchants. But women comprise only 14 percent of Managua's industrial labor force. In most cases women work not to provide a second income, but rather to maintain the home as the sole wage earner. According to the statistics Borge cited in his AMNLAE speech, 83 percent of working women are heads of households. The figures for Managua indicate that women head 49 percent of the families and of these women 85 percent are economically active.[48]

Women Vendors

Women vendors sell food, clothes, and vegetables in their homes, in the street, in tiny stores, or in the markets. Until 1984 the earning capacity of women market vendors was precarious and their earnings minimal. In 1981, of those self-employed people earning less than 800 córdobas a month in Managua, 77 percent were women, most of them market vendors. As with all self-employed people they have no sick or holiday pay, and they work long hours.[49] Claudia, a woman who works in Managua's sprawling eastern market, details the situation that prevailed in 1982.

> I get here about five in the morning (I come from outside Managua) and leave at about six at night. The really tiring days are at the weekend since so many people come to do their week's shopping then. Monday and Tuesday we do less business but we still sell something.

We work from 6 in the morning until 8 at night. I buy the fruit I sell in Masaya, very early in the morning, at about 6. Then I come here by lorry. A group of us come, all from Masaya at 8 or 8:30 if the buses are very full and I have to wait. I work here and not in Masaya because you have to work where you can sell more. In Masaya you sell a little bit, nothing more, in the morning, whereas here things happen all day. Sometimes we sell, sometimes we don't. You know how poor this country is. People sometimes buy and sometimes don't; then you have to give up. We spend the whole day sitting, waiting, working sometimes in vain because we're not selling anything. There are days when we have to give up. We can spend two, three days, sometimes, before we sell anything. It's hard. There are days when you don't earn enough to eat.[50]

In its early stage, the revolution attempted to improve the life of market sellers in two major ways: by incorporating them into the national distribution system and by encouraging them to organize into CDSs. To attract market sellers into its distribution system, ENABAS built new local markets, 36 in Managua alone. These markets are sheltered from the sun and rain, have water and electricity, and are more hygienic than the old markets. They have greatly improved the working conditions of the market vendors. "When people get to know the way things work here," says Elena, of Managua's Eduardo Contreras Market,

especially the hygiene and cleanliness, they see that it's better. Produce lasts longer because it's not out in the sun or rain. We feel happier now we're here. People are leaving the old market now, the Oriental. In that market there used to be a lot of crime— here, no. The government has arranged 24 hour internal security and people can see that it's much safer here—they feel safe and see how clean the place is so they start coming here. We feel better here; we're involved in the organization of the market. We have our own CDSs formed by the market-sellers. We work together and next to the market we have a childcare center where the children can spend the day while their parents work. They eat there, the food is healthy. We also have a nursery in the market which is also used as a center for adult education. We are also going to have a health center and we're working with the people there to develop it.[51]

As Nicaragua's economic crisis deepened in 1983 and 1984, many market vendors benefitted because of shortages and the steep rise in prices. An important study of women in small commerce conducted in

1984 and 1985 showed that many market vendors were earning considerably more than the highest-paid state employees. In May and June 1985, for example, one-third of the women surveyed in the study were earning more than 30,000 córdobas per month (then the maximum salary in the state sector). The study also reported that many women entered small commerce as a solution to unemployment and underemployment. Most women surveyed had only 3 to 5 years education and were the sole support of their families. In addition, the study concluded that through their participation in the CDSs and other organizations, many women vendors were making an active contribution to the revolution.[52]

Domestic Work

One quarter of all Nicaraguan women who work outside their homes are domestics. They are among the most oppressed workers in the country. An August 1981 *Barricada* article desribes their plight.

> The situation of the domestic workers at this moment is one of the most acute indications of the class struggle in the revolutionary process. These women, many of whom became 'Daughters of the House' at the age of 12 or 14, were subjected to an unparalleled denial of elementary rights. . . . And the fact of having to live in the place of exploitation makes—for the majority of them—the struggle much more difficult. They are literally prisoners of their employers.[53]

Domestics work without fixed hours, can be fired at any time, and often experience sexual harassment. They usually live and work in isolation, maintaining little contact with other workers, other women, or people outside their employer's family. Many Nicaraguans fail to recognize that domestic workers are workers with attendant rights and dignity, but militant domestics have challenged this attitude. Soon after the fall of Somoza, domestics from across the country met with the FSLN's National Directorate, demanding the elimination of paid domestic work. Although the Sandinistas persuaded them that this demand could not be met because no alternative work was available, abolition of domestic work remains the domestic workers' ultimate goal. "We are sure," avows Nicolasa Morales, "that domestic service will cease to exist in the future, because as production increases, jobs will increase too."[54]

After the meeting with the FSLN, AMNLAE helped found the Union of Domestics. Although it fought for an eight-hour day, the union settled for 10 hours, "in order to give employers who worked for the state time to come and go to work." The union also won the right for domestics to be paid double for holiday work, overtime, and a minimum wage. In 1982, a union organizer summed up some of union's gains and outlined its problems.

> We have a national contract that sets the minimum wage for domestic workers at 400 córdobas a month and establishes a 10 hour work day. It's also suggested that maids get 800 cordóbas if they do washing and cooking too. Maids have usually been paid 200 to 300 córdobas a month and have been forced to work as much as 15 hours a day. Employers still oppose the 10 hour day and often say, "Well, if you're only going to work 10 hours, you have to leave in the evening." Since many of the maids are farm women, they don't have any other place to go, so they work the 15 hours just to have a place to sleep.[55]

The plight of the domestic workers traps Nicaraguan economy in a double bind. Without the domestic services these women provide, thousands of other Nicaraguan women would be unable to leave their homes to work. Moreover, it is not only well-to-do employers or "reactionaries" that fail to treat domestics respectfully. As *Barricada* reported: "We should be concerned at an ideological level, by the testimony of the *compañeras*, that the treatment they receive in many of the houses of *compañeras* who support the revolution, does not differ much from that imposed by the most recalcitrant reactionaries. At times the form is a little more gentle, but in essence the situation appears to be the same."[56]

Without other alternatives, women will continue to seek domestic employment. Thus far, neither the legislation that calls for men to share housework nor the new child care centers have had any effect on the demand for domestic workers. At the same time, however, the domestic workers' union is having an impact on Nicaraguans. The union's militancy, along with the increasing recognition of women's unpaid domestic labor may yet lead to an improvement in the life of waged domestic workers.

Prostitution

The Sandinista government outlawed prostitution within a month after taking power. Nevertheless, prostitution continues in Nicaragua, and the mass organizations regard it as a problem."Generally," observe Deighton et al., "the view is that it is the prostitutes who constitute the problem, not their male clients or pimps."[57] AMNLAE attributes prostitution to men's involvement in migrant labor and to the high unemployment rate among women—both products of the Somoza economy.

The movement of men between the cities and the countryside meant that women were left to fend for themselves and consequently there are many single mothers. These women who have been left alone are forced onto the streets (i.e, into waged work), to supplement any money that they might receive (from their husbands). Or they might be completely without financial support because their *compañeros* have started a new family elsewhere. Some women therefore fall into the trap of prostitution.[58]

Such an analysis ignores the issues of sexism and sexuality and AMNLAE often adopts a moralistic view of prostitution. But the Association acknowledges the direct link between prostitution and women's economic reality, and works to integrate prostitutes in women's production collectives. AMNLAE's Sylvia Reyes elaborates:

The only way to get a woman out of prostitution is by giving her an economic alternative. We've involved them in these collectives—of course, without saying 'this woman's a prostitute, let's include her to do her a favor'. We include them just like any other workers, making them aware of the need to increase productivity and attending to their political development just as with other women who have already got a basic political education. In this way we are solving, in part, the problem of prostitution in our country. Some women from other organizations, from the United States to be precise, have said to me that this work wasn't suitable rehabilitation work for prostitutes, that they needed a special job. But we believe that if we pay them special attention we are marginalizing them, and it's not their fault that they are prostitutes, it's society's, because it hasn't given them any skills, either technical or cultural, so that they can look after themselves. It was the enormous economic pressure that forced women at certain times to find any means of subsistence.[59]

The Ministry of Social Welfare also attempts to find prostitutes a safe place to live and to train them for alternative employment. But often the government response to prostitution is harsh, aimed at the prostitutes themselves rather than the underlying reasons for prostitution. In February 1981, police smashed their way through the prostitutes' huts in the Mercado Oriental, destroying them. CDS activists had requested this action. Thus, while the revolution has begun to do away with prostitution, it hasn't susbstantially changed matters; prostitution remains financially lucrative for women. Because the public concentrates on prostitutes, not prostitution, questions of sexuality, sexism, and attitudes to sex that create a demand for prostitutes are ignored. Moreover, the law currently asserts that prostitutes can become criminals for their actions while their clients' behavior goes unexamined.[60]

Women in the Rural Sector

As in most Latin American countries, rural women in Nicaragua have been historically marginalized and doubly exploited: as peasant women or agricultural workers and as women. In the rural world, the differences between men's work and women's work are strictly defined. The woman is responsible for the home and the children while the man is responsible for productive work and animal care.

Various studies on the economic participation of rural women in Latin America have shown that the figures, based on international criteria, tend to underestimate the participation of rural women, whether peasants or proletarians. In small farm production the man, as head of the household, is always considered the principal agricultural producer and therefore economically active. The woman and children are considered nonpaid family assistants and only enter the economically active population if agriculture is their principal activity.

However, even when rural women do not work the land, many of them raise animals and transform and process agricultural products. Before the revolution, statistical studies or investigations ignored such activities and sharply underestimated the number of women in the rural EAP. Government studies published since 1979 indicate that women significantly participate in the rural EAP. Some officials estimate, for example, that women represent 36 percent of the labor force that picks cotton and at least 28 percent of the coffee pickers.[61] Moreover, many women work year round in both the banana and tobacco industry in Nicaragua.

AMNLAE AND THE UNIONS

Until the summer of 1981, AMNLAE had no specific policy on women in unions. Concentrating up to that time on helping to raise the social wage, the Association promoted social programs such as literacy and health care. AMNLAE also viewed the community—not the workplace—as the principal arena for women, perhaps because most AMNLAE activists lacked trade union experience. Since 1981, as part of its move to organize within the mass organizations, the Association has targeted the workplace, forming small groups of women to pressure both the unions and employers into meeting women's demands. AMNLAE chose this path because the unions have been slow to respond to women's needs. In a 1981 interview, Glenda Monterrey, then general secretary of AMNLAE, delineated the relationship between women and the unions.

> It is true that there are many longstanding problems that just cannot be resolved right now, because we don't have the economic resources. But we think that with a proper understanding of the role women have played and are playing in the revolution, with a clear understanding of women's responsibilities in the home—because the majority here are single mothers—that yes, the unions can do something. Maybe higher wages are out of the question right now. But it is sometimes possible to take steps to improve working conditions without spending a lot of money. And if they changes aren't made, it will be difficult for the woman worker to participate in the way she should, either in the factory or in the union. This is another problem. It often happens that women do their work, are members of their union, but don't participate in a militant way, don't fight to resolve these problems. And if the women don't do it, the male *compañeros* won't do it.[62]

Nicaraguan women do not have a history of involvement in Nicaraguan trade unionism. This explains why there are few women leaders and union activists. In realms such as defense, where women participated in the war against Somoza, they have continued to organize and to gain leadership positions. But, as Monterrey notes, the situation in the unions is quite different.

> The truth is that in the governing bodies of the Sandinista Workers Federation (CST) and the Rural Workers Association (ATC) there are almost no women leaders at the national level. . . . In the CST it is understandable, because we have some catching up to do. We women did not play much of a role in forming or organizing the trade unions. So it wasn't until after the revolution that the real efforts to involve women workers began. And women are responding. But this is not yet reflected much at the national leadership.[63]

Although AMNLAE now pressures the unions' male hierarchy through its member groups in the factories and farms, the Association has not yet confronted the key problem: the sexual division of labor. Until AMNLAE and the government devise a plan for altering the rigid separation between "female" and "male" occupations, Nicaragua women will continue to suffer the economic consequences of job segregation.

Unemployment

An urgent problem throughout Nicaragua, lack of employment is particularly severe for women. Glenda Monterrey explains, "We think there are still problems with the degree to which women are incorporated into the work force. This isn't because women don't want to work, or because the government doesn't want us to. The problem is the overall lack of jobs. And it is still sometimes true in our country, that when there are two people for only one job, the job is given to the man."[64] To provide immediate sources of income, AMNLAE and the Social Welfare Ministry have set up collectively-run projects such as sewing and laundry co-ops. Now under the responsibility of the Ministry of Labor, these collectives use women's existing skills to bring them into production. Although this project maintains the sexual division of jobs, it attempts to link aspects of production and reproduction in the employment of women. In 1979, Antonio Jarquin, then supervisor of the project at the Ministry of Social Labor, defined the aim of the collectives.

> The program aims to give employment by means of artisan and manufacturing industry. Secondly, it aims to make available to the people a series of basic goods at the lowest possible price. This is because sales will leave out the middlemen, the speculators . . . The participation of women is vital. The problems of women will not be solved simply by incorporating them into productive activity. It's a question of establishing a new mode of production. The collectives depend on the community collectively assuming the domestic tasks of women. That's why we are creating community laundries, dining-rooms, ironing centers, child-care collectives. Production and social services are a single bloc.[65]

Although the collectives project seeks to alter the "mode of production" rather than merely integrate women into traditional productive activity, Nicaragua's economic realities have forced the collectives to operate on a more modest level. The project is now a small but significant advance in job creation, a measure that recognizes women's need to work near their homes, and that also draws on local skills and community sentiment.

POLITICAL REPRESENTATION

In its first platform statement in 1967, the FSLN raised the subject of woman's emancipation, referring to the double exploitation to which she has been subjected throughout history. Women, according the the FSLN statement, suffered from "unequal wages, a double workload (inside and outside of the home), isolation from political and social participation (fundamentally in rural areas), use as a sexual object (prostitution, exploitation. of women in the media, etc.), and to complete the picture, legal discrimination."[66]

Women entered the structures of the FSLN even in its early years, but they did so in small numbers and men did not immediately accept them as equals. Monica Baltodano describes the obstacles that Sandinista women confronted within the revolutionary organization.

> The problem of male chauvinism was evident among comrades in the . . . FSLN. Some men harboured distinctly sexist attitudes toward women. They believed that women were for domestic tasks alone and that we shouldn't go beyond being messengers. There were a lot of arguments. Some comrades were open to dealing with sexism while others remained closed. Some said women were no good in the mountains, that they were only good "for screwing," that they created conflicts—sexual conflicts. But there were also men with very good positions. Carlos Fonseca, for example, was a solid comrade on this issue. It's been a long struggle. We won those battles through discussions and by women comrades demonstrating their ability and their resistance.[67]

Indeed, many women in the FSLN were combatants, including several commanders such as Dora Maria Tellez, Leticia Herrera, Monica Baltodano, and Doris Tijerino. In 1982, 22 percent of the FSLN militants were women and women held 37 percent of the FSLN zonal and regional political administration positions.[68] Although these percentages are still low, they are higher than any European, North American, or Latin American political party. Given the relatively short history of the FSLN, these numbers may also be an indication of future increases in women's participation.

In the government, however, few women hold top political positions. During the Council of State period—1980 to 1985—there were no women in the Government Junta and only seven women in the legislature. As of December 1986 President Daniel Ortega had appointed only one woman to his cabinet, Health Minister Dora Maria Tellez. The overwhelming majority of women employed in the government are secretaries and cleaning women. But the revolution has engendered a shift of power towards women in two ways. First, the Fundmental Statute on the Rights and Guarantees of Nicaraguans directs the government to foster conditions for sexual and racial equality.

All people are equal before the law and have the right to the same protection.

There shall be no discrimination on the grounds of birth, race, color, sex, religion, opinions, origins, economic position or any other social condition. It is a duty of the State to remove, by all means at its disposal, all obstacles that in effect obstruct the equality of citizens and their political, economic, and social participation in the life of the country.[69]

This statute serves as the basis for the many government programs that have improved the status of Nicaraguan women. In addition, women themselves acknowledge that the revolution has endowed them with the capacity to exercise political power.

We feel that political power is beneficial for women as well as men. It's acknowledged that women are worth as much as men, and have the same rights as men. That doesn't mean we are changing everything, but we have the principal thing—the political power. Women's liberation is one of the points of the Sandinista Front's prgram. In other countries, in the USA, for example, you have to fight with the big companies, the television and the radio. But here, we control the key elements. We have the potential. There you feel like a peanut. Here, you don't feel like a peanut but you feel like you are changing the world. We [women] are very important to change in Nicaragua. We are 50.8 percent of the population. We feel there is a place for us here. We have to fight, that's right, we accept that. We think we are going to make a revolution inside this revolution. That's the project we have to work on. But we have the possibility.[70]

CASE STUDY: THE AMNLAE ZONAL OFFICE IN ESTELÍ

The Zonal Executive Committee

At the time of the case study (1983-84) AMNLAE's zonal office in Estelí was run by a five-member executive committee: a secretary-general, a secretary of organization, a secretary of health and social affairs, a secretary of defense and production, and a secretary of propaganda and political eduction. During the time that the author studied the work of the committee, the secretary of propaganda and education was ouside of Estelí carrying out a special assignment. The other four AMNLAE officers divided up her duties. All these women are full-time, professional

members of AMNLAE. "Professional members," according to the secretary-general, "are those who know how to manage the business of the
organization and who receive economic help or a minimal salary."[71]

At the end of each month, the committee met to establish its monthly
work plan. At the end of August 1984, for example, the zonal office
planned activities centering on the following tasks: 1. initiating the election campaign; 2. honoring women for their participation in production;
3. celebrating Sandinista Popular Army day; 4. commemmorating the
anniversary of the National Literacy Campaign; and 5. honoring the
seventh anniversary of AMNLAE. The five secretaries were responsible
for organizing all these tasks and activities.

AMNLAE Membership in the Zone

AMNLAE has thirty-eight work committees in the city of Estelí: twenty-
eight in the barrios and ten in work centers. These work centers include
the state-owned cigar factory, the hospital, the health center, AMNLAE's
sewing collective, a child development center, a spice factory, and the
Ministry of Interior. A work committee comprises a minimum of six
women. Work-committee coordinators meet weekly in the zonal office
of AMNLAE to develop organizational projects and plans for executing
them.

But who are the women who are members of AMNLAE? According
to Luz, secretary of organization, "To be a member you have to share
a part of your life in the work of the society. Also, you have to work
with your husband and children because the woman is the primary ed-
ucator in the family. You may be a member no matter party you are in
or what your faith is."[72] The Association's membership form includes
the following question: "What is the reason that motivated you to be
in AMNLAE?" The women of Estelí respond in different ways to this
question:

> The reason that motivated me to belong to this organization is
> to work more to serve the revolution and to be within it (23-
> year-old worker).
> To be organized and to be a new woman (50-year-old house-
> wife).
> To be each day more organized in consolidating the revolution
> (15-year-old student).
> Because only through organization can we succeed in con-
> solidating the Popular Sandinista Revolution (29-year-old
> teacher).
> Because I feel the necessity to help our people and only

through organization will we defend the revolution (15-year-old student).

To be revolutionary I should be integrated in the mass organizations in order to participate in all forms of work (53-year-old teacher)

To be more organized and help any way I can (48-year-old maid).

The level of participation among AMNLAE members varies greatly. Some women work in all of the organization's projects, while others choose to perform only a single task. Some members fail to attend work committee meetings but participate in AMNLAE activities in their neighborhood. And some women carry out Association tasks at their workplace but never at the neighborhood level.

An AMNLAE Organizational Meeting

In January 1984, Rosario Rivera, AMNLAE's secretary of defense and production arranged a meeting in a rural area south of Estelí.[73] The purpose of this meeting was to form an AMNLAE work committee among interested women in the community.

Before the meeting, Rosario met with Fililena Morena, AMNLAE's contact person in the community. Fililena briefly described herself: "I come from a very poor family. But I know how to operate a sewing machine and I can read and write. I can draw and make things." Fililena then held up a silhouette of Sandino that she had made by pasting beans onto construction paper. Although an enthusiastic AMNLAE supporter, Fililena complained of the organizing difficulties in her community: "To get people here to fight the National Guard was easy. But to get people organized here is now much more difficult. Some are confused mentally and others just don't want to do anything." Rosario attributed many of the community's problems to reactionary evangelical preachers who were active in the area.

Rosario noted that in the revolution's early period many Nicaraguan women who were active in the CDSs considered AMNLAE to be unimportant, secondary. But more recently they have come to see that only by participating in AMNLAE can they resolve thier problems as women: "We have to get used to having meetings as women because we have our own concerns that men are not interested in or don't like." As Rosario waited for more women to gather for the 3:00 meeting, she spoke of some of the recent gains made by the revolution. She mentioned Estelí's special-education school for students with mental and physical problems.

Rosario also discussed the Nurture Law guaranteeing child support, and the need to work with parents who are mistreating their children.

The meeting commenced at 3:00 with thirteen women in attendance, including three teenagers. Rosario began by greeting the women on behalf of AMNLAE's zonal office. She stressed the importance of the upcoming commemoration of Sandino's assassination (February 22), explaining how Carlos Fonseca had revived Sandino's legacy and continued his work. Nicaraguans should undersand who Sandino was, insisted Rosario, especially since his enemies spread so many lies about him, including the charge that he was a "bandit. Rosario concludes: "We must speak about Sandino to everyone, especially our children."

Rosario then turned to the main purpose of the meeting: establishing an AMNLAE work committee staffed by five secretaries. Rosario asked for volunteers to fill the work committee's posts. She explained the different tasks of each of the five secretaries, emphasizing the duties of secretary of defense. "We have to be organized," Rosario declared. "The secretaries will receive orientations and then pass them on to the AMNLAE members. In turn, your work committee will transmit its concerns and problems to the zonal office so that we can assist you." Rosario added: "Because you all know each other well, only you can choose one another to fill the work committee secretariats." Filelena intervened to back up Rosario's point, confirming that the women in the room were quite capable of carrying out the Association's work.

Rosario explained that not only the executive members of the work committee should work and set priorities, but that any interested woman could participate and do the work. One woman, when asked if she would consent to be the Secretary of Health, responded that she would prefer holding the defense position. The other women ratified her for this task. They then decided to nominate as secretary of health a woman absent from the meeting but who had been carrying out community health work. Finally, the women agreed that during the next week they would elect or confirm the women that had been proposed for the various offices that day.

The discussion then turned to the problems involved in mobilizing the women in their zone. Although thirty women in the community had expressed an interest in AMNLAE, they had yet to be organized. One woman conceded that many of the women lost their enthusiasm between meetings. Another woman stressed that the work committee's new leadership had to be active and serve as an example to the other members. Rosario then reminded the women that organizing efforts often began slowly and were part of a long, arduous process. After all, she observed, Carlos Fonseca began the Sandinistas' struggle with only two colleagues, and had to work tirelessly until his efforts multiplied into a war involving hundreds of thousands of Nicaraguans. The meeting ended on this positive note.

A Coordinators Meeting

Every Saturday, the coordinators of AMNLAE's work committees met to discuss the Association's ongoing projects, and to receive orientations from the zonal office. The following is an account of one such coordinators' meeting held on February 4, 1984.[74]

The women present introduced themselves. Of the 15 women attending the meeting, three represented Esteli's female hospital workers, four represented one neighborhood, and the other eight represented eight different barrios. The secretary of organization, Luz Florian, then outlined AMNLAE's role and its importance to Nicaraguan women.

We are a movement that works with peasant women, workers, professionals, intellectuals, and small merchants. We work with women who are housewives as well as women who work outside the home. We are all women, we are all in AMNLAE. . . . All women who have problems as women have to recognize that AMNLAE is *their* organization. So if a working woman has a problem relating to her pregnancy and the union is incapable of resolving it she can come to AMNLAE for help. AMNLAE can negotiate with the ATC, for example, if a woman loses her job because she was sick and lost time at work. We women have problems on top of problems. Peasant women have to struggle together because they have to integrate themselves into the cooperatives. We will be free when we understand ourselves, when we struggle for ourselves.

Women have to understand that they have to participate in the revolution. Maybe we are not entirely equal physically but we're equal in duties and rights. Women are respected who are honest, who attend to the problems in their barrios, who are not indifferent.

Luz then offered a short summary of the family laws that AMNLAE had sponsored in the Council of State. She stressed that in cases where women are working and men are unemployed, the men have to do the housework. "This is a daily political struggle and one of persuasion. Within this revolution we have to make another revolution."

Next, Luz asked the coordinators to report on the concerns of the women they represented. The coordinator from the hospital complained that administrators ask women to fill in for those workers who miss their work shifts, thereby doubling the women's work load. While admitting such a practice represented discrimination against women workers, one AMNLAE secretary suggested that the women hospital workers raise the matter with the Health Workers' Union. One of the neighborhood co-ordinators then discussed the situation of women who file child-support claims at the Ministry of Social Welfare, but who often feel humiliated when dealing with this ministry. Another coordinator reported that women have little access to scholarships awarded by the *Frente*, the government, and foreign countries. The women agreed that AMNLAE should launch a campaign to obtain more scholarships for women.

The next agenda item concerned the street vendors who sold food and wares in and around the main park in Estelí. One AMNLAE leader argued that the street vendors were creating a bad image for the town and that sanitation problems were prevalent. The AMNLAE leadership asked the coordinators to urge the street vendors to pay the 350-córdoba fee required to obtain a market booth. Because a campaign to clean and decorate the park had begun, the AMNLAE secretaries called on the coordinators to try to persuade the street vendors to relocate their busi-nesses as soon as possible. "We don't want to appear as the vendors' oppressors," emphasized one AMNLAE official, "we want to find out their problems and help them with the task of moving."

The Secretary of Health and Social Welfare then reported on the upcoming polio vaccination campaign. She announced that women health brigadistas and others with first aid training would administer the vaccinations. The Secretary of Organization gave notice that in two weeks AMNLAE would hold a special meeting to distribute membership cards to new members of the Association. In addition, the zonal office would honor a number of women for outstanding performance in carrying out revolutionary tasks. The meeting closed with the news that a North Amer-ican woman had donated an accordion to the municipal office and that women were welcome to learn how to play the instrument.

The Luisa Amanda Espinosa Sewing Collective

In 1980, AMNLAE established Estelí's first sewing collective in order to organize women who were unemployed, especially mothers who had lost children in the war, and widows.[75] AMNLAE sought to train women who hadn't had the opportunity to receive an education for a trade that would benefit society. Launched with donations of money, material, and machines from friendly countries, the collective thrived in its early stage. But it encountered stiff resistance from conservative sectors in Estelí. AMNLAE's critics argued that the collective's products would fall apart, that workers weren't paid sufficiently, and that workers wouldn't receive their fringe benefits. But the collective's members soon proved that they could produce quality clothes at the lowest prices in Estelí. As the production manager put it: "This collective was founded to guarantee clothes at fair prices for people. The goal was to eliminate the intermediaries and keep prices low." During its peak business stage, the collective had 90 members but due to economic problems the number fell to 63 in 1986.

All the workers belong to the Sandinista Trade Union Federation and are active in their CDSs and in the militia. The workers elect the administrative staff, all of whom serve on a rotating basis: when their terms expire they return to productive tasks. Administrative members are also subject to recall.

The Committee of Mothers of Heroes and Martyrs

The Committee of Mothers of Heroes and Martyrs, founded in 1980, dedicates its work to the remembrance of those who died—and continue to die—fighting for the liberation and sovereignty of Nicaragua. The Committee is part of AMNLAE but retains a separate organizational structure and sets its own tasks. Like AMNLAE, its base is made up of work committees that carry out the day-to-day affairs of the organization.

According to Carmen Montenegro Zelaya, an activist in Estelí's Committee of Mothers of Heroes and Martyrs, the Committee

> has the idea of defending our country and continuing to fight for the dreams of our heroes and martyrs. We're also organized to help the combatants and their mothers—elderly mothers need to be visited so that we know how they are doing. Are they sick? Do they need anything? We help the families of combatants by seeing what their needs are and then channeling necessities to them. For example, maybe the husband is fighting in the mountains and a child is sick. We visit the family and try—within the barrio—to resolve the situation. If we can't solve it on our own we try to get direct government help to the children.[76]

In the summer of 1984, the Committee was considering the formation of a collective that would raise needed funds for the organization. Some women wished to start a sewing collective while others preferred a florist shop. Carmen noted that each organization in Estelí sends an offering of flowers at funerals, and that these floral gifts were becoming very expensive. The Committee, she felt, could sell flowers at reduced prices, thereby serving the community while accumulating funds for the organization. The Committee's top priority, Carmen stressed, was to raise money to serve the needs of the mothers.[77]

Conclusion

Through the efforts of its zonal executive committee and work committee coordinators, AMNLAE promotes various activities which promote the well-being of Estelí's women. Despite AMNLAE's hard work, however, the contra war limits the organization's effectiveness. AMNLAE must devote scarce resources to aiding the families of mobilized soldiers and expends much of its energies rallying women around defense tasks. Only when peace prevails in Nicaragua will AMNLAE be capable of demonstrating its full strength as a women's organization.

Clearly, the revolution has created conditions that allow women to gain control over their lives.[75] Non-sexist legislation, an open political environment, and the sympathetic backing of the government have made it possible for women to voice and act upon their demands and concerns. Because they now have a nationwide organization campaigning on their behalf, Nicaraguan women exercize power in nearly every social sphere. Women, especially working class and peasant women, have enjoyed the benefits of the literacy and health campaigns; they no longer must fear that half their children might die while infants, or that they will inevitably lose a conflict with an employer. Through their active participation in AMNLAE and other mass organizations, women directly influence the direction and pace of government reforms.

Participation alone, however, provides no guarantee of equality. Hard economic realities narrow the revolution's options. The economy remains based upon women's subordination in low paid, insecure jobs in markets, factories, and other people's homes. Saddled with traditional sexist attitudes, the Sandinista union federations have offered women little support, proving reluctant to press women's demands in their day-to-day struggles. AMNLAE must face the fact that its strategy of "integrating" women into production must confront the difficulties posed by the sexual division of labor.

On the other hand, women have gained significantly from general improvements concerning the family. With childcare centers available, thousands of women can work without worrying about their children. New laws guarantee women child support in cases of abandonment and promote equality in household arrangements. Within both the government and the FSLN, there is a growing awareness that domestic burdens must be shared if women are to participate fully in the revolution.

Thus far, AMNLAE has won important advances for its members, and it has brought women's concerns into the public realm. But its disproportionate emphasis on production sometimes disregards aspects of women's oppression such as their reproductive role. Female participation in the economy will not destroy patriarchy unless it is accompanied by a vigorous challenge to gender-based economic and family roles. AMNLAE's understanding of this feminist assertion will go a long way to ensuring the genuine liberation of Nicaraguan women.

9

SHAPING AGRICULTURAL POLICY: UNAG

The National Union of Farmers and Ranchers (UNAG), with its 120,000 members, plays a major role in shaping the country's agricultural policy.[1] Nicaragua's small- and medium-size farmers and ranchers represent 66 percent of the economically active population in the agricultural sector and 28 percent of that of the entire country. In 1984 there were 259,100 small and medium producers, including 157,600 poor peasants.[2] These producers raise almost all the nation's basic foodstuffs, growing 80 percent of all the beans and corn and 97 percent of the vegetables. In addition, they produce a significant amount of two important exports: coffee and beef.[3] Yet, despite the influence they wield in the national economy, Nicaragua's farmers and ranchers lacked their own organization until 1981.

NEW SOCIAL RELATIONS IN THE COUNTRYSIDE

The transformation of Nicaragua's rural structure began before the 1979 Sandinista victory, as peasants and farmworkers seized Somocista land holdings during the war against the dictatorship.[4] The Rural Workers Association backed these landtakeovers, which mainly occurred around the Pacific Coast city of León during the final months of the popular insurrection. The seizures not only vindicated the economic and political struggles of the rural workers and peasants, but also provided the food necessary to the liberated areas. Between June and August, 1979, peasants collectively farmed the seized land, refraining from converting them into individual holdings.

The day after the dictatorship's collapse, Decree No. 3 of the National Government of Reconstruction authorized the confiscation of all the landholdings of Somoza and his allies. All at once, this decree initiated the nationalization of almost two million acres in approximately 2,000 farms and ranches. Because the bulk of these ex-Somocista farms were modern large-scale enterprises, the Sandinistas feared that productivity would drop if they were parceled up.

> The production units formerly owned by the Somozas, the military and their associates were large, highly mechanized plantations into which huge investments in the millions were channeled, often from the national treasury. Breaking them up into a myriad of parcels would decrease or eliminate the possibility of employing the technology and machinery that had been put into them and, conseqently, would reduce their productivity. We realized that it was absolutely necessary to keep the production units intact. Had we not [acted] immediately, the campesinos would have occupied this land themselves and would have parceled it out in the traditional way.[5]

The state, however, still had to decide whether to transfer the title to these lands to production cooperatives or retain title and manage the farms itself. The Sandinistas decided to create state farms, justifying their decision with three arguments. First, the success of these farms was crucial to guarantee the ongoing receipt of foreign exchange. Second, these highly developed properties had been run with a small permanent labor force and a large seasonal workforce; worker ownership could easily generate a rural elite. If the state had direct control of the surplus created on these farms it could distribute the benefits throughout the population. Third, the Sandinistas thought that it would be easier to generate more jobs—so desperately needed by landless farmworkers—under state administration than on worker-owned lands.

The creation of the state farms placed an important sector of the agro-export economy under state control and created new social relations for a portion of the rural labor force. But other landless agricultural workers and peasants with small holdings were untouched by these measures; these groups began to demand jobs, access to land, and state services. Numerous land seizures, especially in the northern provinces, demonstrated that the peasantry continued to experience economic hardship. Moreover, because the state farms were mainly export-oriented concerns, their creation did nothing to resolve the country's domestic grain shortages.

The FSLN was involved in a delicate balancing act at this juncture. As Deere et al. point out:

It was clear to the Sandinista leadership that the agrarian reform process had to be broadened in order to attack the problems of rural poverty, unemployment and foodstuff production as well as to meet popular demands. But the Sandinista government's options were constrained by the policy of national unity. Its alliance with the private sector, which was seen as necessary in order to reactivate production and preserve foreign political and economic relations, depended upon its commitment to the mixed economy, and specifically to private property. The bulk of export production still remained in the hands of the private sector. The rural bourgeoisie (holdings of over 70 hectares) accounted for over half the production of cotton, coffee, and sugar cane, and some 40% of cattle production. The reactivation of this production was crucial to the economic success of the revolutionary project.[6]

The Sandinistas offered a compromise: expropriating all lands under ATC membership control while assuring private landowners that further land takeovers would be vigorously discouraged. To meet the demand for land, the Ministry of Agriculture allowed landless workers to "borrow" unused plots on state farms, theoretically on a season-to-season basis. The workers had to be willing to work the land collectively and promise to work for wages on the state farm when they were needed. In addition, because a large proportion of the peasantry was sharecropping or renting land at rates that reproduced their poverty and landlessness, the government tried to convince the big growers to change the conditions of land rental.

In the spring of 1980, the government initiated a two-sided policy to deal with the problems of rural poverty and unemployment. The first aspect of the new approach centered on the conditions of land rental. In April and May of 1980, the government established the maximum annual rent for non-cotton-producing land at 100 córdobas per manzana and prohibited tenant evictions. Also, by mid-1980, the state had turned over 19,500 acres of APP land rent-free to about 4,000 rural workers organized into production cooperatives, or *colectivos de trabajo* (work collectives—CTs), for a single growing season.

The second element of the new policy was a massive small farm credit program designed to fulfil four goals: increase food production, build political support among the small producers, improve the economic situation of the poor campesinos, and encourage peasants to form cooperatives or credit associations. The government enticed tenants and owners into forming cooperatives with lower interest rates, providing credit at 7 percent to production cooperatives, at 8 percent to members of credit and service cooperatives, and at 11 percent to unorganized peasant producers. To coordinate the credit program, the government created a joint commission, with representatives from the *Banco Nacional de Desarollo* (National Development Bank—BND) the *Programa Campesina* (Peasant's Program—PROCAMPO), the ATC, the Ministry of Planning, and the *Empresa Nicaraguense de Alimentos Basicos* (National Basic Foods Company—ENABAS) in order to coordinate the credit program.[7]

Although the amount of financing directed to the peasant producers was unprecedented in Nicaraguan history, the disbursal of credit encountered a range of administrative and structural problems. First, some peasants in remote areas received credit so late that they were still harvesting their corn and beans at a time when their labor was desperately needed on the export crop farms. Second, crop yields in a number of regions failed to meet ministry predictions and thus some small producers simply had too little income from their crop to repay the loan. Third, no purchasers appeared to buy harvests from farmers who cultivated their land in the most inaccessible parts of the country. Finally, the credit that many peasants received simply exceeded the economic potential of their land. Not surprisingly, then, the percent of the 1980 debt repaid that year fell to 33.6 percent, from the already low figure of 58.7 percent for 1979.[8]

> These problems can be attributed in part to the lack of government technical expertise, to difficulties in coordinating the activities of the various government agencies involved with the peasant sector, and to a general lack of knowledge of the conditions of the peasant producers. In large part they are also due to the generally *ad hoc* nature of Sandinista policy towards the peasant sector at this time. The State was still concerned with the consolidation and administration of the APP, an enormous undertaking. The ATC, with its increasingly large cooperative membership, had taken up the pressing issues of indebtedness and the need for improved marketing services. Nevertheless it was still at heart a rural workers association, and was finding it difficult to effectively coordinate policy towards its peasant members. While credit had been a useful tool in expanding ATC membership, it was not clear that this was to the benefit of the ATC as an organization, nor to its increasingly diverse membership, nor to the overall goals of the revolution. It was becoming evident that more fundamental changes in the approach to the peasant sector were necessary.[9]

THE RISE OF UNAG

The issue of land ownership continued to pose a problem for the Sandinistas. The new rental decrees failed to meet the poor peasants' demand
for land. Many private landowners defied the rental provisions by refusing
to rent land at the established rates. And in those cases where land was
ceded to the peasants, tenure was too insecure to plan production for
more than one harvest at a time. Thus, during 1980, the ATC began to
press for land tenure guarantees and for firmer action against the moves
of the bourgeoisie.

At the same time, government policy failed to respond to all the
needs of the middle and well-to-do peasants. The credit program had
provided sufficient financing, but technical aid and the speedy provision
of inputs and machinery were absent. The Area of People's Property and
the new cooperative sector continued to receive most of the attention of
the Ministry of Agriculture agencies. In addition, both the state and
cooperative sectors employed labor and often their concerns conflicted
with those of the ATC.

The rural bourgeoisie moved swiftly to take advantage of this short-
coming in Sandinista policy. Although the Sandinistas attempted to work
with the private sector and assure them that their economic interests
would be taken into account, sectors of the rural bourgoisie were campaigning intensively against the revolution. They overcame their initial
period of disorganization and began to rally their economic and political
forces around the producer associations: the coffee growers' association,
the cotton growers' association, and the Union of Agricultural Producers
of Nicaragua. These organizations sought to attract peasant producers,
using credit, the supply of cheap inputs, and propaganda as their main
recruiting devices. And to confuse the peasants, the producer associations
began a smear campaign against the government. "In the mountains,"
said one peasant from Chontales, "reactionary elements go around saying
that the government is going to tax small farmers for every chair and pig
and hut that we own, that then it is going to take way our lands besides."[10]
The bourgeoisie also attempted to organize the peasantry by crop into
their productive associations to prevent them from recognizing their
shared class interests.

The ATC countered this organizing drive with a campaign to actively
recruit the middle and large peasantry. But in August the ATC was deprived of its main organizing weapon when the government, concerned
about a possible labor shortage for the upcoming harvests, drastically
cut credit for the second planting of basic grains. At the same time,
peasants with medium and large holdings no longer viewed the ATC as

an organization that could respond to their concerns. The peasantry's disenchantment with the ATC was reinforced in November 1980 when the Association pressed the government for more state-sector land to form work collectives, a measure which jeopardized the harvest labor supply of both peasant producers and the bourgeoisie.

Activists within the ATC had insisted for months that the peasantry needed their own organization. They realized that the support of the small farmers could not be taken for granted; this important social sector could easily be alienated from the revolution, especially because economic scarcity makes it impossible to deliver immediate improvements to the peasantry. The small farmers' isolation, backwardness, and fear of change made them susceptible to the propaganda of the big growers and their political parties.

After the defection of the bourgeois agricultural organizations from the revolution,[11] the most conscious elements among the peasantry began mobilizing in various regions of the country. A large regional assembly took place in Matagalpa on December 14, 1980, to build the foundation for a new peasant organization. The assembly called for a nationwide union of all small and medium producers. On April 25 and 26, 1981, 360 delegates met in Managua to form the *Union Nacional de Agricultores y Ganaderos* (National Union of Farmers and Ranchers—UNAG). Upon its formation UNAG became the sole representative of the small and medium producers before the state. The union gained representation in the Council of State, in the National and Departmental Committees of Small and Medium Producers, and in the National and Regional Councils of the Ministry of Agriculture.

The creation of UNAG meant that the ATC lost a part of its membership. Peasant producers organized in cooperatives, as well as unorganized peasant landowners, became members of UNAG. Permanent and seasonal agricultural workers stayed with the ATC, including those workers renting APP land in work collectives (CTs). UNAG thus was responsible for organizing all peasant producers except for work collective producers. The ATC was charged with organizing rural workers, and union-building became its principal task. Because a part of its membership was in work collectives, however, the ATC maintained a degree of interest in the problems of peasant producers.

The new political and organizational forms of the peasantry both reflected and subsequently shaped the direction of Sandinista agrarian policy. There was now a clear recognition of the peasants as producers rather than as rural workers. This marked a definite theoretical shift from the original assumption that the semi-proletarians could best be organized as workers. This changing consciousness of the nature of the rural situation was reflected in a shift in terminology: "semi-proletarian" was dropped and the phrase "small and medium producers" (*pequeno y mediano productores*) began to appear in all discussions of the peasantry.[12]

UNAG AND PRODUCTION POLICY

Since its inception, UNAG has proved itself one of the country's most powerful organizations, winning a series of important demands for its large constituency. Through its lobbying efforts, farmers and ranchers have gained access to land, credit, services, and technical assistance, as well as considerable state assistance in marketing their products. In addition, UNAG plays a major role in formulating Nicaragua's agricultural production policy. It has a key voice in determining land distribution under the agrarian reform and in coordinating the cooperativization process. Thus UNAG wields its organizational strength to both shape the nation's agricultural policy and to meet the needs of its membership.

Access to Land

The agrarian reform law, announced in July 1981, had three basic aims: 1. to bring idle land in the private sector into production in order to increase basic grain production; 2. to satisfy peasant demand for secure access to land and therefore consolidate their support for the revolution; and 3. to alleviate the fears of the bourgeoisie by proposing a definitive solution to the land issue.[13]

The new law provided for the expropriation of unused, underutilized, and rented land on farms greater than 865 acres in the Pacific and central interior regions of the country and on farms greater than 1730 acres in the rest of the country. Also affected were lands leased by their owners under precapitalist forms of tenancy (sharecropping and *colono* arrangements) where total farm size either exceeded 865 acres in the Pacific region, or 1,730 acres in the rest of the country. Abandoned land was subject to confiscation regardless of size. The government would compensate owners of expropriated land with agrarian reform bonds based on the average declared value of owners' holdings over the previous three years. Those slated to receive land included peasants who had been farming land under any type of rental arrangements, small holders with insufficient land, landless workers, state farms, and urban residents who wanted to produce basic grains.[14] The government an-

nounced that it would give first priority to those peasants and rural workers willing to establish cooperatives, and to the families of those who
died fighting the dictatorship. The Ministry of Agriculture originally estimated that 1.7 million acres would be available for redistribution under
the agrarian reform.[15] In July 1983 the Ministry increased that figure to
3.4 million acres.[16]

Deere describes other important aspects of the agrarian reform law.

> Nicaraguan tenants will not necessarily receive the land on
> which they presently work since the law is not intended to punish
> small and medium-sized producers who are engaged in land
> renting. Tenants can extricate themselves from rental arrange-
> ments by soliciting land from the pool of expropriated lands in
> the area; they will not be bound to marginal parcels of land.
> Thus, second, tenants and landless workers are guaranteed ac-
> cess to the amount of land necessary to provide an income
> equivalent to the minimum monthly agricultural salary.
> Tenants may receive access to land either individually or col-
> lectively, in both cases receiving agrarian reform titles which
> guarantee dominion possession, and the usufruct of land. Lands
> adjudicated under the agrarian reform cannot be sold, in order
> to avoid the process of peasant dispossession so prevalent during
> the 1950s. Land may be inherited, as long as it is not subdivided
> among the heirs, so as to avoid a process of minifundization in
> future years.[17]

The government cautiously implemented the agrarian reform in its
first year. By July 1982, the Ministry of Agriculture had expropriated 242
properties totaling about 166,000 acres and had redistributed only 40
percent of the land to 6,503 beneficiaries who received titles either
individually or as part of a production cooperative.[18] The National Agrarian Reform Council carefully determined each case of expropriation and
a special Agrarian Reform Tribunal adjudicated all appeals. Although the
Sandinistas attempted to identify and expropriate only the worst cases to
avoid alienating the bourgeoisie, evidence of landowner resistance to
government economic policies mounted daily. By early 1982, both the
ATC and the UNAG were urging the government to hasten the implementation of the agrarian reform process.[19]

Faced with an agrarian bourgeoisie engaged in a campaign of economic sabotage and the growing militancy of the rural mass organizations, the Ministry of Agriculture decided to shift more control over the
agrarian reform process to UNAG and the ATC. The Ministry turned over
final decision on land expropriation to regional commissions that in-

cluded ATC and UNAG representatives. In the fall of 1982, both organizations mobilized their base level activists throughout the country to study the patterns of land tenure and utilization, and to propose detailed plans for the expropriation and redistribution of land in their communities.[20]

The UNAG representatives on the Regional Commissions ofAgrarian Reform now play a decisive role in land adjudications.[21] UNAG has a direct voice in determining the criteria used to decide which land is to be turned over and to whom. If there is a large plot of underutilized or abandoned land, the UNAG regional representative ensures that it is given to the cooperative movement according to the provisions of the Agrarian Reform Law. Union leaders insist that the primary beneficiaries be poor peasants who have no land or who are exploited by landowners. UNAG representatives also propose that those peasants who want to move from marginal land in order to join a cooperative be allowed to do so.[22] According to Nicolas Chavez, director of the Cooperative Development Program in Estelí: "UNAG is the organization that has the most weight, the most social force, in determining the distribution of land because of the great number of peasants it organizes and the overall strength of its organization."[23]

Despite its influence in determining land distribution, UNAG has not yet been able to secure land for all those who need it. Roberto Laguna, UNAG Coordinator in Region I, summarizes the situation in his region.

> Under Somoza the majority of campesinos didn't have land. After August 1981 land began to be handed to the peasants. But many still don't have land. Here peasants lived on marginalized land and suffered precarious conditions. The spirit of the Agrarian Reform Law is to affect the large landowners who neglect the land. Poor peasants have to be moved to places where there is better land and larger plots of land. In this region there isn't much good land. Most of it is up north near Jalapa where the Contras operate. In most other areas the small and medium producers need to receive more services. Those who also need help are peasants who left their land due to Contra attacks. We can't say that these problems are being resolved a hundred percent.[24]

One problem that has been resolved concerns the question of whether the agrarian reform should be implemented slowly or rapidly. The military situation has prompted a definite speed-up of land redistribution. In late 1982 and early 1983, the Somocista counter-revolutionaries stepped up their attacks against Nicaragua as they tried to interfere with the export harvest. The military, seeking to augment the defense capabilities of the war zone, called for settling more peasants on the land, thereby reinforcing UNAG's pressure for redistribution. The Sandinistas also felt that a more rapid implementation of the agrarian reform would strengthen peasant and rural worker commitment to defend the revolution.[25]

As a result of these pressures, the process of land entitlement dramatically accelerated in 1983. While the government had distributed only 91,550 hectares of land in the first eighteen months of the agrarian reform, it turned over 482,430 hectares in 1983 alone. And in 1984 the Ministry of Agricultural Development and Agrarian Reform distributed approximately one million hectares to *campesinos*.[26]

Deere summarizes the significance of the agrarian reform process.

> The Nicaraguan agrarian reform is more than a response to peasant and worker demands; these producers themselves have shaped the course of the agrarian reform. Indicative of this is the great degree of flexibility written into the agrarian reform law. Peasants and rural workers are not being compelled into predetermined forms of production. Rather the degree of individual choice and local autonomy in the process makes this reform process unique in the Latin American reform experience.[27]

Access to Credit

The most common concern of UNAG members has been one familiar to land-holding farmers everywhere—credit. Since the beginning of the revolution, small farmers have had the option of borrowing from the state-owned National Development Bank instead of falling deeper and deeper into debt and eventually turning over their land to the big growers. While rural credit during 1978 (under Somoza) totaled 204 million córdobas distributed to 31,993 producers, by December 1982 rural credit had increased 5.5 times, to 1,620.9 million córdobas, benefitting 94,174 farmers.[28]

This rapid expansion of debt, of course, does not automatically solve the problem of debt service, especially given the extremely small size and low productivity of most of the farms. By the middle of 1983, Nicaragua's small and medium food producers found themselves in debt to the national banking system for a total of $35 million.[29] Nearly all the small peasants in the country owed more money than they could afford to pay. The counterrevolution moved to exploit this situation, spreading rumors that the government was going to confiscate the land of all peasants who couldn't pay their debts.

Consequently, in 1983, UNAG spearheaded a drive to revise the debt situation, especially for peasants who produce basic grains and who work on cooperatives. Both the FSLN and the Government Junta acceded to UNAG's demands, and on July 19, 1983, Ortega announced the formal alleviation of the peasant debt. The measure gave preferential treatment to the most advanced forms of collective production: food producers organized in Sandinista agricultural cooperatives had their debts totally eliminated; members of credit and service cooperatives had all debts up to the 1981–1982 growing season lifted; and small and medium individual producers of basic food items had all debts up to the 1980–1981 growing season cancelled. Finally, in recognition of their contribution to defense, all peasants serving in the reserves or militias as well as all peasants in self-defense settlements had their total debts erased.[30]

UNAG also participates in the process of allocating credits to small and medium farmers and cattlemen. It sits on credit committees at the zonal, regional, and national levels, airing its point of view along with those of the banks and the Ministry of Agriculture. Because so many of its members work on cooperatives, UNAG delegates on these credit committees lobby vigorously to secure loans for the cooperative sector. If a cooperative is seeking a loan, but also needs more land to thrive economically, UNAG will press for both additional land and sufficient credit. In addition, UNAG attempts to coordinate the amount of credit a cooperative receives with the ability of the cooperative to repay the loan.[31]

Access to Services and Technical Assistance

UNAG delegates, along with representatives of various state agencies and the FSLN, participate in the deliberations of the zonal and regional Committees of Small and Medium Production. Among other tasks, these committees must set fair prices for basic grains in order to ensure the economic well-being of peasant producers. Aware of production costs, UNAG delegates try to set prices at levels that guarantee a decent profit margin to its members.[32] UNAG also works to gain services and technical assistance for its membership. To determine the needs of production cooperatives, credit and service associations, and individual producers, the union convenes periodic municipal assemblies. In these assemblies, producers submit their needs for agricultural inputs such as machinery, seeds, fertilizer, and irrigation equipment. The UNAG municipal councils, in conjunction with the UNAG zonal and regional councils, determine a plan of action to secure these inputs, then present the plan to the Committee of Small and Medium Production.[33]

The problem, however, is that MIDINRA frequently cannot meet the service and technical needs of UNAG's membership. This situation dramatizes a major weakness inherited from *Somocismo*: the lack of institutions responding to the needs of the peasant sector. To develop non agro-export production, the government must match the rapid pace of land redistribution with an increase in services to the peasant producers. Because the government now emphasizes the role of peasants as producers, it is obliged to develop institutions that will give it greater control over the generation and distribution of surplus in that sector. But the government is handicapped by a shortage of technical personnel, infrastructure, and technological development in basic foodstuff production. As Deere et al., caution: "There is the danger that the pace of the agrarian reform may outstrip the institutional capacity of the government."[34]

Most *campesinos* employ primitive forms of technology; almost half of peasant credit recipients use only traditional technology, and another 40 percent use only some selected components of a semi-technified standard package. This state of underdevelopment results in extremely low yields for basic grains, even compared to other Central American countries.[35]

UNAG plans to develop technical training programs for its members to help overcome the legacy of underdevelopment in the peasant sector. Until now UNAG has coordinated training programs with MIDINRA, but this too has involved problems.

> We've had problems coordinating classes in different crops— basic grains, vegetables, etc. If a rancher goes to a basic grains seminar he won't understand anything. We try to have classes for different types of peasants. But we're only now concretizing "integral" programs from the technical and organizational point of view. We want our members to have technical capacities. This year we are proposing a regional technical school, but we still don't have the material and technical resources to maintain a school, nor do we have the financial means to set one up.[36]

In 1985 UNAG completed the construction of a school in Region III that provides technical training in cotton production and horticulture. Funded by an Italian foundation, the school has its own fields for agricultural and stockraising experiments.[37]

Commercialization

The majority of UNAG members, especially those on cooperatives, channel their products through the Basic Foods Marketing Company, ENABAS.

Before selling their products, however, cooperative members first decide how much to consume, how much to retain for animal consumption, and how much to use as seed. They then sell the balance to the state or to private intermediaries. According to Nicolas Chavez, selfishness motivates those producers that sell to private intermediaries: "It's mostly individual producers who don't care about the well-being of consumers, who sell to private intermediaries offering higher prices, because if they sell to intermediaries at higher prices, then the retail prices will be higher as well."[38]

ENABAS is in charge of storing all the products it buys from UNAG. Each year UNAG and ENABAS determine together the quantities of goods that need to be stored, and try to establish centrally located storage facilities. In 1981, ENABAS constructed "intermediate storage centers" close to many of the more remote areas of the country. Two or three UNAG members manage each storage center and the union then distributes the products to the country's marketplaces.[39]

Since 1982, UNAG has organized rural supply centers on cooperatives that carry products such as sugar, oil, cooking gas, soap, rice, and matches. Maintained by UNAG members, these centers play the same role as urban outlets, providing basic goods at fixed prices. The Ministry of Internal Commerce works with UNAG to guarantee that the rural supply centers receive sufficient quantities of supplies other than basic grains.[40]

COOPERATIVIZATION

One of UNAG's primary tasks is to help consolidate the cooperativization process that the government initiated as part of the agrarian reform.[41] Because the peasantry in Nicaragua is not monolithic—individual *campesinos* have different interests and ideologies—UNAG convinces peasants to form cooperatives by appealing to a variety of class and personal interests. Peasants have joined cooperatives to gain land, to improve crop sales, to defend themselves against the Contras, and to work alongside family members. Consequently, the cooperative movement has developed a complex and flexible structure.

The cooperativization program has three goals: 1. to consolidate the peasant alliance with the revolutionary project; 2. to expand the efficiency of basic grains and vegetable production; and 3. to begin to develop socialist forms of agricultural development. The governing principles of the program are "voluntary enlistment, graduality, and democracy," and its driving forces are the interests and motivations of the *campesinos* themselves.[42]

Four types of agricultural cooperatives exist in Nicaragua. The two major types are *cooperativas de credito y servicio* (credit and service cooperatives—CCSs) and *cooperativas agrícolas Sandinistas* (Sandinista agricultural cooperatives—CASs). Credit and service cooperatives, which comprise 57 per cent of all cooperatives, are associations of private, individual producers who organize to jointly receive low interest credit, resources, and higher prices for their products.[43] Members negotiate for their loans as a unit, but the cooperative disburses the money individually to each member, who works his/her land separately. The CCS may also organize the joint purchase, rental, and delivery of inputs and then distributes them for individual use on each member's farm. The individual producers retain the entire product of their farms, but CCS members may sell their products jointly in order to receive a higher price.

Private landowners form "dead furrow" cooperatives by removing the divisions between their parcels in order to cooperatively work their land. They collectively manage labor, land, and other means of production, but each of the producers retains ownership of the land and the means of production. Some small producers create dead furrow cooperatives to gain the advantages of cooperative labor and resource management; peasants formed many of the earliest CASs in this manner. At the same time, some credit and service cooperatives establish dead furrow cooperatives as a step toward the creation of a CAS.

Sandinista agricultural cooperatives are the most advanced form of cooperative organization in Nicaragua. All aspects of production are collectively owned and managed on a CAS: labor, land, natural resources, livestock, financing, and the product. As in the cooperative movement as a whole, there is a wide range of flexibility in the actual organization and operation of individual CASs. Though certain requirements, such as collective ownership, are established by law, each cooperative is free to decide its own methods and standards of labor organization, reimbursement, ownership of domestic animals, and other internal matters. As of July 1986, CASs constituted approximately 18 percent of all cooperatives.[44]

In early 1983, a new type of cooperative began to emerge in the northern departments of the country in response to increasing attacks by Honduran-based counterrevolutionaries. Cooperatives are often the target of Contra attacks since they are most often the center of agricultural development programs, health posts, schools, machine shops, and other economic and infrastructural aid from the government. To defend themselves, cooperative members, as well as previously nonintegrated *campesinos*, began to organize themselves for protection. Though all cooperatives throughout Nicaragua maintain a secretary and committee of self-defense, the new *cooperativas de defensa y produccion* (defense and production cooperatives—CDPs) "divide their tasks as much for defense as for production. Depending upon the situation, if there are 30 members, 20 are working and 10 are guaranteeing their defense. But all of them are armed and ready."[45]

Because defense is the defining element of CDPs, this form of cooperative includes a broad range of productive and cooperative relations. According to UNAG's Roberto Laguna, there are essentially three types of CDPs.

> Some are composed of private owners who want arms to defend themselves. They produce individually, but from the point of view of organization they are a cooperative, organized to guarantee defense. There are others made up of *campesinos* who were dislodged from their land by Contra attacks and have received Agrarian Reform land in CDPs for their defense and to protect production. A third type is any previously organized cooperative that has requested arms and organized its entire membership for defensive purposes.[46]

The Nicaraguan agrarian reform is designed to complete the the the first steps toward collectivized production. The government encourages peasants to form cooperatives as an initial step away from individualistic social relations and toward socialist relations. Indeed, many Sandinistas envision the long-term goal of cooperativization as the voluntary transformation of all lower forms of cooperatives into Sandinista agricultural cooperatives.[47]

Women in the Cooperative Movement

Women's participation in the cooperative movement has become a central issue for both UNAG and AMNLAE. Although 44 percent of the cooperatives had women members in 1983, only 6 percent of all cooperative members were women.[48] Cooperatives that included women had an average of only three women as members, while the average number of men per cooperative was 22.[49] The General Regulation of the Law of Cooperatives, however, calls explicitly for the full participation of women in the cooperative movement: "The production cooperatives will promote the full integration of women in the productive tasks of the cooperative, incorporating them as members in the same conditions as men, as one more expression of the participation of women in the construction of the new society.(Reg. Gen Art. 132)"[50]

During the Somoza era, the rural family's survival depended as much on the income of the woman and her children as on the man's. Women were therefore incorporated in wage production, albeit in even worse conditions than men. During the months when there were no harvests—the "dead season"—some women would rent a parcel of land with a man and work it together. And while men have been the principal economic actors in the countryside, women constitute a fundamental component of the family work force. They have traditionally cared for chickens and pigs, and raised animals to be sold on the market. Women have also played an important role in the sale of products grown on the family parcel, and women run the majority of rural stores.

Despite their significant level of participation in agricultural production, however, few women have joined the rapidly growing cooperative movement. A study conducted by the research arm of the Ministry of Agriculture, the *Centro de Investigaciones y Estudios de la Reforma Agraria* (Center for Investigations and Studies of the Agrarian Reform—CIERA), reveals the salient facts concerning women's participation in the new cooperatives.[51]

The study affirms that, because of their experience in the productive sphere and lack of access to land, women farm workers are more interested than female small producers in joining production cooperatives, (CASs). In the majority of the CASs studied, the female members came from the rural proletariat. For example, in the German Pomares CAS of Tola, Rivas, all the women members older than twenty-two once worked as agricultural wage laborers. Thirty percent of these women worked as temporary wage workers in the *Somocista* farm that is now in the hands of the cooperative.

In general, women who are heads of households—both small landowners and agricultural workers—join cooperatives to secure employment and income for their families. In most of the cooperatives studied by CIERA, most female members are the only or principal providers of their families. Women also join credit and service cooperatives to secure low interest loans and to receive technical training available to cooperative members.

Aside from economic factors, political, ideological, and organizational considerations play a role in determining women's participation in the cooperative movement. These considerations include: women's participation in the struggle for land; the demand for labor power on the cooperative; thepolitical/organizational work of the FSLN and the mass organizations; the influence of MIDINRA's technicians; and the cooperative members' political and ideological development.

In three of the CASs in which women have been founding members, long-time collaborators of the FSLN comprised part of the membership.

Members in these cooperatives recognize women's participation as an integral element of the revolutionary process. In only one of these cooperatives, however, did women originally enjoy the same rights as the men. "In the other two," the study comments, "even though women participated in the struggle for the land, their incorporation with equal rights was not easy. This shows the weight of those ideological conceptions that survive political and social changes, and means that the struggle must be waged against these conceptions so that women can achieve full participation in the Agrarian Reform."[52]

The CIERA study indicates that men's traditional sexist views on women's capacities have played a major role in preventing women from participating in the cooperative movement. Men argue that women are unable to equal men's productive capacities in the heavy aspects of the cooperative's work. They also point to the shortage of land and jobs in a particular zone, insisting that only men can be members in such a situation. Furthermore, while women often help acquire a parcel of land on credit and service cooperatives, male partners register the land in their own names, thereby securing exclusive membership rights. Even when the parcel is in both names, cooperative members consider the man to be head of the household and the family's sole representative within the cooperative. The sexual division of labor also inhibits women's participation in agricultural cooperatives. Many of the women interviewed in the study said they were unable to join cooperatives because of their child-care responsibilities. If child care were available, these women insist, they would be able to carry out the daily work required of members.

Male opposition and domestic burdens, however, are not the only obstacles preventing women from assuming an equal role in the cooperative movement. Some women lack previous experience in agricultural work and others do not like the work, while still others have a fear of competing with men's farming experience. This fear is more common among women from small landowning families than among women from the agricultural proletariat, although it constrains women's participation in both cases.

The CIERA study demonstrates that female cooperative members face great difficulties in achieving leadership positions. The obstacles they confront include their role in reproducing family labor power, their child care responsibilities, and their lack of access to education. As one woman stated: "It would be difficult to attend more meetings because of my small children and all that I have to do in the house."[53] When they do attend meetings, women members are more timid than the men. Those few women who regularly offer their opinions are usually older women and others with a high degree of revolutionary consciousness. In some cooperatives, the president and other officials make special efforts to elicit the opinion of women members.

In short, the actual situation of women in the cooperative movement is very far from the legal goal proclaimed in the Cooperative Law's regulations. The discrimination against women in the cooperative movement continues; therefore the political and ideological efforts necessary to overcome this discrimination also continue. In the words of the CIERA study:

> It is of utmost importance not only to publicize the regulations of the Cooperative Law that call for the participation of women, but also to undertake a campaign of consciousness-raising. This campaign to foster the participation of rural women must include state functionaries as well as activists in the mass organizations that work with the agricultural sector. The first step is to recognize the productive work of rural women. The second, if the goal of an egalitarian society is to be attained within the process of transition, is to recognize their demands as producers and as women. . . . Their incorporation in the cooperatives would be a form of consolidating their participation in the revolutionary process.[54]

CASE STUDY: THE GAMEZ-GARMENDIA COOPERATIVE

The task of collectivizing peasant agriculture confronts every Third World country that attempts to transform its socio-economic system. Each of these countries face the monumental problem of rationalizing and socializing agricultural production in societies characterized by cultural and material underdevelopment. In Nicaragua, the state and UNAG are attempting to carry out this process without the use of coercion, by offering material and psychological incentives to peasants of varying backgrounds. The following account of the formation and development of a Sandinista agricultural cooperative, the Gamez-Garmendia cooperative, demonstrates many of the forces shaping collectivization, and shows why this process has met with considerable success since the founding of UNAG in 1981.[55]

History of the Gamez-Garmendia Cooperative

The Gamez-Garmendia Cooperative lies just outside the city of Estelí in north-central Nicaragua. Having emerged just weeks after the triumph, it is one of the oldest cooperatives in Nicaragua. "It was just after the war," relates a founding member, "when we were all rebuilding our streets, that we began thinking about where we could find work. . . . We had heard the Sandinista Front say that the struggle was fought so that the land would belong to the *campesinos*, for them to be able to work it. So, we spoke with some *compañeros* from the FSLN. They told us to look for an idle piece of land and to work it."[56]

The original fourteen members of the cooperative, all friends or relatives, occupied an abandoned ranch named "La Pora" owned by the widow of a former education minister under Somoza. The new tenants renamed the ranch "Noel Gamez" to honor a man who died fighting for the liberation of Estelí. Although eager to make their living on their new land, the cooperative members faced serious problems. In the words of an UNAG organizer: "They lacked resouces. They didn't have a title, and their own people said they were thieves for taking the land. There was a general lack of confidence in what they were doing even among themselves."[57] Soon, however, officials from the state agency PRO-CAMPO and the ATC aided the new cooperative, securing a small, one-year loan and helping the members organize an internal administrative structure—the governing council. After a respectable first harvest, the cooperative attracted twelve additional members in 1980.

But by the end of the year, the cooperative was in trouble again. Because the state had not confiscated the ranch, the owner reasserted her claim through legal action. Unable to guarantee that they would be on the land for the next harvest, the cooperative members found it impossible to obtain long-term bank loans. When the second harvest of corn and beans failed due to bad seeds, the cooperative found itself unable to repay the one-year loan that the ATC had arranged. Unable to cope with these problems, a few of the new members left the cooperative.

Throughout this period the cooperative received little support from either the ATC or the state. Indeed, at one point, some state technical officials attempted to gain personal control over the cooperative:[58]

> At that time there was a mountain of problems, even with employees of our government. They came to tell us that we were incapable of running the ranch, of making it produce, and that it would be better if we work as day laborers. They were going to pay us fifty cordobas a day. They said that they would administer the ranch. . . . We did not fall for it because we had already been working collectively for some time. . . . Then one day one of the members put his machete to the head of one of them and told him: 'You came here to cheat us. You haven't

done any work here. You are not important to us. Go do your
own work. We will see how we end up here.' He then chased
the aide off the ranch with his machete.[59]

In early 1981, the court ordered the cooperative to return the ranch
to the original owner. Convinced that the cooperative was about to
collapse, the majority of members quit, leaving only eleven members.
With the founding of UNAG in April 1981, however, the cooperative's
fortunes began to improve; the new peasant's union became a crucial
ally: "Realizing that we were still organized and that we were prepared
to work the land, UNAG gave us its full support."[60] UNAG, with the aid
of MIDINRA, negotiated a rental agreement with the owner that allowed
the cooperative to legally occupy and work the land. On the basis of the
rental agreement, UNAG renegotiated the overdue 1980 bank loan, roll-
ing it over to the 1982 harvest. UNAG also arranged another one year
bank loan for the 1981–1982 agricultural year.

After the passage of the Agrarian Reform Law in late August 1981,
UNAG worked to secure a title for the Gamez cooperative. In October,
the Ministry of Agriculture formally confiscated the ranch and reimbursed
the owner with government bonds. A short time later the cooperative
received title to the ranch. With title in hand, the cooperative obtained
its first major long-term loans from the National Development Bank. The
loan paid for production costs, a new corral, fences, and forty cows. A
Swiss government development agency also began to assist the cooperative.[61]

In May 1982, however, disastrous rains, which inundated the entire
Central American region, ruined the majority of the crops. After the rains
subsided, most of the replanted crops were lost during an extended
drought. These natural disasters kept Gamez in financial trouble; it could
afford to repay only a portion of its 1982 loans and none of its 1980
loans. The banks allowed the cooperative to carry over the 1982 loans
to 1983. Despite these difficulties, however, each member earned $500
in 1982, the highest annual income most members had ever received.

In 1983, Gamez participated in a national development program
aimed at raising milk production. The cooperative received $11,000 to
purchase an additional forty cows, and a line of long-term credit from
COSUDE for infrastructural improvements and maintenance. The members purchased a hay shredder, added a tin roof and cement feeding
trough to the corral, and continued to upgrade and expand their fencing.

In 1983, the cooperative had its best harvest. Their primary cash
crop, potatoes, produced a large harvest, allowing Gamez to repay all
of its previous debts: approximately 250,000 córdobas plus interest. In

addition, each member earned 21,500 córdobas ($768 dollars) for the
year. Between the beginning of 1983 and February 1984, ninety-three
calves were born, increasing the value of the herd by approximately
275,000 córdobas ($10,000). Now profitable and credit worthy, Gamez
turned to MIDINRA for assistance with medium and long-term development programs. In May 1984 the cooperative received a 150,000
córdoba short-term loan for the production of basic grains, and a long-
term loan of 500,000 córdobas for cattle production.

In June 1984, Gamez merged with a much larger cooperative named
Gregoria Garmendia. A group of farmers established Garmendia in mid-
1983, and by January 1984 its members held title to a 2,000 acre ranch,
with 540 head of cattle and considerable infrastructure. From its creation,
however, the cooperative was plagued by serious organizational problems. Although it received special assistance from MIDINRA soon after
its formation, Garmendia was unable to repay any part of its initial bank
loans. Membership dropped from 33 in February to 21 in June.

In the early Spring of 1984, the Gamez cooperative offered to merge
with Garmendia. The merger became official in June and by August the
new cooperative—now named Gamez-Garmendia—totaled forty-one
members. It held three agrarian reform titles including 2,435 acres and
a livestock herd of approximately 1,200 animals. Since the merger, Gamez-Garmendia has confronted a series of problems related to the Contra
war. At any given time, eight to ten cooperative members are serving in
the armed forces, and the remaining members maintain a 24-hour guard
to protect their property and lives. In 1985 the Estelí region was hit by
a severe drought and Gamez-Garmendia lost its harvest of basic grains.
Despite losses due to the war and adverse weather, the cooperative has
survived, receiving priority assistance from government agencies. In 1986
Gamez-Garmendia secured an 8 million córdoba loan to develop its
infrastructure and pay back taxes.[62]

Women on the Gamez-Garmendia Cooperative

As of December 1986, only men were members of the Gamez cooperative; women had neither voice nor vote in anything related to the cooperative's business. Yet many women worked whenever they were
needed, usually during the harvest and planting seasons. The men hold
contradictory attitudes concerning women's membership in the cooperative. On the one hand, they accept the general principle that women
should be full participants in the cooperative; on the other hand, they
feel that women are incapable of performing the most important productive tasks. During one discussion of how to incorporate women into

the cooperative, the men suggested that women raise chickens: "This would be the women's area of production and the source of their profit."[63] Although this suggestion was a sincere attempt to deal with the issue, it assigned women a traditionally domestic area of sideline production. Furthermore, assigning the profit from such production to women would not be a collective manner of income distribution, especially because it would not equal the profit from the other areas of production.

During another discussion of the incorporation of women, the president of the cooperative stated:

> We [the men] are thinking of the future. Some of our wives want to work as full members. We are planning on building a poultry farm for them to manage and to help us, because there is certainly a lot of work on the cooperative that they can accomplish. They can also harvest potatoes and plant cabbage. All of these things they can do. But other things theys can't—fencing, for example. In order to fence one has to dig the holes and cut and raise the poles. These things they are not able to do.[64]

Fully incorporating women into the Gamez cooperative faces an additional problem: all but one family lived in barrios on the periphery of Estelí. Consequently, many women were drawn toward the daily economic life of their homes, their barrios, and the city, and not toward the cooperative. As some of the men pointed out, the full integration of women would occur only after their families begin living on the ranch. This observation proved correct: cooperative members, with assistance from a construction brigade from the United States, built eight houses in the San Rafael section of Gamez-Garmendia. Once the houses were finished, a group of twelve women, eight of whom lived in San Rafael, formed a commission to plan their own integration into the cooperative. With technical assistance from the Ministry of Agriculture, they planned to begin tending fish and ducks in early 1987.

Internal Organization

On Gamez, as on all cooperatives in Nicaragua, the general membership organized in the "general assembly," makes all the decisions.[65] Formally, a simple majority vote is required, but the members always attempt to reach a consensus on key decisions.[66] In fact, the secretary of organization is charged with establishing consensus and maintaining unity at all meetings. The Gamez secretary of organization says his role is to "maintain internal respect, discipline, and consensus. This must be done with fairness and care so that people are not put off and are heard. He makes clear to those dissenting what the position and reasoning of the majority is. And he explains the reasoning of the dissenters so people can weigh their ideas. . . ."[67]

The administrative body of the cooperative is called the *junta directiva* (governing council); it implements all decisions and oversees all administrative tasks.[68] The governing council consists of seven officers: a president, and secretaries of finances, production, organization, defense, education, and propaganda.[69] The general assembly elects all council officers for open-ended terms, but they are subject to recall at any time by a simple majority vote. Most cooperatives in Nicaragua maintain a system of commissions that correspond to each secretariat. On Gamez, however, the commissions have developed around necessary tasks and function as work teams organized to implement specific, ongoing labor. There are four commissions on the ranch: cattle raising, agriculture, sorghum production, and defense.

In addition to a system of commissions, the cooperative has an FSLN base committee made up of twelve of its own members. The members of the base committee consider their two primary functions as promoting the revolutionary process and supporting the mass organizations, especially UNAG. Specifically, they seek to promote the agrarian reform, cooperativization, and the development of their own cooperative. They also encourage fellow cooperative members and people in their families to participate in other areas of the revolution. At one meeting, for example, the committee discussed how to encourage six cooperative membersto volunteer for their neighborhood watch patrols. They decided to try to persuade these members that it was their civic duty to volunteer for their neighborhood watch patrols. As the FSLN political secretary explains:

> This is our revolution. We receive its benefits, so we have the responsibility to protect it and its gains. The revolution is more than just the cooperative. We all receive its benefits in our neighborhoods as well: schools, health centers, day care, new homes, electricity, water. The rest of our neighbors are doing vigilance. Defending our own cooperative is not enough. We must defend our interests and the interests of our people. It is not fair if we don't.[70]

In February 1984, the cooperative began to write a constitution that would include legal regulations and democratic norms.[71] Internally generated, the norms would establish work standards, work hours, sick leave, salary, permission and sanctions for missing work, rights to individually own domestic animals, emergency medical and disaster loans, and in-surance.[72]

Relationship with UNAG

Since UNAG emerged in April 1981, it has consistently provided Gamez with effective lobbying support, organizational advice, and technical skills workshops. In addition to the action it took to acquire a rental agreement and a loan for the cooperative in 1981, UNAG has backed all of Gamez' subsequent loan requests. This is partly because of UNAG's position on the regional Rural Credit Commission, but mainly due to Gamez' status as a "vanguard" or model cooperative.[73]

UNAG provides the cooperative with important organizational ad-vice. When UNAG came on the scene, the cooperative was in the middle of a crisis. Founding members of the cooperative were having difficulty orienting the new members to the collective activity that cooperative life requires; they became disillusioned and fifteen left the cooperative. In late 1981, UNAG sent an organizer to the cooperative to help stem the tide of departures. The organizer advised the cooperative on conducting effective meetings, promoting group unity, and introducing new members to cooperative life. This advice helped strengthen the cooperative during the following year.

The union's regional office also assists Gamez with monthly work-shops on organizational matters. These workshops are part of the National Program of Basic Courses for Cooperative Organization. The workshops cover the following topics: how to organize and run meetings; how to organize work; organizational problems and mechanisms to confront and overcome them; resolving disagreements; and writing a constitution. The workshops also discuss all aspects of the Agrarian Reform Law and the Law of Cooperatives. To help cooperative members upgrade their tech-nical knowledge, UNAG conducts seminars on subjects such as organ-izing finances and identifying cattle diseases. Moreover, the peasants' union occasionally sends cooperative members abroad to receive courses on cooperative farm management and the theory of cooperative organization.

Relationship to MIDINRA

The Gamez cooperative receives three kinds of technical aid from the Ministry of Agriculture, MIDINRA. An agricultural extension adviser visits the cooperative at least twice a week. This adviser monitors the technical development of all aspects of the cooperative: finances, cattle production, agricultural production, and infrastructure. He also assists the cooperative with development programs offered by the regional MIDINRA office. In addition, MIDINRA technicians aid Gamez in specific areas of agricultural production. These technicians work within national or regional technical development programs, specializing in various areas of agricultural production such as the national milk production program, the regional potato project, fruit orchard development, and the garlic production project. In a one month period in early 1984, Gamez received assistance from four teams of MIDINRA specialists in cattle nutrition and health, infrastructural development, fruit orchard development, and vegetable production. In earlier years, the cooperative received assistance in potato, cattle, and cabbage production; the application of chemical fumigants; and financial management. Finally, MIDINRA holds a series of weekly classes for Gamez members covering topics such as common livestock diseases, fertilization processes, and the gestation, birthing, and weaning of cattle.

The Initiative of Cooperative Members

The members of the Gamez cooperative have consistently taken the initiative in promoting the development of their holdings. Their continued occupation and operation of the La Pora ranch in the face of all the early difficulties attests to their collective initiative and motivation during the cooperative's first year. The founding members' tenacity was also evident in the second year when they persevered during worsening conditions: an increasing debt, a court order returning the ranch to its original owner, a cutoff of bank loans, and the resignation of more than half of the membership.

But their most dramatic display of initiative occurred in 1984 when they arranged the merger with the failing Gregorio Garmendia cooperative. In his role as the local UNAG representative, the president of Gamez participated in the advisory team that worked with the Garmendia cooperative. He attributed many of Garmendia's problems to its late start and its easy access to state support, explaining that he and his fellow cooperative members had struggled to learn how to work and survive collectively for two years before they received a title, a long-term loan, or cattle. In contrast, the president noted, the Garmendia cooperative received a title, abundant land, a herd of cattle, and a 10-year loan— all in its first year. He argued that the Garmendia members could not learn to work effectively under such conditions because they had no incentive to work collectively and organize themselves. If they were serious about cooperative life, they would have to learn from others who already knew how to work collectively. He discussed Garmendia's problems with the members of his own cooperative and they decided to suggest that their cooperative, successful and experienced, merge with the Garmendia cooperative.[74]

Although the advisory team continued to work with Garmendia through the spring of 1984, the situation continued to deteriorate. The cooperative was unable to repay its first short-term loan and membership decreased by 30 percent between February and June. During the latter part of this period, the Gamez members discussed merger arrangements with the remaining members of the Garmendia cooperative. They then met with representatives of UNAG, MIDINRA, and the FSLN to discuss their merger proposal. Aside from presenting their president's views, they argued that uniting the two cooperatives would provide a more rational economy of scale for cattle-raising. In light of Garmendia's troubled situation, all the agencies agreed to the merger proposal and the two cooperatives united in June 1984. The merger illustrates that even with considerable state and union involvement in their operations, the Gamez members are capable of maintaining their self-motivation and initiative. Indeed, with encouragement from UNAG and MIDINRA, their ability to act autonomously is being transformed into an additional source of local leadership within the process of cooperativization; both the ministry and the union have asked the cooperative's members to help advise other production cooperatives in the zone of Estelí.

Conclusion

This case study demonstrates that effective coordination betweeen a mass organization and its base constituency can lead to positive results, especially with added assistance from a state agency (MIDINRA). Exercizing constant pressure from below, the members of the Gamez-Garmendia cooperative have so far achieved organizational cohesion and modest economic gains in the face of a deteriorating national economy and a costly war of attrition. At the same time, the zonal and regional offices of UNAG can claim credit for helping to convert a failing project into a model for other production cooperatives.

Although UNAG is the only mass organization to appear after Somoza's defeat, it has become the most powerful mass organization in the country, winning a series of demands for its constituency, most notably the cancellation of debts, increases in producer prices, and generous credit terms. No aspect of government policy toward the agricultural sector is enacted without prior consulation with UNAG.

Moreover, as of October 1985, the peasant union's members farmed 61 percent of the area under cultivation and producing 45 percent of the total value of agricultural production.[75]

In 1984 UNAG decided to open its membership to large producers. In an October interview that year, Daniel Nuñez, the union's president, avowed that "We aspire to unite all the producers of this country. . . . we want large producers, because the more we produce the more wealth the country will have. The revolution was not made to bring degradation, but rather social wealth, to all the sectors."[76] Asked if a capitalist grower who employs up to 500 workers during the coffee or cotton harvest could join UNAG, Nuñez replied:

> Yes, why not? If he is a patriotic man he is in the UNAG. Just like there are priests here in the revolution, such as [Foreign Minister Miguel] D'Escoto and Ernesto and Fernando Cardenal [ministers of culture and education]. This revolution is making contributions to the world on this. The framework should not be philosophical questions, but rather the conduct of men. No matter whether they are atheists, Marxists, or Christians, the important thing is their attitude toward life.[77]

Opening its ranks to all farmers is expected to strengthen UNAG, allowing it to better confront Nicaragua's legacy of agricultural underdevelopment.

10
PRODUCTION AND PARTICIPATION: CST AND ATC

Since July 19, 1979, the Sandinistas have stressed that political power in Nicaragua is exercised in the interests of the workers and peasants. The country's capitalists must therefore respect not only trade union rights, but also other gains the workers have won through the revolution—including the right to exercise vigilance over the capitalists themselves. At the same time, however, the FSLN and the revolutionary government repeatedly call on Nicaraguan workers to forsake immediate benefits in order to increase labor productivity. Xavier Gorostiaga, a leading economic adviser, outlines the framework in which the government views the problem of productivity:

> All social changes bring about a decrease in productivity because they require adjustment. For more than 400 years, our labor force has been under the oppression of the colonial system, the capitalist system, and, on top of that, the Somocista dynastic system. Productivity was obtained from the workers through oppression. Now that we are eliminating oppression, there is a relaxed atmosphere among the workers and productivity has decreased. We need to develop new conditions for productivity and these new conditions depend on political consciousness, organization, and new relations of production.[1]

For the Sandinistas, "new relations of production" means, above all, worker participation in the country's enterprises. Workers will respond to appeals for increased productivity only if they have a stake in decision-making at their workplace. Moreover, genuine worker participation can only emerge through initiatives that workers themselves take—

not through measures that managers implement. How, then, do the two pro-Sandinista trade union federations—the CST and the ATC—strive to increase worker productivity and to involve workers in transforming the nation's productive relations?

THE NICARAGUAN WORKING CLASS

The Nicaraguan working class developed relatively slowly until the 1950s when the cotton industry's rapid expansion fueled its growth. In the 1960s the proletarianization process received another boost with the creation of the Central American Common Market.[2] By the end of the 1970s, the Nicaraguan working class consisted of 210,000 workers—less than 30 percent of the economically active population (EAP).[3] The proletariat was unequally divided into an urban and rural sector: 80,000 urban wage workers (around 20 percent of the nonagricultural EAP), and 130,000 rural wage workers (a third of the agricultural EAP).

Under Somoza, the rural proletariat faced extremely precarious conditions. Fifty thousand workers had year-round employment, and the rest were employed only during the harvest season.[4] After the harvests, the latter group of workers labored in construction, worked in urban services, or farmed for the domestic market. These workers were involved in a process of rural-urban and rural-rural labor circulation that generally-maintained their wage condition.

Two other segments of the work force complete this portrait of Nicaragua's working class: an extensive rural semiproletariat made up of peasants with very small holdings who worked in the harvests, and a mass of artisanal workers and salaried workers in the cities. Together, artisans and salaried workers comprised nearly two-thirds of the nonagricultural EAP.

The Nicaraguan working class maintains close links to the rest of the working population, especially in the cities. Studies show that the working class family cannot sustain itself solely or even principally from wage-earning. In many cases, family members who are engaged in peddling, personal services, and petty commercial activities earn more income than do wage-earning family members.

These structural aspects, as well as Somocista political repression, kept the union movement weak during the last years of the dictatorial regime. In July 1979 there were only 138 registered unions in the country, totaling 27,000 affiliated workers. Moreover, many of these unions had a merely formal existence, having been inactive for years.

Since the fall of Somoza, the unionization of the work force has increased rapidly. Between August 1979 and December 1983, labor federations registered 1,400 unions with the Ministry of Labor. These unions had a combined membership of more than 120,000 workers. Almost half of these new organizations are in the agricultural sector, and just under 20 percent are in the industrial sector. Workers in a single enterprise comprise some 75 percent of all the unions. Since 1981, however, the large union confederations and the FSLN have been promoting the formation of industrywide unions. Almost 90 percent of the new unions and their members are affiliated with the CST or with the ATC. In 1979–1980, 75 percent of the new unions affiliated with the CST, marking the peak of the unionization of urban and industrial workers. By contrast, almost 80 percent of the new unions in 1981–1982 affiliated with the ATC, since rapid unionization in the countryside occurred in that period. Although there are several union confederations besides the CST and ATC, together they account for a little more than 10 percent of all the unions and union members.[5]

THE SANDINISTA WORKERS FEDERATION

The CST's Strategy

As Nicaragua's economic crisis deepened in 1981 and 1982, the CST focused its attention on raising production and responding to the FSLN demand for "revolutionary austerity." The CST attempted to convince workers that high productivity and the acceptance of austerity do not serve the interests of the factory owner but, in the long run, benefit the interests of the working class as a whole. The Sandinistas designed their policies to aid the CST in its task. As George Black has written:

> The workers and peasants must have solid proof that the initial redistributive policies of the state, as well as the long-term strategy, directly benefit the working class. In the Frente's own words: "Austerity must be the answer to a concrete problem and not an externally imposed principle. We must distinguish clearly between the austerity produced by an unjust structural situation, and the austerity required to make the revolutionary project a reality. The sacrifice itself must be given a class content."[6]

CST contributions to raising production and sharing the burden of austerity include: participating in harvest campaigns; reaching optimal labor efficiency; establising specific production goals; and sponsoring training programs for *innovadores* (innovators), workers who manage to adapt, refurbish, repair, or maintain productive equipment.[7] In May 1982, the CST's general secretary, Lucio Jiminez, summarized the labor federation's goals.

> In general . . . the strategy of the CST to reach a new stage of production is to build a strong union organization that continually links its activity to the problems of production, that makes its central concern such questions as labor discipline; fulfilment of production goals; effective operation of the institutions that administer the national economy and the budgets of local enterprises; and the fight against bureaucratism, against administrative inefficiency, and for a new consciousness toward work.
>
> We also want to see the unions make it their special concern to promote a fundamental savings—that of important resources that we do not produce, such as energy, fuel, and paper, as well as raw materials, which are in many cases wasted.
>
> This in general is the long-term line of action of our unions. Only in this way can we play a dynamic, active role in building a society that breaks with dependency.[8]

In September 1984 the national leadership of the CST drafted ten resolutions in connection with the Third National Assembly of Unions. These resolutions were designed to confront what the CST leadership called "new situations and larger and more serious problems that require of us higher levels of consciousness and organization, greater united efforts, and a more active, dynamic, and combative presence of the unions."[9] The CST's ten resolutions were:

> 1. To strengthen and consolidate the military defense forces, from the patriotic military service to revolutionary vigilance.
> 2. To struggle so that in all workplaces norms of production are worked out that permit us to achieve the highest possible productivity per worker, in line with the productive experience of each workplace.
> 3. To resolve labor problems and conflicts by means of negotiations, without halting production.
> 4. To support distribution on a territorial basis, making sure that there is a correct distribution of stocks of goods.
> 5. To ask the revolutionary government to finalize the application of the first subsystem of the National System for the Organization of Work and Wages, dealing with categorization, and that the government immediately begin the revision of wage scales.
> 6. To review the purchase at cost of goods produced in our work centers.

7. To organize Sandinista emulation in the work centers.

8. To recognize international solidarity.

9. Absolute support for the FSLN Plan of Struggle.

10. To fulfill these great challenges, the leaders participating in the National Assembly of Unions commit ourselves to maintain close ties with our rank and file, to constantly explain the main problems no matter how hard they are, and to overcome organizational failings and deficiencies in order to meet this historic challenge.[10]

In its 1986 workplan the CST once again committed itself to strengthening the nation's defense by ensuring a 100 percent success rate in signing up new enlistees in the military draft. The Federation called upon its member unions to institute permanent mechanisms to ensure the well-being of families whose members serve in the warfront. The 1986 plan also calls for worker discussion and education aimed at finding ways to lower production costs, increase productivity, and maintain equipment. Finally, the CST urges its locals to back the Federation's constitutional proposals guaranteeing the right to strike, worker participation in economic management, and healthy and safe working conditions at the workplace.[11]

Health and Safety

The CST's emphasis on raising production is reflected in its attention to health and safety issues. In its monthly newspaper, *Trabajadores*, the Federation regularly discusses health and safety concerns, emphasizing that unhealthy and unsafe working conditions lead to a decline in productivity and cause work accidents and professional illnesses. As one editorial put it: "A work accident or a professional illness is not a personal problem; it is a social problem that affects all of production and therefore our entire population."[12]

The CST seeks to overcome the dangerous and unhealthy work environment that prevailed during the dictatorship. Under Somoza, workers labored in conditions that included intense noise, excessive heat, and toxic substances. Employers refused to improve these conditions because they would have required considerable "unproductive" investments. Consequently, Nicaraguan workers suffered exhausting workdays, forced speed-up of the work pace, and uncompensated overtime—all with the aim of extracting the most profit from their labor power.

The CST, along with the government, attempts to protect the physical and mental well-being of the country's industrial workers. In the view of the CST, health and safety programs can succeed only if the workers themselves actively participate in their execution. Only the workers can monitor their workplaces to detect those dangers that can damage their health. Moreover, the CST believes that workers must learn the technical aspects concerning their working conditions: the risks present in different work centers, how to detect them, and how to avoid their threat to workers' health. To inform workers, every issue of *Trabajadores* carries articles on such dangers as heat, noise, toxic vapors, electric shock, and pesticides. These articles—in the "Work and Health" section of the newspaper—tell readers about new laws and decrees that guarantee the right of workers to work in a healthy, safe, and dignified environment. In addition, *Trabajadores* provides information on the various state institutions that help defend workers' health and safety.

Many workers in the textile industry suffer health problems due to excessive machine noise. For example, in the loom section of FANATEX, one of the largest textile factories in Managua, the noise decibels approach 115, a level that threatens the hearing of the 300 working people in this section. In 1982, the CST secured a donation of ear protection devices for the FANATEX workers. Most of the workers, however, refuse to use them; they feel uncomfortable wearing them and claim they cause headaches. The CST holds educational forums to persuade the workers to wear these devices, explaining that the incessant noise can cause loss of hearing, damage to the nervous system, and diminution in the capacity to concentrate.

The CST devotes considerable energies to urging the use of personal protection equipment in the workplace. Union activists concerned with the health of industrial workers stress that such equipment is indispensable in workplaces with high-volume noise, dangerous machinery, and a high level of exposure to toxic chemicals. As *Trabajadores* puts its:

> Personal protection equipment must always be viewed as a last resort. Administrators must allocate such equipment to workers after they have exhausted all possibilities to correct the dangers at their point of origin.
> We should not forget that this equipment is no guarantee against accidents, but it does diminish the degree of risk at the work post.
> The use of personal protection equipment should not be imposed, but rather its importance should be explained to the workers, along with the economic cost that it entails for our country.[13]

The CST views health and safety concerns as a major priority. Due to the economic crisis and the military situation, however, the CST cannot dramatically improve the poor working conditions that harm its membership. Just as in other Federation tasks, the CST must rely on rank-and-file mobilization and consciousness for health and safety improvements.

The CST and the New Salary Policy

Under Somoza Nicaragua suffered from an anarchic salary system that was part of the dictator's deliberate tactics to divide workers. As early as 1980 the Ministry of Labor considered a national reorganization of salaries but decided against making the necessary commitment of resources. After an outbreak of (illegal) strike activity in 1982 following a wage freeze and a substantial drop in purchasing power of wages in 1983, the Ministry again began the task of reordering salaries. The goal was to create a fair salary scale based on the specific tasks that workers perform. The promoters of the new system believed that workers engaged in the same task—independent of where they work, the location of their enterprise, the ownership of their enterprise, or their union affiliation—should receive the same salary.

Special commissions organized according to the country's different economic sectors developed the *Sistema Nacional de Organización del Trabajo y los Salarios* (National System of Ordering Work and Salaries—SNOTS). Each commission included administrative representatives, union representatives, Labor Ministry representatives, and experienced workers and technicians. The Commission members first organized workshops to train each other in how to devise the new system in their sector. Next, they determined a work plan that included the number of businesses in each sector, the total number of occupations, and the sector's occupational breakdown. The Commissions then formed subcommisions to establish job descriptions and salary scales. Defining each occupation according to its work functions, the subcommissions analyzed its degree of complexity in order to place it within a salary scale. After setting the value of each occupation, they submitted the new salary scale to the workers for their review and approval. Finally, the sector's administrative representatives, Ministry of Labor officials, and union leaders signed the salary accords.[14]

The CST played a major role in implementing the new system. A 1983 *Trabajadores* article expressed the CST's strong commitment to backing the salary policy.

> The success in the application of this salary policy will depend on the serious and responsible work of the CST union leadership

at all its levels, from the national council down to the union sections. It will also depend on the close communication between rank-and-file base members and their leaders.

This work requires an extraordinary effort and we should work slowly, with firm steps, careful to avoid errors in the application of the policy.[15]

Applying the new wage and salary policy has indeed required an extraordinary effort, and, unfortunately, some errors did occur in its application. Before the government published the new wage and salary scales, workers were led to believe that the scales would mean across-the-board pay increases. In fact, however, only about 80 percent of the workers included in the SNOTS program actually received higher wages.[16] Consequently, thousands of workers who failed to receive pay hikes were disappointed when the new wage scales appeared. The SNOTS program was poorly received by most workers and employees in the private sector because this sector had the financial resources to pay higher wages and salaries than stipulated in the new salary scales. Consequently, private sector employers often resist implementation of the SNOTS program thereby enabling them to lure both workers and professionals away from the state sector.

At the same time, however, many workers are satisfied with the new wage scales. The standardization of job categories and pay has eliminated much of the chaos that previously reigned in the wage labor sector and the SNOTS program guarantees equity in pay increases whenever they occur. In 1985 the government granted three wage increases totalling 107 percent, and in the first three months of 1986 alone workers received two wage increases totalling almost 140 percent. Although such increases lag considerably behind inflation, workers at least know that they are applied fairly since the wage scales are widely disseminated.

In addition to defining job categories in terms of difficulty, level of training, and required experience, the SNOTS program is implementing a "norm system" which attempts to established a daily or weekly goal that a worker should be able to achieve if he/she works diligently and with little resource waste. Once a norm is established a worker can receive a wage bonus as an incentive for surpassing the norm. But setting norms has proven to be an immensely difficult task, especially in the industrial sector where spare parts are lacking and power shortages frequent. Moreover, establishing norms requires meticulous analysis by technicians already overburdened with tasks. As a result, norms have yet to be established in many job categories, and the norms that do exist are often unrealistic. In 1985 and 1986 the CST and the Ministry of Labor met freqently to improve and expand the norm system.

The Innovators Movement

The United States trade embargo, the foreign exchange shortage, and the lack of skilled technicians have stimulated Nicaraguan workers' creativity. Faced with the prospect of widespread unemployment, workers have responded to the economic crisis by developing their own machines and industrial processes. Such activity has led to the Innovators Movement.[17] Innovators are workers who develop new tools or new production processes, thereby allowing industrial production to continue at reduced cost to the nation. José Lopez, a member of the CST's Secretariat of International Relations, explains why the Innovators Movement is important to Nicaragua.

> The Innovators' Movement is an answer to the problems we're facing. By changing the line of production to necessities and to products that use Nicaraguan materials, or by inventing small machines that permit production to go forward, we can avoid unemployment and reopen factories. In practice, this means that we must push forward the revolution, the same revolution that we workers are making.[18]

The rise of the Innovators Movement reflects the country's economic problems and workers' attempts to confront these problems. The CST credits the innovators with a number of important achievements, particularly in the manufacture of machine parts and tools that Nicaragua previously imported. At the agrarian reform repairshops, for example, workers reconstructed two 40-year-old lathes and used them to make replacement parts for over 600 tractors.[19] At the German Pomares Engineering Works, Jose del Carmen Filetes used pieces of scrap to make a sheet metal bender, a tool that had been imported at a cost of 90,000 córdobas.[20]

The government and the Sandinista trade unions have supported the growing Innovators Movement. At an October 1981 meeting with government officials, CST and ATC innovators requested workshops, material supplies, and a training institute. They also called for the formation of a technical advisory council to aid their efforts. The government responded by providing the innovators with machine shops and preferential admission to government-sponsored technical education courses. In addition, the Ministry of Labor initiated a series of conferences in which innovators met with one another to compare and coordinate their research.[21]

The CST and ATC conduct training seminars for innovators, sometimes sending them to special courses abroad. The federations have also built repair workshops, especially designed for innovators, in the departments of Leon and Zelaya. But much remains to be done; the commission that assists the Innovators' Movement stresses that careful planning and evaluation are needed to incorporate the innovators' efforts into a longer-term economic strategy. Furthermore, at the end of 1985, the number of innovators nationwide was still unknown, and no figures were available on foreign exchange savings attributable to innovators' inventions.

The trade union federations and the Sandinistas emphasize that the importance of the Innovators Movement transcends its role in overcoming the nation's economic crisis. In a 1983 editorial, *Barricada* argued that because the innovators were no longer dependent on capitalist owners, they were free to begin exercising their human abilities.

> The capitalist system is based on the separation of manual labor from mental labor. As ownership of the means of production is reserved in that system to the capitalist, so too do they seize scientific knowledge and technology. Around this they install an aura of mystery, a barrier, in order to maintain the workers in ignorance. And this is not only in the technology of production, but they also extend it to administration. . . . The worker innovator, when he is not subject to dependence on the capitalist, who is going to take advantage of his ingenuity and skill in order to extract more surplus value, begins to travel the road which will eliminate the separation of manual labor from intellectual labor. . . . The construction of socialism happens, among other reasons, because workers reach a higher level of technical ability; because, by dominating technology—and science with it— the worker is able to give work its true creative character, is able for the first time to dominate and transform nature and its products and put the fruit of that work to the service of human development.[22]

With its emphasis on popular education and inventiveness, the Innovators Movement is an important counterweight to the approach that development can only occur by creating a stratum of experts. The Movement exemplifies the attempt to achieve "popular power" in Nicaragua and its future course will reveal much about the nature of the revolutionary process.

THE RURAL WORKERS ASSOCIATION

The Rural Workers Association (ATC) includes 50,000 permanent workers and 55,000 temporary workers organized in over 700 unions.[23]

The ATC campaigns for union rights, salary increases, improved working conditions, education and health benefits, technical training, an equitable food distribution system for its members, and higher production.

Employment Stability

During the first three years of the revolutionary process, the ATC pressed state farm administrators to create permanent jobs for its workers. The Association's efforts met with considerable success; thousands of agricultural workers on state farms now secure employment during the "dead season" by repairing houses, buildings and roads, and others work permanently in the scores of new clinics and stores that the government created on state farms.[24] The Association also bolsters employment stability for farmworkers by negotiating less intensive work days for agricultural workers. In addition, the ATC negotiates agreements guaranteeing that a minimum number of workers will be assigned to a given land area. In the case of cotton, for example, one worker is responsible for each 100 sown acres. Finally, ATC-supported production projects in sugar cane, milk, tobacco, African palm, and basic grains employ thousands of permanent workers.

The ATC and the New Salary Policy

When the Sandinistas assumed power in July 1979, the salary situation in rural Nicaragua was in a state of chaos. The salary differential between two agricultural technicians—each with the same amount of experience and academic training—could vary substantially. For example, some technicians who worked for wealthy landowners earned as much as 30,000 córdobas a year, while others earned only 7,000. Many unskilled workers earned only 210 córdobas per month, while an owner's favorite employee received as much as 1,200 córdobas per month. In addition, women farm workers never earned as much as their male counterparts in the same jobs.[25]

The ATC's first post-Somoza demand called for a government-enforced minimum wage. In 1980, the Ministry of Labor established a minimum wage of 25.30 córdobas per day. (Somoza had set the minimum agricultural wage at 20 córdobas per day. Most workers, however, never received this amount.)[26] The ATC also insisted that women farmworkers receive equal pay for equal work. Although the government declared a comparable-worth policy shortly after July 1979, the Labor

Ministry failed to enforce it until the creation of the 1984 work and salary system. To close the enormous gap between workers with the lowest salaries and technicians with the highest salaries, the state set a 10,000 córdoba per month limit on public sector salaries. Finally, the ATC negotiated scores of collective bargaining agreements for agricultural workers in the rice, coffee, and cotton sectors. The contracts included substantial social wage benefits such as free health care and education, subsidized meals, and transportation to and from the work site.

The wage and salary system introduced in 1984 ended the gross disparities in farmworkers' wage scales. The system sets work norms for the entire agrarian sector, recognizing such factors as work skills, educational background, intensity of work, and types of soil and terrain. The new system also includes an incentive scheme designed to reward workers who surpass work norms or production goals. During the 1985–1986 harvest season, for example, coffee pickers received 80 córdobas for each basket they picked above the weekly quota.[27] This incentive program encourages workers to surpass production goals, thereby compensating for the shortage of labor power during the harvest season.

The ATC and Production

The Association contends that increasing production is vital both for the revolutionary process as a whole and the particular interests of agricultural workers. Consequently, the ATC engages in a wide variety of activities that promote the goal of increasing agricultural production. To promote coffee and cotton production, the ATC participates in commissions responsible for monitoring the harvests of these two key export crops. Union representatives constantly track labor power needs for both crops. For example, in late September 1985, the ATC announced that 30,000 traditional workers and 25,000 volunteer workers would be needed to bring in the 1985–1986 coffee harvest. That same month ATC leaders met with coordinators of the Sandinista Youth's Student Production Battallions to plan the mobilization of more than 18,000 secondary and university students.[28] ATC officials also assist the government's attempts to resolve transportation and food supply problems during the harvest season.

When necessary, ATC officials pressure state ministries to meet their responsibilities in carrying out the crucial sugar, cotton, and coffee harvests. For example, in October 1985, Edgardo García, ATC General Secretary, called on the government to 1. guarantee the distribution of basic products at fair prices to coffee harvesters and their families; 2. improve the food served to workers on state farms; 3. provide essential medical supplies to the coffee pickers; and 4. revise the salary scale for those ATC members who work at coffee-drying facilities.[29]

In March 1984, an ATC national official presented a paper to a Managua conference on the agrarian reform's impact on rural employment.[30] The paper listed three principal factors limiting the availability of labor power in the coffee and cotton harvests. First, because tens of thousands of peasants have benefited from the agrarian reform, many of them no longer need to sell their labor power during the harvest season; land entitlements, improvements in commercialization, and credit and technical assistance have created economic conditions that permit small peasants to remain on their farms year-round. In addition, many members of the semiproletariat have received financing for cultivating their small plots of land, and no longer need to work in the harvest. The agrarian reform has also created more possibilities for permanent wage employment through agricultural projects in tobacco, milk, sugar, African palm, rice, and corn. Consequently, there are fewer temporary workers available during the harvest season.

Second, the continuing migration from the countryside to the city has reduced the number of traditional workers for the harvests. The informal urban sector continues to attract unemployed and underemployed rural workers.[31] Finally, fewer workers are available for the harvests because of the massive mobilization of traditional cutters that began during the 1983–1984 harvest. For example, in Region VI, 40 percent of the ATC-affiliated workers, 5,000 out of 12,000, volunteered for defense duties during the 1983–1984 harvest cycle. Furthermore, when male members of the family enlist for military duty, the other family members usually fail to join the harvest campaigns, thereby adding to the labor power shortage.

To resolve the labor shortage the state sector recruits thousands of volunteer workers. In the 1985–86 harvest, for example, the government mobilized 25,000 nontraditional cutters, mainly students and government employees. In the Association's view, the volunteer work of thousands of young people is an important gain for the revolution, helping to overcome the tremendous gap between the countryside and city. The ATC observes, however, that serious organizational problems have impeded the rational use of the volunteer labor force. Moreover, the ATC report reveals that when nontraditional harvesters such as students replace traditional workers, average productivity falls. Traditional workers, for example, can pick 150 pounds of cotton a day, other workers can only pick 60 per day. With so many nontraditional workers in the harvests, more workers with experience are needed to fulfill production goals.[32]

Emulation Campaigns

Emulation campaigns are a primary vehicle through which the Rural Workers Association stimulates production. The ATC pamphlet "Emulación Sandinista," defines "emulation" this way:

> To emulate means to surpass goals through the conscious participation of workers in production; to work better; to be vigilant concerning the use of the enterprise's social resources; to aid the proper conduct of our fellow workers on the job; to put extra effort in fulfilling and over-fulfilling the goals of production, in quantity and quality; and to have great personal and collective disposition to maintain and develop production.[33]

The pamphlet sharply differentiates emulation from competition:

> Emulation is the conscious and fraternal effort to attain production, organizational, and social goals in order to benefit the entire population; in contrast, competition is individualistic rivalry carried out for personal benefit. Emulation seeks the development of all, attaining material achievements for social benefit while developing new attitudes toward work which will do away with the concept that workers are mere work instruments that generate profits for the capitalists. Bourgeois competition is no more than a mechanism to exploit workers. We see therefore that emulation is made to benefit the population as opposed to competition which exploits the people.[34]

Emulation campaigns begin with the dissemination of the norms and principles that govern the campaign: its objectives, content, and incentives. The ATC issues updates during the course of a campaign, showing the workers' progress. Once the campaign is over, workers compare the results to determine which of them have surpassed goals and which of them may need help in upgrading their performance. Workers also review the work methods that achieved the most success in the campaign.

Emulation campaigns rest on two basic principles. The first principle holds that the best workers' attainments are within reach of all workers. Groups of workers that achieve the best production results share their work methods with other collectives in order to ensure the success of future emulation campaigns. The second principle emphasizes that collective efforts are needed to attain the campaign's proposed economic and political-organizational goals. To reach these goals, the unions attempt to organize work so that the workers understand all their assigned tasks. A corollary of this principle is that workers should embrace voluntary work and eschew individualistic positions.

Emulation campaigns culminate in the distribution of moral and material awards to those workers and work collectives that obtain the best results. In 1984, for example, a state farm awarded the nation's "vanguard" coffee cutter 40,000 córdobas to buy a new house and sent him on a trip abroad, while the "outstanding" cutter received 20,000 cordobas for the repair of his house and a free trip abroad.[35]

Emulation campaigns advance a number of ATC objectives: 1. they contribute to workers' education; 2. increase the quality and quantity of agricultural production and lessening production costs; 3. contribute to saving primary materials, inputs, and labor time; 4. foster a sense of solidarity among workers; and 5. stimulate worker participation in economic decision making.[36]

WORKER PARTICIPATION IN MANAGEMENT

Worker participation in management is a key aspect of Nicaragua's developing system of participatory democracy. Although many writers on economic management use the concept of worker "participation," they seldom define the term, or if they do, the definition is imprecise. McGregor, for example, after complaining how often the idea of "participation" is misunderstood, asserts that participation consists

> . . . basically in creating opportunities under suitable conditions for people to influence decisions affecting them. That influence can vary from a little to a lot . . . participation is a special case of delegation in which the subordinate gains greater control, freedom of choice, with respect to his own responsibilities. The term participation is usually applied to the subordinate's greater influence over matters within the superior's responsibilities.[37]

Another common view of participation holds that it is "any or all of the processes by which employees other than managers contribute positively towards the reaching of managerial decisions which affect their work."[38] A third definition argues that participation in decision making is "the totality of such forms of upward exertions of power by subordinates in organizations as are perceived to be legitimate by themselves and their superiors."[39]

But these definitions fail to offer a rigorous analysis of participation. As Carole Pateman points out, true participation in management "involves a modification, to a greater or lesser degree, of the orthodox authority structure; namely one where decision making is the 'preroga-tive' of management, in which workers play no part."[40] Many writers on management use the term "participation" to refer not just to a method of decision making, but also to cover techniques used to persuade employees to accept decisions that have *already* been made by man-agement. This type of situation is *pseudo participation*. Pseudo-partici-pation occurs, for example, when a supervisor, instead of merely announcing a decision, allows workers to question him/her about it and to discuss it.

Genuine participation in management, however, involves partici-pation in decision making itself. Moreover, there are two fundamental types of participation: "partial participation" and "full participation." Partial participation occurs when workers affect the decisions of man-agement but management retains the power to make the final decision. Full participation takes place when each individual member of a decision-making body has equal power to determine the outcome of decisions. Moreover, partial participation and full participation can exist at both the "lower" and "higher" levels of management. The lower level refers broadly to those management decisions relating to control of day-to-day shop floor activity, while the higher level refers to decisions that relate to running the whole enterprise, decisions on such matters as investment and marketing.[41]

In Nicaragua, worker participation began as a defensive response to the bourgeoisie's massive campaign of decapitalization during the 1980–1982 period. As the word indicates, decapitalization is a mech-anism by which capital is lost. It is the opposite of the accumulation of capital. Decapitalization occurs when a business or a country loses its capital reserves or foreign exchange. Decapitalization of a business, therefore, involves the loss of part of its productive capital, thereby impeding the continuation of production. "Decapitalization," writes journalist Arnold Weissberg, "is like a strike by the bosses, who refuse to invest in their own enterprises. They fail to hire enough workers, refuse to purchase raw materials, ignore equipment maintenance, sell off assets, and carry out fraudulent dealings. The aim is to milk the enterprise for everything it is worth before abandoning it."[42]

Decapitalization is not a new phenomenon in Nicaragua. Aspects of decapitalization such as capital flight formed an essential part of the economy under Somoza. During the mass struggle against the Somoza regime, business sectors took huge sums of money—estimates put the total at $800 million—out of the country. When the Sandinistas took power, only 3 million dollars remained in the Central Bank. The new government immediately began to rebuild the Nicaraguan economy, setting increased production as the central goal. "But," as Arnold Weiss-berg asserts, "decapitalization means cutting production, thus directly confronting the ability of the Government of National Construction and the FSLN to carry out the social programs the country so desperately needs. Decapitalization expresses the employing class's complete dis-interest in the standard of living of Nicaragua's working masses."[43]

Owners can decapitalize their businesses in a myriad of ways; some are obvious, while others are more subtle and difficult to prove. Nica-raguan capitalists have carried out decapitalization in six principal forms: 1. refusing to cultivate land; 2. reducing the productive capacity of factories. 3. transporting productive machinery out of the country; 4. refusing to reinvestprofits; 5. manipulating business transactions with the aim of depositing dollars in foreign bank accounts; and 6. failing to deposit payments in foreign currency to the Nicaraguan Central Bank.[44]

Sectors of Nicaragua's capitalist class began their decapitalization campaign in late 1979. They launched the campaign out of their frus-tration at the FSLN's dominant role in the country's political life. During the first three months of 1980, pro-Sandinista unions reported numerous cases of economic sabotage. Workers accused the Plastinic factory of falsifying invoices and tax evasion, the U.S. multinational Sears of con-cealing capital and unjustifiably firing workers, and the Sovipe engi-neering company of threatening to shut its plant because of an alleged lack of raw materials. In addition, the government charged a number of companies with undercutting their Nicaraguan businesses in favor of operations in other countries.[45]

In early 1980, the San Martin slaughter house laid off 188 workers and announced it was closing for at least two months. The owners had already sent checks for more than 100,000 U.S. dollars to Miami and had withdrawn seven million cordobas from the company accounts to buy more dollars on the black market. The IGOSA slaughterhouse sacked more than 300 workers after selling off 6,375 acres, two jeeps, three microbuses, two cars, and spare parts. The CST reported that 29,000 workers in Managua alone were not receiving the minimum wage levels laid down under the Somocista labor code. Furthermore, hundreds of employers ignored the Junta's June decree that called for wage increases for most industrial workers.[46]

Workers met the capitalist sabotage with strong action, including plant seizures. In November 1979, the work force occupied the FANISA pharmaceutical plant. On the Atlantic Coast, 283 workers seized the Bluefields Manufacturing Corporation clothing factory, forcing manage-ment to improve working conditions. In March 1980, 135 workers oc-cupied Polymer SA, a local subsidary of United Brands, to demand full payment of promised wage increases and the end of interference in union activity.[47]

The most famous of all factory occupations occurred at the food-processing plant of El Caracol. In late November 1979, the Campos family, owners of the plant, had signed a contract with the union. After six weeks of management's failure to implement the pact, the workers struck and halted production. But after intensive debate and self-criticism, they returned to work the same day. By February, they had collected sufficient data to denounce management for economic crimes and connections with the counterrevolution. While most members of the Campos family had fled to Miami, two had remained behind in Managua with the specific task of decapitalizing the plant. On February 19, the work force voted by a majority of 121 to 10 to occupy the factory. The following day, the workers invited Commandante Carlos Nuñez to a meeting, where they accused management of 1. refusing to stock sufficient raw materials; 2. refusing to maintain machinery and repair company vehicles; 3. reducing the distribution of El Caracol products; 4. removing "unprofitable" vitamin additives from children's food products; 5. reducing production to a single work shift; and 6. unfairly dismissing twenty-eight workers. After locking out management, the workers immediately raised production levels by 20 percent. The union introduced industrial safety measures and established a defense commission to guard the plant twenty-four hours a day against physical sabotage. On February 21, state judicial authorities, using their emergency powers, sealed off management offices for investigation.[48]

Two weeks later, on March 2, 1980, Junta member Sergio Ramirez announced a new antidecapitalization decree that called for prosecution of anyone "who by action or omission employs deceitful or fraudulent means to remove from the country the fixed or circulating assets of enterprises." Those convicted under the law faced stiff fines and jail terms. Capitalists found guilty of economic sabotage also risked confiscation of their factories by the state.[49]

Before the law was announced, the FSLN weekly *Poder Sandinista* asserted that the workers' own initiatives were "as or more important than the legal measures taken to control the illegal practices of various unpatriotic businessmen." The article continued:

> In the event situations of this type [decapitalization] are detected it is necessary to denounce them immediately, defend the means of production, demand maintenance of production levels, and call for a review of the real accounts of the enterprise. . . .
> The working class has to begin to be concerned with main-

taining the economic balance, understanding that this is not a problem for the private owners, but rather an axis of the workers' class interests—an eminently popular question and thus cause for concern and study on the part of the workers.[50]

The FSLN later appealed for the implementation of "workers' control . . . so as to prevent a halt in production or the destruction of enterprises by their owners or other reactionary forces."[51] Indeed, the FSLN viewed factory occupations as the most effective way of combating counterrevolutionary activity in the private sector. A week after the new antidecapitalization decree was enacted, *Barricada* devoted a full page to detailed explanations of how workers could detect decapitalization.

Many capitalists complained that the anticapitalization decree, which allowed worker access to company records, undermined traditional private sector prerogatives. Jaime Chamorro, editor of *La Prensa*, registered this objection: "All decisions count on the help and cooperation of what they [the Sandinistas] call the 'progressive bourgeoisie.' They are indispensable because a country can't maintain production or run an economy without the cooperation of the class which knows about production."[52]

During the first half of 1981, "the class which knows about production" retaliated with a new wave of economic sabotage. The 1980 antidecapitalization law proved ineffectual against this sabotage campaign because that decree failed to cover such forms of decapitalization as distributing profits as dividends before the end of the year or inflating management salaries. Moreover, while workers gathered evidence of decapitalization to meet the requirements of the 1980 law, many owners stripped their enterprises of capital before the law could be applied. "Against decapitalization, confiscation," asserted ATC General Secretary Edgardo García, "but timely, not just when there's nothing left but ruins, debts, and bankrupt enterprises."[53]

In June 1981, the Ministry of Justice proposed tougher legislation against the capitalists' renewed campaign of economic sabotage. Workers welcomed the proposal, insisting that it include rapid enforcement procedures. Fernando Cedeno, ATC labor director, argued that the new law

. . . should be based upon the experiences and contributions of the workers who feel most immediately the effects of decapitalization that has caused unemployment and that constitutes an attack against the national economy. . . . Proposed modifications are not aimed so much at the content of the actual law as at the implementation measures. The new law should permit the government, through the Ministry of Justice, to intervene immediately in production units based on claims filed by the employees stating that decapitalization is taking place.[54]

Both the ATC and the CST demanded that the new law include measures enabling labor to play the fundamental role in its implementation. In the view of the two labor federations, workers had demonstrated their ability to investigate decapitalization, file complaints against owners, and, if necessary, take over and run entire enterprises. The CST's Lucio Jiminez outlined the solution to decapitalization in a speech to the government workers' union.

> We are all aware of the conscious participation of the workers, sometimes even including taking on tasks that are part of administration. We value the immense sacrifices of the working class and all the workers, but, working aginst these sacrifices and this effort is the criminal hand of imperialism and its lackeys, the sellout capitalists that in a thousand and one ways are decapitalizing the national economy.
>
> By looking at a huge number of private enterprises, we have learned about two fundamental forms of decapitalization. The first and most important is the refusal to invest, in spite of the profits they make. And as if that weren't enough, not only do they rob the people through phony bank loans, but they also allow themselves the privilege of decapitalizing their enterprises both by overbilling imports and by buying dollars and sending them to Miami, surely to arm the counterrevolutionary bands there and here on our northern frontier. . . .
>
> We are of the opinion that the workers cannot remain on the defensive, because on our shoulders rests the future of the revolution. And we should immediately go over to the offensive, to an open struggle not just against anybody or against one or two bosses, but go over to an immediate struggle to strike a profound blow at the bourgeoisie as a class.[55]

On July 19, 1981, the government announced the new law against decapitalization. The law allows the government to intervene whenever workers submit formal charges of decapitalization. While authorities investigate the charges, the enterprise remains under government control. In addition, the law bans owner reprisals against those workers who make charges of decapitalization. The legislation also expands the definition of decapitalization to include practices that escaped prosecution in the old decree.[56]

First Steps Toward Worker Participation

In response to the decapitalization campaign, the Sandinistas proposed "workers' control," which they defined in terms of workers' rights to inspect or check management decisions. Although control in this sense represents "partial participation" in management and clearly implies a limitation to workers' sovereignty, capitalists opposed it. "The private sector's nightmare," wrote Black in 1981, "is how long it will continue to monopolize knowledge about production, when all around it is the evidence of direct state support for worker control—a mixture of legislation, propaganda and specific structures for popular participation—and the correspondingly rapid increase in workers' consciousness."[57]

In the first year of the revolution, the principal form of worker control took place during regular meetings of all the workers and administrators. These meetings were called *Asambleas de Reactivación Económica* (economic reactivation assemblies—AREs). Assembly discussions centered on problems of the national economy, productive difficulties in each enterprise, and matters involving both these concerns: the lack of spare parts, the lack of foreign exchange, and shortages of raw materials and other inputs. The purpose of the reactivation assemblies was to move the workers beyond their immediate work sphere and expand their participation in the entire production process. Planners set three objectives for the assemblies: 1. to disclose the plant's production plan to the workers in every section and department; 2. to ensure that workers continually monitor the production process according to the goals of each section, department, and work brigade; and 3. to urge workers to detect problems, maintain tools and machinery, and properly use the enterprise's resources.[58]

The assemblies were scheduled to meet three times a year: first for production planning, then for mid-year monitoring, and finally for evaluation and criticism. According to the CST, the assemblies represented ". . . the forum which guarantees that workers will know how an enterprise is being run. And the workers have the power to dismiss any administrator, whether on the grounds of inefficient management of the company or malpractice of workers."[59]

Although the AREs frequently engendered worker self-confidence, their long-term benefits were limited. Writing in *Barricada* in May, 1981, Sandinista economist Nathan Sevilla explained that the reactivation assemblies failed to accomplish their goals because many workers refrained from participating in decision-making after the assemblies were over.[60] A government report published in 1984 enumerated additional difficulties encountered in the assemblies. In the agricultural sector, for example, assemblies often ended in heated and stormy discussions between workers and managers. Workers used the meetings to air long-standing complaints, sometimes demanding the dismissal of administrators. The report affirms, however, that the assembly experience expanded workers' knowledge of production problems and familiarized them with the technical resources available on state farms.[61]

In a more recent assessment of the assemblies, Argentinian sociologist Carlos Vilas observes:

> The results of these assemblies depended upon the way they were conceived and carried out. The AREs which functioned best, in terms of workers participation in the discussion of important issues, were those which were set up at the urging of the local union, where the union carried out effective political work among the rank-and-file, and where the latter demanded, sometimes belligerently, information on and discussion about issueswhich up to this time had been forbidden to them. In other words, the existence of a strong union, with a firm base in the rank-and-file, proved to be the main condition favoring the development of genuine participation. In contrast, where the AREs were vertically organized from the top by management, the results were poor and tended to hinder the development of the process of workers participation.[62]

The Economic Reactivation Assemblies ended in the midst of the 1981 industrial crisis that included many cases of bankruptcy and temporary shutdowns of important enterprises. The chief causes of this crisis were 1. deteriorating industrial machinery; 2. inherited financial burdens; 3. foreign exchange shortages; and 4. workers' salary demands.[63]

Obstacles to Worker Participation

Worker participation in Nicaragua involves a dramatic break from the social relations that prevailed under the dictatorship. But do the workers, in fact, grasp their participation as a dramatic break? Workers commonly hold one or another of three views on their work's effect upon their lives. They can see it simply as a means of securing the income necessary to satisfy material or status needs. They can derive a sense of fulfillment from the work process itself or from the status connected with it. Or, workers can perceive their work in the context of the whole society, understanding its importance in the economic, social, and political development of their country. Workers in advanced capitalist countries usually hold these attitudes.

In Nicaragua, where unemployment or underemployment has been the norm, most workers continue to view their work as merely a way of meeting their material needs. For the unemployed under Somoza, the most menial job could mean survival. In such a context, attempts to develop any form of trade-union consciousness faced formidable obstacles.

> For three months of the year, the rural poor were thrown up against the brutalities of Nicaraguan captialism, with a brief opportunity to organise and share experiences. For the other nine, they dispersed once more to their homes to scratch out a living through subsistence farming. The few who found year-round work in cotton gins or sugar refineries worked in isolated locations, easily divided and repressed. Their revolutionary potential as a class came not from their tradition of organisation, but from the objective facts of their misery.[64]

Immersed in their everyday struggle for material survival and deprived of educational opportunities, most Nicaraguan workers face severe limitations on their ability to assume the tasks of administering production. In a three-part *Barricada* series in May 1981, Ives Chaix, a state-sector production manager, cited some of the main obstacles to workers participation: lack of confidence and unwillingness on the part of workers to challenge administrators; divisions within the working class; a fear of the rank and file by some union leaders; indiscipline at work; and unfamiliarity with the technical side of production. Chaix suggested three measures to counter these obstacles. First, he proposed that workers establish simple initial goals, and then gradually tackle more complex projects. Second, Chaix urged workers to question management whenever there was something they didn't like or understand. Third, he called for higher levels of organization and discipline in the working class, and more widespread use of democratic forms such as councils, section meetings, and plant meetings.

But obstacles to workers' participation cannot be attributed solely to workers' historically-rooted weaknesses. State-appointed administrators have frequently resisted meaningful workers' input into management-level decisions. Although many administrators in the state sector are neophytes, possessing little or no managerial training or experience, they frequently adopt elitist attitudes toward workers. While welcoming workers' contributions to maintaining labor discipline and raising productivity, these administrators often ignore workers' proposals concerning the operations of the production process itself. In 1983, Selgado Membreno, General Secretary of the CGT-I, registered this complaint:

Workers' participation should not be limited to problems such as productivity, savings, austerity, but it should also be extended to management-level decisions. Only in this way will workers be able to assume a greater responsibility for the entire operation. This is where we run into obstacles; there is even some opposition on the part of government administrators. Many times management decisions of the People's Industrial Corporation (COIP) or the APP cannot be questioned. By the very fact that they are management-level decisions, the workers have no voice. So what happens? Many times the workers reject the decisions. Why? Because first they're told to participate fully, to incorporate themselves completely in their work, but when the workers want to point out the faults of management, they find they're without voice or vote. When workers ask to participate in administrative management, it's because they see errors being committed. The administrators are not infallible.[65]

Upgrading Worker Participation: The Pilot Projects

In June 1982, the Sandinista Workers Federation and the People's Industrial Corporation (COIP) took an important step toward confronting the various barriers to workers' participation. After intensive discussions, the two organizations launched a pilot project designed to increase worker participation in the operations of eight public-sector enterprises. According to Sergio Molina, COIP Director of Industrial Relations, the object of the plan was to "upgrade the level of workers' involvement from a mere audit level to one of greater knowledge and domination of the global problematic of the enterprise."[66] The project attempts to go beyond partial worker participation in state enterprises to forms of full participation; instead of merely checking management decisions, workers in these eight plants help determine production objectives and, at the same time, ensure that management uses the appropriate means to achieve them.

The idea that working people should themselves make decisions concerning production matters is crucial to the plan. When the pilot project was announced, Ruben Ulloa, CST Secretary of Production, explained that it would allow workers to discuss with management both production plans and goals, that is, the entire process of production: how much to produce, for whom to produce, and how to obtain raw materials. Ulloa emphasized that "discussion" with management includes the opportunity for workers to enrich or even revise production plans.[67]

The project began in June 1982. First, each factory's Enterprise Committee, which comprises the factory director, the plant department heads, and the union leadership, established the annual production goals. Next, the plant's Production Committee, a new body created by the pilot plan, reviewed the production goals. The Production Committee is made up of three union leaders, the members of the various union sections, and the plant manager and department heads. Finally, "commitment assemblies," made up of all the workers in the factory, discussed the production goals. In the assemblies, the manager and union leaders discussed all the aspects relevant to meting production goals, including supply problems, production costs, and estimates of production. Because of their previous participation in the earlier stages of review, workers frequently added their suggestions and criticisms to the analysis of the production goals. To guarantee continual worker involvement, the earlier stages of review, workers frequently added their suggestions and criticisms to the analysis of the production goals. To guarantee continual worker involvement, the Enterprise and Production Committees met every fifteen days to review production goals, and the Commitment Assemblies held monthly sessions.[68]

How did the unions react to the pilot project? In July 1982, Nancy Aguirre Vargas, the general secretary of the CST-affiliated union at Texnicsa, Nicaragua's largest factory, reflected on her union's participation in the pilot plan.

> In our factory there is still very little support from management for union participation in production. But that doesn't hold us back. Here there are worker comrades at the base who know the production process like the back of their hands; perhaps the administration doesn't know all that we know. And, in time, we're going to acquire even greater knowledge because the CST now provides all the workers with regular technical instruction.
>
> We, the union executive committee, meet with management, that is, the enterprise committee meets. We discuss productivity goals for each month, the production problems which we have, and what interferes with the raising of production. We then meet with each union department and its leadership to hear the workers' problems and concerns so that we can bring them up in the Production Committtee.
>
> The union executive committee is an organ of popular power because it represents all the workers of this enterprise. The administration has to listen to us and seriously analyze and discuss problems with us.[69]

In an interview one year later, Vargas asserted that the level of worker participation at Texnicsa had doubled in the previous year. The biweekly

Production Committees and monthly Commitment Assemblies had continued their functions. During the 1982–1983 production cycle, the Production Committee had examined every aspect of factory administration, including reviewing production goals and supply shortages. The Production Committee reported the results of its work to all the workers during the monthly Commitment Assembly gatherings.

In addition to participating in meetings concerning the factory's production process, Texnicsa workers and technicians receive formal instruction to upgrade their general understanding of the textile industry, and to increase their specific job skills. In 1983, 10 workers attended a special government-sponsored course on textile production. In the same year, 180 workers attended two classes held in the factory, one on mechanics and the other on technical theory.[70]

One Texnicsa technician reported that union members had contributed markedly to the decision-making process in the factory. Their contributions, he said, included assissting management in improving production, and making decisions that affected both specific and general aspects of the production process. In addition, the technician noted that, although administrators and technicians have the last word concerning production decisions, they always conveyed their decisions in a respectful manner: "We don't order people around here; we explain exactly why a decision was made. This is part of our educational process. In fact, our whole process in the factory is one large school for all of us."[71]

Many enterprises have duplicated the pilot project's participatory model. The CST and COIP help factories implement worker-participation plans that make use of workers' prior experiences. The expansion of the pilot project will have a series of long-term effects that enhance the capabilities, determination, and power of Nicaragua's industrial workers.

The ATC Pilot Project

In February 1983, the Ministry of Agriculture, aided by the Rural Workers Association, selected ten state enterprises to participate in a worker participation project in the agricultural sector. The Ministry chose these ten enterprises because of the compactness of their productive units, their financial solvency, and their high level of union organization. In addition to upgrading worker participation, planners expect the project to improve administrative efficiency on the state farms. The National Council of Agrarian Reform supervises the project, while the Regional Councils of Agrarian Reform monitor its implementation at the regional level.[72]

The project established three administrative councils: the management council, the extended council, and the production councils. The management council is the project's principal decision-making body. It is made up of the Director and the Assistant Director of the enterprise, an Agriculture Ministry representative, two union delegates, and a representative of the Regional Council of Agrarian Reform. The Management Council meets monthly to revise and evaluate the state farm's technical-economic plan and annual budgets. The Council reports alterations in the plan to the Ministry of Agriculture. The extended council meets every three months and is made up of the Management Council members, directors and union leaders of state Complexes and UPES, and union leaders of the enterprise. The Extended Council reviews and ratifies the Director's production report, and monitors the work of the Management Councils. The production councils councils meet at least once a month in the complexes and UPEs to revise proposed production goals, to participate in the hiring or discharging of the labor force, to revise the organization of the production process, and to discuss and evaluate the technical/economic plan. Complex and UPE admiministrators sit on the Production Councils.[73]

Oscar Turcios, a large tobacco enterprise in the Nueva Segovia Region, participates in the pilot project. In a 1984 interview, Alcides Montoya, director of one complex within the enterprise, disclosed the project's achievements and problems. What follows is a summary of Montoya's assessment.[74] After elaborating the 1983–1984 technical/economic plan, management submitted the plan to the workers. The plan proposed a 10 percent cut in expenses over 1982–1983, a cut that the workers' representatives insisted was too ambitious. Although union officials recommended a return to the previous year's budget, management stuck to its budget. The enterprise then set in motion its production plan. Both workers and management evaluated the plan at each production stage, and management periodically reported expense figures to the workers. By the end of the tobacco cycle, the union delegates had been vindicated: the enterprise had spent the same amount as the previous year.

Oscar Turcios' management council meets every two weeks to make financial decisions on economic matters and technical aspects of production. According to Montoya, union participants usually limit their contribution to telling management how many workers will be needed during the different phases of the production cycle. The union officials are unable to assist management with technical or financial matters: "The union leaders had a lot of problems understanding the technical plans and the figures discussed in the production council meetings."[75]

In 1983, the directors of the enterprise's four complexes attended project-sponsored classes in Managua, and intermediate technicians received training at MIDINRA's regional office. Because these courses required a high level of technical competence, union representatives did not attend. But MIDINRA held classes for all members of the management and production councils, including workers.

> Our problem is that it has only been four years since the literacy campaign and therefore the workers don't have the ability to pass directly to accounting school. But they are often able to manipulate figures after completing the fifth level of the adult education program. Also, many farm administrators have a lot of technical knowledge and can handle figures even though they too are still students in the adult education classes. Their experience has given them a lot of knowledge.
> Here, in this enterprise, there is a lot of acceptance of worker participation. Workers are helping us rationalize the financing of the business and they are able to concretize our figures. They have definitely influenced our budgets through their suggestions. All of us have been affected by worker participation. Although 20 percent of the permanent workers who were mobilized [for defense] we achieved 100 percent of our production goals for 1983–84.[76]

To date, union leaders have more vigorously championed worker participation in management than have rank-and-file workers. In most cases, both union cadres and workers display a limited capacity to participate in management-level decisions. The need for increased political conviction and training remains paramount. A major part of union activity still consists of motivating the rank and file to involve themselves in such forms of participation as attending assemblies, participating in discussions, demanding reports from union delegates, and monitoring the production process.

Both the CST and the ATC are engaged in efforts to expand workers' training in order to augment their level of participation. But these efforts confront many difficulties because in many cases the union leadership suffers from the same limitations as the workers. Few experienced cadres are available and their level of training is meager. Carlos Vilas wrote:

> These conditions have created a context within which paternalistic practices have developed among certain sectors of the state apparatus and the administration of the APP, as well as among the union leaders themselves. There is a tendency toward leadership by substitution, i.e., decisions are made for the workers instead of by them. Or participation is omitted in an effort to avoid overloading the workers or their organizations; or be-

cause the functionaries have better technical knowledge; or because of the slowness of the union's response due to the factors we have already mentioned—all of which in the end lead to decisions being taken at the top and the workers representatives are left simply with endorsing these decisions.[77]

In short, Nicaraguan workers have thus far engaged in partial participation in management: they contribute to management decisions and can restrict what managers do. But the country's workers do not exercise full participation in management, and face formidable obstacles to such participation. To ensure workers' support for the revolution, they must share in the key economic decisions facing the country; if they are unable to do so, productivity will decline because of the workers' disinterest and resistance, thereby imperiling the revolution itself.

11
DEFENDING THE REVOLUTION

THE MILITARY STRUCTURE

At the time of its victory over Somoza, the FSLN had a total of 15,000 combatants. Of this number, 2,000 fought in regular army units, 3,000 served in guerrilla columns, and 10,000 battled in urban militia forces.[1] Many of these combatants joined the Sandinista regime's new army, the *Ejercito Popular Sandinista* (Sandinista Popular Army—EPS), created on September 2, 1979. Fifty-two years earlier on that date Sandino had established his guerrilla army that fought the U.S. Marines. The Sandinistas considered the creation of an army like Sandino's—nationalist, defensive, anti-imperialist, the foundation of the revolution.

During the first six months of the revolutionary process, the new regime disarmed those who had participated in the insurrection and integrated many of them into the EPS. Because 45 percent of the soldiers in the new army were illiterate, the Ministry of Defense launched a literacy campaign within the armed forces; literate troops provided on-going instruction in educational basics to illiterate troops. To deal with the lack of adequate political orientation among some of the recruits, the EPS established political-cultural sections at all levels and in all regional commands. These sections embarked on an intensive political training program. Professor Stephen M. Gorman describes the content of this training:

> The responsibility of soldiers to set moral examples for the pop-
> ulation, to take advantage of every opportunity to work with
> members of the popular classes, and to avoid developing par-

ticularistic interests that might weaken their identification with the disadvantaged were especially significant elements of political-cultural training. The ideal soldier, according to the model projected by the Sandinista leadership, was one willing to oppose any and all threats to the material and spiritual well-being of the masses. A particularly interesting facet of the training was the attention given to working with children. Accordingly, the military sponsored a variety of recreational and cultural programs aimed at bringing soldiers and children together, which had a predictable socializing impact on both groups.[2]

In February 1980, the Defense Ministry began to form the *Milicias Populares Sandinistas* (Sandinista People's Militias—MPS) to support the EPS and to involve all Nicaraguans in national defense. The MPS were voluntary and accepted men and women between the ages of sixteen and sixty. During their first year, the militias carried out a number of tasks. Militia members guarded public installations or aided police in major operations. Militias which were organized in factories protected workplaces and equipment from destruction by ultraleftist elements engaged in labor disturbances, or from owners who attempted to decapitalize their property. The MPS also fought alongside the regular army combating the ex-National Guardsmen in the north.[3]

Shortly after the fall of Somoza, the Ministry of Interior created the Sandinista police. In their first year the police received sufficient military training to aid in national defense. Minister of Interior Tomás Borge explained that if Nicaragua suffered an attack "the police and soldiers of the Sandinista Popular Army are going to go to the same trenches and shed the same blood."[4] But under normal conditions the army and police would perform separate functions. According to Borge,

> The members of the State Security Forces, the Sandinista Police and the Sandinista Popular Army form part of the same family and regardless of where they go they must be coordinated. United in the same force, the only thing that has to be understood is that their functions are distinct. The police are responsible for maintaining order, protecting the people—especially children and the weak—from delinquents and from antisocial enemies. . . . The army should concentrate on constant military training in order to be ready as a vanguard force in the hour of combat to confront the armed enemies of our Revolution.[5]

During the first year of the revolution, defense was not yet a daily priority. The Defense Ministry organized and trained both the EPS and the MPS, and both groups participated in the harvests and other social and economic projects. By late 1981, the counter-revolutionaries had escalated their attacks against Nicaragua, and the Defense Ministry broadened and strengthened the defense structure.

THE CONTRA WAR

In March 1982, President Ronald Reagan, in a secret move revealed only to the Senate Intelligence Committee, reaffirmed the existing covert programs against Nicaragua began under President Carter and extended them by authorizing the start of a new covert military operation. The alleged purpose of this action was to halt Nicaraguan arms shipments to El Salvador.[6]

The Central Intelligence Agency assigned 150 agents to begin organizing the anti-Sandinista operation. CIA operatives contacted Somocista exiles in Miami, Florida, where since the Sandinista victory in 1979, paramilitary forces had been training for an invasion of Nicaragua. In return for U.S. aid, the CIA compelled the different anti-Sandinista elements, including many former Somoza National Guardsmen and the disident Miskitu Indian group, Misura, to unite in a counterrevolutionary organization called the *Frente Democratico Nicaraguense* (Nicaraguan Democratic Front—FDN).

In November 1981, the National Security Council (NSC) adopted a 10-point proposal for increased U.S. intervention in Central America and the Caribbean, which included a plan to markedly escalate covert operations against Nicaragua. In addition to reaffirming existing covert aid to "moderate political and economic forces" inside Nicaragua, the NSC authorized a $19.5 million initial budget for the CIA to begin training a 500-man contingent to engage in paramilitary operations against Nicaragua. Joining this group was a 1,000-strong paramilitary force already being trained by Argentina whose cooperation had been gained earlier that year by former CIA director General Vernon Walters, a secret Reagan emissary. The NSC, while not precluding CIA involvement, called for third country participation, mainly Argentinian and Honduran, and "third parties," namely the anti-Sandinista exiles. This NSC decision launched the undeclared war against Nicaragua.

By 1983, U.S. support had transformed a motley band of poorly armed ex-guardsmen into a well-organized counter-revolutionary army (the Contra) equipped with automatic rifles, mortars, heavy caliber machine guns, trucks, and small aircraft. The FDN had approximately 4,000 troops; the 3,000 Indians of Misura were less well trained and disciplined.

In the late spring of 1983, former Sandinista commander Eden Pastora, who had refused to join with the FDN, initiated incursions against the Sandinistas from bases along the Costa Rican border. Pastora at first vehemently denied links to the CIA, but published reports alleged that he was receiving laundered CIA money through various Latin American sources.

Although Reagan administration officials scoffed at Sandinista charges that the United States sought a Honduran-Nicaraguan war as a pretext for American intervention against the Sandinistas, U.S. policies created a dangerous situation along the border. The Honduran army's assistance to the Contras increased as the covert war developed. In addition to serving as an intermediary for supplies, Honduran forces aided the Contras with artillery fire and frequently engaged in direct clashes with the Nicaraguans.

In the winter and spring of 1983, the Contras, at the behest of the CIA, launched their first major offensive in northern Nicaragua. Besides assaulting rural settlements and disrupting the coffee harvest, the Contra tried to establish military "task forces" deep inside Nicaraguan territory. They also had a more ambitious goal in mind: occupying the strip of land in northern Jinotega province that juts up into Honduras. This would be the first step toward declaring a provisional government. Contra leaders even boasted that they would march into Managua before the end of the year.

By summer, however, the FDN's Contra army proved to be no more than a harassment to the Sandinistas. Although it inflicted $70 million in economic destruction and forced thousands of Nicaraguan peasants to abandon their farms, the invasion failed both militarily and politically. The Contras were unable to hold any territory and could not keep their task forces inside the country. The thousands of Contra infiltrators retreated to their camps in Honduras "in such bad shape," admitted one FDN leader, "that some of them straggled back to their bases literally without shoes."[7]

The Sandinistas had successfully withstood the Contra attack. Indeed, as a House Intelligence Committee report concluded in May 1983, United States aid to the Contras was backfiring. Popular support for the Sandinista government had increased in the face of the U.S. alliance with the universally despised Somocistas.

To revitalize the defeated Contra forces, the Reagan administration decided to double the number of FDN forces. In the summer of 1983, it asked Congress for an additional $50 million and permitted the CIA to take charge of choosing targets and planning attacks. The CIA official directing the covert operation in Tegucigalpa ordered the Contras to focus their attacks on strategic installations in Nicaragua. In late 1983, ARDE planes furnished by the CIA bombed the Managua airport, and CIA operatives struck the country's vital oil storage facilities at Corinto and Puerto Sandino. In March 1984, the CIA supervised the mining of Nicaragua's main ports.

In 1984 and 1985 Contra attacks severely damaged important parts of Nicaragua's economic infrastructure—bridges, granaries, water and oil storage facilities, electrical power stations, telephone lines, saw mills, health centers, agricultural cooperatives, schools, and dams. Between November 1984 and March 1985 the Contras concentrated their attacks in the coffee harvest zones, killing 200 farmers and destroying fifty-nine coffee production centers. The Contra raids inflicted losses totalling $69 million.[8]

During the first two months of 1985, the Contras hit targets in half of Nicaragua's sixteen departments, and during January alone, the Nicaraguan army fought seventy-one battles with the Contra.[9] Most of the fighting in the first half of 1985 took place in the northern departments of Matagalpa, Jinotega, Madriz, and Zelaya, but in July Contra units made strikes along the Panamerican Highway in the department of Estelí. However, in the second half of 1985, a Sandinista army counteroffensive severely crippled the Contra forces, driving most of their units back into Honduras. By early 1986 most Contra bands were fighting in central Zelaya and the departments of Boaco and Chontales.

THE NICARAGUANS RESPOND

The State of Emergency and the Expansion of the Militias

On March 15 1982, the Nicaraguan government declared a state of emergency after the bombing of two bridges near the Hounduran border, an attack on two fishing vessels in Nicaraguan territorial waters, and the killing of three soldiers' in a clash with a counterrevolutionary band. The response to appeals for militia volunteers later that month was massive. Eighteen thousand members of the Sandinista Youth enrolled in the MPS. In León, a city of 250,000, five centers of militia training were required to accomodate all the volunteers.[10]

In the second half of 1983, the Ministry of Defense reorganized the urban MPSs into territorial battalions. The Ministry inaugurated the first territorial battalions, established on the basis of Managua's geographical zones on July 26. At a rally of 3,500 militia members held that day, Humberto Ortega, Nicargua's Minister of Defense, stressed the CST's role in the creation of these battalions.

The CST is taking the lead in mobilizing people for military defense. Obviously, the militia battalions organized on a territorial basis include a large proportion of workers. Among them are both industrial and agricultural workers, as well as other working people.

The battalions must guard the cities, the industries, and the schools so that the invaders will not be able to take any street. . . . What the national leadership [of the FLSN] is preparing for is the most massive counterattack against the threat we think we now face—that is, conventional military assaults backed up by the landing of commando forces directed against strategic points such as the airport or the telecommunications building.[11]

Ortega went on to assert, "The counterrevolution will find the country 'mined' with better organized and better armed militia in specific places of the military theater. . . ."[12] That image reflects the new strategy's pragmatic nature: decentralize, specialize, and extend the militias, and familiarize them with the locations or strategic targets which they must defend.

Patriotic Military Service

Until 1983, the Defense Ministry organized national defense on four distinct levels: nonarmed revolutionary vigilance; armed militias organized to defend neighborhoods, villages, and enterprises; reserve battalions ready to be sent to combat zones; and the standing army. Volunteers filled the ranks of all four levels of this defense structure, serving wherever they were needed.[13] Volunteers in the reserve brigade received at least one month training before engaging in combat while militia members trained once a week near their homes.

In 1983, however, the system of recruiting volunteers to meet defense requirements began to have adverse economic and political effects. As an increasing number of the most committed activists left for the border areas, the urban and rural economies began to feel their absence. Moreover, the loss of outstanding activists weakened the organizing efforts of the unions and the Sandinista Defense Committees. In response to these problems as well as to meet the need to recruit more skilled personnel, Daniel Ortega announced a proposal for a military draft law on July 19, 1983.[14] This law, calling for Patriotic Military Service, drew on the historical legacy of Sandino's army, on the government platform (points 1 and 12), and on the Fundamental Statute of the Republic (art. 24) promulgated on July 20, 1979. These stipulate that the new army "will be formed by a minimum of permanent cadres and by Nicaraguans able to give obligatory military service, with the goal of lessening the costs which defense generates and setting aside said financial resources for the economic and social development of the country."[15]

The Council of the State passed the military service law in September 1983. Defined as "the institutionalization of the military service which the reservists and the militia have been doing voluntarily since the revolution,"[16] the law covers both active and reserve duty. Active duty implies direct and continuous service in some branch of the Ministry of Defense, while reserve duty includes military training and readiness. All Nicaraguan males between eighteen and forty years of age are obliged to serve active or reserve duty. Military service for women is voluntary but women between eighteen and forty may request to serve.

Military service lasts for a two-year period, but the law allows the Ministry of Defense to reduce or or extend it by six months. New recruits are designated "military personnel" and receive food, clothing, medical attention, and a monthly stipend. If they are employed when drafted, the government guarantees their job after their service commitment. Once their active duty is finished, they automatically become a part of the reserves.

The Patriotic Military Service greatly strengthened the Sandinista armed forces allowing the Ministry of Defense to launch an offensive against the contras in December 1984. Newly formed "irregular fighting battalions," made up of draftees, continually pursued detected contra units in search and destroy missions that by late 1985 made it impossible for the contras to launch any effective attacks. In early 1985 the Sandinista military began to employ MI-8 and MI-24 Soviet helicopters which allow the army's batallions to deploy themselves faster than the contras can flee on the ground. The helicopters also give the army the advantage of air fire support. With the addition of some 25,000 draftees between February 1984 and February 1986 the Sandinista army grew in strength to some 62,000 soldiers. The Ministry of Defense also bolstered its reserve units with the passage of the Patriotic Military Reserve law in October 1985. In January 1986 the Ministry began forming army reserve units drawing heavily from recently demobilized draftees. The Contra strength is estimated to be between 9,000 and 14,000 men.

MASS ORGANIZATION PARTICIPATION IN DEFENSE

Throughout the war the Reagan Administration has pursued three inter-related objectives: to destroy the economy, to build the Contras into a force capable of occupying the country, and to expand the social base for the counterrevolution. The Sandinista decision in December 1984 to mobilize its resources for this war takes account of this comprehensive strategy. "We will meet the U.S. head on, on all fronts, including the economic and political" declared a government foreign policy strategist.

To meet the United States head on, the Sandinistas rely heavily on the mass organizations' contributions to the defense efforts. Although the mass organizations had been heavily involved in defense tasks ever since the fall of Somoza, they increased their involvement after March 15, 1982, the day the government declared the state of emergency. From March 15 to April 4, Nicaragua suffered twenty-three armed attacks, including two in which units of the Honduran army participated; twenty-three violations of its air space, including four RC-135 U.S. spy flights and one attack by Honduran war planes on a coast guard vessel; and five violations of its territorial waters.[17] At a memorial service for a 17-year old Sandinista soldier killed by counterrevolutionaries at a northern border post, Defense Minister Humberto Ortega stressed the importance of defense mobilization:

> Our revolutionary government was forced to decree the state of emergency and with it we showed the imperialists that despite difficulties we are capable of organizing to push the revolutionary process ahead under the most trying conditions.
>
> Imperialism is trying to prevent the people of our country from carrying out their normal activities. They are trying to create chaos, to keep us from carrying through the tasks posed by the revolution. But we have shown them we are capable of confronting a difficult situation without halting production, cultural activities, or religious services.
>
> So long as imperialism continues to consolidate the thousands of counterrevolutionaries based in Honduran territory, defense will remain a top priority, If these camps are shut down, in accordance with proposals for peace we have made, then the high state of readiness can be lessened.
>
> If the CIA halts its efforts to destabilize the revolution, the tension can be relaxed somewhat. But as long as we continue to be threatened, murdered, and have our bridges blown up, our defense will remain in high gear as well.[18]

As the border war heated up during the end of March, the mass organizations devoted their attention to guaranteeing the continued supply and distribution of food. After an emergency meeting of his organization on March 17, UNAG president Narciso Gomez warned: "If we don't assure our people *gallo pinto* [literally, "spotted rooster," a popular

Nicaraguan term for rice and beans], especially those on the frontline, it will be a disaster. Hunger, not the enemy's bullets will defeat us."[19] UNAG held the meeting to discuss the precautionary measures that the government had taken to assure food supplies as well as to establish plans for supplying the cities during an invasion.

The National Executive Committee of the ATC also met on March 17 to discuss how branches of the ATC would ensure continued agricultural production, particularly of such major items as coffee, cotton, rice, and beef. The Association leadership also established vigilance committees of ATC members to prevent sabotage of crops and machinery, and attacks by counterrevolutionary bands.[20]

The mass organizations were especially concerned with food distribution in the cities. In the large central markets where most food is sold, the CDSs recruited market vendors for the militia and vigilance committees. CDS activists fortified the markets against military attack: vendors dug trenches at the Roberto Huembes outdoor market in Managua, where two-thirds of the market stall proprietors had already joined the militia or the CDS. The CDSs also created special price-watch committees to make sure that no one took advantage of the increased tension to artificially increase food prices. Managua's Eastern Market had thirty-four CDSs responsible for this task.[21]

In addition to guaranteeing supplies and the distribution of food during a time of crisis, the popular associations perform two other principal defense tasks: they recruit most of the volunteers for the reserve infantry battalions and the militias, and they provide substantial financial and material aid to combatants and their families. The mass organizations recruit the vast majority of volunteers to the reserve infantry battalions and militias. Indeed, in evaluating their organizational achievements, the popular associations emphasize their members' contributions to the defense effort. In March 1984, for example, the ATC office in Estelí released figures concerning the number of farmworkers who had recently volunteered in defense tasks: 335 had joined the reserve battalions, 1,085 had signed up for the militias, and 1,695 had enrolled in revolutionary vigilance.[22]

The ATC's national magazine, El Machete, regularly features articles on farmworker participation in military defense. These articles are designed to inspire ATC members to continue their military involvement. In December 1983, El Machete printed interviews with three association members serving in infantry reserve batallion 31–17, a unit that fights the contras in the Segovia mountains. Asked to explain why he was fighting, Leonidas Acuna replied: "I am an agricultural worker. I am in these mountains fighting and annihilating the enemy because I'm committed to the defense of the conquests that agricultural workers have achieved through our revolution."[23] The article ends by noting that reserve battalion 31-17 is named after Jose Benito Jiminez, an outstanding ATC union leader who was killed by "somocista beasts" in the zone of San Juan de Rio Coco.[24]

The CST also recruits thousands of its members to the reserves and militias. In July 1984, to honor the fifth anniversary of Somoza's overthrow, the CST in the Managua region formed six military companies made up of industrial workers. Orlando Cruz Baltodano, a worker in the Coca Cola bottling plant, explained why he had volunteered for one of these companies: "Our working class consciousness is not for sale nor is it a plaything; we must either be in the first line of fire or working hard." Baltodano added: "We want peace and to achieve peace we have no other alternative but to fight against imperialism."[25]

Among the CST volunteers in the July 1984 mobilization were two top union leaders: Donald Silva, the CST's Secretary of Production, and Leoncio Altamirano, Secretary General of the CST-affiliated union at the Selim Shible milk complex. Damaso Vargas, the CST's Secretary General in Managua, affirmed that the example of the two union leaders motivated other Managua factory, commercial, and service workers to volunteer for the reserve units.[26] Many Nicaraguans unaffiliated with unions sign up for military duties at the behest of the Sandinista Defense Committees. The CDSs constantly stress the importance of national and territorial defense. And although their primary defense responsibility lies in revolutionary vigilance, since 1983 they have played a vital role in filling the ranks of the territorial militias. Each Sandinista Barrio Committee recruits volunteers from among those adults who have not been mobilized in SMP or reserve battalion units.

As the Contras increased their attacks in early 1984, the national office of the CDSs called upon each of the nation's neighborhood committees to name a "secretary of defense" to coordinate all community defense matters. The defense secretaries serve as laison officers between residents and local military authorities. They must be familiar with all questions pertaining to military regulations and procedures so that they can present their constituency with regular reports concerning both national and local defense needs.

The three class-based mass organizations, UNAG, the ATC, and the CST, frequently mobilize their memberships to carry out volunteer work in order to raise funds for the nation's combatants. Instead of receiving their day's wages, workers who participate in a voluntary work campaign contribute the money to a national defense fund. In July 1984, for example, ATC workers in Region II contributed 22,400 córdobas—3,200 hours of work—to support the war front.[27] And in November 1986 thousands of UNAG farmers in Region VI donated 110 million córdobas to the war effort.[28]

In addition to such monetary aid, all the popular associations collect clothes and food to send to the battle zones. Throughout the country, mass organization representatives sit on local commissions called Aid Commissions for Combatants that review the material needs of combatants who live in the commissions' jurisdictions. They then report back to their base and mobilize activists to gather the needed supplies. In many cases, grassroots organization members themselves take the provisions all the way to the front. The popular associations also assist the families of mobilized combatants. It is not unusual for the associations to help pay the bills incurred by poor families whose bread-winners are engaged in combat. If a family has not received mail from a mobilized soldier, mass organization activists will attempt to learn of the soldier's whereabouts and reestablish communication. Furthermore, both the CST and the ATC constantly monitor the law that guarantees full pay to workers who are mobilized, ensuring that the workers' families receive their paychecks.

CIVIL DEFENSE

In 1982, after the escalation of Contra attacks, the government added CDS civil defense groups to the defense structure to help defend communities against sabotage. "Civil defense," according to Captain Moreno, the national head of civil defense, "is the collective and organized participation of our people in the task of guaranteeing their own protection and survival."[29] In Nicaragua, all nonserving, able-bodied adults are expected to contribute to civil defense tasks. Captain Moreno notes that "it takes courage and strength to evacuate people amid bombing, to rescue the injured, or to clear debris. To accomplish these tasks, one must be in good shape."[30]

In September 1983, CIA operatives attacked oil storage tanks at the port of Corinto, setting off a dangerous conflagration. Immediately, civil defense units went into action, evacuating 1,500 residents who lived close to the thirty-five burning tanks. By nightfall civil defense brigades had succeeded in the orderly removal of the nearly 25,000 inhabitants of Corinto. Aiding Corinto's CDS civil brigade units were fifty-five CDS and twenty-one CST civil defense brigades from the neighboring city of Chinandega. The next day, *Barricada* praised the extraordinary efforts of Corinto's civil defense untis: "This criminal act served as a test by fire for Corinto's civil defense which yesterday morning, amid a suffocating evil, successfully passed a test that all had anticipated."[31]

Just after the 1983 school year ended in November, the government introduced obligatory civil defense courses for teachers and students. Primary and secondary school teachers first received civil defense instruction and then served as "multipliers," giving the same courses to high school and university students between December 2 and 23. In order to register for the 1984 school year, the Ministry of Education required students to present certificates of attendance in civil defense courses.[32]

The Ministry of Health and the National Fire-Fighting System conducted the bulk of civil defense courses during the fall of 1983. CDS regional executive committees recruited the bulk of the students. In the zone of Matagalpa, for example, 756 neighborhood residents volunteered to receive the first series of courses in fire fighting, rubble clearance, first aid, and supplies.[33]

In November and December 1983, trade unions affiliated with the CST and the ATC worked to strengthen the defense of economic objectives. Thousands of workers entered civil defense brigades and contributed unpaid labor on Sundays to construct air-raid shelters. Workers also donated blood to the Nicaraguan Red Cross, carried out fire drills, and developed shelters for machinery and equipment. In coordination with management, union leaders elaborated production plans to be followed in the case of full-scale war.[34]

WOMEN IN THE MILITARY

Thousands of Nicaraguan women participate in military defense, an involvement stemming from three factors: women's contributions to the war against Somoza; the government's need to involve as many people as possible in the defense effort; and AMNLAE's ability to raise the issue of women's rights within the military structure.

Women in the Anti-Somoza Struggle

Women made up more than 30 percent of the combatants in the armed struggle against Somoza, a proportion of women in a liberation war that has seldom been equalled. In addition to their participation in guerrilla units in the mountains, women held key leadership positions in the ranks of the FSLN. Dora Maria Tellez, for example, helped lead the audacious Sandinista seizure of the National Palace in 1978. She later became one of three women *comandantes* ("revolutionary heroes") and headed operations on one of the most important fronts of the war, the Rigoberto Lopez Western Front.

It took twenty years for Nicaraguan women to attain such a significant presence within the Sandinista forces. In the 1960s, during the early years of the FSLN, women carried out few military tasks. Tito Valle of the FSLN recalls this period:

> When Luisa Amanda was a member of the Organization there were very few women in the FSLN. In those days, a woman had to make tremendous sacrifices to be a member. It was the end of the sixties and the beginning of the seventies and the FSLN was going through a period of reorganization. Those were very hard years. The women who participated had to face special problems, more difficult perhaps than those faced by the men. Military tasks weren't the general rule; organizational work was what was needed. The job was to recruit people, to politicize them. Most of the women involved at that point were students. Luisa was one of the few working class women.[35]

As the FSLN itself became more active in the early 1970s, a few women joined the guerrilla forces, most of them from educated middle-class families.

But most women became involved in the military conflict more gradually. Inspired by their children's involvement, and infuriated by the repressive actions of the National Guard, they adopted a support role for those in the "front line" of the guerrilla war. Many women turned their homes into safehouses at a time when even those suspected of FSLN sympathies were imprisoned or shot. Many of these women then joined the thousands who engaged in combat in the last stages of the war, a fact which reflects a profound attitude change toward women. Yet the very speed of the change raised the possibility that it would be short-lived. The vast majority of women saw combat at the height of the insurrection when every additional combatant was urgently needed, regardless of gender. After the war some sectors attributed women's participation as exceptional, due only to the emergency of war.

Men have provided such rationalizations in other post-war situations. In Western Europe and the United States after the Second World War, for example, women returned to their homes and husbands almost immediately—albeit after an intense government propaganda campaign. In Nicaragua, however, there has been little opportunity for this retrenchment to the traditional gender roles. Almost overnight the Sandinista regime confronted a new military threat. The subsequent growth of

the armed forces and the escalating contra war necessitated the continuing participation of women in Nicaragua's defense. As Deighton et
al., comment: "The drive to recruit people into the military has produced
a situation for women which runs contrary to that usual in the rest of
society. Rather than being squeezed out as a result of greater military
and economic pressures (as day care centers have been, for example),
women's opportunities in the armed forces have expanded because of
the overarching military threat."[36]

Just after the victory, women constituted 25 percent of the Sandinista
Popular Army.[37] The women who chose to remain in the army possessed
a new mentality, not always shared by their colleagues. Women insisted
they receive the same basic training as men in physical fitness, combat,
arms deployment, arms maintenance, and political theory. Women officers reported that men showed no resentment when receiving orders.

Nevertheless, most male soldiers did not regard women as their
equals.

> While military men conceded that women combatants won their
> respect for the excellent job they did during the insurrection and
> that women would be called on again to defeat a foreign invader,
> they encouraged women to accept technical and administrative
> positions. Furthermore, unlike their male counterparts, not all
> women lived in barracks. Instead, they were allowed to live off-
> base, usually with the family, giving evidence of lingering chau-
> vinism on the part of some men.[38]

As a result of these and other factors, the number of women in the
army dropped considerably during the first year of the revolution, to
between 8 and 10 percent. Because many women left the army to serve
in the Sandinista Police and others joined the reserves, this reduction is
not as drastic as it may seem. Moreover, since July 1979, many more
men than women signed up for the army as a result of an enlistment
campaign. At the same time, there were clear signs that women had
failed to consolidate their place in the regular army: only six percent of
the officers were women, and women began to be trained separately
from the men.

"It's not that the women comrades aren't capable," explained the
director of the Carlos Aguero Military School in Managua,

> and it's not that we're thinking of excluding women from the
> army. There are women with excellent military talents, and there
> is room for them in our ranks. But right now we see the need
> for training them separately. There are exceptions of course,

there are women who because of their excellence must be left
in the regular army and given every opportunity to advance. The
need to train women separately is not because of any limitations
the women have. In fact, you might say it's because of failings
on the part of some men. Our army has many new soldiers,
comrades who haven't had the experience of fighting alongside
women, and they aren't always able to relate to a woman as
just another soldier. They still tend to see them as women.[39]

The Reserve Battalions

Reservists are drawn from the militias, and there is much more room for
women's participation in these military units. Originally, however, only
men's battalions were created. Military authorities later formed one wom-
en's battalion in the traditionally militian area of Leon. But the move to
make women's battalions an essential part of the reserves only occurred
after an incident in 1982. A reserve unit on the border asked AMNLAE
in Estelí to send a dozen members—not as military reinforcements, but
to cook for the troops. AMNLAE refused, insisting that women go to the
front as soldiers, not as cooks. Martha Munguia, AMNLAE's general
secretary in Estelí, forcefully voiced her organization's stance.

> We women are in the Sandinista Popular Militia. In the Madriz
> district 60 percent of the militia are women, in Nueva Segovia
> we make up half the total, and in all districts of the country
> women of the militias have made their presence felt. We have
> military squadrons in Siuna, Masaya, Granada, Rivas, Chinan-
> dega, Jinotega, Matagalpa—the entire nation. But we have only
> seen the mobilization of one women's reserve battalion. In this,
> our region, where women have been outstanding for their com-
> bativity and dedication to the liberation of our people, where
> women are in the militia, the voluntary police, and where they
> watch over the streets of our cities, we haven't been given the
> opportunity to become reservists. Sandino's country is being
> threatened. We women cannot restrict our participation in its
> defence to duties that will place us again in a secondary role. If
> we did, we would be leaving empty the space left to us by those
> women who died for the country.[40]

AMNLAE's pursued the issue of women's reserve battalions, launching a successful national campaign to pressure the government to change
its policy. It also initiated reservists' training especially for women. In
1985, there were battalions in Managua, Carazo, and Chontales.

CASE STUDY: DEFENDING JALAPA

On January 11, 1984, members of the Sandinista Popular Army and militia units from the Jalapa region opened fire on a U.S. helicopter that had violated Nicaraguan air space.[41] The helicopter was shot down and its pilot killed. People in the region said: "This is the first time we've brought down one of those big butterflies." The oldest people in Jalapa, however, disagreed: "This wasn't the first time. Sandino shot down some of the marines' planes not far from here."[41] (On October 7, 1927, Sandino's guerrillas used a makeshift antiaircraft mortar to down their first U.S. aircraft in Las Cruces.)

For two years, from March 1982 to early 1984, Jalapa was the scene of the heaviest fighting in the Contra war. Visitors from abroad frequently visited the area and the Sandinista military often referred to it in their military reports. It was also the main target of the counterrevolutionaries from the time of their "silent war, strategy of terror" until the so-called Sierra Plan. During this period Jalapa became the symbol of Nicaragua under attack.

The "beak of Jalapa" protrudes into Honduras and is surrounded by that country except at one spot: the old dirt road leading to the city of Ocotal. This road is crossed by dozens of brooks which the Nicaraguans have covered with small and fragile bridges. The bridges seem very vulnerable, as does Jalapa because of its isolation. But the counterrevolutionaries have always failed in their repeated attempts to seize it.

Jalapa is one of the twelve municipalities of the department of Nueva Segovia, which, together with Madriz and Estelí, makes up Region I, called Las Segovias. In 1981 Jalapa had 22,835 inhabitants, 82 percent of which lived in rural areas. The farmland in Jalapa is very fertile. A Jalapa resident describes the agricultural richness of the land.

As far as agriculture's concerned, I'd say that Jalapa's the most important zone here in Las Segovias. We produce tobacco, which is a delicate plant that can easily be damaged by the counterrevolutionaries. Jalapa has 48,000 acres of flatlands and an excellent climate. Experts say that it has the best rainfall in all Nicaragua. Even though we're still not using the full productive capacity of these 48,000 acres, you can understand why we have high expectations. We haven't received much economic aid. We've probably averaged less aid than the rest of the region or even the rest of the country. Still, what we've been given has been enough because the land is good. For years and years Las Segovias has been Nicaragua's main tobacco region, and 65 percent of the tobacco grown in Las Segovias comes from Jalapa.

That comes to about 750 tons. All the region's rice is also produced in Jalapa. And now we're beginning to work seriously on
basic grains: 6,000 tons of corn, 2,500 tons of beans . . . and
what's more, we're only farming 30 percent of the arable land.[43]

Its agricultural capacity and strategic geographical location have
placed Jalapa, both politically and militarily, in the forefront of Nicaragua's revolutionary process. "Our tasks are clear: we have to make
this land produce all that we need to live; and we have to defend this
land because our sovereignty is at stake here in Jalapa."[44]

Between 1950 and 1965, the population of Jalapa increased dramatically. While between 1906 and 1940 the population only grew from
1,149 to 1,948 inhabitants, from 1950 to 1963 the population quadrupled
from 2,088 to 8,602 inhabitants. The introduction of new crops (tobacco
and coffee) required additional labor and attracted poor peasants from
different areas of the country. During the dictatorship, agricultural workers and poor peasants comprised the overwhelming majority of Jalapa's
residents. The rural workers earned wages on the large haciendas and,
to a lesser extent, on the medium-sized farms. Because the poor campesinos owned plots of land no larger than eight acres, they had to work
for wages in order to survive. The large landowners and wealthy peasants
dominated the workers and peasants. Many residents of Jalapa's urban
center worked as agricultural laborers on the large haciendas. All the
farms and haciendas were spread out along the dusty road that stretches
across Jalapa. The workers traversed this road, earning a few pesos for
long hours of work. An end to *Somocismo* seemed impossible to most
of Jalapa's inhabitants.

Life was very tough under Somoza. We didn't even earn enough
to eat. They paid us 14.40 pesos, and it was hard to buy even
a pound of rice. They paid us every two weeks, but after just
one week we were already in debt. All we did was ask for loans
. . . we had the impression that even our lives were borrowed.

There were a bunch of political parties when I was young.
Truckloads of people would leave Jalapa to go and vote, to go
to the dances that Somoza organized at election time, and to
eat popsicles and tamales. Sure, there were a lot of Somocistas
around here. They might not have cared much for Somoza, but
there didn't seem to be anyone who could represent our interests.
If there had been elections here six months before the victory in
1979, Somoza would have won. People would have gone the
way of the cakes, the soft drinks, and the five pesos; they would
have voted for Somoza.

René Molina, Rosa Quinonez, and the Somozas controlled

the land and livestock around here. They were real Somocistas. They took off for Honduras. Then there were also Cubans who supported Batista and left Cuba when the revolution came along there. When I came into this world, this place was full of those Cubans. They first showed up when tobacco growing started. They had nice houses, servants, vehicles, parties for their people, everything. Somoza used them as administrators on his farms. I worked in tobacco with them. I made 14 pesos and the Cuban administrator earned thousands. That's how things were. They treated us badly and beat the kids. If a woman complained and asked to be paid for her hour of overtime, they'd fire her. They had their orders, and they were the ones who carried out the repression.[45]

After the fall of Somoza, many people celebrated by looting the houses of the Cubans and the large landowners; amid the confusion and indiscipline many thought that the revolution meant that no one would have to work anymore. State farm officials wasted fuel, wrecked vehicles, and embezzled funds. During the literacy campaign, however, the people of Jalapa began to gain political awareness. They learned about the cooperative movement and about all the other changes brought about by the revolution.

After Reagan's approval of covert operations against Nicaragua, the people of Jalapa began to suffer attacks every two or three days. The Contras came into the communities, trying to convince the peasants to join them. They had some success in the zones located very close to the border where there were no roads and no communication by radio, telephone, or telegraph with the rest of Nicaragua. Because a road in Honduras runs parallel to the border, the Contras could visit all the different communities in a short period.

Jalapa residents who had direct encounters with the counterrevolutionaries recall their experiences:

The guardsmen arrived at our small house. They grabbed my youngest son to take him away. "Don't take him away from me," I begged them as I threw myself down on my knees. The guardsmen shoved and kicked me out of the way. He didn't pay any attention to me. He told my boy: "Get up on that horse, hurry up." I just had enough time to say: "May God protect you, son." "Don't worry, Mom, I'll be back soon." I couldn't get up off the ground. I just watched as they took my son away. I don't know if he's dead or alive, but I imagine that they've killed him by now. Those guardsmen are animals.
They took her away. She'd just given birth one month before.

They gang-raped her. My son tried to resist them, so they killed him, pulled out his intestines, and filled them with stones. Then they busted up his head and his legs and left his body, along with others, on the other side of the ravine. They cut my aunt's and uncle's throats and carved out their eyes. They also took one woman's seven-year-old daughter, raped her, and then killed her.

They've left mothers without their children just because they've felt like it. They say that they're going to liberate Nicaragua again, but Nicaragua already was liberated. We mothers have been filled with grief. We've lost half of the fruits of our wombs to those bastards that the U.S. government supports. They come and take away our men, shamelessly carry away our daughters, and burn homes. Many people have lost everything they had. That U.S. government should soften its heart of stone and admit that Nicaragua is already free, that we want peace.

They were laying ambushes and putting four-pronged iron bars on the road from Jalapa to Ocotal. They wanted the rice to remain here and be wasted, because we thresh our rice outside Jalapa. The ambushes were a real pain in the ass because the truckdrivers didn't want to come into this region; they were too afraid. The contras were also going into certain villages. More people were getting scared. That's when we decided to start handing out guns in the different communities.

Weapons had to be given to a population that was very scattered and isolated. The attacks forced thousands of people to move, damaged the economy, and cast a shadow on agricultural plans for the zone. It was time to change direction and implement resettlement programs, self-defense, and an acceleration of the cooperative plans.[46]

In 1982, Jalapa had ten border posts. The Contras attacked all of them repeatedly but failed to capture even one of them. They assaulted communities, burning homes and farms, kidnapping and killing people. Jalapa residents near the border area had to move down toward the valley. More than twenty communities were left abandoned. Four thousand people had to be relocated in 1982 alone.

In response to the aggression, the people of Jalapa built new settlements for those who were relocated. They established agricultural cooperatives, built health care centers, dining halls, day-care centers, and schools. To protect themselves from future attacks, the people organized a self-defense system. They built bomb shelters, organized civil defense brigades, and established communications signals to let others know where the enemy was. To maintain a continual state of alert, residents created surveillance units that patrolled twenty-four hours a day. Fully aware of the Contras' aims, the people of Jalapa worked feverishly to defend their lives and property: "The whole war of terror and their dreams about capturing Jalapa ended up working against the Contras like a boomerang and defeating them. When we saw what they were after, we began to organize our defense and production like never before.[47]

In response to the attacks, the government and mass organizations accelerated the agrarian reform process; peasants created new cooperatives on the fertile land of the valley. UNAG distributed weapons to the cooperatives, which soon developed good working relationships with MIDINRA administrators and technicians as well as army officers. An UNAG member testifies to the peasants' growing spirit of confidence and cooperation: "We reacted to each attack with new strength: strength for the battalions, the cooperative, the union, and for education. The attacks have changed our lives. We used to live far apart, way up on top of a hill or way down in the hollow. Now we live together, and we all watch out for the good of the group.[48]

Late 1982 was a difficult period for Nicaragua. Both the U.S. government and the counterrevolutionaries spoke of a "final offensive." The people of Jalapa had to resist increasingly fierce attacks. The Contras planned to make Jalapa part of their "liberated" territory. They also sought to disrupt the coffee harvest and weaken the Nicaraguan army which had begun to fight alongside the militia units and reserve brigades.

> The attacks were getting worse. Before, there would be 80, 100, or 150 counterrevolutionaries armed with rifles. Then things became very serious. They wanted to take Jalapa. Now there were 1,000 or more men. They made it three kilometeres into Nicaragua, and we defeated them. They were very well armed, but they suffered a lot of casualties. We captured rocket launchers, 60 and 80-mm. mortars . . . The battalions from Jalapa fought alongside soldiers from León, Managua, Masaya, and Chinandega.[49]

The heaviest fighting in Jalapa took place between March and June 1983. For ten straight days, the Contras mortared Teotecacinte, on the tip of Jalapa. The entire population participated in organizing self-defense, civil defense, and circular defense in all the different zones. The militias doubled their strength and people dug thousands of yards of trenches. As one resident commented: "It was really something to see people digging shelters and trenches after sweating through a whole day of regular work. That kind of thing can only be done when everybody works together and when it's done with consciousness."[50]

Members of the Rural Workers Association proved their mettle at the state farm in El Porvenir, where tobacco is grown. The farm grows tobacco right up to the fence that divides Nicaragua and Honduras. Attacked by a large Contra force, 40 ATC members resisted until the counterrevolutionaries ran out of ammunition and withdrew. But the Contras inflicted 8 million córdobas in damages on El Porvenir, destroying the tobacco sheds and newly-built workers' homes. One farm worker describes his sentiments concerning the fighting:

> We thought that we were going to be afraid during the shooting, but we weren't. We actually felt brave. You feel that the truth is on your side, and you forget your fear. You also feel a strong tendency that tells you not to kill, but then you see that they're the ones who are going to kill you and you think that we need to live in a just society. You have a bunch of different feelings at the same time. There's nobody around here who wants to kill. If they don't attack us, no one's going to kill them. Nobody in Jalapa wants to kill. We'd much rather be producing instead of being here right on the border where things are so difficult. But if we abandon the border area, they'll destroy everything, and we can't allow that.[51]

After the attack on El Porvenir, Sandinista leaders visited the farm to offer the workers a new location away from the border where they could work in safety. But the workers declined to leave, saying that they prefered to remain on the border. "Now that we're in battle formation," declared one worker, "we won't retreat. Nobody ran during the fighting in El Porvenir and Teotecinte. We know what it would have meant to give up even a little land to the Contras. We knew that moving back would mean giving up El Porvenir, and giving up El Porvenir would mean giving up Teotacinte, and so on until they reached Managua. No, we won't yield even one inch of our land."[52]

The counterrevolutionary attacks on Jalapa have stimulated popular participation in all tasks of the revolution, especially in defense. Out of an active population of 6,222 in the Jalapa municipality, 2,000 participate in reserve battalions. These reservists not only defend the Jalapa region; they are also available to fight anywhere in Nicaragua. Moreover, both the ATC and UNAG have witnessed significant increases in their memberships. An ATC member describes his reactions to the Contras' activitities:

> The war of aggression has helped us develop our awareness as workers. We have also been affected as an organization because

our best leaders had to be mobilized, as is only natural. But this fact really pushed our consciousness forward. The enemies themselves have provided us workers with the tools that we need to learn how to defend our work places and our country. We understand very clearly that we can't do much alone; we have to work together, and we have to organize ourselves.

Now we're all in the union. We elect the board of directors for a certain period of time. We elect those who are most capable and most conscious. They have to inform the members every month about how the cooperative is running. Whenever there are problems or new things come up, we hold special meetings. The whole union meets with the administration when there are very special problems. We'd never experienced anything like that before.

Here we are in the trenches. It's too bad if we die, but, as Sandino said, others will follow us. Dying for the people is what I call being a Christian. In Nicaragua we've got something to defend, so if we die, it's not so important.[53]

In Nicaragua, Jalapa has become the symbol for defense and production. The tenacity of its residents is representative of the spirit that pervades the poor majority of the country's population. Determined to fight for the gains they themselves participate in achieving, the people of Jalapa—organized in their popular associations—continue to make sacrifices. For all these reasons, Jalapa is Nicaragua.

The Reagan administration, in defiance of U.S. public opinion, remains determined to destroy the Nicaragua revolution, pushing vigorously in Congress for military aid to the Contras. On June 23, 1986, the U.S. House of Representatives voted to send $110 million in military aid to the Contras. Unless cancelled as a result of the the Iran arms deal scandal that began to unfold in November 1986, such an aid package guarantees the continuation of a war which in 1985 cost 1,900 lives.[54] If the revolution survives the U.S.-sponsored aggression, it will be due largely to the defense efforts of hundreds of thousands of Nicaraguans organized in the mass organizations.

CONCLUSION

The mass organizations in Nicaragua constitute an essential element in the revolutionary process. They continue to grow both in numbers and organizational strength; yet they also face numerous obstacles in their bid to increase their participation in the revolutionary process. The conclusion evaluates the extent to which the popular organizations exercize autonomy, democracy, and power in the Nicaraguan revolution.

The mass organizations are organizationally and financially independent of the FSLN. Although they tend to follow Sandinista policies, the popular associations sometimes forcefully oppose the party in the interests of their constituencies. And although the grassroots organizations work hand-in-hand with state institutions, they also closely monitor the government, blowing the whistle on corruption and mismanagement. Generally, the Sandinistas have promoted the autonomous development of the mass organizations, feeling that their independence strengthens the revolutionary process. However, when the grassroots organizations pursue a path that contradicts the FSLN's attempt to maintain national unity, the Sandinistas withdraw their support.

As the mass organizations continue to expand their influence in shaping social policy, they face the need to institutionalize their political role in the revolution. Setting the bounds of grassroots power in the new constitution will benefit popular association activists as well as those Nicaraguans wary of mass organization abuses. Above all, the mass organizations must receive concrete guarantees of their autonomy to protect them from state and party encroachment.

The mass organizations have made significant advances in democratizing their internal structures. All the grassroots organizations employ democratic procedures to choose their leaders and assess their behavior in office; but they have not yet implemented fixed terms of office. That the CDSs intend to limit their coordinators to one-year terms is an important precedent; the other mass organizations will need to consider this measure as a means to check the power of incumbents.

Lack of political equality within the popular organizations is a major problem. Due to the "double shift" and unequal access to education, many women are unable to fully participate in the life of the grassroots organizations. Inequality within these organizations also stems from educational differences among members. The vast majority of popular association leaders possess sufficient formal education to write reports and conduct meetings. The mass organizations must constantly work to raise the capacities of their least educated members and afford them access to leadership positions.

There are signs that the mass organizations are aware of the need to overcome inequalities, for they have established study circles and training workshops for both rank-and-file members and leaders. In these study circles and workshops, popular association activists study the history, structure, and functions of their organizations. This educational process is designed to broaden the participation of the entire membership and, in the long run, extend the democratization process.

Even though hundreds of thousands of Nicaraguans are newly literate and possess only a short history of political experience, they have felt the exhilaration and power that comes from direct involvement in the revolutionary process; they will not accept anything less than political equality within their organizations.

The mass organizations have demonstrated their power to the extent that they have been able to win some of the demands of their membership and influence certain revolutionary policies; but there are three basic reasons that the power of the popular associations remains somewhat circumscribed. First, the limited development of the productive forces in Nicaragua acts as a brake on all social and political organizations in the country. Generally, mass organizations operating in societies that have the most meager resources of capital, technology, and skilled personnel face tremendous obstacles in developing their capacity to act as a counterweight to state and party organs; and they inevitably have to compete with these power centers amid this situation of scarcity.

Second, to the extent that they subordinate their tasks to those set by party policy and mobilize their constituencies only to fulfill state goals, the popular associations will be unable to realize their full potential to influence the revolutionary process. This is especially obvious in the case of AMNLAE. Despite AMNLAE's deliberate efforts to avoid the path taken by women's organizations in the socialist countries, its priorities tend to reflect party policies only.[1] This is not to deny AMNLAE's contributions to health campaigns, women's education, child care, and so on; but AMNLAE's projects remain firmly tied to women's prescribed roles. For example, the organization's long-range goal of socializing domestic work does not address the fundamental problem: the equalization of male and female responsibilities for domestic labor.

Finally, the power of the mass organizations is limited to the extent that they lack full representation throughout the various levels of the state apparatus; their representation on some bodies is merely token. The continued advance of the revolutionary process is best guaranteed by the constant expansion of mass participation in all aspects of public life.

The first seven years of the Nicaraguan revolution have been marked by an incredible explosion of popular mobilization and organization. The central question is whether the country's peasants, workers, artisans, and merchants will continue to consolidate and expand their participation in every aspect of revolutionary life. To achieve this objective, mass organization members will have to rely on their capacity for creativity and organization that led them to victory.

NOTES

Introduction

1. *Washington Post*, July 20, 1979, quoted in Dilling et al., *Nicaragua: A People's Revolution* (Washington D.C.: EPICA Task Force, 1980), p. 71.

2. In Spanish *masas*, "masses," does not have an inherently pejorative cast, particularly in a revolutionary context; it simply means "majority."

3. "Nicaragua—Strategy of Victory," in *Sandinistas Speak*, Bruce Marcus, ed., (New York: Pathfinder Press, 1982), p. 58.

4. Throughout the text "mass organizations" is used interchangeably with "grassroots organizations" and "popular associations."

5. *New York Times*, April 16, 1985.

6. (New York, Harper & Row Publishers, 1978), p. 269.

7. For a detailed discussion of the theories of democracy held by Rousseau and Mill, see Carole Pateman, *Participation and Democratic Theory* (New York: Cambridge University Press, 1970), pp. 22–35.

8. Quoted in Henri Weber, *Nicaragua: The Sandinist Revolution*, trans. Patrick Camiller (London: Verso Editions and NLB, 1981), p. 112.

9. In U.S. Out of Central America, *Declaration of Managua* (San Francisco, n.d.), p. 14.

10. At a November 1984 media forum on Central American coverage, George Melloan, deputy editor of *The Wall Street Journal*'s editorial page, said: "The Sandinistas are Marxist Leninist, a fact of which we should have been apprised three years ago." When asked, "Exactly what is a Marxist-Leninist?" he answered: "I don't have the foggiest idea." (Quoted in Sarah Ann Friedman, "Eyes Right," *The Quill*, January 1985, p. 15.)

11. For a thorough analysis of the November 1984 elections in Nicaragua, see Latin American Studies Association, "The Electoral Process in Nicaragua: Domestic and International Influences," (November 19, 1984).

12. Quoted in Friedman, "Eyes Right," p. 15.

13. The July 19th Sandinista Youth, although often referred to as a mass organization, is the youth wing of the FSLN. It has strict membership requirements and does not consider itself a mass organization.

14. For a comprehensive study of Sandino and the guerrilla war he waged against the United States Marines, see Gregorio Selser, *Sandino*, (New York and London: Monthly Review Press, 1981).

15. Pateman, *Participation*, p. 77.

16. Rudolf Bahro, for example, argues that given the massive task of restructuring the economy and of hastening the process of industrialization, the construction of a bureaucratic state apparatus in the Soviet Union was unavoidable. "Without the apparatus of force that the Bolsheviks set in motion," declares Bahro, "Russia today would still be a peasant country, most probably on the capitalist road." See Bahro's *The Alternative in Eastern Europe*, trans. David Fernbach (London: NLB and Verso Editions, 1978), p. 49.

1. The FSLN and the Mass Movement

1. "Nicaragua—The Strategy of Victory," p. 71.

2. For summaries of Nicaraguan history see George Black, *Triumph of the People, The Sandinista Revolution in Nicaragua* (London: Zed Press, 1981); John A. Booth, *The End and the Beginning: The Nicaraguan Revolution* (Boulder, Colorado: Westview Press, 1982); Henri Weber, *Nicaragua, The Sandinist Revolution* (London: NLB and Verso Editions, 1981); Jaime Biderman, "The Development of Capitalism in Nicaragua: A Political Economic History," *Latin American Perspectives* (Winter 1983).

3. H. Ofilio Argirello, advisor to Nicaraguan Vice President Juan Batista Sacasa, quoted in Weber, *Nicaragua, The Sandinist Revolution*, p. 10.

4. *Cinceunta años de lucha sandinista* (Habana, Editorial de ciencias sociales, 1980), pp. 166–67.

5. *El Principio del Fin* (Managua, SENAPEP, 1979), p. 25.

6. "For us," writes Tomás Borge, "Fidel was the resurrection of Sandino . . . the justification of our dreams." *Carlos El Amanecer Ya No Es una Tentacion* (Managua, SENAPEP, 1979), p. 23.

7. Quoted in Amalia Chamorro, *The Hegemonic Content of Somocismo and the Sandinista Revolution* (unpublished manuscript, INIES, Managua, 1982), p. 71.

8. See Black, *Triumph of the People*, pp. 17–21.

9. Quoted in Chamorro, *The Hegemonic Content of Somocismo*, p. 72.

10. Quoted in Chamorro, p. 72.

11. Ibid., p. 73.

12. For an account of Sandinista ideology, see Harry E. Vanden, "The Ideology of the Insurrection," in Thomas W. Walker, ed., *Nicaragua in Revolution* (New York: Praeger Publishers), pp. 41–62.

13. Weber, *Nicaragua: The Sandinist Revolution*, p. 36.

14. Quoted in Chamorro, *The Hegemonic Content of Somocismo*, p. 74.

15. Henry Ruiz, quoted in Ibid., p. 75.

16. See Black, *Triumph of the People*, p. 78.

17. Norma Stoltz Chinchilla defines the "foco" strategy: "The guerrilla *foco*—a small group of militarily trained armed professional revolutionaries—was seen as capable of creating the subjective conditions for convincing the masses of people to revolt, of setting off the spark that would light the revolutionary fire. . . . The foco would accomplish this, for example, by contributing to a general breakdown in law and order . . . which would cause a general political crisis." "Class Struggle in Central America: Background and Overview," *Latin American Perspectives*, Spring 1980, pp. 9–10.

18. Quoted in *Nicaragua: Revolucion, relatos de combatientes del frente sandinista*, ed. by Pilar Arias (Mexico: Editorial Siglo XXI, 1980, p. 35. My translation.

19. Quoted in Arias, *Nicaragua*, p. 39. My translation.

20. Quoted in Ibid., p. 35. My translation.

21. "Zero Hour," in Tomás Borge et al., *Sandinistas Speak*, ed. by Bruce Marcus (New York: Pathfinder Press, 1982), p. 38.

22. "Zero Hour," p. 35.

23. This section draws on Black, *Triumph of the People*, pp. 81–86.

24. Fonseca, quoted in "Zero Hour," p. 37.

25. Ibid., pp. 36–37.

26. *Carlos, el amanecer ya ni es una tentacion* (Managua, Editorial Nueva Nicaragua, 1982), p. 41.

27. Rene Nuñez, quoted in Arias, *Nicaragua*, p. 57.

28. Borge, *Carlos*, p. 44.

29. Ortega, quoted in *Cincuenta Años*, pp. 167–68.

30. Quoted in Arias, *Nicaragua*, p. 77.

31. "The Churches in the Nicaraguan Revolution," in *Nicaragua in Revolution*, p. 169.

32. See Fernando Cardenal, testimony before the International Organizations Sub-Committee, Washington D.C., June 8–9, 1976.

33. Quoted in Arias, *Nicaragua*, p. 113. My translation.

34. This section draws on Black, *Triumph of the People*, pp. 91–97, and Alejandro Bendana, "Crisis in Nicaragua," *NACLA Report on the Americas* 12 (November-December 1978), p. 20–23.

35. Quoted in Arias, *Nicaragua*, p. 118. My translation.

36. Quoted in Black, *Triumph of the People*, p. 93.

37. Unidad de Combate "Juan Jose Quezada," *Mensaje no. 2 Al Pueblo de Nicaragua*, quoted in Ibid., pp. 94–95.

38. FSLN circular, signed by Humberto Ortega, Daniel Ortega, and Victor Tirado, somewhere in Nicaragua, July 1978, quoted in Ibid., p. 97.

39. Quoted in Bendana, "Crisis in Nicaragua," p. 23.

40. Humberto Ortega describes the context in which this concession was made: "Somoza and the Yankees swore that they had eliminated us and, therefore, that we would be unable to serve as the catalyst for this crisis. When they felt that we were hard hit, scattered and divided, they decided it was time for a

democratization plan," "Nicaragua—Strategy of Victory," in *Sandinistas Speak*, p. 57.

41. *New York Times*, 20 October 1977.

42. For details on Costa Rican support of the Sandinistas see Mitchell A. Seligson and William J. Carroll III, "The Costa Rican Role in the Sandinist Victory," in *Nicaragua in Revolution*, pp. 331–44.

43. Dilling et al., *Nicaragua: A People's Revolution*, p. 19.

44. Ibid., p. 64.

45. Ortega, quoted in "Nicaragua—Strategy for Victory," p. 64.

46. This section relies on Bendana, "Crisis in Nicaragua," p. 24; Black, *Triumph of the People*, p. 144; and Dilling et al., *Nicaragua: A People's Revolution*, pp. 57–58.

47. Chapter two offers a complete account of the founding of the ATC.

48. Dilling et al., *Nicaragua: A People's Revolution*, pp. 46–47.

49. "Crisis in Nicaragua", p. 41.

50. This Communist Party of Nicaragua emerged in the early seventies as a result of a split in the Nicaraguan Socialist Party.

51. Quoted in Arias, *Nicaragua*, p. 158. My translation.

52. See Black, *Triumph of the People*, p. 127.

53. Dilling et al., *Nicaragua: A People's Revolution*, p. 60.

54. See Institute for Sandinista Studies, *La insurreccíon popular sandinista en Masaya* (Managua: Editorial Nueva Nicaragua, 1983) p. 115.

55. Quoted in Bendana, "Crisis in Nicaragua," p. 26.

56. Ortega, "Nicaragua—Strategy for Victory," pp. 68–69.

57. See FPN, "Constitution of the National Patriotic Front" (Managua: January 1979).

58. *La Nación*, Costa Rica, January 26, 1979, cited in Dilling et al., *Nicaragua: A People's Revolution*, p. 52.

59. Orlando Nuñez Soto, "The Third Social Force in National Liberation Movements," *Latin American Perspectives* 8 (Spring 1981), p. 1.

60. Quoted in EPICA Task Force, "Nicaragua," p. 57.

61. Black, *Triumph of the People*, p. 136.

62. *Ideario Sandinista*, Secretaria Nacional de Propoganda y Educacion Politica, FSLN, p. 5, quoted in Dilling et al., *Nicaragua: A People's Revolution*, p. 57.

63. Comunicado del FSLN, quoted in Ibid., p. 58.

64. Comunicado del FSLN, quoted in Ibid., p. 59.

65. *Unidad Sandinista*, p. 1, quoted in Ibid., p. 60.

66. *Unidad Sandinista*, p. 12, quoted in Ibid., p. 62.

67. Black, *Triumph of the People*, p. 146.

68. Ibid., pp. 149–50.

69. Quoted in Ibid., p. 150.

70. Ortega, "Nicaragua—Strategy for Victory," p. 77.

71. Black, *Triumph of the People*, p. 153.

72. "Nicaragua—Strategy for Victory," p. 75.

73. Black, *Triumph of the People*, p. 167.

74. Dilling et al., *Nicaragua: A People's Revolution*, p. 63.

75. *Washington Post*, June 7, 1979, in Ibid., p. 64.

76. *Washington Post*, June 6, 1979, quoted in Ibid., p. 65.

77. See Institute of Sandinista Studies, *La insurrección*, pp. 174–75; and Dilling et al., *Nicaragua: A People's Revolution*, p. 64.

78. *Washington Post*, June 7, 1979, in Dilling et al.; *Nicaragua: A People's Revolution*, p. 65.

79. Quoted in Black, *Triumph of the People*, p. 162.

80. Ibid., p. 163.

81. *Washington Post*, June 19, 1979, in Dilling et al., *Nicaragua: A People's Revolution*, p. 66.

82. Black, *Triumph of the People*, pp. 166–67.

83. *Washington Post*, June 28, 1979, quoted in Dilling et al., *Nicaragua: A People's Revolution*, p. 68.

84. Ibid., p. 69.

85. Comandante Henry Ruiz, quoted in *The Guardian*, July 21, 1979.

2. The Mass Organizations Emerge

1. Carmen Diana Deere et al., "Agrarian Reform and the Transition in Nicaragua: 1979–1983," (unpublished mimeo, November 1983), pp. 5–6.

2. Orlando Nuñez Soto, "The Third Social Force in National Liberation Movements," *Latin American Perspectives*, 29 (Spring 1981), p. 11.

3. Carmen Diana Deere and Peter Marchetti, "The Worker-Peasant Alliance in the First Year of the Nicaraguan Agrarian Reform," *Latin American Perspectives*, 29 (Spring 1981), p. 49.

4. Ibid., p. 47.

5. *Triumph*, pp. 79–80.

6. Jacinto Suarez, in *Nicaragua: Revolución*, p. 34.

7. *Nicaragua: A People's Revolution*, p. 23.

8. Bayardo Arce, in Arias, *Nicaragua*, p. 92.

9. Ibid., p. 116.

10. This section draws on Dilling et al., *Nicaragua: A People's Revolution*, pp. 23–26.

11. See Phillip Berryman, *The Religious Roots of Rebellion: Christians in Central American Revolutions* (New York: Orbis Books, 1984), p. 60.

12. "The Churches in the Revolution," Thomas W. Walker, ed., *Nicaragua in Revolution* (New York: Praeger Publishers, 1982), p. 170.

13. Dilling et al., *Nicaragua: A People's Revolution*, p. 14.

14. *La ATC, Organizacion Sandinista de los Trabajadores del Campo*, quoted in Ibid., pp. 24–25.

15. *La ATC*, quoted in Ibid., p. 26.

16. ATC General Secretary Edgardo García, speech to ATC Assembly, *Memorias*, p. 17, quoted in Black, *Triumph*, p. 273.

17. Ibid., p.

18. Ibid., p. 68.

19. Ibid., p. 69.

20. Carlos Vilas, "The Workers Movement in the Sandinista Revolution," *Nicaragua Under Siege* (London: Zed Press, 1985), p. 122.

21. Arnold Weissberg, *The Nicaraguan Revolution* (New York: Pathfinder Press, 1981), p. 12.

22. "The Third Social Force," p. 11.

23. Booth, *The End and the Beginning*, p. 90.

24. "Zero Hour," p. 32.

25. Interview with Luis Sanchez, PSN general secretary, in *El Dia*, November 26, 1977, quoted in Black, *Triumph*, p. 72.

26. The Democratic Union of Liberation, UDEL, represented a broadly pluralistic convergence of political forces, including conservatives, liberal democrats, Christian and social democrats, united around a platform calling for the recovery of democratic rights and a social and economic transformation of the society. Its leader was Pedro Joaquin Chamorro, editor of *La Prensa*.

27. Black, *Triumph*, p. 72.

28. Ibid., p. 71.

29. Ibid., p. 72.

30. Ibid., p. 93.

31. Central Sandinista de Trabajadores, "El Papel de los Sindicatos en la Revolución" (Managua: Instituto Jonathan Gonzalez, March 1981), p. 2. My translation.

32. Elizabeth Maier, *Nicaragua, La Mujer en la Revolución* (Mexico D.F.: Ediciones de Cultura Popular, 1980), p. 73.

33. Black, *Triumph*, p. 70.

34. Megan Martin and Susie Willett eds., *Women in Nicaragua* (London: Nicaragua Solidarity Campaign, 1980), p. 8.

35. *Nicaragua*, p. 73.

36. Ibid., p. 73.

37. Ibid., p. 74.

38. Black, *Triumph*, p. 60.

39. *Nicaragua*, p. 75.

40. Quoted in Randall, *Sandino's Daughters*, p. 2.

41. Maier, *Nicaragua*, p. 74.

42. Martin and Willett, eds., *Women in Nicaragua*, p. 11.

43. Lea Guido, in Randall, *Sandino's Daughters*, pp. 2–3.

44. Ibid., p. 5.

45. Dilling et al., *Nicaragua: A People's Revolution*, p. 29–30.

46. Ibid., p. 29.

47. Lea Guido, in Randall, *Sandino's Daughters*, p. 6.

48. Ibid., p. 6.

49. Ibid., pp. 6–7.

50. Ibid., p. 7.

51. Ibid., p. 8.

52. Ibid., pp. 7–8.

53. EPICA Task Force, *Nicaragua*, p. 30.

54. Martin and Willett, eds., *Women in Nicaragua*, p. 12.
55. Ibid., p. 14.
56. Lea Guido, in Randall, *Sandino's Daughters*, p. 16.
57. Dilling et al., *Nicaragua: A People's Revolution*, p. 31.
58. Martin and Willett, eds., *Women in Nicaragua*, p. 14.
59. Maier, *Nicaragua*, p. 65.
60. Ibid.
61. Lea Guido, in Randall, *Sandino's Daughters*, pp. 16–17.
62. Ibid., p. 17.
63. Ibid., p. 23.
64. Martin and Willett eds., *Women in Nicaragua*, p. 15.
65. Ibid., p. 16.
66. Martin and Willett, eds., *Women in Nicaragua*, p. 15.
67. Deighton et al., *Sweet Ramparts*, p. 43.
68. Quoted in Randall, *Sandino's Daughters*, p.16.
69. Instituto Historico Centroamericano, "Young People in a Young Country: A Look At Nicaraguan Youth," *Envio* 28 (October 1983), p. 3c.
70. *Inside the Nicaraguan Revolution (As Told to Margaret Randall)*, Elinore Randall, trans. (Vancouver: New Star Books, 1978), pp. 61–62.
71. Instituto Historico Centroamericano, "Young People in a Young Country," p. 2c.
72. Tijerino, *Inside*, p. 61. Sergio Ramirez, vice president of Nicaragua, speaks of the effect the July 23 demonstration had on his political development: "I myself was a survivor of that massacre. I was there when the Guard opened fire, and I helped take the wounded to a hospital; I saw the dead lying in the street. All that had a tremendous impact on my life. It was probably the most decisive event up to that time. It changed my political and ideological criteria completely, as well as how I saw my future." Also quoted in Margaret Randall, *Risking a Somersault in the Air: Conversations with Nicaraguan Writers* (San Francisco: Solidarity Publications, 1984), p. 26.
73. Ibid., p. 27.
74. Tijerino, *Inside*, p. 60.
75. Ibid.
76. Ibid., p. 69.
77. Berryman, *Religious Roots*, p. 61–62.
78. The following account of the Christian Youth Movement draws on Margaret Randall, *Christians in the Nicaraguan Revolution* (Vancouver: New Star Books, 1983), pp. 127–66.
79. Ibid., pp. 128–29.
80. Ibid., p. 130.
81. Ibid., p. 156.
82. Ibid., pp. 161–62.
83. Ibid., p. 162.
84. Ibid., pp. 163–64.
85. The following section draws on the EPICA Task Force, *Nicaragua*, pp. 26–29.

86. Nicaraguan Revolutionary Youth (JRN), "Participación de la Juventud en la Lucha Popular Contra la Dictadura Somocista," November 1978, p. 5., n.p. (mimeographed document), quoted in Ibid., pp. 26–27.

87. "The parents organized themselves in different commissions in order to give logistic support to the student movement: they served as messengers between different institutions and churches, provided food to the students, carried out actions in support of their demands, and maintained permanent guards around the building occupied by the young people to try to impede National Guard attacks," *La insurrección popular sandinista en Masaya*, p. 91.

88. Orlando Nuñez comments on the militancy of Nicaraguan students: "It is often claimed that students are able to be so combative because they are not repressed as severely as the workers. In Nicaragua, however, during the revolutionary struggle there were more martyrs among the students than among the workers. Of course they were being repressed not for being students but for being *combative* . . . for being revolutionaries . . . for being Sandinistas . . . in the same manner that a worker is repressed for being a unionist or a communist," "Third Social Force," p. 13.

89. *Lucha Sandinista*, Publication of the Foreign Affairs Commission of the FSLN, June 3, 1978, quoted in Dilling et al., *Nicaragua*, p. 29.

90. "Third Social Force," p. 12.

91. Jacinto Suarez, in Arias, *Nicaragua*, p. 36.

92. Tijerino, *Inside*, p. 125.

93. Ibid., p. 126.

94. Harvey Williams, "Housing Policy in Revolutionary Nicaragua," in *Nicaragua in Revolution*, p. 274.

95. Ibid.

96. Ibid., p. 275.

97. Tijerino, *Inside*, p. 130. For a description of the Housing Institute's urban projects, see Williams, "Housing Policy," pp. 275–76.

98. Black, *Triumph*, p. 60.

99. The following section draws from Dodson and Montgomery, "The Churches in the Nicaraguan Revolution," in *Nicaragua in Revolution*, pp. 166–69.

100. Quoted in Ibid., p. 169.

101. "*Atención!!! Pueblo de Nicaragua*," FSLN Proletariano, September 1978, cited in Dilling et al., *Nicaragua*, p. 45.

102. Quoted in IES, *La Insurreccion*, p. 142.

103. These *adoquines* were commonly referred to as "Somoza's Bricks" because his private factory monopolized their manufacture. All major roads in Nicaragua were paved with them.

104. "Strategy," p. 58.

105. Quoted in Chamorro, *The Hegemonic Content of Somocismo*, p. 97.

3. The Setting

1. See Booth, *The End and the Beginning*, p. 198.

2. For the advantages of analyzing social reality according to these four

spheres, see Michael Albert and Robin Hahnel, *Marxism and Social Theory* (South End Press, 1981).

3. Black, *Triumph*, p. 201.

4. Booth, *The End and the Beginning*, p. 181.

5. Ibid., p. 203.

6. The rest of this section draws from Richard Harris, "The Role of Industry in Revolutionary Nicaragua's Mixed Economy," in *Nicaragua under Siege* (London: Zed Press, 1985).

7. Quoted in Ibid.

8. Richard Dellobuono, "Nicaragua's Emergency Laws: A In-Depth Look," *Nicaraguan Perspectives* 3 (Winter 1982): 10.

9. Goran Therborn's phrase, in *What Does the Ruling Class Do When It Rules?* (London: NLB. 1978), p. 146.

10. Quoted in Paul Le Blanc, *Permanent Revolution in Nicaragua* (New York: Fourth Internationalist Tendency, 1984), p. 18.

11. Ministry of Labor, *Estimación de PEA y Ocupación por Sectores Económicos*, 1985.

12. These are large landowners who own 500 manzanas or more in basic grains; more than 65 manzanas of coffee; more than 200 manzanas of cotton; more than 1000 manzanas of cattle with more than an average of 912 heads of cattle. (A manzana is equal to 1.76 acres.)

13. These are landowners with 50–500 manzanas in basic grains; 15–65 manzanas of coffee; 50–200 manzanas of cotton; 200–1000 manzanas dedicated to ranching with an average of 311 heads of cattle.

14. These are farmers with up to 15 manzanas of coffee; 15–50 manzanas of basic grains; 20–50 manzanas of cotton; 50–200 manzanas dedicated to ranching with 50–300 heads of cattle.

15. These are farmers with around 15 manzanas of basic grains; 5–20 mazanas of cotton; and from 10–50 heads of cattle.

16. These are farmers with less than 15 manzanas of land.

17. These are owners of large industrial and commerical enterprises with more than 100 employees.

18. These are owners of medium-size industrial and commercial enterprises with between 15 and 100 employees.

19. These are people earning at least four times more than a manual worker.

20. These are people earning between two and four times more than a manual worker. They fall within categories X–XXII of the Ministry of Labor's wage and salary scale.

21. These are small property owners that employ one or two assistants.

22. For an interesting discussion that argues that high-grade functionaries and highly qualified experts constitute a new bureaucratic class in both capitalist and socialist societies, see Donald C. Hodges, *The Bureaucratization of Socialism* (Amherst, Mass.: The University of Massachusetts Press, 1983).

23. Quoted in Harris, "The Role of Industry," p. 51.

24. *Barricada*, March 23, 1986.

25. *Barricada Internacional*, February 21, 1985.

26. Quoted in Latin American Studies Association, "The Electoral Process in Nicaragua: Domestic and International Influences," (November 1984), p. 6.

27. *Barricada Internacional*, February 13, 1986.

28. Quoted in Ibid.

29. Ibid.

30. Ibid.

31. In Latin America, "propaganda" is the neutral equivalent of "information."

32. See Instituto Historico Centroamericano, "The Elections Reagan Would Like To Forget," *Envio* 46 (April 1985), pp. 1–8.

33. Quoted in Roger Burbach and Tim Draimin, "Nicaragua's Revolution," *NACLA Report on the Americas* 14 (May–June, 1980), pp. 29–30.

34. "Revolution and Crisis in Nicaragua," in *Trouble In Our Back Yard*, Martin Diskin, ed. (New York: Pantheon Books, 1983), p. 128.

35. Interview with Sandinista militant, in Estelí, February 1984.

36. See Jaime Wheelock, "The Great Challenge," in *Nicaragua: The Sandinista People's Revolution*, Bruce Marcus, ed. (New York: Pathfinder Press, 1985), pp. 125–29.

37. On January 9, 1985, Daniel Ortega became President of Nicaragua and a new political era began.

38. Booth, *The End and the Beginning*, pp. 184–85.

39. This section derives from Ibid., pp. 186–88.

40. Chapter 4 offers a full treatment of the formation of the Council of State.

41. This section draws from Latin American Studies Association, "The Electoral Process in Nicaragua."

42. Ibid., p. 3.

43. Ibid.

44. Ibid., p. 12.

45. Ibid.

46. See Instituto Historico Centroamericano, "The National Assembly: First Steps Toward a New Political Model," *Envio*, 47 (May 1985), pp. 1–8.

47. Davis and Martinez, "Nicaragua's Election," *Nicaraguan Perspectives* (Fall 1984), p. 21.

48. Instituto Historico Centroamericano, "Analysis of Electoral Results," *Envio*, Issue 13 (July 1985), p. 12.

49. *Barricada Internacional*, March 6, 1985.

50. This phrase is attributed to Gloria Carrión, former AMNLAE leader.

51. Instituto Historico Centroamericano, "The Nicaraguan Family in a Time of Transition," *Envio* 34 (April 1984), p. 2a.

52. Quoted in Randall, *Sandino's Daughters*, p. 14.

53. Patricia Flynn, Aracelly Santana, Helen Shapiro, "Latin American Women: One Myth—Many Realities," *NACLA Report on the Americas* 5 (September–October, 1980)), p. 30.

54. See Batya Weinbaum, *The Curious Courtship of Women's Liberation and Socialism* (Boston: South End Press, 1978).

55. Quoted in *Barricada*, March 23, 1980.

56. "Socialist Countries Old and New: Progress Toward Women's Emancipation," *Monthly Review* (July-August 1982): pp. 74.56. Quoted in *Barricada*, March 23, 1980, Translation by W.I.R.E. Service.

57. Quoted in AMNLAE, *Una Mujer Donde Este Debe Hacer Revolución* (Centro de Publicaciones "Silvio Mayorga," n.d.), p. 8. My translation.

58. Deighton et al., *Sweet Ramparts: Women In Revolutionary Nicaragua* (London: War on Want and Nicaraguan Solidarity Campaign, 1983), p. 45.

59. Ibid., p. 46.

60. Instituto Historico Centroamericano, "Women In Nicaragua: A Revolution Within a Revolution," *Envio* 25 (July 1983), p. 5c.

61. Ibid., p. 6c.

62. This section draws from Deighton et al., *Sweet Ramparts*, p. 124.

63. Ibid., p. 125.

64. Instituto Historico Centroamericano, "The Nicaraguan Family," p. 2c.

65. Ibid., p. 5c.

66. Ibid., p. 6c.

67. *The End and the Beginning*, p. 199.

68. Black, *Triumph*, p. 315.

69. This section relies on Booth, *The End and the Beginning*, pp. 200–201, and the Center for the Study of the Americas (CENSA), *CENSA's Strategic Reports* 3 (March 1985), p. 9.

70. See Tomás Borge, "We Speak to You from a Country at War," in *Nicaragua: The Sandinista People's Revolution*, p. 253.

71. *Barricada Internacional*, March 6, 1986.

72. See Randall, *Christians in the Nicaraguan Revolution*.

73. Interview with Tercer Cine (Managua, 1980), quoted in Hermione Harris, "Nicaragua: Two Years of Revolution," *Race and Class* XXIII, No. 1 (Summer 1981), p. 20.

74. Berryman, *The Religious Roots of Rebellion*, pp. 252–53.

75. Ibid., p. 253.

4. Developing a National Presence

1. Lynn Silver, "Nicaraguan Women Organize to Defend the Revolution," *Intercontinental Press* (October 15, 1979), quoted in Roger Burbach and Tim Draimin, "Nicaragua's Revolution," *NACLA Report on the Americas* 14 (May-June 1980), p. 5.

2. For an interesting analysis of why the Sandinistas adopted a transitional strategy, see Ibid., pp. 7–8.

3. Black, *Triumph*, p. 230.

4. EPICA Task Force, *Nicaragua*, p. 79. Chapter 5 presents a more detailed account of the CDSs' role during this emergency period.

5. From a 1980 CDS pamphlet, "Linea Organizativa de los Comites de Defensa Sandinista," quoted in Luis Serra, "The Sandinist Mass Organizations," in *Nicaragua in Revolution*, Thomas W. Walker, ed. (New York: Praeger, 1982), p. 105.

6. Ibid., pp. 105–06.

7. Interview with Uriel Guzman, Monimbó shoemaker and CDS activist, quoted in Black, *Triumph*, pp. 240–41.

8. Ibid., p. 242.

9. Ronald Paredes of the National Office of the CDS, in *El Nuevo Diario* (an independent progovernment newspaper), July 9, 1980, quoted in Ibid., p. 244.

10. Serra, "The Sandinist Mass Organizations," p. 106.

11. Instituto Historico Centroamericano, "Sandinista Defense Committees (CDSs): Impressions after Four Years of Existence," *Envio*, 16 (October 15, 1982), p. 19.

12. Ibid., p. 21.

13. Black, *Triumph*, p. 243.

14. Interview quoted in Ibid., p. 243.

15. Quoted in Ibid., p. 244.

16. Serra, "The Sandinist Mass Organizations," p. 106.

17. For a fascinating account of Luisa Amanda Espinosa's participation in the FSLN, see Margaret Randall, *Sandino's Daughters*, pp. 24–33.

18. Susan E. Ramirez-Horton, "The Role of Women in the Nicaraguan Revolution," in *Nicaragua in Revolution*, pp. 154–55.

19. See AMNLAE, *Una Mujer Onde Este Debe Hacer Revolución* (n.p., n.d.).

20. Ramirez-Horton, "The Role of Women."

21. Ibid.

22. Ibid.

23. Ibid.

24. Quoted in Harry Fried, "Nicaraguan women demand rights," *Guardian*, December 2, 1981, p. 3.

25. Ibid., p. 4.

26. *Sweet Ramparts: Women in Revolutionary Nicaragua*, p. 47.

27. Margaret Randall, "Nicaragua: A Struggle for Dignity," *Guardian Women's Day Supplement*, Spring 1982.

28. Deighton et al., *Sweet Ramparts*, p. 48.

29. Interview in AMNLAE national office, July 1981, quoted in Ibid, p. 48.

30. "Nicaragua: A Struggle for Dignity."

31. *Sweet Ramparts*, p. 49.

32. See, for example, Batya Weinbaum, *The Curious Courtship of Women's Liberation and Socialism*.

33. Interview in Leon, in Deighton et al., *Sweet Ramparts*, p. 49.

34. Black, *Triumph*, pp. 272–73.

35. David Kaimowitz and Joseph R. Thome, "Nicaragua's Agrarian Reform: The First Year," in Walker ed. *Nicaragua in Revolution*, p. 237.

36. Black, *Triumph*, p. 272.

37. Ibid., p. 273.

38. Speech to ATC Assembly, *Memorias*, pp. 37–38, quoted in Ibid.

39. The following account of the INRA system draws on the EPICA Task Force, *Nicaragua*, p. 82, and Deere and Marchetti, "The Worker-Peasant Alliance," *Latin American Perspectives* 8 (Spring 1981), p. 53.

40. "The Worker-Peasant Alliance," pp. 54–55.

41. Black, *Triumph*, p. 274.

42. Deere and Marchetti, "The Worker-Peasant Alliance," p. 60.

43. Black, *Triumph*, p. 274.

44. Ibid.

45. Ibid., pp. 274–75.

46. Ibid., pp. 276–77.

47. Ibid., p. 275.

48. Ibid., p. 277.

49. Ibid., pp. 277–78.

50. Ibid., p. 278.

51. Ibid., p. 279.

52. Carlos Vilas, "The Workers Movement in the Sandinista Revolution," in *Nicaragua: A Revolution Under Siege* (London: Zed Press, 1985), p. 123.

53. Black, *Triumph*, p. 278.

54. Vilas, "The Workers Movement," p. 124.

55. Black, *Triumph*, p. 277.

56. *Nicaragua: The Sandinist Revolution*, Patrick Camiller, trans. (London: Verso Editions and NLB, 1981), pp. 122–23.

57. Pedro Camejo, "How FSLN Handled Strike at Managua Construction Project," *Intercontinental Press* (February 11, 1980): 110–11, and Black, *Triumph*, pp. 280–81.

58. Lars Palmgren, "Nicaraguan Unions Take First Big Step Toward Unity, *Intercontinental Press* (December 1, 1980), p. 111.

59. Ibid., p. 113.

60. Vilas, "The Workers Movement," p. 134.

61. See Black, *Triumph*, pp. 244–45.

62. The Pact of Espino Negro, arranged by the United States, ended the Liberal-Conservative civil war in 1927. Because the United States had sent in more than 5,000 troops to shore up their political allies during the war, Sandino refused to sign the pact and vowed to keep fighting until the United States removed its troops.

63. Black, *Triumph*, p. 245.

64. *Barricada*, November 4, 1979.

65. *Barricada*, November 5, 1979.

66. *Barricada*, May 3, 1980.

67. Ibid.

68. *Barricada*, April 28, 1980.

69. Ibid.

70. Ibid.

71. *Barricada*, May 3, 1980.

72. Ibid.

73. Ibid.

74. Black, *Triumph*, p. 244.

75. Ibid., p. 245.

76. *Barricada*, May 3, 1984.

77. Booth, *The End and the Beginning*, p. 187, and Black, *Triumph*, p. 249.

78. Interview in *Perspectiva Mundial*, July 28, 1980, quoted in Black, p. 249.

79. Ibid., p. 250.

80. This section relies on Valerie Miller, "The Nicaraguan Literacy Campaign," in *Nicaragua in Revolution*, pp. 241–57.

81. Ibid., pp. 241–42.

82. Cruzada Nacional de Alfabetización, *La Alfabetización en Marcha* (Managua: Ministry of Education, 1980), p. 1, quoted in Ibid., p. 246.

83. Cruzada Nacional de Alfabetización, *Cuaderno de Orientaciones* (Managua: Ministry of Education, 1979), p. 1, quoted in Ibid., p. 253.

84. Black, *Triumph*, p. 312.

85. "The Nicaraguan Literacy Campaign," p. 257.

86. This section draws from Richard Garfield, "Malaria Control in Nicaragua: Health Promotion Through a Mass Drug Administration Program," (Managua, 1983, mimeograph).

87. Ibid.

88. Ibid.

89. Ibid.

90. Ibid.

91. See, for example, Instituto Historico Centroamericano, "The Health Situation in Revolutionary Nicaragua," *Envio* 23 (May 1983), p. 3c.

92. Deighton et. al., *Sweet Ramparts*, p. 47.

5. Building Internal Democracy

1. "The Sandinist Mass Organizations," p. 100.

2. Ibid., p. 101.

3. Ibid., p. 102.

4. Chapter 6 discusses this administrative division in greater detail.

5. Serra, "The Sandinist Mass Organizations," p. 101.

6. Vilas, "The Workers' Movement in the Sandinista Revolution."

7. Ibid.

8. Ibid.

9. Black, *Triumph*, p. 284.

10. Vilas, "The Workers' Movement in the Sandinista Revolution," p. 156.

11. James Petras, "Nicaragua: The Transition to a New Society," *Latin American Perspectives* 8 (Spring 1981), pp. 87–88.

12. Ibid., pp. 87–89.

13. Ibid., pp. 87–88.

14. *Barricada*, October 5, 1980, quoted in Weber, *Nicaragua*, p. 124.

15. Ibid.

16. Black, *Triumph*, p. 274.

17. ATC, "Declaración de Principios," *Memorias*, p. 54, quoted in Black, *Triumph*, p. 273.

18. Report to ATC Assembly, *Memorias*, p. 4, quoted in Ibid., p. 274.

19. Interview in Estelí, November 1984.

20. Chapter 7 offers a detailed account of the founding of UNAG.

21. Matilde Zimmermann, "Nicaragua's Farmers and Ranchers form Union" *Intercontinental Press*, (May 16, 1983), p. 552.

22. *Trabajadores*, February 1983.

23. Quoted in Ibid., p. 2.

24. Ibid., p. 3.

25. Ibid., p. 5.

26. "The Sandinist Mass Organizations," p. 103.

27. Interview with ATC secretary of propaganda and political education, in Estelí, November 1983.

28. Fred Judson, "Political Morale in the Sandinista Armed Forces," (unpublished manuscript, 1985), p. 5.

29. Ibid., p. 6.

30. Ibid., p. 7.

31. Ibid., p. 8.

32. Interview with Octavio Obregon Blandon, in Estelí, January 1984.

33. Ibid.

34. UNAG, *Nuestros Organismos Muncipales de UNAG* (n.p., n.d.).

35. Ibid.

36. Judson, "Political Morale," p. 10.

37. "Letter to Leaders of the Sandinista Defense Committees," in *Nicaragua: The Sandinista People's Revolution* (New York: Pathfinder Press, 1985), pp. 61–63.

38. Quoted in Instituto Historico Centroamericana, *Envio* 16 (October 15, 1982), p. 10.

39. *Barricada*, September 10, 1985.

40. CDS, November 1985, p. 3.

41. *Barricada*, November 25, 1985.

42. Interview in Estelí, January 16, 1984.

43. "If the Peasantry Did Not Trust the Revolution," in *Nicaragua: The Sandinista People's Revolution*, Bruce Marcus ed. p. 369.

44. CIERA, *La Mujer en las Cooperativas Agropecuarias en Nicaragua* (Managua: MIDINRA, May 1984).

45. The following discussion draws from Jane Harris, "Women Farm Workers Meet," *Intercontinental Press* (May 16, 1983), p. 257.

46. ATC, *El Machete* (December 1983).

47. Jorge G. Casteneda, *Nicaragua: Contradicciones en la Revolucion* (Mexico: Tiempo Extra, 1980), p. 15.

48. "The Sandinista Mass Organizations," p. 102.

6. Relations with the Party and State

1. The following statement, taken from AMNLAE's "Declaration of Principles," is typical of mass organization statements concerning the FSLN's vanguard role: "We recognize the FSLN as the indisputable vanguard that led the people to its liberation and that today leads the construction of the new society. AMNLAE

will work toward the fulfilment of the historical program of the FSLN and the decisions of its National Directorate." AMNLAE, *Documentos de la Asamblea Constitutiva*, n.d., p. 12.

2. The mass organizations are financed only by members' dues and nongovernmental aid from organizations abroad. As a result, their financial resources are extremely limited.

3. Quoted in Burbach and Draimin, "Nicaragua's Revolution," p. 19.

4. Interview by George Black with FSLN militant, in Managua, March 1980, *Triumph of the People*, p. 200.

5. No. 6, November 22, 1979, quoted in Ibid., p. 231.

6. Quoted in Ibid., p. 232.

7. *El Papel de las organizaciones de masa en el proceso revolucionario* (Managua: SNPEP del FSLN, 1980), p. 21.

8. Interview in *Estelí*, January 20, 1984.

9. *Triumph of the People*, p. 233.

10. Ibid., p. 234.

11. Tomás Borge, *El Partido Sandinista y las Cualidades del Militante*, (Managua:SENAPEP, 1980), p. 15. My translation.

12. Black, *Triumph of the People*, p. 232.

13. "Papel de los trabajadores en el cumplimiento del Plan '80," *Barricada*, quoted in Burbach and Draimin, "Nicaragua's Revolution," p. 30.

14. Interview with Vivian Perez, ATC zonal secretary of propaganda and political education, in Estelí, August 13, 1984.

15. Interview with CDS zonal secretary, February 26, 1984.

16. Interview with Vivian Perez, August 13, 1984.

17. Interview in Estelí, February 18, 1984.

18. This account relies on Joseph Collins, *What Difference Could a Revolution Make?* (San Francisco: Institute for Food and Development Policy, 1982), pp. 81–82.

19. Quoted in Ibid., p. 81.

20. Quoted in Ibid., p. 82.

21. Black, *Triumph of the People*, p. 251.

22. *Barricada*, August 18, 1983, p.

23. Instituto Historico Centroamericano, "Nicaragua's New Army: Fighting to Achieve Peace," *Envio* 28 (October 1983), p. 8b.

24. *Barricada*, December 5, 1983.

25. Interview, quoted in Eric Weaver, "Nicaraguans Go to the Polls," *Central American Bulletin* 4 (November 1984), p. 25.

26. Quoted in Ibid., p. 27.

27. Quoted in Ibid., p. 28.

28. Ibid., p. 29.

29. Ibid., p. 30.

30. Interview with AMNLAE zonal secretary, in *Estelí*, August 1984.

31. Interview with CDS regional secretary, in *Estelí*, August 1984.

32. Interview in *Estelí*, January 20, 1984.

33. Ibid.

34. Interview with Javier Molina, member of ATC national training staff in Estelí, November 1984.

35. The Sandinista Assembly is the advisory body to the FSLN's National Directorate.

36. Interview in Managua, March 22, 1984.

37. For example, Lucio Jiminez, secretary general of the CST, Leticia Herrera, general secretary of the CDSs, and Daniel Nunez, president of UNAG, all have seats in the National Assembly.

38. See, for example, AMNLAE, *Documentos de la Asamblea Constitutiva*, p. 12.

39. This section draws on Dilling et al., *Nicaragua*, p. 79.

40. See Nuñez, *El Papel*, p. 5.

41. This section draws on Charles Downs and Fernando Kusnetsoff, "The Changing Role of Local Government in the Nicaraguan Revolution," *International Journal of Urban and Regional Research* 6 (1982), pp. 533–47.

42. Ibid., p. 536.

43. Ibid., p. 537.

44. Ibid., p. 538.

45. Quoted in Ibid., p. 538.

46. Quoted in Ibid., pp. 538–39.

47. Quoted in Ibid., p. 543.

48. *El Papel*, p. 16.

49. Instituto Historico Centroamericano, *Envio* 27 (September 1983), p. 3c.

50. Ibid.

51. Ibid.

52. Ibid.

53. Ibid., p. 6c

54. Ibid., p. 4c.

55. *Barricada*, December 26, 1983.

56. Ibid.

57. Ibid.

58. Ibid.

59. Interview with CDS regional official, in Estelí, August 1984.

60. Ibid.

61. Interview with CDS regional secretary in Estelí, February 18, 1984.

62. *El Papel*, p. 21. My translation.

63. *Barricada*, February 15, 1984.

64. As Philip Martinez notes: "The goal [of the decentralization] was to reduce the dependency of regional and local government on the national structure in Managua. In the event of an invasion . . . each region was to have the ability to function independently." Philip Martinez, "Five Years of Agrarian Reform in Nicaragua: The Case of the Noel Gamez Cooperative," (M.A. thesis, University of California, Berkeley, 1984), p. 33).

65. Interview in Esteli, November 30, 1984.

66. Ibid.

67. Interview with Vivian Perez, in Estelí, August 18, 1984.

68. Ibid.

69. "La Participación de las Organizaciones Populares en la Gestion de Salud," (n.p., March 1984), p. 9. My translation.

70. Ibid., p. 10.

71. Ibid., p. 11.

72. Serra, "The Sandinist Mass Organizations," p. 104.

73. Interview in Estelí, January 20, 1984.

74. *El Papel*, p. 13.

7. Community Development: The CDSs

1. See, for example, Dan Williams, "Sandinistas Tightening State Rule," *Los Angeles Times*, May 7, 1985.

2. Instituto Historico Centroamericano, "Sandinista Defense Committees (CDSs): Impressions after Four Years of Existence," *Envio* 16 (October 15, 1982), p. 16.

3. CDS, *Los CDS Somos: Poder Popular* (n.d., n.p.,), p. 3.

4. Rebecca Gordon, "We're All One Army: Nicaragua's Strategy of Self-Defense," *Nicaraguan Perspectives* (Summer-Fall 1985).

5. Ibid.

6. "The Organized People Are the Backbone of the Sandinista Police," in *Nicaragua: The Sandinista People's Revolution*, p. 375–76.

7. Ibid., p. 377.

8. Governing Junta of National Reconstruction, "Address of Daniel Ortega to The Council of State," May 1983.

9. Borge, "The Organized People," in *Nicaragua*, p. 377.

10. Richard M. Garfield and Eugenio Tabaoda, "Health Services Reforms in Revolutionary Nicaragua," *American Journal of Public Health*, 74 (October 1984), p. 1143.

11. Mary Elsberg, "Trail Blazing on the Atlantic Coast: A Report on the Health Care Brigadistas in Nicaragua," *Science for the People* (November/December 1983), p. 15.

12. Ibid., p. 16.

13. Consejo Nacional Popular de Salud, *La Participación de las Organizaciones Populares en la Gestion de Salud* (Managua: 1984), pp. 7–8.

14. Ibid., p. 12.

15. Ibid., p. 13.

16. David Siegel, "The Effects of the War on Health Care," *Nicaraguan Perspectives*, 10 (Spring-Summer 1985): 22.

17. World University Service Educational Project, *Nicaragua*, (n.p., n.d.), p. 1.

18. Interview with CDS secretary of political education and propaganda, in Managua, March 1984.

19. W.U.S., *Nicaragua*, p. 2.

20. Interview with CDS Secretary of Political Education and Propaganda, in Managua, March 1982.

21. The following section is drawn from Instituto Historico Centramericano, "Sequel to the Literacy Campaign," *Envio* 17 (November 15, 1982), pp. 14–21.

22. Williams, "Housing Policy in Revolutionary Nicaragua," in Thomas Walker ed., *Nicaragua in Revolution*, p. 274.

23. Ibid., p. 279.

24. Ministerio de Planificación, *Plan de Reactivación Economico en el Beneficio del Pueblo* (Managua: Secretario Nacional de Propaganda y Educación Politica del F.S.L.N., 1980), pp. 109–10, quoted in Ibid., p. 281.

25. Ibid., p. 282.

26. *Convenio: CDS-MINVAH*, September 1983, p. 1.

27. Ibid., p. 3.

28. The following section draws on William Robinson, "Sandinistas Seek to Abolish Landlords and Rent," *Guardian*, July 13, 1983.

29. *Nuevo Diario*, January 31, 1984, p.

30. Ibid.

31. The following discussion draws on Solon Barraclough, *A Preliminary Analysis of the Nicaraguan Food System* (Geneva: United Nations Research Institute for Social Development, 1982), pp. 15–40.

32. August 6, 1984.

33. *Barricada*, May 21, 1986.

34. *Barricada*, July 5, 1984.

35. *Barricada*, August 3, 1984.

36. *Barricada*, July 5, 1984.

37. *Barricada*, August 3, 1984.

38. *Barricada*, August 9, 1984.

39. *Barricada*, August 16, 1984.

40. Ibid.

41. MICOIN, "The ABCs of Supply", p. 2.

42. Interview with CDS Secretary of International Relations, in Managua, August 1984.

43. Quoted in Deighton et al., *Sweet Ramparts*, pp. 30–31.

44. Quoted in Ibid., pp. 31–33.

45. Quoted in Ibid., p. 34.

46. Quoted in Ibid.

47. The author studied Georgino Andrade between July 1983 and July 1986.

48. From the author's notes taken at the meeting, August 17, 1983

49. From the author's notes taken at the meeting, March 11, 1984.

50. Personal communication to the author from Hugo Saenz, barrio coordinator, March 1984.

51. Interview with Hugo Saenz, barrio coordinator, January 22, 1986.

8. The Liberation of Women

1. I follow Heidi I. Hartmann's definition of patriarchy: "We can usefully define patriarchy as a set of social relations between men, which have a material

base, and which, though hierarchical, establish or create interdependence and solidarity among men that enable them to dominate women." ("The Unhappy Marriage of Marxism and Feminism: Towards a More Progressive Union," *Capital and Class* 8 (Summer 1979, p. 11).

2. From "Woman-as-Object to Woman as Revolutionary Force," quoted in Nicaragua Network, "Women in Nicaragua Information Packet" (Washington, D.C., n.d.), p. 3.

3. Quoted in *Our Socialism* (June/July 1983), p. 13.

4. Interview with Angela Cerda, in Managua, July 1983.

5. "The Role of Women in Building Democracy in Nicaragua," delivered February 21, 1984, in Berkeley, California.

6. Interview with AMNLAE officer in the Managua Office of Legal Assistance for Women, February 18, 1986.

7. AMNLAE, *Exposición de AMNLAE ante la Comision Especial Constitutional de la Asamblea Nacional*, Managua, January 8, 1986, pp. 6–7.

8. Ibid., pp. 9–12.

9. Ibid., pp. 12–13.

10. *Sweet Ramparts*, p. 127.

11. Ibid, p. 129.

12. Quoted in Ibid., p. 130.

13. *Somos*, November 1983.

14. Deighton et al., *Sweet Ramparts*, p. 129.

15. Instituto Historico, "The Nicaraguan Family," p. 7c.

16. Instituto Historico Centroamericano, "Women in Nicaragua: A Revolution Within a Revolution," *Envio* (July 1983), p. 5c.

17. Quoted in Instituto Historico, "The Nicaraguan Family," p. 7c.

18. Instituto Historico, "Women in Nicaragua," p. 5c.

19. Interview in Managua, July 1984.

20. This section draws from Instituto Historico, "The Nicaraguan Family," p. 8c.

21. Instituto Nicaraguense de Seguridad Social y Bienestar, *Logros 85* (Managua: 1986), p.5.

22. "La Educación Pre-Escolar," *Somos* (July 1983), p. 4.

23. Interview with Arquimides Colindus, delegate from the Ministry of Social Welfare and Social Security to Region I, in Estelí, November 30, 1981.

24. Instituto Historico, "The Nicaraguan Family," p. 9c.

25. Quoted in Martin and Willett, *Women in Nicaragua*, p. 35–36.

26. *Ventana*, September 26, 1981, quoted in Deighton et al., *Sweet Ramparts*, pp. 156–57.

27. Quoted in Ibid., p. 157.

28. Quoted in Ibid.

29. Ibid., p. 159.

30. *Barricada*, November 19, 1985.

31. *Barricada*, November 22, 1985.

32. Ibid.

33. Ibid.
34. Quoted in Instituto Historico, "The Nicaraguan Family," p. 9c.
35. *Nuevo Diario*, January 26, 1986.
36. AMNLAE, *Documentos de la Asamblea Constitutive*, p. 7.
37. Ibid., p. 8.
38. Quoted in Deighton et al., *Sweet Ramparts*, p. 107.
39. In *La Prensa*, June 8, 1980, quoted in Ibid., pp. 107–08.
40. Ibid., p. 108.
41. Nicaraguan Household Survey, INEC, 1981.
42. *Somos*, (November 1979), p. 3.
43. *Sandino's Daughters*, p. vi.
44. Instituto Historico, "Women in Nicaragua," p. 1c.
45. Ibid., p. 2c.
46. "Women in the Nicaraguan Revolution," in *Nicaragua: The Sandinista People's Revolution*, pp. 52–53.
47. Deighton et al., *Sweet Ramparts*, p. 65.
48. Instituto Historico, "Women in Nicaragua," p. 2c.
49. Deighton et al., *Sweet Ramparts*, p. 81.
50. Quoted in Ibid.
51. Quoted in Ibid., p. 78.
52. Aida Redondo, "Women Market Vendors in Nicaragua's Informal Sector," (unpublished mimeo).
53. Quoted in *Sweet Ramparts*, p. 82.
54. Quoted in Ibid., p. 83.
55. Quoted in "Learning from Our Compañeras," *Voices from Nicaragua 2–3*, p. 31.
56. Quoted in *Sweet Ramparts*, p. 86.
57. Ibid.
58. Quoted in Ibid., p. 87.
59. *El Topo*, Madrid, 1980, quoted in Ibid.
60. Ibid., p. 88.
61. Instituto Historico, "Women in Nicaragua," p. 3c.
62. *Intercontinental Press*, October 26, 1981, p. 314.
63. Ibid., p. 315.
64. Ibid., p. 316.
65. In *Barricada*, December 20, 1979, quoted in Black, *Triumph*, p. 294.
66. Quoted in Instituto Historico, "Women in Nicaragua," p. 4c.
67. In *Sandino's Daughters*, p. 66.
68. Instituto Historico, "Women in Nicaragua," p. 4c,
69. Quoted in Deighton et al., *Sweet Ramparts*, p. 21.
70. Milu Vargas, legal director, Council of State, August 1981, quoted in Ibid., pp. 21–22.
71. Interview in Estelí, November 1983.
72. Interview in Estelí, December 1983.
73. This section is based on observations made at the meeting.

74. This account is taken from the author's notes.

75. This section is based on an interview with the production manager of the collective, held in Estelí, January 1984.

76. Interview in Estelí, August 1984.

77. Interview in Estelí, August 1984.

9. Shaping Agricultural Policy

1. UNAG bulletin, no title, September 1984, p. 5.

2. UNAG, Las Pequeñas y Mediana Poductores, (n.p.), p.3.

3. UNAG bulletin, p. 3.

4. The first two sections of this chapter draw on Carmen Diana Deere, Peter Marchetti, S.J., and Nola Reinhardt, "Agrarian Reform and the Transition in Nicaragua: 1979–1983," (unpublished mimeo, November 1983), pp. 5–18.

5. Quoted in Joseph Collins, What Difference Could a Revolution Make? Food and Farming in the New Nicaragua (San Francisco: Institute for Food and Development Policy, 1982,) p. 60.

6. "Agrarian Reform," pp. 10–11.

7. PROCAMPO—Programa Campesina was originally a state agency to oversee all technical aid to peasants. It is now formally a department of MININRA.

8. Deere et al., "Agrarian Reform," p. 14.

9. Ibid., pp. 14–15.

10. Quoted in Matilde Zimmerman, "How Sandinistas Won Over the Nicaraguan Farmers," Intercontinental Press (April 20, 1981): 391.

11. COSEP, the Superior Council of Private Enterprise, withdrew from the Council of State in November 1980, after its vice president, Jorge Salazar, who was also president of UPANIC, was killed in a shoot-out with police. Salazar was linked to a counterrevolutionary plot that exposed the links between Somocista elements outside Nicaragua and certain sectors of the private sector.

12. "Agrarian Reform," p. 18.

13. The law was subsequently promulgated by the Council of State and the Junta of National Reconstruction.

14. Carmen Diane Deere, "Agrarian Reform as Revolution and Counter-Revolution: Nicaragua and El Salvador," in Roger Burbach and Patricia Flynn, eds. The Politics of Intervention: The United States in Central America (New York: Monthly Review Press, 1984), p. 181.

15. Deere et al., "Agrarian Reform," p. 23.

16. Ibid.

17. Deere, "Agrarian Reform as Revolution and Counter-Revolution," pp. 182–83.

18. Ibid., p. 182.

19. Deere et al., pp. 28–29.

20. Ibid., p. 29.

21. The other members of the regional commissions are the regional director

of the Agrarian Reform, the regional director of MIDINRA, the regional delegate of the Government Junta, and a member of the regional office of the FSLN.

22. Interview with Roberto Laguna, UNAG regional coordinator, in Estelí, January 16, 1984.

23. Interview in Estelí, January 27, 1984.

24. Interview in Estelí, January 16, 1984.

25. Deere, "Agrarian Reform as Revolution and Counter-Revolution," p. 183. Jaime Wheelock, Minister of Agriculture and Agrarian Reform, stated in 1983: "If the [Nicaraguan] revolution has benefited a particular social sector, it is the peasantry. This explains why the vast majority of those who have taken up arms against the counter-revolutionary bands are peasants" (quoted in Ibid., p. 164).

26. Instituto Historico Centroamericano, Envio (July 1984), pp. 31–32.

27. "Agrarian Reform as Revolution and Counter-Revolution," p. 182.

28. UNAG, op. cit., p. 6.

29. Intercontinental Press, August 8, 1983, p. 438.

30. Ibid.

31. Interview with Nicolas Chavez, in Estelí, January 27, 1984.

32. Interview with Nicolas Chavez, in Estelí, Jaunary 27, 1984.

33. Interview with Nicolas Chavez, in Estelí, January 27, 1984.

34. "Agrarian Reform," p. 32.

35. Ibid., p. 32.

36. Interview with Roberto Laguna, in Estelí, January 16, 1984.

37. Interview with Archimedes Rivera Rivera, coordinator of international relations in UNAG's national office, in Managua, December 22, 1983.

38. Interview in Estelí, January 27, 1984.

39. Ibid.

40. Ibid.

41. The following discussion of cooperativization draws on Philip Martinez, "Five Years of Agararian Reform in Nicaragua: The Case of the Noel Gamez Cooperative," (M.A. thesis, University of California, Berkeley, 1984), pp. 21–22.

42. Interview with Roberto Laguna.

43. Martinez, "Five Years of Agrarian Reform," p. 21.

44. Ibid., p. 22.

45. Interview with Roberto Laguna, in Estelí, February 1984.

46. Ibid.

47. This is a subject of much controversy within the FSLN.

48. CIERA, La Mujer en las Cooperativas Agropecuarias en Nicaragua (Managua: April, 1984), p. 26.

49. Ibid.

50. Quoted in Ibid., p. 27.

51. Ibid., p. 36.

52. Ibid., p. 68.

53. Quoted in Ibid., p. 70.

54. Ibid., pp. 81, 82.

55. This case study is drawn from Martinez, op. cit., pp. 35–75. Martinez

collected most of his data on Gamez-Garmendia over a four-week period. During that time he lived with the family of the president of the cooperative, worked daily on the farm, and participated in all the daily activities of the cooperative. He also conducted more than twelve hours of interviews.

56. Interview with Rafael Flores, president of Junta Directiva, Noel Gamez Cooperative, Estelí, February 1984, quoted in Martinez, op. cit., p. 35

57. Interview with Octavio Obregon Blandón, UNAG organizer, Region I, in Estelí, February 1984, quoted in Ibid, p. 36.

58. "Due to the low level of technical education, the Agrarian Reform has had to rely on the services of bureaucrats and technicians who are holdovers from the Somoza administration. This was particularly true during the first years of reconstruction. In fact, the advisers in question were independent, large ranchers who were recruited specifically to help the smaller recipients of land redistribution. Some of these administrators and technicians continue to think in the old way, believing that state employment entitles a person to rights of official corruption. All of the advisers in question were transferred to another region. Eventually all but one retired to their own ranches." (Martinez, draft of M.A. thesis, p. 19.)

59. Interview with Rafael Flores, quoted in Martinez, Ibid., p. 2.

60. Ibid., p. 3.

61. This Swiss agency is called COSUDE: Comision Suiza de Desarrollo Economico, Swiss Commission of Economic Development.

62. Interview with Rafael Flores, in Estelí, July 3, 1986.

63. Interview with Production Committee members, February 1984, quoted in Martinez, draft of M.A. thesis, p. 7.

64. Interview with Rafael Flores in February 1984, quoted in Ibid., pp. 7–8.

65. The general assembly meets once a month.

66. In the event of a split vote, the president has the authority to decide the issue.

67. Interview with the Secretary of Organization, Noel Gamez Cooperative, February 1982, quoted in Martinez, M.A. Thesis, p. 58.

68. The directing junta meets every fifteen days.

69. Most governing councils consist of these seven officers.

70. Political Secretary of Gamez cooperative, February 1984, quoted in Martinez, draft of M.A. thesis, p. 11.

71. The constitution will include about twenty-three statutes required by law. These statutes govern who is eligible to enter the cooperative, standardize membership dues, establish a legal procedure for reprimanding and removing a member from the cooperative, establish retirement rights, and establish a formal voting procedure. For details see "Reglamento General de la Ley de Cooperativas Agropecuarias," in Marco Juridico de la Reforma Agraria Nicaraguense, CIERA, Managua, October 1982: Article 39, p. 96.

72. "Some of the specific norms to be included in the constitution are:

a) An unexcused absence will lose a days wages. In the event of a frivolous absence (e.g. drunkeness) the member may lose a portion of his profit share.

b) Express criticism.

c) Everyone is equal. Do not place yourself above others.

d) Work hours are from 7 A.M. to 4 P.M.

e) Members will receive a weekly wage of 60 córdobas per day worked. Each member will also receive a share of the profit proportional to the number of days worked.

f) Maintain discipline in the areas of:

1. respecting decisions and authority of the General Assembly and directing junta;

2. attending adult education classes and study groups;

3. respecting each other;

4. working cooperatively.

g) Private ownership of domestic animals (chickens, pigs, ducks, etc.) is permitted. Private ownership of livestock is permitted only if the livestock uses none of the cooperatively owned resources and the owner receives permission from the General Assembly. In both cases the animals must be raised off of cooperative property.

h) All members are required to work at least one night a week in defensive vigilance of the ranch." (Martinez, op. cit., p. 90.)

73. Given the growth of the cooperative movement and the country's scarce technical resources, MIDINRA decided to select the 500 best organized ones in the thirty-five areas of agricultural development. These 500, called vanguard cooperatives, receive special attention in all areas.

74. Interview with Rafael Flores, quoted in Martinez, p. 8.

75. Daniel Nuñez, "The Producers of this Country Support Our Revolutionary Government," in *Nicaragua: The Sandinista People's Revolution*, p. 362.

76. "If the Peasantry Did Not Trust the Revolution, We Would Be Through," in Ibid., pp. 369–70.

77. Ibid., p. 370.

10. Production and Participation: CST and ATC

1. Quoted in Instituto Historico, *Envio* 12 (June 1982), p. 4.

2. This section draws on Carlos Vilas, "The Workers Movement in the Sandinista Revolution," in Harris and Vilas eds. *Nicaragua: A Revolution Under Siege*, pp. 122–23.

3. The last official census was carried out in 1971; consequently, all the figures concerning total population, economically active population, etc., are estimates.

4. The major harvests were sugar, coffee, and cotton.

5. For a discussion of these other trade union confederations, see Instituto Historico Centroamericano, *Envio*, (June, 1982), pp. 1–12.

6. *Triumph*, p. 291.

7. The innovators' movement is discussed later in this chapter.

8. Quoted in Intercontinental Press, May 10, 1982, p. 389.

9. "Economic Production Is the Rear Guard of the Battle Front," in *Nicaragua: The Sandinista People's Revolution*, p. 340.

10. Ibid., pp. 345–47.

11. *Trabajadores*, Numero 22, p. 8.

12. Numero 28, p. 2

13. Numero 30, p. 3

14. Ibid., p. 5.

15. Numero 33., p. 2.

16. Personal communication from Richard Stahler-Scholk.

17. This section draws on Central American Historical Institute, "Innovators in the Factories: A Small Step Towards Economic Independence," *Update* 30 (December 13, 1983); and Peter Downs, "Towards a People's Science, The Innovators Movement in Nicaragua," *Science for the People*, (November/December, 1983).

18. Quoted in Downs, "Towards a People's Science," p. 21.

19. Ibid., p.22.

20. Ibid.

21. Historical Institute, "Innovators," p. 2.

22. Quoted in Downs, "Towards a People's Science," p. 24.

23. Interview with ATC statistician in Managua, February 1986.

24. *El Machete*, July 1984, p. 4.

25. *El Machete*, November 1983., p. 2.

26. Ibid., p. 3.

27. *El Machete*, November, 1985, p. 3.

28. *Barricada*, September 26, 1985.

29. *El Machete*, November, 1985. p. 3.

30. ATC, "Los Trabajadores del Campo y el impacto de la Reforma Agraria sobre el empleo rural," March 1984. The following discussion is drawn from this paper.

31. For a discussion of this growing informal urban sector, see Instituto Historico, *Envio*, February 1985, pp. 9–16.

32. ATC, "El Empleo Rural," p. 8.

33. (Managua, 1983), p. 3.

34. Ibid., pp. 3–5.

35. *El Machete*, April 1984, pp. 6–7.

36. *Emulación Sandinista*, p. 5.

37. Quoted in Carole Pateman, *Participation and Democratic Theory*, p. 67.

38. Sawtell, quoted in Ibid.

39. Lammers, quoted in Ibid.

40. Ibid., p. 68.

41. Ibid., p. 70.

42. "Unions Discuss Workers Control," Intercontinental Press, July 20, 1981, p. 757.

43. Ibid.

44. Central American Historical Institute, *Envio*, November 1981, p. 2.

45. Black, *Triumph*, p. 215.

46. Ibid.

47. Ibid., pp. 285–86.

48. Ibid., p. 286.

49. Weissberg, p. 757.

50. Quoted in Ibid., p. 757.

51. Quoted in Ibid.

52. Quoted in Black, *Triumph*, p. 287.

53. Quoted in Weissberg, p. 757.

54. Quoted in Central American Historical Institute, *Envio*, (November 1981), pp. 3–4.

55. Quoted in Weissberg, p. 758.

56. *Intercontinental Press*, August 3, 1981, p. 760.

57. Black, p. 287.

58. Vilas, "The Workers' Movement in the Sandinista Revolution," p. 136.

59. Quoted in Black, p. 287.

60. *Barricada*, May 23, 29, 30, 1980.

61. CIERA, *Participatory Democracy in Nicaragua*, p. 103.

62. "The Workers' Movement," p. 136.

63. CIERA, *Participatory Democracy*, pp. 113–14.

64. Black, *Triumph*, p. 70.

65. Quoted in Instituto Historico *Envio*, June 1982, p. 21.

66. Quoted in *Barricada*, June 29, 1982.

67. Ibid.

68. Ibid.

69. Interview in Managua, July, 1982.

70. Interview in Managua, August, 1983.

71. Ibid.

72. The following description of the pilot project is drawn from *Barricada*, July 11, 1983.

73. Ibid.

74. Based on an interview in Estelí, January 23, 1984.

75. Ibid.

76. Ibid.

77. "The Workers' Movement," pp.142–43.

11. Defending the Revolution

1. This section draws from Instituto Historico Centroamericano, "Nicaragua's New Army: Fighting To Achieve Peace," *Envio* 28 (October 1983), pp. 4b–6b.

2. "The Role of the Revolutionary Armed Forces," in *Nicaragua in Revolution*, p. 123.

3. "Nicaragua's New Army," p. 5b.

4. *Discurso del Comandante Tomás Borge durante la promocion policial de la escuela Carlos Aguero E.* (Managua: Oficina de Divulgacion y Prensa, Ministerio del Interior, December 16, 1979), p. 1. Quoted in Gorman, "The Role of the Revolutionary Armed Forces," p. 128.

5. Quoted in Gorman "The Role of the Revolutionary Armed Forces,"p. 128.

6. This section draws on Patricia Flynn, "The United States at War in Central America: Unable to Win, Unwilling to Lose," in Roger Burback and Patricia

Flynn, eds. *The Politics of Intervention: The United States in Central America* (New York: Monthly Review Press/Center for the Study of the Americas, 1984), pp. 93–127.

7. *Washington Post,* September 29, 1983, quoted in Ibid., p. 118.
8. *El Machete,* April 1985, p. 5.
9. Richard Harris, *Nicaragua: A Revolution Under Siege,* p. 236.
10. *Intercontinental Press* (March 29, 1982), p. 244
11. Quoted in *Intercontinental Press* (August 3, 1983), p. 572.
12. Ibid.
13. Instituto Historico, "Nicaragua's New Army," p. 6b.
14. Ibid.
15. Quoted in Ibid.
16. Quoted in Ibid.
17. *Intercontinental Press* (April 19, 1982), p. 321.
18. Quoted in Ibid.
19. Quoted in *Intercontinental Press* (March 29, 1982), p. 245.
20. Ibid.
21. Ibid.
22. *Barricada,* March 12, 1984.
23. P. 5.
24. Ibid.
25. *Barricada,* July 11, 1984.
26. Ibid.
27. *El Machete,* August 1984, p. 5.
28. *Barricada,* November 28, 1986.
29. *Somos* (August-September 1983), p. 10.
30. Ibid.
31. *Barricada,* September 24, 1983.
32. *Nuevo Diario,* November 26, 1983.
33. *Barricada,* November 15, 1983.
34. *Barricada,* passim, October-November 1983.
35. Quoted in Randall, *Sandino's Daughters,* p. 27.
36. *Sweet Ramparts,* p. 52.
37. Ibid., p. 50.
38. "The Role of Women in the Nicaraguan Revolution," p. 156.
39. In Randall, *Sandino's Daughters,* pp. 138–39.
40. *Mujer y Revolucion,* (Managua: AMNLAE, July 1982), quoted in Deighton et al., *Sweet Ramparts,* pp. 56–57.
41. This case study is based on Instituto Historico, "Jalapa is Nicaragua," *Envio* (November, 1984), pp. 1b–14b.
42. Ibid., 1b.
43. Quoted in Ibid., p. 2b.
44. Quoted in Ibid.
45. Ibid., p. 5b
46. Ibid., pp. 9b–10b.
47. Ibid., p. 10b.

48. Ibid., 11b.
49. Ibid.
50. Ibid., 12b.
51. Ibid.
52. Ibid.
53. Ibid., 14b.
54. *Barricada*, July 2, 1986.

Conclusion

1. Although for obvious reasons Maxine Molyneaux does not include an analysis of AMNLAE in her article, "Socialist Societies Old and New: Progress Toward Women's Emancipation," her comments on women's organizations in socialist societies can be applied to the Nicaraguan women's association: "These organizations do not generally encourage radical thinking or action, and many of the more subtle discriminatory structures are not tackled unless they are considered to be survivals from the pre-revolutionary period and obstacles to development," *Monthly Review* (July–August 1982), pp. 93–94.

SELECT BIBLIOGRAPHY

Books

Arias, Pilar. *Nicaragua: Revolucion, relatos de combatientes del frente sandinista*. Mexico: Editorial Siglo XXI, 1980.

Berryman, Philip. *The Religious Roots of Rebellion: Christians in Central American Revolutions*. New York: Orbis Books, 1984.

Black, George. *Triumph of the People*. London: Zed Press, 1981.

Booth, John A. *The End and the Beginning: The Nicaraguan Revolution*. Boulder, Colorado: Westview Press, 1982.

Borge, Tomás. *Carlos, el amanecer ya ni es una tentacion*. Managua: Editorial Nueva Nicaragua, 1982.

Burbach, Roger; Flynn, Patricia. *The Politics of Intervention: The United States in Central America*. New York: Monthly Review Press, 1984.

CIERA. *Participatory Democracy in Nicaragua*. Managua: CIERA, 1984.

Collins, Joseph. *What Difference Could a Revolution Make: Food and Farming in the New Nicaragua*. San Francisco: Institute for Food and Development Policy, 1982.

Deighton, Jane; Horsley, Rossana; Stewart, Sarah; and Cain, Cathy. *Sweet Ramparts: Women in Revolutionary Nicaragua*. London: War on Want and the Nicaraguan Solidarity Campaign, 1983.

Epica Task Force. *Nicaragua: A People's Revolution*. Washington: Epica Task Force, 1980.

Escobar, Jose Benito. *El Principio del Fin*. Managua, Nicaragua: SENA-PEP, 1979.

Harris, Richard, and Vilas, Carlos. *Nicaragua: A Revolution Under Siege*. London: Zed Press, 1985.

Instituto de Estudios del Sandinismo. *La insurreccion popular sandinista en Masaya*. Managua: Editorial Nueva Nicaragua, 1983.

Le Blanc, Paul. *Permanent Revolution in Nicaragua*. New York: Fourth Internationalist Tendency, 1983.

Maier, Elizabeth. *La Mujer en la Revolucion*. Mexico D.F. : Ediciones de Cultura Popular, 1980.

Marcus, Bruce, ed. *Sandinistas Speak*. New York: Pathfinder Press, 1982.

——. *Nicaragua: The Sandinista People's Revolution*. New York: Pathfinder Press, 1985.

Martin, Megan; Willett, Susie, eds. *Women in Nicaragua*. London: Nicaragua Solidarity Campaign, 1980.

Pateman, Carole. *Participation and Democratic Theory*. New York: Cambridge University Press, 1970.

Randall, Margaret. *Risking a Somersault in the Air*. San Francisco: Solidarity Publications, 1984.

——. *Christians in the Nicaraguan Revolution*. Vancouver: New Star Books Ltd., 1983.

——. *Sandino's Daughters*. Vancouver: New Star Books Ltd., 1981.

Rosset, Peter; Vandermeer, John, eds., *The Nicaragua Reader: Documents of a Revolution Under Fire*. New York: Grove Press, 1983.

Selser, Gregorio. *Sandino*. New York: Monthly Review Press, 1981.

Tijerino, Doris. *Inside the Nicaraguan Revolution*. Vancouver: New Star Books Ltd., 1978.

Walker, Thomas T., ed. *Nicaragua in Revolution*. New York: Praeger, 1982.

——. *Nicaragua: The First Five Years*. New York: Praeger, 1985.

Weber, Henri. *Nicaragua: The Sandinista Revolution*. Translated by Patrick Camiller. London: Verso Editions and NBL, 1981.

Weissberg, Arnold. *Nicaragua: An Introduction to the Sandinista Revolution*. New York: Pathfinder Press, 1981.

Articles, Documents, Reports

Asociación de Trabajadores del Campo. "A pesar de la agresión imperialista, la jornada de Emulacion Sandinista fue un exito." *El Machete*. Managua: Abril 1984.

——. *Asociación de Trabajadores del Campo*. n.p.; n.d.

——. *Emulación Sandinista*. Managua: 1983.

——. *Los Trabajadores del Campo y el impacto de la Reforma Agraria sobre el empleo rural*. Managua: Marzo 1984.

Asociación de Mujeres Nicaraguenses Luisa Amanda Espinosa. "Documentos de la Asamblea Constitutiva," n.p.; n.d.

Barraclough, Solon. *A Preliminary Analysis of Nicaraguan Food System.* Geneva: United Nations Research Institute for Social Development, 1982.

Burbach, Roger; Draimin, Tim. "Nicaragua's Revolution." *NACLA.* XIV, number 3 (May/June 1980), pp. 2–30.

Camejo, Pedro. "How FSLN Handled Strike at Managua Construction Project," *Intercontinental Press* (February 1980), pp. 110–11.

Central Sandinista de Trabajadores. *La ATC y CST, su organizacion y Funciones en el Actual Proceso.* n.p.; n.d.

——. "El Papel de los Sindicatos en la Revolución." Managua: Instituto Jonathan Gonzales, March 1981, p. 2.

Centro de Investigaciones y Estudios de la Reforma Agraria. *La Mujer en las Cooperativas Agropecuarias en Nicaragua.* Managua: CIERA, 1984.

Chamorro, Amalia. *The Hegemonic Content of Somocismo and the Sandinista Revolution.* Managua: INIES, September 1982.

Consejo Nacional Popular de Salud, *La Participación de las Organizaciones Populares en la Gestion de Salud.* Managua: 1984.

Dellobuono, Richard. "Nicaragua's Emergency Laws: A In-Depth Look." *Nicaraguan Perspectives.* (Winter 1982).

Deere, Carmen Diane. "Agrarian Reform as Revolution and Counter-Revolution: Nicaragua and El Salvador." In Burbach, Roger and Flynn, Patricia. *The Politics of Intervention: The United States in Central America.* New York: Monthly Review Press, 1984.

Deere, Carmen Diane; Marchetti, S. J.; Peter; and Reinhardt, Nola. "Agrarian Reform and the Transition in Nicaragua: 1979–1983" November 1983.

Deere, Carmen Diane; Marchetti, S. J., Peter. "The Worker-Peasant Alliance in the First Year of the Nicaraguan Agararian Reform." *Latin American Perspectives.* (Spring 1982), pp. 42–55.

Downs, Charles and Kusnetsoff, Fernando. "The Changing Role of Local Government in the Nicaraguan Revolution." *International Journal of Urban and Regional Research.* 1982, pp. 533–47.

Downs, Peter. "Towards a People's Science: The Innovators Movement in Nicaragua." *Science for the People* (November/December 1983), p. 21.

Eitel, Jim. "Gains and Struggles of Women Workers."*Intercontinental Press.* (October 12, 1984), p. 1002.

Ellsberg, Mary. "Trail Blazing on the Atlantic Coast: A Report on the Health Care Brigadistas in Nicaragua." *Science for the People.* (November/December 1983).

Fagen, Richard. "Revolution and Crisis in Nicaragua." In *Trouble In Our*

Backyard: Central American and the United States in the Eighties, ed. Martin Diskin. New York: Pantheon Books, 1983, pp. 125–54.

Flynn, Patricia. "The United States at War In Central America: Unable to Win, Unwilling to Lose." In ed. Burbach, Roger and Flynn, Patricia. *The Politics of Intervention: The United States in Central America* New York: Monthly Review Press/Center for the Study of the Americas, 1984, pp. 93–127.

Flynn, Patricia; Santana, Aracelly; Shapiro, Helen. "Latin American Women: One Myth—Many Realities." *NACLA Report on the Americas*. (September-October, 1980), pp. 2–35.

Friedman, Sarah Ann. "Eyes Right." *The Quill*. (January 1985).

Garfield, Richard M. and Tabaoda, Eugenio, "Health Services Reforms in Revolutionary Nicaragua." *American Journal of Public Health*. (October 1984).

Harris, Jane. "Women Farm Workers Meet." *Intercontinental Press* (May 16, 1983), p. 257.

Harris, Jane; Martinez, Antigona. "Farmers form cooperatives." *Intercontinental Press* (March 29, 1982), p. 258.

Instituto Historico Centroamericano. "Sandinista Defense Committees (CDS): Impressions after Four Years of Existence." *Envio*, (October 15, 1982).

———. "Sequel to the Literacy Campaign." *Envio* (November 15, 1982), pp. 14–21.

———. "The Health Situation in Revolutionary Nicaragua." *Envio* (May 1983).

———. "Women in Nicaragua: A Revolution Within a Revolution." *Envio* (July, 1983), pp. 1c–9c

———. "Nicaragua's New Army: Fighting to Achieve Peace."*Envio* (October 1983).

———. "Young People in a Young Country: A Look at Nicaraguan Youth." *Envio* (October, 1983), pp. 1c–9c.

———. "Jalapa: A Symbol for all Nicaragua." *Envio* (February, 1984), pp. 1b–11b.

———. "The Nicaraguan Family in a Time of Transition." *Envio* (April 1984), pp. 1c–11c.

———. "The Right of the Poor to Defend their Unique Revolution: Five Years of Sandinista Government." *Envio* (July 1984), pp. 31–32.

———. "The Elections Reagan Would Like to Forget." *Envio* (April, 1985), pp.1b–29b.

———. "The National Assembly: First Steps Toward a New Political Model." *Envio* (May, 1985), pp. 1b–9b.

Latin American Studies Association. *The Report of the Latin American*

Studies Association Delegation to Observe the Nicaraguan General Election of November 4, 1984. November 19, 1984.

Martinez, Philip. "Five Years of Agrarian Reform in Nacaragua: The Case of the Noel Gamez Cooperative." M. A. thesis, University of California, Berkeley, 1984.

Ministry of Planning. Defensa de la Economia Popular. Managua, 1984.

Molyneaux, Maxine. "Socialist Countries: Old and New: Progress Toward Women's Emancipation." Monthly Review (July-August 1982), pp. 56–100.

Palmgren, Lars. "Nicaragua: New Efforts Toward Trade Union Unity." Intercontinental Press (November 17, 1980), p. 1189.

Petras, James. "Nicaragua: The Transition to a New Society."Latin American Perspectives (Spring 1981), pp. 87–88.

Siegel, David. "The Effects of the War on Health Care." Nicaraguan Perspectives (Spring/Summer 1985).

Soto, Orlando Nuñez. "The Third Social Force in National Liberation Movements." Latin American Perspectives (Spring 1981), pp. 5–21.

Tellez, Carlos Nuñez. El Papel de las Organizaciones de Masas en el Proceso Revolucionario. Managua: Secretaria Nacional de Propaganda y Educacion Politica del FSLN, 1980.

Thiebaud, Lorraine. "Nicaraguan Workers Make Gains in Health and Society." Intercontinental Press (March 23, 1983), p. 269.

Union Nacional de Agricultores y Ganaderos. Asamblea Nacional de los Pequenos y Medianos Productores Agropecuarios Afiliados a la UNAG. Managua: UNAG, September 10, 1982.

———. Las Pequeñas y Medianas Productores Agropecuarios. Managua: UNAG, 1983.

———. Programa de Fortalecimiento de los Consejos Municipales: Nuestros Organismos Municipales de la UNAG. Coleccion Pablo Ubeda. Managua, 1983.

———. Programa de Fortalecimiento de los Consejos Municipales: Nuestra Organization La UNAG. Coleccion Pablo Ubeda. Managua: UNAG, 1984.

U.S. Out Of Central America. Declaration of Managua. San Francisco. n.d.

Weaver, Eric. "Nicaraguans Go to the Polls." Central American Bulletin. (November 1984).

Weissberg, Arnold. "Unions Discuss Workers Control." Intercontinental Press (July 20, 1981), p. 757.

Zimmerman, Matilde. "How Sandinistas Won Over the Nicaraguan Farmers." Intercontinental Press (April 26, 1981), pp. 391–92.

————. "Nicaragua's Farmers and Ranchers form Union". *Intercontinental Press* (May 16, 1982), p. 552.

Newspapers and Journals

Barricada, 1979–1986.
Barricada Internacional, 1984–1986.
Central America Update, 1983–1986.
El Machete, 1984–1986.
El Nuevo Diario, 1983–1986.
Envio, 1983–1986.
La Prensa, 1983–1986.
Latin American Perspectives, 1982–1985.
Nicaraguan Perspectives, 1983–1985.
Somos, 1983–1986.
Trabajadores, 1983–1985.

Interviews

Blandon, Octavio Obregon, UNAG regional secretary of propaganda and political education, January 1984

Cerda Angela, member of CDS national commission of international affairs, July 1983

Chavez, Nicolas, director of MIDINRA Region I office of cooperative development, January 1984

Colindus, Arquimides, regional delegate of INSSBI, November 1983

Flores, Rafael, president of Gamez-Garmendia cooperative, June 1986

Florian, Luz, AMNLAE zonal secretary of organization in Estelí, December 1983

García, Edgardo, ATC general secretary, March 1984

Henderson, Helen, general secretary of AMNLAE's zonal office in Estelí, November 1983

Laguna, Roberto, UNAG coordinator in Region I, January 1984

Lara, Agustín, FSLN political secretary in Region I, January 1984

Molina, Javier, member of ATC national training staff, November 1984

Montoya, Alcides, director of complex in Esteli's Oscar Turcios tobacco enterprise, January 1984

Quintillana, Leonel Enrique, CDS secretary of economic defense, November 1984

Perez, Vivian, ATC secretary of propaganda and political education, November 1983

Rivera, Archimedes Rivera, UNAG coordinator of international relations, December 1983

Rugama, Nora Marlene, secretary of production in AMNLAE's sewing collective in Esteli, January 1984

Zelaya, Carmen Montenegro, activist in Estelí's Committee of Mothers of Heroes and Martyrs, August 1984

INDEX

Agrarian Promotion and Educational Center (CEPA), 39–40
Aguero, Fernando, 43
American Institute for Free Labor Development (AIFLD), 45
AMNLAE, See Association of Nicaraguan Women "Luisa Amanda Espinosa"
AMPRONAC, See Association of Women Confronting the National Problem
Annunciata, Lucia, 5
Arce, Bayardo, 10, 129
Area of People's Property (APP), 66, 143, 268
Argentina, 68
Association of Nicaraguan Women "Luisa Amanda Espinosa" (AMNLAE), 113, 114, 134, 142, 146, 154, 156, 157, 166, 177, 178, 180, 217, 297–98; case study of, 209–16; and Council of State, 106–7; and draft law, 144; and education, 197–99; and employment, 199–205; evolution of, 94–97; and the family, 190–97; ideology of, 187–89; and literacy crusade, 111; political education in, 126–27; political equality in, 133–35; and reserve battalions, 288; role in legislation of, 189–90; and unemployment, 207; and the unions, 205–6

Association of Rural Workers (ATC), 42, 49, 114, 118, 124, 140, 142, 146, 147, 151, 154, 157, 254; and employment stability, 255; and innovators movement, 253; land conflict with FSLN, 143; leadership selection process in, 122–23; and literacy campaign, 111; and new salary policy, 255–56; and production, 256–59; problems of women in, 134–35
Association of Women Confronting the National Problem, 2, 41, 48–51, 59, 79, 94
ATC, See Association of Rural Workers

Baltodano, Alvaro, 56
Baltodano, Monica, 107, 138, 208
Barricada, 84, 106, 107, 126, 132, 144, 196, 265, 267, 284
Barricada Internacional, 72
Belli, Giaconda, 28
Bendaña, Alejandro, 24
Bolivia, 33
Booth, John A., 84
Borge, Tomás, 9, 56, 59, 68, 140, 164, 200; on hardships of guerrilla life, 11; on FSLN's early urban activity, 12–13; on Christianity and religion, 87; on electoral process, 145; on mixed economy, 68; on role of army and police,